Points of View

Readings in American Government and Politics

Points of View

Readings in American Government and Politics

TENTH EDITION

Edited by

Robert E. DiClerico
Allan S. Hammock
West Virginia University

Boston   Burr Ridge, IL   Dubuque, IA   Madison, WI   New York
San Francisco   St. Louis   Bangkok   Bogotá   Caracas   Kuala Lumpur
Lisbon   London   Madrid   Mexico City   Milan   Montreal   New Delhi
Santiago   Seoul   Singapore   Sydney   Taipei   Toronto

POINTS OF VIEW: READINGS IN AMERICAN GOVERNMENT AND POLITICS

Published by McGraw-Hill, a business unit of The McGraw-Hill Companies, Inc., 1221 Avenue of the Americas, New York, NY, 10020. Copyright © 2007, 2004, 2001, 1998, 1995, 1992, 1989, 1986, 1983, 1980 by The McGraw-Hill Companies, Inc. All rights reserved. No part of this publication may be reproduced or distributed in any form or by any means, or stored in a database or retrieval system, without the prior written consent of The McGraw-Hill Companies, Inc., including, but not limited to, in any network or other electronic storage or transmission, or broadcast for distance learning.

Some ancillaries, including electronic and print components, may not be available to customers outside the United States.

This book is printed on acid-free paper.

1 2 3 4 5 6 7 8 9 0 DOC/DOC 0 9 8 7 6 5

ISBN-13: 978-0-07-310681-6
ISBN-10: 0-07-310681-X

Editor in Chief: *Emily Barrosse*
Publisher: *Lyn Uhl*
Senior Sponsoring Editor: *Monica Eckman*
Freelance Developmental Editor: *Larry Goldberg*
Freelance Permissions Coordinator: *Anne Wallingford*
Marketing Manager: *Katherine Bates*
Managing Editor: *Jean Dal Porto*
Senior Project Manager: *Diane M. Folliard*
Associate Designer: *Marianna Kinigakis*
Cover Design: *Marianna Kinigakis*
Senior Production Supervisor: *Carol A. Bielski*
Composition: *International Typesetting & Composition*
Printing: *R.R. Donnelley/Crawfordsville, IN.*

Library of Congress Cataloging-in-Publication Data

Points of view: readings in American government and politics/edited by Robert E. DiClerico, Allan S. Hammock.—10th ed.
     p. cm.
   Includes bibliographical references.
   ISBN 0-07-310681-X (softcover: alk. paper)
   ISBN 978-0-07-310681-6
   1. United States—Politics and government. I. DiClerico, Robert E. II. Hammock, Allan S., 1938–
JK21.P59 2007
320.973—dc21   2005052252

www.mhhe.com

About the Editors

ROBERT E. DiCLERICO is the Eberly Distinguished Professor of Political Science at West Virginia University. An Indiana University (Bloomington) Ph.D. and a Danforth fellow, he is author of *Voting in America* (2004) and *The American President*, 5th edition (2000); co-author of *Choosing Our Choices* (2000) and *Few Are Chosen* (1984); and editor of *Political Parties, Campaigns, and Elections* (2000) and *Analyzing the Presidency* (1985).

ALLAN S. HAMMOCK is an Associate Professor and former Chairman of the Department of Political Science at West Virginia University. He received his Ph.D. from the University of Virginia and is co-author of *West Virginia Politics and Government* (1996). He served as chairman of the West Virginia Election Commission from 1983 to 2004.

Contents

Preface

Reflecting the press of events and editorial judgments, the changes made for the Tenth Edition of *Points of View* are substantial. We have added five new topics. Under the general subject of Federalism in Chapter 3, we address federal mandates and gay marriage; for Elections in Chapter 7, we have included the presidential nominating process; for Congress in Chapter 10, we have included redistricting; and Chapter 14 on Civil Liberties now addresses civil liberties and terrorism. In addition to these changes, we have added a third article on Voting in Chapter 5, and new pairs of articles for Political Parties (Chapter 8), Interest Groups (Chapter 9), and The Presidency (Chapter 11). Finally, under the general subject of Civil Rights (Chapter 15), we have included a new pair of articles on affirmative action.

The basic goals of the book remain the same, namely, to provide students with a manageable number of selections that present readable, succinct, thoughtful, and diverse perspectives across a broad range of issues related to American Government.

Acknowledgments

We would like to extend our thanks to a number of individuals who made valuable contributions to this project. A special debt of gratitude is owed to Larry Goldberg, who had primary editorial responsibility for this latest edition and in that capacity did absolutely everything possible to make the editorial process flow smoothly and effectively.

We would also like to express our appreciation to the sponsoring editor, Monica Eckman, who had overall responsibility in coordinating this latest revision and did a superb job of expediting the publishing process, and to Diane Folliard, the project manager, whose guidance throughout the production process was exemplary.

In the course of revising and updating this manuscript, we repeatedly called upon the typing skills of administrative associate Lee Ann Greathouse, who cheerfully reproduced manuscripts with unfailing accuracy and in less time than we had any reason to expect.

Finally, we would like to express our deep appreciation to the following academicians who carefully read the previous edition of *Points of View.* Their detailed and constructive suggestions guided several of the changes made for this latest revision:

Julianne F. Flowers—Loyola University Chicago

Joanne S. Grasso—Hofstra University

James D. King—University of Wyoming

Terrence A. Lenio—McHenry County College

Peter J. Longo—University of Nebraska at Kearney

Frederick R. Neikirk, Jr.—Geneva College

Ryan Petersen—College of the Redwoods

William M. Salka—Eastern Connecticut State University

Robert E. DiClerico
Allan S. Hammock
Morgantown, West Virginia

Internet Resources
Visit our Web site at www.mhhe.com/diclerico10 for links and resources relating to chapter topics.

A Note to the Instructor

For some years now, we have jointly taught the introductory course to American government. Each year we perused the crop of existing readers, and while we adopted several different readers over this period, we were not wholly satisfied with any of them. It is our feeling that many of the readers currently on the market suffer from one or more of the following deficiencies: (1) Some contain selections that are difficult for students to comprehend because of the sophistication of the argument, the manner of expression, or both. (2) In many instances, readers do not cover all of the topics typically treated in an introductory American government course. (3) In choosing selections for a given topic, editors do not always show sufficient concern for how—or whether—one article under a topic relates to other articles under the same topic. (4) Most readers contain too many selections for each topic—indeed, in several cases the number of selections for some topics exceeds ten. Readers are nearly always used in conjunction with a textbook. Thus, to ask a student to read a lengthy chapter—jammed with facts—from a textbook and then to read anywhere from five to ten selections on the same topic from a reader is to demand that students read more than they can reasonably absorb in a meaningful way. Of course, an instructor need not assign all the selections under a given topic. At the same time, however, this approach justifiably disgruntles students who, after purchasing a reader, discover that they may only be asked to read one-half or two-thirds of it.

Instead of continuing to complain about what we considered to be the limitations of existing American government readers, we decided to try our own hand at putting one together. In doing so, we were guided by the following considerations.

Readability

Quite obviously, students will not read dull, difficult articles. We feel that, as well as having something important to say, each of the articles in *Points of View* is clearly written, well-organized, and free of needless jargon.

Comprehensiveness

The fifteen chapters of *Points of View* cover all the major topics of concern that are typically treated in the standard introductory course on American government.

Economy of Selections

We decided, generally, to limit the number of selections to two per topic, although we did include three selections on topics in Chapters 5, 7, and 10. The limitation on selections will maximize the likelihood that students will read them. It has been our experience that when students are assigned four, five, or more selections under a given topic, they simply do not read them all. In addition, by limiting the selections for each topic, there is a greater likelihood that students will be able to associate an argument with the author who made it.

Juxtaposition

The two selections for each topic will take *opposing* or *different* points of view on some aspect of a given topic. This approach was chosen for three reasons. First, we believe that student interest will be enhanced by playing one article off against the other. Thus, the "interest" quality of a given article will derive not only from its own content, but also from its juxtaposition with the other article. Second, we think it is important to sensitize students to the fact that one's perspective on an issue will depend upon the values that he or she brings to it. Third, by having both selections focus on a particular issue related to a given topic, the student will have a greater depth of understanding about that issue. We think this is preferable to having five or six selections under a topic, with each selection focusing on a different aspect, and with the result that the student ultimately is exposed to "a little of this and a little of that"—that is, if the student even bothers to read all five or six selections.

While the readers currently available take into account one or, in some instances, several of the considerations identified, we believe that the uniqueness of *Points of View* lies in the fact that it has sought to incorporate *all* of them.

chapter 1

Democracy

*A*ny assessment of a society's democratic character will be fundamentally determined by what the observer chooses to use as a definition of democracy. Though the concept of democracy has commanded the attention of political thinkers for centuries, the following selections by Howard Zinn and Sidney Hook demonstrate that there continues to be considerable disagreement over its meaning. Each of them has scanned the American scene and reached different conclusions regarding the democratic character of our society. This difference of opinion is explained primarily by the fact that each approaches his evaluation with a different conception of what democracy is.

For Zinn, the definition of democracy includes criteria that bear not only upon how decisions get made but also upon what results from such decisions. Specifically, he argues that such results must lead to a certain level of human welfare within a society. In applying these criteria of human welfare to the United States, he concludes that we fall short of the mark in several areas.

Although Sidney Hook is willing to acknowledge that democracy might indeed function more smoothly in societies where the conditions of human welfare are high, he insists that these conditions do not themselves constitute the definition of democracy. Rather, he maintains that democracy is a process—a way of making decisions. Whether such decisions lead to the conditions of human welfare that Zinn prescribes is irrelevant. The crucial test, according to Hook, is whether the people have the right, by majority rule, to make choices about the quality of their lives—whatever those choices might be.

How Democratic Is America?
Howard Zinn

To give a sensible answer to the question "How democratic is America?" I find it necessary to make three clarifying preliminary statements. First, I want to define "democracy," not conclusively, but operationally, so we can know what we are arguing about or at least what I am talking about. Second, I want to state what my criteria are for measuring the "how" in the question. And third, I think it necessary to issue a warning about how a certain source of bias (although not the only source) is likely to distort our judgments.

Our definition is crucial. This becomes clear if we note how relatively easy is the answer to our question when we define democracy as a set of formal institutions and let it go at that. If we describe as "democratic" a country that has a representative system of government, with universal suffrage, a bill of rights, and party competition for office, it becomes easy to answer the question "how" with the enthusiastic reply, "Very!" . . .

I propose a set of criteria for the description "democratic," which goes beyond formal political institutions, to the quality of life in the society (economic, social, psychological), beyond majority rule to a concern for minorities, and beyond national boundaries to a global view of what is meant by "the people," in that rough, but essentially correct view of democracy as "government of, by, and for the people."

Let me list these criteria quickly, because I will go on to discuss them in some detail later:

1. To what extent can various people in the society participate in those decisions which affect their lives: decisions in the political process and decisions in the economic structure?

2. As a corollary of the above: do people have equal access to the information which they need to make important decisions?

3. Are the members of the society equally protected on matters of life and death—in the most literal sense of that phrase?

4. Is there equality before the law: police, courts, the judicial process—as well as equality *with* the law-enforcing institutions, so as to safeguard equally everyone's person, and his freedom from interference by others, and by the government?

Howard Zinn is professor emeritus of political science at Boston University. This essay was originally published in Robert A. Goldwin, ed., *How Democratic Is America?* (Chicago: Rand McNally, 1971), pp. 39–60. The author revised and updated the original for *Points of View* in 1985 and again in 1997.

5. Is there equality in the distribution of available resources: those economic goods necessary for health, life, recreation, leisure, growth?
6. Is there equal access to education, to knowledge and training, so as to enable persons in the society to live their lives as fully as possible, to enlarge their range of possibilities?
7. Is there freedom of expression on all matters, and equally for all, to communicate with other members of the society?
8. Is there freedom for individuality in private life, in sexual relations, family relations, the right of privacy?
9. To minimize regulation: do education and the culture in general foster a spirit of cooperation and amity to sustain the above conditions?
10. As a final safety feature: is there opportunity to protest, to disobey the laws, when the foregoing objectives are being lost—as a way of restoring them? . . .

Two historical facts support my enlarged definition of democracy. One is that the industrialized Western societies have outgrown the original notions which accompanied their early development: that constitutional and procedural tests sufficed for the "democracy" that overthrew the old order; that democracy was quite adequately fulfilled by the Bill of Rights in England at the time of the Glorious Revolution, the Constitution of the United States, and the declaration of the Rights of Man in France. It came to be acknowledged that the rhetoric of these revolutions was not matched by their real achievements. In other words, the limitations of that "democracy" led to the reformist and radical movements that grew up in the West in the middle and late nineteenth century. The other historical note is that the new revolutions in our century, in Africa, Asia, Latin America, while rejecting either in whole or in part the earlier revolutions, profess a similar democratic aim, but with an even broader rhetoric. . . .

My second preliminary point is on standards. By this I mean that we can judge in several ways the fulfillment of these ten criteria I have listed. We can measure the present against the past, so that if we find that in [2005] we are doing better in these matters than we were doing in 1860 or 1910, the society will get a good grade for its "democracy." I would adjure such an approach because it supports complacency. With such a standard, Russians in 1910 could point with pride to how much progress they had made toward parliamentary democracy; as Russians in 1985 could point to their post-Stalin progress away from the gulag; as Americans could point in 1939 to how far they had come toward solving the problem of economic equality; as Americans in the South could point in 1950 to the progress of the southern African-American. Indeed, the American government has given military aid to brutal regimes in Latin America on the ground that a decrease in the murders by semiofficial death squads is a sign of progress.

Or, we could measure our democracy against other places in the world. Given the high incidence of tyranny in the world, polarization of wealth, and lack of freedom of expression, the United States, even with very serious defects, could declare itself successful. Again, the result is to let us all off easily; some of our most enthusiastic self-congratulation is based on such a standard.

On the other hand, we could measure our democracy against an ideal (even if admittedly unachievable) standard. I would argue for such an approach, because, in what may seem to some a paradox, the ideal standard is the pragmatic one; it affects what we *do*. To grade a student on the basis of an improvement over past performance is justifiable if the intention is to encourage someone discouraged about his ability. But if he is rather pompous about his superiority in relation to other students (and I suggest this is frequently true of Americans evaluating American "democracy"), and if in addition he is a medical student about to graduate into a world ridden with disease, it would be best to judge him by an ideal standard. That might spur him to an improvement fast enough to save lives. . . .

My third preliminary point is a caution based on the obvious fact that we make our appraisals through the prism of our own status in society. This is particularly important in assessing democracy, because if "democracy" refers to the condition of masses of people, and if we as the assessors belong to a number of elites, we will tend (and I am not declaring an inevitability, just warning of a tendency) to see the present situation in America more benignly than it deserves. To be more specific, if democracy requires a keen awareness of the condition of black people, of poor people, of young people, of that majority of the world who are not American—and we are white, prosperous, beyond draft age, and American—then we have a number of pressures tending to dull our sense of inequity. We are, if not doomed to err, likely to err on the side of complacency—and we should try to take this into account in making our judgments.

1. PARTICIPATION IN DECISIONS

We need to recognize first, that whatever decisions are made politically are made by representatives of one sort or another: state legislators, congressmen, senators, and other elected officials, governors and presidents; also by those appointed by elected officials, like Supreme Court justices. These are important decisions, affecting our lives, liberties, and ability to pursue happiness. Congress and the president decide on the tax structure, which affects the distribution of resources. They decide how to spend the monies received; whether or not we go to war; who serves in the armed forces; what behavior is considered a crime; which crimes are prosecuted and which are not. They decide what limitations there should be on our travel, or on our right to speak freely. They decide on the availability of education and health services.

If representation by its very nature is undemocratic, as I would argue, this is an important fact for our evaluation. Representative government is *closer* to democracy than monarchy, and for this reason it has been hailed as one of the great political advances of modern times; yet, it is only a step in the direction of democracy, at its best. It has certain inherent flaws—pointed out by Rousseau in the eighteenth century, Victor Considerant in the nineteenth century, Robert Michels in the beginning of the twentieth century, Hannah Arendt in our own time. No representative can adequately represent another's needs;

the representative tends to become a member of a special elite; he has privileges which weaken his sense of concern at others' grievances; the passions of the troubled lose force (as Madison noted in *The Federalist 10*) as they are filtered through the representative system; the elected official develops an expertise which tends toward its own perpetuation. Leaders develop what Michels called "a mutual insurance contract" against the rest of society. . . .

If only radicals pointed to the inadequacy of the political processes in the United States, we might be suspicious. But established political scientists of a moderate bent talk quite bluntly of the limitations of the voting system in the United States. Robert Dahl, in *A Preface to Democratic Theory*, drawing on the voting studies of American political scientists, concludes that "political activity, at least in the United States, is positively associated to a significant extent with such variables as income, socio-economic status, and education." He says:

> By their propensity for political passivity the poor and uneducated disfranchise themselves. . . . Since they also have less access than the wealthy to the organizational, financial, and propaganda resources that weigh so heavily in campaigns, elections, legislative, and executive decisions, anything like equal control over government policy is triply barred to the members of Madison's unpropertied masses. They are barred by their relatively greater inactivity, by their relatively limited access to resources, and by Madison's nicely contrived system of constitutional checks.[1]

Dahl thinks that our society is essentially democratic, but this is because he expects very little. (His book was written in the 1950s, when lack of commotion in the society might well have persuaded him that no one else expected much more than he did.) Even if democracy were to be superficially defined as "majority rule," the United States would not fulfill that, according to Dahl, who says that "on matters of specific policy, the majority rarely rules."[2] After noting that "the election is the critical technique for insuring that governmental leaders will be relatively responsive to nonleaders," he goes on to say that "it is important to notice how little a national election tells us about the preferences of majorities. Strictly speaking, all an election reveals is the first preferences of some citizens among the candidates standing for office."[3] About 45 percent of the potential voters in national elections, and about 60 percent of the voters in local elections do not vote, and this cannot be attributed, Dahl says, simply to indifference. And if, as Dahl points out, "in no large nation state can elections tell us much about the preferences of majorities and minorities," this is "even more true of the interelection period." . . .

Dahl goes on to assert that the election process and interelection activity "are crucial processes for insuring that political leaders will be *somewhat* responsive to the preferences of *some* ordinary citizens."[4] I submit (the emphasized words are mine) that if an admirer of democracy in America can say no more than this, democracy is not doing very well.

Dahl tells us the election process is one of "two fundamental methods of social control which, operating together, make governmental leaders so responsive to nonleaders that the distinction between democracy and dictatorship still makes sense." Since his description of the election process leaves that dubious, let's look at his second requirement for distinguishing democracy: "The other method of social control is continuous political competition among individuals, parties, or both." What it comes down to is "not minority rule but minorities rule."[5]

If it turns out that this—like the election process—also has little democratic content, we will not be left with very much difference—by Dahl's own admission—between "dictatorship" and the "democracy" practiced in the United States. Indeed, there is much evidence on this: the lack of democracy within the major political parties, the vastly disproportionate influence of wealthy groups over poorer ones. What antismoking consumer group in the election year of 1996 could match the five million dollars donated to the Republican Party by the tobacco interests? What ordinary citizen could have the access to President Bill Clinton that a group of bankers had in May of that election year when they were invited to the White House?[6] All of this, and more, supports the idea of a "decline of American pluralism" that Henry Kariel has written about. What Dahl's democracy comes down to is "the steady appeasement of relatively small groups."[7] If these relatively small groups turn out to be the aircraft industry far more than the aged, the space industry far more than the poor, the Pentagon far more than the college youth—what is left of democracy?

Sometimes the elitism of decision-making is defended (by Dahl and by others) on the ground that the elite is enacting decisions passively supported by the mass, whose tolerance is proof of an underlying consensus in society. But Murray Levin's studies in *The Alienated Voter* indicate how much nonparticipation in elections is a result of hopelessness rather than approval. And Robert Wiebe, a historian at Northwestern University, talks of "consensus" becoming a "new stereotype." He approaches the question historically.

> Industrialization arrived so peacefully not because all Americans secretly shared the same values or implicitly willed its success but because its millions of bitter enemies lacked the mentality and the means to organize an effective counterattack.[8]

Wiebe's point is that the passivity of most Americans in the face of elitist decision-making has not been due to acquiescence but to the lack of resources for effective combat, as well as a gulf so wide between the haves and have-nots that there was no ground on which to dispute. Americans neither revolted violently nor reacted at the polls; instead they were subservient, or else worked out their hostilities in personal ways. . . .

Presidential nominations and elections are more democratic than monarchical rule or the procedures of totalitarian states, but they are far from some reasonable expectation of democracy. The two major parties have a monopoly of presidential power, taking turns in the White House. The candidates of minority parties don't have a chance. They do not have access to the financial backing of the major parties, and there is not the semblance of equal attention in the mass media; it is only the two major candidates who have free access to prime time on national television.

More important, both parties almost always agree on the fundamentals of domestic and foreign policy, despite the election-year rhetoric which attempts to find important differences. Both parties arranged for United States inter-vention in Vietnam in the 1950s and 1960s, and both, when public opinion changed, promised to get out (note the Humphrey-Nixon contest of 1968). In 1984, Democratic candidate Walter Mondale agreed with Republican candidate Ronald Reagan that the United States (which had ten thousand thermonuclear warheads) needed to continue increasing its arms budget, although he asked for a smaller increase than the Republicans. Such a position left Mondale unable to promise representatives of the black community (where unemploy-ment was over 20 percent) that he would spend even a few billion dollars for a jobs program. Meanwhile, Democrats and Republicans in Congress were agree-ing on a $297 billion arms bill for the 1985 fiscal year.[9]

I have been talking so far about democracy in the political process. But there is another serious weakness that I will only mention here, although it is of enormous importance: the powerlessness of the American to participate in economic decision-making, which affects his life at every moment. As a con-sumer, that is, as the person whom the economy is presumably intended to serve, he has virtually nothing to say about what is produced for him. The cor-porations make what is profitable; the advertising industry persuades him to buy what the corporations produce. He becomes the passive victim of the mis-allocation of resources, the production of dangerous commodities, the spoiling of his air, water, forests, beaches, cities.

2. ACCESS TO INFORMATION

Adequate information for the electorate is a precondition for any kind of action (whether electoral or demonstrative) to affect national policy. As for the voting process, Berelson, Lazarsfeld, and McPhee tell us (in their book, *Voting*) after extensive empirical research: "One persistent conclusion is that the public is not particularly well informed about the specific issues of the day." . . .

Furthermore, there are certain issues which never even reach the public because they are decided behind the scenes. . . .

Consider the information available to voters on two major kinds of issues. One of them is the tax structure, so bewilderingly complex that the corporation, with its corps of accountants and financial experts, can prime itself for lob-bying activities, while the average voter, hardly able to comprehend his own income tax, stands by helplessly as the president, the Office of Management and Budget, and the Congress decide the tax laws. The dominant influences are those of big business, which has the resources both to understand and to act.

Then there is foreign policy. The government leads the citizenry to believe it has special expertise which, if it could only be revealed, would support its position against critics. At the same time, it hides the very information which would reveal its position to be indefensible. The mendacity of the government on the Bay of Pigs operation and the withholding of vital information about the

Tonkin Gulf events are only two examples of the way the average person becomes a victim of government deception.*

In 1990, historian Warren Cohen resigned as adviser to the State Department in its publication of the series *Foreign Relations of the United States*, pointing out that the government was refusing to cover events less than thirty years old. And even what it did publish was not trustworthy. "The United States government is publishing blatantly fraudulent accounts of its activities in Guatemala, Iran, and Southeast Asia in the 1950s" (*World Monitor Magazine*, 1990).

When the United States invaded the tiny island of Grenada in the fall of 1983, no reporters were allowed to observe the invasion, and the American public had little opportunity to get independent verification of the reasons given by the government for the invasion. As a result, President Reagan could glibly tell the nation what even one of his own supporters, journalist George Will, admitted was a lie: that he was invading Grenada to protect the lives of American medical students on the island. He could also claim that documents found on the island indicated plans for a Cuban-Soviet takeover of Grenada; the documents showed no such thing.[10]

Furthermore, the distribution of information to the public is a function of power and wealth. The government itself can color the citizens' understanding of events by its control of news at the source: the presidential press conference, the "leak to the press," the White Papers, the teams of "truth experts" going around the country at the taxpayers' expense. As for private media, the large networks and mass-circulation magazines have the greatest access to the public mind. There is no "equal time" for critics of public policy. . . .

3. EQUAL PROTECTION

Let us go now from the procedural to the substantive, indeed to the most substantive of questions: the right of all people to life itself. Here we find democracy in America tragically inadequate. Not only Locke, one of the leading theorists of the democratic tradition, declared the ultimate right of any person to safeguard his own life when threatened by the government; Hobbes, often looked on as the foe of democratic thought, agreed. Yet, in matters of foreign policy, where the decisions involve life or death for large numbers of Americans, power rests in the hands of the president and a small group of advisers. Despite the constitutional provision that war must be declared by Congress, in reality the President can create situations (as in the Mexican War, as in both world wars) which make inevitable congressional votes for war. And in all post-World War II conflicts (Korea, Vietnam, Iraq) there was no declaration of war by Congress.

It is in connection with this most basic of rights—life itself, the first and most important of those substantive ends which democratic participation is

---

*The Bay of Pigs operation was an unsuccessful, United States-backed invasion of Cuba by Cuban exiles in 1961; the Gulf of Tonkin Resolution, passed by Congress in 1965 on the occasion of an alleged attack on U.S. ships by the North Vietnamese, authorized the deployment of thousands of U.S. troops to Vietnam—*Editors*.

designed to safeguard—that I would assert the need for a global view of democracy. One can at least conceive of a democratic decision for martial sacrifice by those ready to make the sacrifice; a "democratic" war is thus a theoretical possibility. But that presumption of democracy becomes obviously false at the first shot because then *others* are affected who did not decide. . . . Nations making decisions to slaughter their own sons are at least theoretically subject to internal check. The victims on the other side fall without any such chance. For the United States today, this failure of democracy is total; we have the capacity to destroy the world without giving it a chance to murmur a dissent; we did, in fact, destroy a part of southeast Asia on the basis of a unilateral decision made in Washington. There is no more pernicious manifestation of the lack of democracy in America than this single fact.

4. EQUALITY BEFORE THE LAW

Is there equality before the law? At every stage of the judicial process—facing the policeman, appearing in court, being freed on bond, being sentenced by the judge—the poor person is treated worse than the rich, the black treated worse than the white, the politically or personally odd character is treated worse than the orthodox. A defendant's poverty affects his preliminary hearing, his right to bail, the quality of his counsel. The evidence is plentiful in the daily newspapers, which inform us that an African-American boy fleeing the scene of a two-dollar theft may be shot and killed by a pursuing policeman, while a wealthy man who goes to South America after a million-dollar swindle, even if apprehended, need never fear a scratch. The wealthy price-fixer for General Motors, who costs consumers millions, will get ninety days in jail, the burglar of a liquor store will get five years. An African-American youth, or a bearded white youth poorly dressed, has much more chance of being clubbed by a policeman on the street than a well-dressed white man, given the fact that both respond with equal tartness to a question. . . .

Aside from inequality among citizens, there is inequality between the citizen and his government, when they face one another in a court of law. Take the matter of counsel: the well-trained government prosecutor faces the indigent's court-appointed counsel. Four of my students did a study of the City Court of Boston several years ago. They sat in the court for weeks, taking notes, and found that the average time spent by court-appointed counsel with his client, before arguing the case at the bench, was seven minutes.

5. DISTRIBUTION OF RESOURCES

Democracy is devoid of meaning if it does not include equal access to the available resources of the society. In India, democracy might still mean poverty; in the United States, with a Gross National Product of more than $3 trillion a year, democracy should mean that every American, working a short work-week, has adequate food, clothing, shelter, health care, education for himself and his family—in short, the material resources necessary to enjoy life and freedom. Even if only 20 percent of the American population is desperately poor . . . in a country so rich, that is an inexcusable breach of the democratic principle. Even if there is a large, prosperous middle class, there is something grossly unfair in the fact that in 1995 the richest 1 percent of the population owned over 40 percent of the total wealth, a figure that, throughout our history, has rarely been under 33 percent.

Whether you are poor or rich determines the most fundamental facts about your life: whether you are cold in the winter while trying to sleep, whether you suffocate in the summer; whether you live among vermin or rats; whether the smells around you all day are sweet or foul; whether you have adequate medical care; whether you have good teeth; whether you can send your children to college; whether you can go on vacation or have to take an extra job at night; whether you can afford a divorce, or an abortion, or a wife, or another child. . . .

6. ACCESS TO EDUCATION

In a highly industrialized society, education is a crucial determinant of wealth, political power, social status, leisure, and the ability to work in one's chosen field. Educational resources in our society are not equitably distributed. Among highschool graduates of the same IQ levels, a far higher percentage of the well-to-do go on to college than the poor.[11] A mediocre student with money can always go to college. A mediocre student without money may not be able to go, even to a state college, because he may have to work to support his family. Furthermore, the educational resources in the schools—equipment, teachers, etc.—are far superior in the wealthy suburbs than in the poor sections of the city, whether white or black.

7. FREEDOM OF EXPRESSION

Like money, freedom of expression is available to all in America, but in widely varying quantities. The First Amendment formally guarantees freedom of speech, press, assembly, and petition to all—but certain realities of wealth, power, and status stand in the way of the equal distribution of these rights. Anyone can stand on a street corner and talk to ten or a hundred people. But someone with the resources to buy loudspeaker equipment, go through the necessary red tape, and post a bond with the city may hold a meeting downtown and reach a thousand or five thousand people. A person or a corporation with $100,000 can buy time on television and reach 10 million people. A rich person simply has much more freedom of speech than a poor person. The government has much more freedom of expression than a private individual, because the president can command the airwaves when he wishes, and reach 60 million people in one night.

Freedom of the press also is guaranteed to all. But the student selling an underground newspaper on the street with a nude woman on the cover may be arrested by a policeman, while the airport newsstand selling *Playboy* and ten magazines like it will remain safe. Anyone with $10,000 can put out a newspaper to reach a few thousand people. Anyone with $10 million can buy a few newspapers that will reach a few million people. Anyone who is penniless had better have a loud voice; and then he might be arrested for disturbing the peace.

8. FREEDOM FOR INDIVIDUALITY

The right to live one's life, in privacy and freedom, in whatever way one wants, so long as others are not harmed, should be a sacred principle in a democracy. But there are hundreds of laws, varying from state to state, and sometimes joined by federal laws, which regulate the personal lives of people in this country: their marriages, their divorces, their sexual relations. Furthermore, both laws and court decisions protect policemen and the FBI in their use of secret devices which listen in on private conversations, or peer in on private conduct.

9. THE SPIRIT OF COOPERATION

The maintenance of those substantive elements of democracy which I have just sketched, if dependent on a pervasive network of coercion, would cancel out much of the benefit of that democracy. Democracy needs rather to be sustained by a spirit in society, the tone and the values of the culture. I am speaking of something as elusive as a mood, alongside something as hard as law, both of which would have to substitute cooperation tinged with friendly competition for the fierce combat of our business culture. I am speaking of the underlying drive that keeps people going in the society. So long as that drive is for money and power, with no ceiling on either, so long as ruthlessness is built into the rules of the game, democracy does not have a chance. If there is one crucial cause in the failure of American democracy—not the only one, of course, but a fundamental one—it is the drive for corporate profit, and the overwhelming influence of money in every aspect of our daily lives. That is the uncontrolled libido of our society from which the rape of democratic values necessarily follows.

The manifestations are diverse and endless: The drug industry's drive for profit has led to incredible overpricing of drugs for consumers (700 percent markup, for instance, for tablets to arthritic patients). It was disclosed in 1979 that Johns-Manville, the nation's largest asbestos manufacturer, had deliberately withheld from its workers X-ray results that showed they were developing cancer. In 1984, a company making an intrauterine birth control device—the Dalkon Shield—was found by a Minnesota court to have allowed tens of thousands of women to wear this device despite knowing that it was dangerous to their health (*Minneapolis Star and Tribune,* May 18, 1984). In the mid-1990s, it was revealed that tobacco companies had concealed information showing the narcotic nature of cigarettes. All in the interest of maximizing profit.

If these were isolated cases, reported and then eliminated, they could be dismissed as unfortunate blemishes on an otherwise healthy social body. But the major allocations of resources in our society are made on the basis of money profit rather than social use. . . .

. . . News items buttress what I have said. The oil that polluted California's beautiful beaches in the 1960s . . . was produced by a system in which the oil companies' hunger for profit has far more weight than the ordinary person's need to swim in clean water. This is not to be attributed to Republicanism over-riding the concern for the little fellow of the Democratic Party. Profit is master whichever party is in power; it was the liberal Secretary of the Interior Stewart Udall who allowed the dangerous drilling to go on. . . .

In 1984, the suit of several thousand veterans against the Dow Chemical Company, claiming that they and their families had suffered terrible illnesses as a result of exposure in Vietnam to the poisonous chemical Agent Orange, was settled. The Dow corporation avoided the disclosures of thousands of doc-uments in open court by agreeing to pay $180 million to the veterans. One thing seemed clear: The company had known that the defoliant used in Vietnam might be dangerous, but it held back the news, and blamed the government for ordering use of the chemical. The government itself, apparently wanting to shift blame to the corporation, declared publicly that Dow Chemical had been motivated in its actions by greed for profit.

10. OPPORTUNITY TO PROTEST

The first two elements in my list for democracy—decision-making and infor-mation to help make them—are procedural. The next six are substantive, deal-ing with the consequences of such procedures on life, liberty, and the pursuit of happiness. My ninth point, the one I have just discussed, shows how the money motive of our society corrupts both procedures and their consequences by its existence and suggests we need a different motive as a fundamental requisite of a democratic society. The point I am about to discuss is an ultimate requisite for democracy, a safety feature if nothing else—neither procedures nor conse-quences nor motivation—works. It is the right of citizens to break through the impasse of a legal and cultural structure, which sustains inequality, greed, and murder, to initiate processes for change. I am speaking of civil disobedience, which is an essential safeguard even in a successful society, and which is an absolute necessity in a society which is not going well.

If the institutional structure itself bars any change but the most picayune and grievances are serious, it is silly to insist that change must be mediated through the processes of that legal structure. In such a situation, dramatic expressions of protest and challenge are necessary to help change ways of thinking, to build up political power for drastic change. A society that calls itself democratic (whether accurately or not) must, as its ultimate safeguard, allow such acts of disobedience. If the government prohibits them (as we must expect from a government committed to the existent) then the members of a society concerned with democracy must not only defend such acts, but encourage them. Somewhere near the root of democratic thought is the theory of popular sovereignty, declaring that government and laws are instruments for certain ends, and are not to be deified with absolute obedience; they must constantly be checked by the citizenry, and challenged, opposed, even overthrown, if they become threats to fundamental rights.

Any abstract assessment of *when* disobedience is justified is pointless. Proper conclusions depend on empirical evidence about how bad things are at the moment, and how adequate are the institutional mechanisms for correcting them. . . .

One of these is the matter of race. The intolerable position of the African-American, in both North and South, has traditionally been handled with a few muttered apologies and tokens of reform. Then the civil disobedience of militants in the South forced our attention on the most dramatic (southern) manifestations of racism in America. The massive African-American urban uprisings of 1967 and 1968 showed that nothing less than civil disobedience (for riots and uprisings go beyond that) could make the nation see that the race problem is an American—not a southern—problem and that it needs bold, revolutionary action.

As for poverty: It seems clear that the normal mechanisms of congressional pretense and presidential rhetoric are not going to change things very much. Acts of civil disobedience by the poor will be required, at the least, to make middle-class America take notice, to bring national decisions that begin to reallocate wealth.

The war in Vietnam showed that we could not depend on the normal processes of "law and order," of the election process, of letters to the *Times*, to stop a series of especially brutal acts against the Vietnamese and against our own sons. It took a nationwide storm of protest, including thousands of acts of civil disobedience (14,000 people were arrested in one day in 1971 in Washington, D.C.), to help bring the war to an end. The role of draft resistance in affecting Lyndon Johnson's 1968 decision not to escalate the war further is told in the Defense Department secret documents of that period. In the 1980s and 1990s civil disobedience continued, with religious pacifists and others risking prison in order to protest the arms race and the plans for nuclear war.

The great danger for American democracy is not from the protesters. That democracy is too poorly realized for us to consider critics—even rebels—as the chief problem. Its fulfillment requires us all, living in an ossified system which sustains too much killing and too much selfishness, to join the protest.

NOTES

1. Robert A. Dahl, *A Preface to Democratic Theory* (Chicago: University of Chicago Press, 1963), p. 81.
2. *Ibid.,* p. 124.
3. *Ibid.,* p. 125.
4. *Ibid.,* p. 131.
5. *Ibid.,* pp. 131–32.

6. *The New York Times*, January 25, 27, 1997.
7. Dahl, *A Preface to Democratic Theory*, p. 146.
8. Robert Wiebe, "The Confinements of Consensus," *TriQuarterly*, 1966. Copyright by TriQuarterly 1966. All rights reserved.
9. *The New York Times*, September 25, 1984.
10. *The New York Times* reported, November 5, 1983: "There is nothing in the documents, however, that specifically indicates that Cuba and the Soviet Union were on the verge of taking over Grenada, as Administration officials have suggested."
11. See the Carnegie Council on Children study, *Small Futures*, by Richard deLore, 1979.

How Democratic Is America?
A Response to Howard Zinn
Sidney Hook

Charles Peirce, the great American philosopher, once observed that there was such a thing as the "ethics of words." The "ethics of words" are violated whenever ordinary terms are used in an unusual context or arbitrarily identified with another concept for which other terms are in common use. Mr. Zinn is guilty of a systematic violation of the "ethics of words." In consequence, his discussion of "democracy" results in a great many methodological errors as well as inconsistencies. To conserve space, I shall focus on three.

I

First of all, he confuses democracy as a political process with democracy as a political *product* or state of welfare; democracy as a *"free society"* with democracy as a *"good society,"* where good is defined in terms of equality or justice (or both) or some other constellation of values. One of the reasons for choosing to

Sidney Hook (1902–1989) was head of the department of philosophy at New York University from 1934 to 1969 and was a senior research fellow at the Hoover Institution on War, Revolution, and Peace at Stanford University from 1973 to 1989. This essay was originally published in Robert A. Goldwin, ed., *How Democratic Is America?* (Chicago, Rand McNally, 1971), pp. 62–75. The author revised and updated the original for *Points of View* in 1985.

live under a democratic political system rather than a nondemocratic system is our belief that it makes possible a better society. That is something that must be empirically established, something denied by critics of democracy from Plato to Santayana. The equality which is relevant to democracy as a *political process* is, in the first instance, political equality with respect to the rights of citizenship. Theoretically, a politically democratic community could vote, wisely or unwisely, to abolish, retain, or establish certain economic inequalities. Theoretically, a benevolent despotism could institute certain kinds of social and even juridical equalities. Historically, the Bismarckian political dictatorship introduced social welfare legislation for the masses at a time when such legislation would have been repudiated by the existing British and American political democracies. Some of Mr. Zinn's proposed reforms could be introduced under a dictatorship or benevolent despotism. Therefore, they are not logically or organically related to democracy.

The second error in Mr. Zinn's approach to democracy is "to measure our democracy against an ideal (even if admittedly unachievable) standard . . . even if utopian . . ." without *defining* the standard. His criteria admittedly are neither necessary nor sufficient for determining the presence of democracy since he himself admits that they are applicable to societies that are not democratic. Further, even if we were to take his criteria as severally defining the presence of democracy—as we might take certain physical and mental traits as constituting a definition of health—he gives no operational test for determining whether or not they have been fulfilled. For example, among the criteria he lists for determining whether a society is democratic is this: "Are the members of the society equally protected on matters of life and death—in the most literal sense of that phrase?" A moment's reflection will show that here—as well as in other cases where Mr. Zinn speaks of equality—it is impossible for all members to be equally protected on matters of life and death—certainly not in a world in which men do the fighting and women give birth to children, where children need *more* protection than adults, and where some risk-seeking adults require and deserve less protection (since resources are not infinite) than others. As Karl Marx realized, "in the most literal sense of that phrase," there cannot be absolute equality even in a classless society. . . .

The only sensible procedure in determining the absence or presence of equality from a democratic perspective is comparative. We must ask whether a culture is more or less democratic in comparison to the past with respect to some *desirable* feature of equality (Zinn ignores the fact that not all equalities are desirable). It is better for some people to be more intelligent and more knowledgeable than others than for all to be unintelligent and ignorant. There never is literally equal access to education, to knowledge and training in any society. The question is: Is there more access today for more people than yesterday, and how can we increase the access tomorrow?

Mr. Zinn refuses to take this approach because, he asserts, "it supports complacency." It does nothing of the sort! On the contrary, it shows that progress is possible, and encourages us to exert our efforts in the same direction if we regard the direction as desirable.

It will be instructive to look at the passage in which Mr. Zinn objects to this sensible comparative approach because it reveals the bias in his approach:

"With such a standard," he writes, "Russia in 1910 could point with pride to how much progress they had made toward parliamentary democracy; as Russians in 1985 could point to their post-Stalin progress away from the gulag; as Americans could point in 1939 to how far they had come in solving the problem of economic equality; as Americans in the South could point in 1950 to the progress of the southern African-American."

a. In 1910 the Russians were indeed moving toward greater progress in local parliamentary institutions. Far from making them complacent, they moved towards more inclusive representative institutions which culminated in elections to the Constituent Assembly in 1918, which was bayoneted out of existence by Lenin and the Communist Party, with a minority party dictatorship established.

b. Only Mr. Zinn would regard the slight diminution in terror from the days of Stalin to the regime of Chernenko as progress toward democracy. Those who observe the ethics of words would normally say that the screws of repression had been slightly relaxed. Mr. Zinn seems unaware that as bad as the terror was under Lenin, it was not as pervasive as it is today.* But no one with any respect for the ethics of words would speak of "the progress of democracy" in the Soviet Union from Lenin to Stalin to Khrushchev to Chernenko. Their regimes were varying degrees of dictatorship and terror.

c. Americans could justifiably say that in 1939 progress had been made in giving workers a greater role, not as Mr. Zinn says in "solving the problem of economic equality" (a meaningless phrase), but in determining the conditions and rewards of work that prevailed in 1929 or previously because the existence of the Wagner Labor Relations Act made collective bargaining the law of the land. They could say this *not* to rest in complacency, but to use the organized force of their trade unions to influence further the political life of the country. And indeed, it was the organized labor movement in 1984 which in effect chose the candidate of the Democratic Party.

d. Americans in the South in 1950 could rightfully speak of the progress of the southern African-American over the days of unrestricted Jim Crow and lynching bees of the past, not to rest in complacency, but to agitate for further progress through the Supreme Court decision of Brown v. Board of Education in Topeka and through the Civil Rights Act of Congress. This has not made them complacent, but more resolved to press further to eliminate remaining practices of invidious discrimination.

Even Mr. Zinn should admit that with respect to some of his other criteria this is the only sensible approach. Otherwise we get unhistorical answers, the hallmark of the doctrinaire. He asks—criterion 1—"To what extent can various people in the society participate in those decisions which affect their

---

*These words and subsequent references to the Soviet Union preceded the reforms initiated under Mikhail Gorbachev and continued under Boris Yeltsin and Vladimir Putin—*Editors.*

lives?" and—criterion 7—"Is there freedom of expression on all matters, and equally for all, to communicate with other members of the society?" Why doesn't Mr. Zinn adopt this sensible comparative approach? Because it would lead him to inquire into the extent to which people are free to participate in decisions that affect their lives *today,* free to express themselves, free to organize, free to protest and dissent today, *in comparison with the past.* It would lead him to the judgment *which he wishes to avoid at all costs,* to wit, that despite the grave problems, gaps, and tasks before us, the United States is more democratic today than it was a hundred years ago, fifty years ago, twenty years ago, five years ago with respect to every one of the criteria he has listed. To recognize this is not an invitation to complacency. On the contrary, it indicates the possibility of broadening, deepening, and using the democratic political process to improve the quality of human life, to modify and redirect social institutions in order to realize on a wider scale the moral commitment of democracy to an equality of concern for all its citizens to achieve their fullest growth as persons. This commitment is to a process, not to a transcendent goal or a fixed, ideal standard.

In a halting, imperfect manner, set back by periods of violence, vigilantism, and xenophobia, the political democratic process in the United States has been used to modify the operation of the economic system. The improvements and reforms won from time to time make the still-existing problems and evils more acute in that people become more aware of them. The more the democratic process extends human freedoms, and the more it introduces justice in social relations and the distribution of wealth, the greater grows the desire for *more* freedom and justice. Historically and psychologically, it is false to assume that reforms breed a spirit of complacency. . . .

The third and perhaps most serious weakness in Mr. Zinn's view is his conception of the nature of the formal political democratic process. It suffers from several related defects. First, it overlooks the central importance of majority rule in the democratic process. Second, it denies in effect that majority rule is possible by defining democracy in such a way that it becomes impossible. . . .

"Representation by its very nature," claims Mr. Zinn, "is undemocratic." This is Rousseauistic nonsense. For it would mean that no democracy—including all societies that Mr. Zinn ever claimed at any time to be democratic—could possibly exist, not even the direct democracies or assemblies of Athens or the New England town meetings. For all such assemblies must elect officials to carry out their will. If no representative (and an official is a representative, too) can adequately represent another's needs, there is no assurance that in the actual details of governance, the selectmen, road commissioners, or other town or assembly officials will, in fact, carry out their directives. No assembly or meeting can sit in continuous session or collectively carry out the common decision. In the nature of the case, officials, like representatives, constitute an elite and their actions *may* reflect their interests more than the interests of the governed. This makes crucial the questions whether and how an elite can be removed, whether the consent on which the rule of the officials or representatives rests is free or coerced, whether a minority can peacefully use these mechanisms, by which freely given consent is registered, to win over or become a majority. The existence of representative assemblies makes democracy difficult, not impossible.

Since Mr. Zinn believes that a majority never has any authority to bind a minority as well as itself by decisions taken after free discussion and debate, he is logically committed to anarchy. Failing to see this, he confuses two fundamentally different things—the meaning or definition of democracy, and its justification.

1. A democratic government is one in which the general direction of policy rests directly or indirectly upon the freely given consent of a majority of the adults governed. Ambiguities and niceties aside, that is what democracy means. It is not anarchy. The absence of a unanimous consensus does not entail the absence of democracy.

2. One may reject on moral or religious or personal grounds a democratic society. Plato, as well as modern totalitarians, contends that a majority of mankind is either too stupid or vicious to be entrusted with self-government, or to be given the power to accept or reject their ruling elites, and that the only viable alternative to democracy is the self-selecting and self-perpetuating elite of "the wise," or "the efficient," or "the holy," or "the strong," depending upon the particular ideology of the totalitarian apologist. The only thing they have in common with democrats is their rejection of anarchy.

3. No intelligent and moral person can make an *absolute* of democracy in the sense that he believes it is always, everywhere, under any conditions, and no matter what its consequences, ethically legitimate. Democracy is obviously not desirable in a head-hunting or cannibalistic society or in an institution of the feeble-minded. But wherever and whenever a principled democrat accepts the political system of democracy, he must accept the binding authority of legislative decisions, reached after the free give-and-take of debate and discussion, as binding upon him whether he is a member of the majority or minority. Otherwise the consequence is incipient or overt anarchy or civil war, the usual preface to despotism or tyranny. Accepting the decision of the majority as binding does not mean that it is final or irreversible. The processes of freely given consent must make it possible for a minority to urge amendment or repeal of any decision of the majority. Under carefully guarded provisions, a democrat may resort to civil disobedience of a properly enacted law in order to bear witness to the depths of his commitment in an effort to *reeducate* his fellow citizens. But in that case he must voluntarily accept punishment for his civil disobedience, and so long as he remains a democrat, voluntarily abandon his violation or noncompliance with law at the point where its consequences threaten to destroy the democratic process and open the floodgates either to the violent disorders of anarchy or to the dictatorship of a despot or a minority political party.

4. That Mr. Zinn is not a democrat but an anarchist in his views is apparent in his contention that not only must a democracy allow or tolerate civil disobedience within limits, but that "members of a society concerned with democracy must not only defend such acts, but encourage them."

On this view, if southern segregationists resort to civil disobedience to negate the long-delayed but eminently just measures adopted by the government to implement the amendments that outlaw slavery, they should be encouraged to do so. On this view, any group that defies any law that violates its conscience—with respect to marriage, taxation, vaccination, abortion, education—should be encouraged to do so. Mr. Zinn, like most anarchists, refuses to generalize the principles behind his action. He fails to see that if all fanatics of causes deemed by them to be morally just were encouraged to resort to civil disobedience, even our imperfect existing political democracy would dissolve in chaos, and that civil disobedience would soon become quite uncivil. He fails to see that *in a democracy the processes of intelligence, not individual conscience, must be supreme.*

II

I turn now to some of the issues that Mr. Zinn declares are substantive. Before doing so I wish to make clear my belief that the most substantive issue of all is the procedural one by which the inescapable differences of interests among men, once a certain moral level of civilization has been reached, are to be negotiated. The belief in the validity of democratic procedures rests upon the conviction that where adult human beings have freedom of access to relevant information, they are, by and large, better judges of their own interests than are those who set themselves up as their betters and rulers, that, to use the homely maxim, those who wear the shoes know best where they pinch and therefore have the right to change their political shoes in the light of their experience. . . .

Looking at the question "How democratic is America?" with respect to the problems of poverty, race, education, etc., we must say "Not democratic enough!", but not for the reasons Mr. Zinn gives. For he seems to believe that the failure to adopt *his* solutions and proposals with respect to foreign policy, slum clearance, pollution, etc., is evidence of the failure of the democratic process itself. He overlooks the crucial difference between the procedural process and the substantive issues. When he writes that democracy is devoid of meaning if it does not include "equal access to the available resources of the society," he is simply abusing language. Assuming such equal access is desirable (which some might question who believe that access to *some* of society's resources—for example, to specialized training or to scarce supplies—should go not equally to all but to the most needful or sometimes to the most qualified), a democracy may or may not legislate such equal access. The crucial question is whether the electorate has the power to make the choice, or to elect those who would carry out the mandate chosen. . . .

When Mr. Zinn goes on to say that "in the United States . . . democracy should mean that every American, working a short work-week, has adequate food, clothing, shelter, health care, . . ." he is not only abusing language, he is revealing the fact that the procedural processes that are essential to the meaning of democracy, in ordinary usage, are not essential to his conception. He is violating the basic ethics of discourse. If democracy "should mean" what Mr. Zinn says it should, then were Huey Long or any other dictator to seize power and introduce a "short work-week" and distribute "adequate food, clothing, shelter, health care" to the masses, Mr. Zinn would have to regard his regime as democratic.

After all, when Hitler came to power and abolished free elections in Germany, he at the same time reduced unemployment, increased the real wages of the German worker, and provided more adequate food, clothing, shelter, and health care than was available under the Weimar Republic. On Zinn's view of what democracy "should mean," this made Hitler's rule more democratic than that of Weimar. . . .

Not surprisingly, Mr. Zinn is a very unreliable guide even in his account of the procedural features of the American political system. In one breath he maintains that not enough information is available to voters to make intelligent choices on major political issues like tax laws. (The voter, of course, does not vote on such laws but for representatives who have taken stands on a number of complex issues.) "The dominant influences are those of big business, which has the resources both to understand and to act." In another breath, he complains that the electorate is at the mercy of the propagandist. "The propagandist does not need to lie; he overwhelms the public with so much information as to lead it to believe that it is all too complicated for anyone but the experts."

Mr. Zinn is certainly hard to please! The American political process is not democratic because the electorate hasn't got enough information. It is also undemocratic because it receives too much information. What would Mr. Zinn have us do so that the public gets just the right amount of information and propaganda? Have the government control the press? Restrict freedom of propaganda? But these are precisely the devices of totalitarian societies. The evils of the press, even when it is free of government control, are many indeed. The great problem is to keep the press free and responsible. And as defective as the press and other public media are today, surely it is an exaggeration to say that with respect to tax laws "the dominant influences are those of big business." If they were, how can we account for the existence of the income tax laws? If the influence of big business on the press is so dominant and the press is so biased, how can we account for the fact that although 92 percent of the press opposed Truman's candidacy in 1948, he was reelected? How can we account for the profound dissatisfaction of Vice President Agnew with the press and other mass media?* And since Mr. Zinn believes that big business dominates our educational system, especially our universities, how can we account for the fact that the universities are the centers of the strongest dissent in the nation to public and national policy, that the National Association of Manufacturers bitterly complained a few years ago that the economics of the free enterprise system was derided, and often not even taught, in most Departments of Economics in the colleges and universities of the nation?

---

*Spiro Agnew, former governor of Maryland and vice president of the United States before being forced to resign in 1973 during the second term of President Richard Nixon, was a frequent and vociferous critic of the "liberal" press—*Editors.*

Mr. Zinn's exaggerations are really caricatures of complex realities. Far from being controlled by the monolithic American corporate economy, American public opinion is today marked by a greater scope and depth of dissent than at any time in its history, except for the days preceding the Civil War. The voice and the votes of Main Street still count for more in a democratic polity than those of Wall Street. Congress has limited, and can still further limit, the influence of money on the electoral process by federal subsidy and regulations. There are always abuses needing reforms. By failing to take a comparative approach and instead focusing on some absolute utopian standard of perfection, Mr. Zinn gives an exaggerated, tendentious, and fundamentally false picture of the United States. There is hardly a sentence in his essay that is free of some serious flaw in perspective, accuracy, or emphasis. Sometimes they have a comic effect, as when Mr. Zinn talks about the lack of "equal distribution of the right of freedom of expression." What kind of "equal distribution" is he talking about? Of course, a person with more money can talk to more people than one with less, although this does not mean that more persons will listen to him, agree with him, or be influenced by him. But a person with a more eloquent voice or a better brain can reach more people than you or I. What shall we do to insure equal distribution of the right of freedom of expression? Insist on equality of voice volume or pattern, and equality of brain power? More money gives not only greater opportunity to talk to people than less money but the ability to do thousands of things barred to those who have less money. Shall we then decree that all people have the same amount of money all the time and forbid anyone from depriving anyone else of any of his money even by fair means? "The government," writes Mr. Zinn, "has much more freedom of expression than a private individual because the president can command the airwaves when he wishes, and reach 60 million people in one night."

Alas! Mr. Zinn is not joking. Either he wants to bar the president or any public official from using the airwaves or he wants all of us to take turns. One wonders what country Mr. Zinn is living in. Nixon spoke to 60 million people several times, and so did Jimmy Carter. What was the result? More significant than the fact that 60 million people hear the president is that 60 million or more can hear his critics, sometimes right after he speaks, and that no one is compelled to listen.

Mr. Zinn does not understand the basic meaning of equality in a free, open democratic society. Its philosophy does not presuppose that all citizens are physically or intellectually equal or that all are equally gifted in every or any respect. It holds that all enjoy a *moral* equality, and that therefore, as far as is practicable, given finite resources, the institutions of a democratic society should seek to provide an equal opportunity to all its citizens to develop themselves to their full desirable potential.

Of course, we cannot ever provide complete equal opportunity. More and more is enough. For one thing, so long as children have different parents and home environments, they cannot enjoy the same or equal opportunities. Nonetheless, the family has compensating advantages for all that. Let us hope that Mr. Zinn does not wish to wipe out the family to avoid differences in opportunity. Plato believed that the family, as we know it, should be abolished because it did not provide equality of opportunity, and that all children should be brought up by the state.

Belief in the moral equality of men and women does not require that all individuals be treated identically or that equal treatment must be measured or determined by equality of outcome or result. Every citizen should have an equal right to an education, but that does not mean that, regardless of capacity and interest, he or she should have the same amount of schooling beyond the adolescent years, and at the same schools, and take the same course of study. With the increase in national wealth, a good case can be made for an equal right of all citizens to health care or medical treatment. But only a quack or ideological fanatic would insist that therefore all individuals should have the same medical regimen no matter what ails them. This would truly be putting all human beings in the bed of Procrustes.

This conception of moral equality as distinct from Mr. Zinn's notions of equality is perfectly compatible with intelligent recognition of human inequalities and relevant ways of treating their inequalities to further both the individual and common good. Intelligent and loving parents are equally concerned with the welfare of all their children. But precisely because they are, they may provide different specific strategies in health care, education, psychological motivation, and intellectual stimulation to develop the best in all of them. The logic of Mr. Zinn's position—although he seems blissfully unaware of it—leads to the most degrading kind of egalitarian socialism, the kind which Marx and Engels in their early years denounced as "barracks socialism."

It is demonstrable that democracy is healthier and more effective where human beings do not suffer from poverty, unemployment, and disease. It is also demonstrable that to the extent that property gives power, private property in the means of social production gives power over the lives of those who must live by its use, and, therefore, that such property, whether public or private, should be responsible to those who are affected by its operation. Consequently one can argue that political democracy depends not only on the extension of the franchise to all adults, not only on its active exercise, but on programs of social welfare that provide for collective bargaining by free trade unions of workers and employees, unemployment insurance, minimum wages, guaranteed health care, and other social services that are integral to the welfare state. It is demonstrable that although the existing American welfare state provides far more welfare than was ever provided in the past—my own lifetime furnishes graphic evidence of the vast changes—it is still very far from being a genuine welfare state. Political democracy can exist without a welfare state, but it is stronger and better with it.

The basic issue that divides Mr. Zinn from others no less concerned about human welfare, but less fanatical than he, is how a genuine welfare state is to be brought about. My contention is that this can be achieved by the vigorous exercise of the existing democratic process, and that by the same coalition politics through which great gains have been achieved in the past, even greater gains can be won in the future.

For purposes of economy, I focus on the problem of poverty, or since this is a relative term, hunger. If the presence of hunger entails the absence of the democratic political process, then democracy has never existed in the past—which would be an arbitrary use of words. Nonetheless, the existence of hunger is always a threat to the continued existence of the democratic process because of the standing temptation of those who hunger to exchange freedom for the promise of bread. This, of course, is an additional ground to the even weightier moral reasons for gratifying basic human needs.

That fewer people go hungry today in the United States than ever before may show that our democracy is better than it used to be but not that it is as good as it can be. Even the existence of one hungry person is one too many. How then can hunger or the extremes of poverty be abolished? Certainly not by the method Mr. Zinn advises: "Acts of civil disobedience by the poor will be required, at the least, to make middle-class America take notice, to bring national decisions that begin to reallocate wealth."

This is not only a piece of foolish advice, it is dangerously foolish advice. Many national decisions to reallocate wealth have been made through the political process—what else is the system of taxation if not a method of reallocating wealth?—without resort to civil disobedience. Indeed, resort to civil disobedience on this issue is very likely to produce a backlash among those active and influential political groups in the community who are aware that normal political means are available for social and economic reform. The refusal to engage in such normal political processes could easily be exploited by demagogues to portray the movement towards the abolition of hunger and extreme poverty as a movement towards the confiscation and equalization of all wealth.

The simplest and most effective way of abolishing hunger is to act on the truly revolutionary principle, enunciated by the federal government, that it is responsible for maintaining a standard of relief as a minimum beneath which a family will not be permitted to sink. . . .

For reasons that need no elaboration here, the greatest of the problems faced by American democracy today is the race problem. Although tied to the problems of poverty and urban reconstruction, it has independent aspects exacerbated by the legacy of the Civil War and the Reconstruction period.

Next to the American Indians, African-Americans have suffered most from the failure of the democratic political process to extend the rights and privileges of citizenship to those whose labor and suffering have contributed so much to the conquest of the continent. The remarkable gains that have been made by African-Americans in the last twenty years have been made primarily through the political process. If the same rate of improvement continues, the year 2000 may see a rough equality established. The growth of African-American suffrage, especially in the South, the increasing sense of responsibility by the white community, despite periodic setbacks resulting from outbursts of violence, opens up a perspective of continuous and cumulative reform. The man and the organization he headed chiefly responsible for the great gains made by African-Americans, Roy Wilkins and the NAACP, were convinced that the democratic political process can be more effectively used to further the integration of African-Americans into our national life than by reliance on any other method. . . .

The only statement in Mr. Zinn's essay that I can wholeheartedly endorse is his assertion that the great danger to American democracy does not come from the phenomena of protest as such. Dissent and protest are integral to the democratic process. The danger comes from certain modes of dissent, from the substitution of violence and threats of violence for the mechanisms of the political process, from the escalation of that violence as the best hope of those who still have grievances against our imperfect American democracy, and from views such as those expressed by Mr. Zinn which downgrade the possibility of peaceful social reform and encourage rebellion. It is safe to predict that large-scale violence by impatient minorities will fail. It is almost as certain that attempts at violence will backfire, that they will create a climate of repression that may reverse the course of social progress and expanded civil liberties of the last generation. . . .

It is when Mr. Zinn is discussing racial problems that his writing ceases to be comic and silly and becomes irresponsible and mischievous. He writes:

> The massive African-American urban uprisings of 1967 and 1968 showed that nothing less than civil disobedience (for riots and uprisings go beyond that) could make the nation see that the race problem is an American—not a southern—problem and that it needs bold, revolutionary action.

First of all, every literate person knows that the race problem is an American problem, not exclusively a southern one. It needs no civil disobedience or "black uprisings" to remind us of that. Second, the massive uprisings of 1967 and 1968 were violent and uncivil, and resulted in needless loss of life and suffering. The Civil Rights Acts, according to Roy Wilkins, then head of the NAACP, were imperiled by them. They were adopted despite, not because, of them. Third, what kind of "revolutionary" action is Mr. Zinn calling for? And by whom? He seems to lack the courage of his confusions. Massive civil disobedience when sustained becomes a form of civil war.

Despite Mr. Zinn and others, violence is more likely to produce reaction than reform. In 1827 a resolution to manumit slaves by purchase (later, Lincoln's preferred solution) was defeated by three votes in the House of Burgesses of the State of Virginia. It was slated to be reintroduced in a subsequent session with excellent prospects of being adopted. Had Virginia adopted it, North Carolina would shortly have followed suit. But before it could be reintroduced, Nat Turner's rebellion broke out. Its violent excesses frightened the South into a complete rejection of a possibility that might have prevented the American Civil War—the fiercest and bloodiest war in human history up to that time, from whose consequences American society is still suffering. Mr. Zinn's intentions are as innocent as those of a child playing with matches.

III

One final word about "the global" dimension of democracy of which Mr. Zinn speaks. Here, too, he speaks sympathetically of actions that would undermine the willingness and capacity of a free society to resist totalitarian aggression.

The principles that should guide a free democratic society in a world where dictatorial regimes seek to impose their rule on other nations were formulated by John Stuart Mill, the great defender of liberty and representative government, more than a century ago:

> To go to war for an idea, if the war is aggressive not defensive, is as criminal as to go to war for territory or revenue, for it is as little justifiable to force our ideas on other people, as to compel them to submit to our will in any other aspect. . . . *The doctrine of non-intervention, to be a legitimate principle of morality, must be accepted by all governments.* The despots must consent to be bound by it as well as the free states. Unless they do, the profession of it by free countries comes but to this miserable issue, that the wrong side may help the wrong side but the right may not help the right side. Intervention to enforce non-intervention is always right, always moral *if not always prudent.* Though it may be a mistake to give freedom (or independence—S.H.) to a people who do not value the boon, it cannot be right to insist that if they do value it, they shall not be hindered from the pursuit of it by foreign coercion (*Fraser's Magazine,* 1859, emphasis mine).

Unfortunately, these principles were disregarded by the United States in 1936 when Hitler and Mussolini sent troops to Spain to help Franco overthrow the legally elected democratic Loyalist regime. The U.S. Congress, at the behest of the administration, adopted a Neutrality Resolution which prevented the democratic government of Spain from purchasing arms here. This compelled the Spanish government to make a deal with Stalin, who not only demanded its entire gold supply but the acceptance of the dread Soviet secret police, the NKVD, to supervise the operations. The main operation of the NKVD in Spain was to engage in a murderous purge of the democratic ranks of anti-Communists which led to the victory of Franco. The story is told in George Orwell's *Homage to Catalonia.* He was on the scene.

The prudence of American intervention in Vietnam may be debatable but there is little doubt that [UN ambassador] Adlai Stevenson, sometimes referred to as the liberal conscience of the nation, correctly stated the American motivation when he said at the UN on the very day of his death: "My hope in Vietnam is that resistance there may establish the fact that changes in Asia are not to be precipitated by outside force. This was the point of the Korean War. This is the point of the conflict in Vietnam."

. . . Mr. Zinn's remarks about Grenada show he is opposed to the liberal principles expressed by J. S. Mill in the passage cited above. His report of the facts about Grenada is as distorted as his account of present-day American democracy. On tiny Grenada, whose government was seized by Communist terrorists, were representatives of every Communist regime in the Kremlin's orbit, Cuban troops, and a Soviet general. I have read the documents captured by the American troops. They conclusively establish that the Communists were preparing the island as part of the Communist strategy of expansion.[1]

It is sad but significant that Mr. Zinn, whose heart bleeds for the poor Asians who suffered in the struggle to prevent the Communist takeover in Southeast Asia, has not a word of protest, not a tear of compassion for the hundreds of thousands of tortured, imprisoned, and drowned in flight after the victory of the North Vietnamese "liberators," not to mention the even greater number of victims of the Cambodian and Cuban Communists. . . .

NOTE

1. *The Grenada Papers: The Inside Story of the Grenadian Revolution—and the Making of a Totalitarian State as Told in Captured Documents* (San Francisco: Institute of Contemporary Studies, 1984).

Rebuttal to Sidney Hook
Howard Zinn

Mr. Hook *does* have the courage of his confusions. I have space to point out only a few.

1. He chooses to define democracy as a "process," thus omitting its substance. Lincoln's definition was quite good—"government of, by, and for the people." Mr. Hook pooh-poohs the last part as something that could be done by a despot. My definition, like Lincoln's, requires "of" and "by" as well as "for," process as well as content. Mr. Hook is wild about voting, which can also be allowed by despots. Voting is an improvement over autocracy, but insufficient to make any society democratic. Voting, as Emma Goldman said (true, she was an anarchist), and as Helen Keller agreed (true, she was a socialist), is "our modern fetish." It is Mr. Hook's fetish.

   Mr. Hook's "democracy" is easily satisfied by hypocrisy, by forms and procedures which look good on paper, and behind which the same old injustices go on. Concealed behind the haughty pedant's charge of "methodological errors" is a definition of democracy which is empty of human meaning, a lifeless set of structures and procedures, which our elementary school teachers tried to pawn off on us as democracy—elections, checks and balances, how a bill becomes a law. Of course, we can't have the perfect democracy, and can't avoid representation, but we get closer to democracy when representation is supplemented by the direct action of citizens.

Howard Zinn's rebuttal was written specifically for this volume.

The missing heart, the flowing blood, the life-giving element in democracy is the constant struggle of people inside, around, outside, and despite the ordinary political processes. That means protest, strikes, boycotts, demonstrations, petitions, agitation, education, sometimes the slow buildup of public opinion, sometimes civil disobedience.

2. Mr. Hook seems oblivious of historical experience in the United States. His infatuation with "political process" comes out of ancient textbooks in which presidents and congresses act in the nick of time to save us when we're in trouble. In fact, that political process has never been sufficient to solve any crucial problem of human rights in our country: slavery, corporate despotism, war—all required popular movements to oppose them, movements outside those channels into which Mr. Hook and other apologists for the status quo constantly invite us, so we can get lost. Only when popular movements go into action do the channels themselves suddenly come to life.

The test is in history. When Mr. Hook says African-Americans got their gains "primarily through the political process" he simply does not know what he is talking about. The new consciousness of the rights of African-Americans, the gains made in the past twenty years—were they initiated by the "political process"? That process was dead for one hundred years while five thousand African-Americans were lynched, segregation flourished, and presidents, Congress, and the Supreme Court turned the other cheek. Only when African-Americans took to the streets by the tens of thousands, sat-in, demonstrated, even broke the law, did the "political process" awaken from its long lethargy. Only then did Congress rush to pass civil rights laws, just in time for Mr. Hook to say, cheerily, "You see, the process works."

Another test. Mr. Hook talks about the progress made "because the existence of the Wagner Labor Relations Act made collective bargaining the law of the land." He seems unaware of the wave of strikes in 1933–34 throughout the nation that brought a dead labor relations act to life. Peter Irons, in his prize-winning study, *The New Deal Lawyers*, carefully examines the chronology of 1934, and concludes: "It is likely that the existing National Labor Relations Board would have limped along, unable to enforce its orders, had not the industrial workforce erupted in late April, engulfing the country in virtual class war . . . Roosevelt and the Congress were suddenly jolted into action." Even after the act was passed in 1935, employers resisted it, and it took the sitdown strikes of 1936–37—yes, civil disobedience—to get contracts with General Motors and U.S. Steel.

A third test. The political process was pitifully inept as a handful of decision-makers, telling lies, propelled this country into the ugly war in Vietnam. (Mr. Hook joins them, when he quotes Adlai Stevenson that we were in Vietnam to act against "outside force"; the overwhelming "outside force" in Vietnam was the United States, with 525,000 troops, dropping 7 million tons of bombs on Southeast Asia.) A president elected in 1964 on his promises to keep the peace took us into war; Congress, like sheep, voted the money; the Supreme Court enveloped itself in its black robes and refused to discuss the constitutionality of the war. It took an unprecedented movement of protest to arouse the nation, to send a surge of energy moving through those clogged processes, and finally bring the war to an end.

3. Mr. Hook doesn't understand civil disobedience. He makes the common error of thinking that a supporter of Martin Luther King's civil disobedience must also support that of the Ku Klux Klan. He seems to think that if you believe civil disobedience is sometimes justified, for some causes, you must support civil disobedience done any time, by any group, for any reason. He does not grasp that the principle is not one of absolute civil disobedience; it simply denies absolute obedience. It says we should not be fanatics about "law and order" because sometimes the law supports the disorder of poverty, or racism, or war.

   We can certainly distinguish between civil disobedience for good causes and for bad causes. That's what our intelligence is for. Will this lead to "chaos," as Mr. Hook warns? Again, historical experience is instructive: Did the civil disobedience of African-Americans in the sixties lead to chaos? Or the civil disobedience of anti-war protesters in the Vietnam years? Yes, they involved some disorder, as all social change does; they upset the false tranquility of segregation, they demanded an end to the chaos of war.

4. Mr. Hook thinks he is telling us something new when he says we can't, and sometimes should not, have perfect equality. Of course. But the point of having ideals is not that they can be perfectly achieved, but that they do not let us rest content, as Mr. Hook is, with being somewhat better off today than yesterday. By his standard, we can give just enough more to the poor to appease anger, while keeping the basic injustice of a wealthy society. In a country where some people live in mansions and others in slums, should we congratulate ourselves because the slums now have TV antennas sticking out of the leaky roofs? His prescription for equality would have us clean out the Augean stables with a spoon, and boast of our progress, while comparing us to all the terrible places in the world where they don't even have spoons. Mr. Hook tries to avoid this issue of inequality by confusing inequality in intellect and physique, which obviously can't be helped much, with inequality of wealth, which is intolerably crass in a country as wealthy as ours.

   Mr. Hook becomes ludicrous when he tries to deny the crucial importance of wealth in elections and in control of the media. When he says, "The voice and votes of Main Street still count for more in a democratic polity than those of Wall Street," I wonder where he has been. If Main Street counts more than Wall Street, how come congressional cutbacks in social programs in 1981–82 brought the number of people officially defined as poor to its highest level since 1965–25.3 million—while at the same time eight thousand millionaires saved a billion dollars in lowered taxes? And how can we account for this news item of October 16, 1984, in *The New York Times:* "Five of the nation's top dozen military contractors earned profits in the years

1981, 1982, and 1983, but paid no Federal income taxes." Can you name five schoolteachers or five social workers who paid no federal income taxes?

What of the system of justice—has it not always favored Wall Street over Main Street? Compare the punishment given to corporation executives found guilty of robbing billions from consumers by price-fixing with the punishment given to auto thieves and house burglars.

Money talks loudly in this "democratic polity." But, Mr. Hook says, in an absurd defense of the control of the media, you don't have to listen! No, the mother needing medical aid doesn't have to listen, but whether her children live or die may result from the fact that the rich dominate the media, control the elections, and get legislation passed which hurts the poor. *A Boston Globe* dispatch, May 24, 1984:

> Infant mortality, which had been declining steadily in Boston and other cities in the 1970s, shot up suddenly after the Reagan Administration reduced grants for health care for mothers and children and cut back sharply on Medicaid eligibility among poor women and children in 1981, according to new research.

5. As for "the global dimension of democracy," Mr. Hook's simple view of the world as divided between "free society" and "totalitarian aggression" suggests he is still living back in the heroic battles of World War II. We are now in the nuclear age, and that neat division into "free" and "totalitarian" is both factually wrong and dangerous. Yes, the United States is a relatively free society, and the Soviet Union is a shameful corruption of Marx's dreams of freedom.* But the United States has established or supported some of the most brutal totalitarian states in the world: Chile, South Africa, El Salvador, Guatemala, South Korea, the Philippines. Yes, the Soviet Union has committed cruel acts of aggression in Hungary, Czechoslovakia, and especially Afghanistan. But the United States has also, whether by the military or the CIA, committed aggression in Iran, Guatemala, Cuba, and the Dominican Republic, and especially in Vietnam, Laos, and Cambodia.

You cannot draw a line across the globe, as Mr. Hook does, to find good on one side and evil on the other. We get a sense of Mr. Hook's refusal to face the complexities of evil when he passes off the horror of the American invasion of Southeast Asia, which left a million dead, with: "The prudence of American intervention in Vietnam may be debatable." One can hear Mr. Hook's intellectual counterparts in the Soviet Union saying about the invasion of Afghanistan: "Our prudence . . . may be debatable." Such moral blindness will have to be overcome if there is to be movement toward real democracy in the United States, and toward real socialism in the Soviet Union. It is the fanaticism on both sides, justifying war "to defend freedom," or "to defend socialism," or simply, vaguely, "national security," that may yet kill us all. That will leave the issue of "how democratic we are" for archeologists of a future era.

---

*This rebuttal was written prior to the collapse of the Communist regime in the former Soviet Union—*Editors*.

Rejoinder to Howard Zinn
Sidney Hook

I may have been mistaken about Mr. Zinn's courage. I am not mistaken about his confusion—his persistent confusion of a free or democratic society with a good society as he defines a good society. Zinn has not understood my criticism and therefore not replied to it. Perhaps on rereading it he will grasp the point.

1. Of course, there is no guarantee that the democratic process will yield a good society regardless of how Zinn or anyone else defines it. Democracies, like majorities, may sometimes be wrong or unwise. But if the decision is a result of a free and fair discussion and vote, it is still democratic. If those who lose in the electoral process resort to civil disobedience, democratic government ultimately breaks down. Even though the processes of democracy are slow and cumbersome and sometimes result in unwise action, its functioning Bill of Rights makes it possible to set them right. That is why Churchill observed, "Democracy is the worst of all forms of government except all the others that have been tried," including, we should add, anarchism.

   Zinn dismisses our democratic processes as "a lifeless set of structures and procedures." But it is these very structures and procedures which have enabled us to transform our society from one in which only white men with property voted to one in which all white men voted, then all men, then all men and women. It is these structures and procedures which have extended and protected the right to dissent, even for all sorts of foolishness like Zinn's. They currently protect Mr. Zinn in his academic freedom and post, in his right to utter any criticism of the democratic system under which he lives—a right he would never enjoy in any so-called socialist society in the world today.

   Mr. Zinn gives his case away when he refers to the democratic process, which requires voting in *free* elections, as a "fetish." A fetish is an object of irrational and superstitious devotion which enlightened persons reject. Like Marx, Zinn rejects "the fetishism of commodities." Is he prepared to reject the democratic process, too, if its results do not jibe with *his* conception of the good society?

   How, one wonders, does Zinn know that his conception is inherently more desirable than that of his fellow citizens? The democrat says: *Let us leave this choice to the arbitrament of the democratic process.* Zinn has a shorter way. He labels any conception other than his own as undemocratic; and if it prevails, he urges the masses to take to the streets.

Sidney Hook's rejoinder was written specifically for this volume.

2. The space allotted to me does not permit adequate discussion of the international aspects of the struggle for a free society. (I refer students to my *Philosophy and Public Policy and Marxism and Beyond.*) Suffice it to say here that sometimes when the feasible alternatives are limited, the wisest choice between evils is the lesser one. This is the same principle, supported by Zinn, that justified military aid to the Soviet Union when Nazi Germany invaded, although Stalin's regime at the time oppressed many more millions than Hitler's. From the standpoint of the free society, Stalin was the lesser evil then. Today Nazism is destroyed and globally expanding communism has taken its place. If, and only if, we are anywhere confronted by a choice of support between an authoritarian regime and a totalitarian one, the first is the lesser evil. This is not only because the second is far more oppressive of human rights (compare Batista to Castro, Thieu to Hanoi, Syngman Rhee to North Korea, Lon Nol to Pol Pot) but because authoritarian regimes sometimes develop peacefully into democracies (Spain, Portugal, Greece, Argentina) whereas no Communist regime allied to the Kremlin so far has.*

3. Within narrowly prescribed limits, a democracy may tolerate civil disobedience of those who on grounds of conscience violate its laws and willingly accept their punishment. (Cf. the chapter in my *Revolution, Reform and Social Justice.*) But Zinn does not advocate civil disobedience in this sense. He urges what is clearly *uncivil* disobedience like the riotous actions that preceded the Civil Rights Acts from which African-Americans, not white racists, suffered most, and the extensive destruction of property from factory sit-ins. Roy Wilkins, who should know, is my authority for asserting that the Civil Rights Acts were adopted by Congress not because of, but despite of, these disorders. The most significant racial progress since 1865 was achieved by *Brown* v. *Topeka Board of Education* without "the disorders" Zinn recommends—a sly term that covers broken heads, loss of property, and sometimes loss of life, which are no part of civil disobedience.

   Until now, the most charitable thing one could say of Zinn's position is what Cicero once said of another loose thinker: there is no absurdity to which a person will not resort to defend another absurdity. But when Zinn with calculated ambiguity includes "disorders" in the connotation of civil disobedience, *without denouncing violence as no part of it as Gandhi and Martin Luther King did,* he is verging on moral irresponsibility. From the safety of his white suburbs, he is playing with fire.

   Law and order are possible without justice; but Mr. Zinn does not seem to understand that justice is impossible without law and order.

Internet Resources

/diclerico10   Visit our Web site at www.mhhe.com/diclerico10 for links and resources relating to Democracy.

---

*Again, this rejoinder was written prior to the breakup of the former Soviet Union—*Editors.*

 chapter 2

The Constitution

Of the many books that have been written about the circumstances surrounding the creation of our Constitution, none generated more controversy than Charles Beard's An Economic Interpretation of the Constitution of the United States *(1913). An historian by profession, Beard challenged the belief that our Constitution was fashioned by men of democratic spirit. On the contrary, in what appeared to be a systematic marshaling of evidence, Beard sought to demonstrate (1) that the impetus for a new constitution came from individuals who saw their own economic interests threatened by a growing trend in the population toward greater democracy; (2) that the Founding Fathers themselves were men of considerable "personalty" (i.e., holdings other than real estate), who were concerned not so much with fashioning a democratic constitution as with protecting their own financial interests against the more democratically oriented farming and debtor interests within the society; and (3) that the individuals charged with ratifying the new Constitution also represented primarily the larger economic interests within the society. Although space limitations prevent a full development of Beard's argument, the portions of his book that follow should provide some feel for both the substance of his argument and his method of investigation.*

Beard's analysis has been subject to repeated scrutiny over the years. The most systematic effort in this regard came in 1956 with the publication of Robert Brown's Charles Beard and the Constitution: A Critical Analysis of "An Economic Interpretation of the Constitution." *Arguing that the rigor of Beard's examination was more apparent than real, Brown accuses him of citing only the facts that supported his case while ignoring those that did not. Moreover, he contends that even the evidence Beard provided did not warrant the interpretation he gave to it. Brown concludes that the best evidence now available does not support the view that "the Constitution was put over undemocratically in an undemocratic society by personal property."*

An Economic Interpretation of the Constitution of the United States
Charles A. Beard

Suppose it could be shown from the classification of the men who supported and opposed the Constitution that there was no line of property division at all; that is, that men owning substantially the same amounts of the same kinds of property were equally divided on the matter of adoption or rejection—it would then become apparent that the Constitution had no ascertainable relation to economic groups or classes, but was the product of some abstract causes remote from the chief business of life—gaining a livelihood.

Suppose, on the other hand, that substantially all of the merchants, money lenders, security holders, manufacturers, shippers, capitalists, and financiers and their professional associates are to be found on one side in support of the Constitution and that substantially all or the major portion of the opposition came from the nonslaveholding farmers and the debtors—would it not be pretty conclusively demonstrated that our fundamental law was not the product of an abstraction known as "the whole people," but of a group of economic interests which must have expected beneficial results from its adoption? Obviously all the facts here desired cannot be discovered, but the data presented in the following chapters bear out the latter hypothesis, and thus a reasonable presumption in favor of the theory is created.

Of course, it may be shown (and perhaps can be shown) that the farmers and debtors who opposed the Constitution were, in fact, benefited by the general improvement which resulted from its adoption. It may likewise be shown, to take an extreme case, that the English nation derived immense advantages from the Norman Conquest and the orderly administrative processes which were introduced, as it undoubtedly did; nevertheless, it does not follow that the vague thing known as "the advancement of general welfare" or some abstraction known as "justice" was the immediate, guiding purpose of the leaders in either of these great historic changes. The point is, that the direct, impelling motive in both cases was the economic advantages which the beneficiaries

Charles A. Beard (1874–1948) was professor of history and political science at Columbia University and former president of the American Political Science Association. Reprinted with the permission of Scribner, an imprint of Simon & Schuster Adult Publishing Group, from *An Economic Interpretation of the Constitution of the United States* by Charles A. Beard. Copyright 1935 by The Macmillan Company; copyright renewed © 1963 by William Beard and Mrs. Miriam Beard Vagts.

expected would accrue to themselves first, from their action. Further than this, economic interpretation cannot go. It may be that some larger world process is working through each series of historical events: but ultimate causes lie beyond our horizon. . . .

THE FOUNDING FATHERS: AN ECONOMIC PROFILE

A survey of the economic interests of the members of the Convention presents certain conclusions:

A majority of the members were lawyers by profession.

Most of the members came from towns, on or near the coast, that is, from the regions in which personalty was largely concentrated.

Not one member represented in his immediate personal economic interests the small farming or mechanic classes.

The overwhelming majority of members, at least five-sixths, were immediately, directly, and personally interested in the outcome of their labors at Philadelphia, and were to a greater or less extent economic beneficiaries from the adoption of the Constitution.

1. Public security interests were extensively represented in the Convention. Of the fifty-five members who attended no less than forty appear on the Records of the Treasury Department for sums varying from a few dollars up to more than one hundred thousand dollars. . . .

    It is interesting to note that, with the exception of New York, and possibly Delaware, each state had one or more prominent representatives in the Convention who held more than a negligible amount of securities, and who could therefore speak with feeling and authority on the question of providing in the new Constitution for the full discharge of the public debt. . . .
2. Personalty invested in lands for speculation was represented by at least fourteen members. . . .
3. Personalty in the form of money loaned at interest was represented by at least twenty-four members. . . .
4. Personalty in mercantile, manufacturing, and shipping lines was represented by at least eleven members. . . .
5. Personalty in slaves was represented by at least fifteen members. . . .

It cannot be said, therefore, that the members of the Convention were "disinterested." On the contrary, we are forced to accept the profoundly significant conclusion that they knew through their personal experiences in economic affairs the precise results which the new government that they were setting up was designed to attain. As a group of doctrinaires, like the Frankfort assembly of 1848, they would have failed miserably; but as practical men they were able to build the new government upon the only foundations which could be stable: fundamental economic interests.[1] . . .

RATIFICATION

New York

There can be no question about the predominance of personalty in the contest over the ratification in New York. That state, says Libby, "presents the problem in its simplest form. The entire mass of interior counties . . . were solidly anti-Federal, comprising the agricultural portion of the state, the last settled and the most thinly populated. There were however in this region two Federal cities (not represented in the convention [as such]), Albany in Albany county and Hudson in Columbia county. . . . The Federal area centred about New York city and county: to the southwest lay Richmond county (Staten Island); to the southeast Kings county, and the northeast Westchester county; while still further extending this area, at the northeast lay the divided county of Dutchess, with a vote in the convention of 4 to 2 in favor of the Constitution, and at the southeast were the divided counties of Queens and Suffolk. . . . These radiating strips of territory with New York city as a centre form a unit, in general favorable to the new Constitution; and it is significant of this unity that Dutchess, Queens, and Suffolk counties, broke away from the anti-Federal phalanx and joined the Federalists, securing thereby the adoption of the Constitution."[2]

Unfortunately the exact distribution of personalty in New York and particularly in the wavering districts which went over to the Federalist party cannot be ascertained, for the system of taxation in vogue in New York at the period of the adoption of the Constitution did not require a state record of property.[3] The data which proved so fruitful in Massachusetts are not forthcoming, therefore, in the case of New York; but it seems hardly necessary to demonstrate the fact that New York City was the centre of personalty for the state and stood next to Philadelphia as the great centre of operations in public stock.

This somewhat obvious conclusion is reinforced by the evidence relative to the vote on the legal tender bill which the paper money party pushed through in 1786. Libby's analysis of this vote shows that "no vote was cast against the bill by members of counties north of the county of New York. In the city and county of New York and in Long Island and Staten Island, the combined vote was 9 to 5 against the measure. Comparing this vote with the vote on the ratification in 1788, it will be seen that of the Federal counties 3 voted against paper money and 1 for it; of the divided counties 1 (Suffolk) voted against paper money and 2 (Queens and Dutchess) voted for it. Of the anti-Federal counties none had members voting against paper money. The merchants as a body were opposed to the issue of paper money and the Chamber of Commerce adopted a memorial against the issue."[4]

Public security interests were identified with the sound money party. There were thirty members of the New York constitutional convention who voted in favor of the ratification of the Constitution and of these no less than sixteen were holders of public securities. . . .

South Carolina

South Carolina presents the economic elements in the ratification with the utmost simplicity. There we find two rather sharply marked districts in antagonism over the Constitution. "The rival sections," says Libby, "were the coast or lower district and the upper, or more properly, the middle and upper country. The coast region was the first settled and contained a larger portion of the wealth of the state; its mercantile and commercial interests were important; its church was the Episcopal, supported by the state." This region, it is scarcely necessary to remark, was overwhelmingly in favor of the Constitution. The upper area, against the Constitution, "was a frontier section, the last to receive settlement; its lands were fertile and its mixed population was largely small farmers. . . . There was no established church, each community supported its own church and there was a great variety in the district."[5]

A contemporary writer, R. G. Harper, calls attention to the fact that the lower country, Charleston, Beaufort, and Georgetown, which had 28,694 white inhabitants, and about seven-twelfths of the representation in the state convention, paid £28,081:5:10 taxes in 1794, while the upper country, with 120,902 inhabitants, and five-twelfths of the representation in the convention, paid only £8390:13:3 taxes.[6] The lower districts in favor of the Constitution therefore possessed the wealth of the state and a disproportionate share in the convention—on the basis of the popular distribution of representation.

These divisions of economic interest are indicated by the abstracts of the tax returns for the state in 1794 which show that of £127,337 worth of stock in trade, faculties, etc. listed for taxation in the state, £109,800 worth was in Charleston, city and county—the stronghold of Federalism. Of the valuation of lots in towns and villages to the amount of £656,272 in the state, £549,909 was located in that city and county.[7]

The records of the South Carolina loan office preserved in the Treasury Department at Washington show that the public securities of that state were more largely in the hands of inhabitants than was the case in North Carolina. They also show a heavy concentration in the Charleston district.

At least fourteen of the thirty-one members of the state-ratifying convention from the parishes of St. Philip and Saint Michael, Charleston (all of whom favored ratification) held over $75,000 worth of public securities. . . .

Conclusions

At the close of this long and arid survey—partaking of the nature of catalogue—it seems worthwhile to bring together the important conclusions for political science which the data presented appear to warrant.

The movement for the Constitution of the United States was originated and carried through principally by four groups of personalty interests which had been adversely affected under the Articles of Confederation: money, public securities, manufactures, and trade and shipping.

The first firm steps toward the formation of the Constitution were taken by a small and active group of men immediately interested through their personal possessions in the outcome of their labors.

No popular vote was taken directly or indirectly on the proposition to call the Convention which drafted the Constitution.

A large propertyless mass was, under the prevailing suffrage qualifications, excluded at the outset from participation (through representatives) in the work of framing the Constitution.

The members of the Philadelphia Convention which drafted the Constitution were, with a few exceptions, immediately, directly, and personally interested in, and derived economic advantages from, the establishment of the new system.

The Constitution was essentially an economic document based upon the concept that the fundamental private rights of property are anterior to government and morally beyond the reach of popular majorities.

The major portion of the members of the Convention are on record as recognizing the claim of property to a special and defensive position in the Constitution.

In the ratification of the Constitution, about three-fourths of the adult males failed to vote on the question, having abstained from the elections at which delegates to the state conventions were chosen, either on account of their indifference or their disfranchisement by property qualifications.

The Constitution was ratified by a vote of probably not more than one-sixth of the adult males.

It is questionable whether a majority of the voters participating in the elections for the state conventions in New York, Massachusetts, New Hampshire, Virginia, and South Carolina, actually approved the ratification of the Constitution.

The leaders who supported the Constitution in the ratifying conventions represented the same economic groups as the members of the Philadelphia Convention; and in a large number of instances they were also directly and personally interested in the outcome of their efforts.

In the ratification, it became manifest that the line of cleavage for and against the Constitution was between substantial personalty interests on the one hand and the small farming and debtor interests on the other.

The Constitution was not created by "the whole people" as the jurists have said; neither was it created by "the states" as southern nullifiers long contended; but it was the work of a consolidated group whose interests knew no state boundaries and were truly national in their scope.

NOTES

1. The fact that a few members of the Convention, who had considerable economic interests at stake, refused to support the Constitution does not invalidate the general conclusions here presented. In the cases of Yates, Lansing, Luther Martin, and Mason, definite economic reasons for their action are forthcoming; but this is a minor detail.

2. O. G. Libby, *Geographical Distribution of the Vote of the Thirteen States on the Federal Constitution*, p. 18. Libby here takes the vote in the New York convention, but that did not precisely represent the popular vote.
3. *State Papers: Finance*, vol. 1, p. 425.
4. Libby, *Geographical Distribution*, p. 59.
5. *Ibid.*, pp. 42–43.
6. "Appius," *To the Citizens of South Carolina* (1794), Library of Congress, Duane Pamphlets, vol. 83.
7. *State Papers: Finance*, vol. 1, p. 462. In 1783 an attempt to establish a bank with $100,000 capital was made in Charleston, S.C., but it failed. "Soon after the adoption of the funding system, three banks were established in Charleston whose capitals in the whole amounted to twenty times the sum proposed in 1783." D. Ramsey, *History of South Carolina* (1858 ed.), vol. 2, p. 106.

Charles Beard and the Constitution
A Critical Analysis
Robert E. Brown

At the end of Chapter XI [of *An Economic Interpretation of the Constitution of the United States*], Beard summarized his findings in fourteen paragraphs under the heading of "Conclusions." Actually, these fourteen conclusions merely add up to the two halves of the Beard thesis. One half, that the Constitution originated with and was carried through by personalty interests—money, public securities, manufactures, and commerce—is to be found in paragraphs two, three, six, seven, eight, twelve, thirteen, and fourteen. The other half—that the Constitution was put over undemocratically in an undemocratic society— is expressed in paragraphs four, five, nine, ten, eleven, and fourteen. The lumping of these conclusions under two general headings makes it easier for the reader to see the broad outlines of the Beard thesis.

Before we examine these two major divisions of the thesis, however, some comment is relevant on the implications contained in the first paragraph. In it

Robert E. Brown is professor emeritus of history at Michigan State University. From Brown, Robert E., *Charles Beard and the Constitution.* Copyright © 1956 Princeton University Press, renewed 1984 by Princeton University Press. Reprinted by permission of Princeton University Press.

Beard characterized his book as a long and arid survey, something in the nature of a catalogue. Whether this characterization was designed to give his book the appearance of a coldly objective study based on the facts we do not know. If so, nothing could be further from reality. As reviewers pointed out in 1913, and as subsequent developments have demonstrated, the book is anything but an arid catalogue of facts. Its pages are replete with interpretation, sometimes stated, sometimes implied. Our task has been to examine Beard's evidence to see whether it justifies the interpretation which Beard gave it. We have tried to discover whether he used the historical method properly in arriving at his thesis.

If historical method means the gathering of data from primary sources, the critical evaluation of the evidence thus gathered, and the drawing of conclusions consistent with this evidence, then we must conclude that Beard has done great violation to such method in this book. He admitted that the evidence had not been collected which, given the proper use of historical method, should have precluded the writing of the book. Yet he nevertheless proceeded on the assumption that a valid interpretation could be built on secondary writings whose authors had likewise failed to collect the evidence. If we accept Beard's own maxim, "no evidence, no history," and his own admission that the data had never been collected, the answer to whether he used historical method properly is self-evident.

Neither was Beard critical of the evidence which he did use. He was accused in 1913, and one might still suspect him, of using only that evidence which appeared to support his thesis. The amount of realty in the country compared with the personalty, the vote in New York, and the omission of the part of *The Federalist*, No. 10, which did not fit his thesis are only a few examples of the uncritical use of evidence to be found in the book. Sometimes he accepted secondary accounts at face value without checking them with the sources; at other times he allowed unfounded rumors and traditions to color his work.

Finally, the conclusions which he drew were not justified even by the kind of evidence which he used. If we accepted his evidence strictly at face value, it would still not add up to the fact that the Constitution was put over undemocratically in an undemocratic society by personalty. The citing of property qualifications does not prove that a mass of men were disfranchised. And if we accept his figures on property holdings, either we do not know what most of the delegates had in realty and personalty, or we know that realty outnumbered personalty three to one (eighteen to six). Simply showing that a man held public securities is not sufficient to prove that he acted only in terms of his public securities. If we ignore Beard's own generalizations and accept only his evidence, we have to conclude that most of the country, and that even the men who were directly concerned with the Constitution, and especially Washington, were large holders of realty.

Perhaps we can never be completely objective in history, but certainly we can be more objective than Beard was in this book. Naturally, the historian must always be aware of the biases, the subjectivity, the pitfalls that confront him, but this does not mean that he should not make an effort to overcome these obstacles. Whether Beard had his thesis before he had his evidence, as some have said, is a question that each reader must answer for himself. Certain it is that the evidence does not justify the thesis.

So instead of the Beard interpretation that the Constitution was put over undemocratically in an undemocratic society by personal property, the following fourteen paragraphs are offered as a possible interpretation of the Constitution and as suggestions for future research on that document.

1. The movement for the Constitution was originated and carried through by men who had long been important in both economic and political affairs in their respective states. Some of them owned personalty, more of them owned realty, and if their property was adversely affected by conditions under the Articles of Confederation, so also was the property of the bulk of the people in the country, middle-class farmers as well as town artisans.

2. The movement for the Constitution, like most important movements, was undoubtedly started by a small group of men. They were probably interested personally in the outcome of their labors, but the benefits which they expected were not confined to personal property or, for that matter, strictly to things economic. And if their own interests would be enhanced by a new government, similar interests of other men, whether agricultural or commercial, would also be enhanced.

3. Naturally there was no popular vote on the calling of the convention which drafted the Constitution. Election of delegates by state legislatures was the constitutional method under the Articles of Confederation, and had been the method long established in this country. Delegates to the Albany Congress, the Stamp Act Congress, the First Continental Congress, the Second Continental Congress, and subsequent congresses under the Articles were all elected by state legislatures, not by the people. Even the Articles of Confederation had been sanctioned by state legislatures, not by popular vote. This is not to say that the Constitutional Convention should not have been elected directly by the people, but only that such a procedure would have been unusual at the time. Some of the opponents of the Constitution later stressed, without avail, the fact that the Convention had not been directly elected. But at the time the Convention met, the people in general seemed to be about as much concerned over the fact that they had not elected the delegates as the people of this country are now concerned over the fact that they do not elect our delegates to the United Nations.

4. Present evidence seems to indicate that there were no "propertyless masses" who were excluded from the suffrage at the time. Most men were middle-class farmers who owned realty and were qualified voters, and, as the men in the Convention said, mechanics had always voted in the cities. Until credible evidence proves otherwise, we can assume that state legislatures were fairly representative at the time. We cannot condone the fact that a few men were probably disfranchised by prevailing property qualifications, but it makes a great deal of difference to an interpretation of the Constitution whether the disfranchised comprised 95 percent of the adult men or only 5 percent. Figures which give percentages of voters in terms of

the entire population are misleading, since less than 20 percent of the people were adult men. And finally, the voting qualifications favored realty, not personalty.

5. If the members of the Convention were directly interested in the outcome of their work and expected to derive benefits from the establishment of the new system, so also did most of the people of the country. We have many statements to the effect that the people in general expected substantial benefits from the labors of the Convention.

6. The Constitution was not just an economic document, although economic factors were undoubtedly important. Since most of the people were middle class and had private property, practically everybody was interested in the protection of property. A constitution which did not protect property would have been rejected without any question, for the American people had fought the Revolution for the preservation of life, liberty, and property. Many people believed that the Constitution did not go far enough to protect property, and they wrote these views into the amendments to the Constitution. But property was not the only concern of those who wrote and ratified the Constitution, and we would be doing a grave injustice to the political sagacity of the Founding Fathers if we assumed that property or personal gain was their only motive.

7. Naturally the delegates recognized that protection of property was important under government, but they also recognized that personal rights were equally important. In fact, persons and property were usually bracketed together as the chief objects of government protection.

8. If three-fourths of the adult males failed to vote on the election of delegates to ratifying conventions, this fact signified indifference, not disfranchisement. We must not confuse those who could *not* vote with those who *could* vote but failed to exercise their right. Many men at the time bewailed the fact that only a small portion of the voters ever exercised their prerogative. But this in itself should stand as evidence that the conflict over the Constitution was not very bitter, for if these people had felt strongly one way or the other, more of them would have voted.

Even if we deny the evidence which I have presented and insist that American society was undemocratic in 1787, we must still accept the fact that the men who wrote the Constitution believed that they were writing it for a democratic society. They did not hide behind an iron curtain of secrecy and devise the kind of conservative government that they wanted without regard to the views and interests of "the people." More than anything else, they were aware that "the people" would have to ratify what they proposed, and that therefore any government which would be acceptable to the people must of necessity incorporate much of what was customary at the time. The men at Philadelphia were practical politicians, not political theorists. They recognized the multitude of different ideas and interests that had to be reconciled and compromised before a constitution would be acceptable. They were far too practical, and represented far too many clashing interests themselves, to fashion a government weighted in favor of personality or to believe that the people would adopt such a government.

9. If the Constitution was ratified by a vote of only one-sixth of the adult men, that again demonstrates indifference and not disfranchisement. Of the one-fourth of the adult males who voted, nearly two-thirds favored the Constitution. Present evidence does not permit us to say what the popular vote was except as it was measured by the votes of the ratifying conventions.

10. Until we know what the popular vote was, we cannot say that it is questionable whether a majority of the voters in several states favored the Constitution. Too many delegates were sent uninstructed. Neither can we count the towns which did not send delegates on the side of those opposed to the Constitution. Both items would signify indifference rather than sharp conflict over ratification.

11. The ratifying conventions were elected for the specific purpose of adopting or rejecting the Constitution. The people in general had anywhere from several weeks to several months to decide the question. If they did not like the new government, or if they did not know whether they liked it, they could have voted no and there would have been no Constitution. Naturally the leaders in the ratifying conventions represented the same interests as the members of the Constitutional Convention—mainly realty and some personalty. But they also represented their constituents in these same interests, especially realty.

12. If the conflict over ratification had been between substantial personalty interests on the one hand and small farmers and debtors on the other, there would not have been a constitution. The small farmers comprised such an overwhelming percentage of the voters that they could have rejected the new government without any trouble. Farmers and debtors are not synonymous terms and should not be confused as such. A town-by-town or county-by-county record of the vote would show clearly how the farmers voted.

13. The Constitution was created about as much by the whole people as any government could be which embraced a large area and depended on representation rather than on direct participation. It was also created in part by the states, for as the *Records* show, there was strong state sentiment at the time which had to be appeased by compromise. And it was created by compromising a whole host of interests throughout the country, without which compromises it could never have been adopted.

14. If the intellectual historians are correct, we cannot explain the Constitution without considering the psychological factors also. Men are motivated by what they believe as well as by what they have. Sometimes their actions can be explained on the basis of what they hope to have or hope that their children will have. Madison understood this fact when he said that the universal hope of acquiring property tended to dispose people to look favorably upon property. It is even possible that some men support a given economic system when they themselves have nothing to gain by it. So we

would want to know what the people in 1787 thought of their class status. Did workers and small farmers believe that they were lower class, or did they, as many workers do now, consider themselves middle class? Were the common people trying to eliminate the Washingtons, Adamses, Hamiltons, and Pinckneys, or were they trying to join them?

As did Beard's fourteen conclusions, these fourteen suggestions really add up to two major propositions: the Constitution was adopted in a society which was fundamentally democratic, not undemocratic; and it was adopted by a people who were primarily middle-class property owners, especially farmers who owned realty, not just by the owners of personalty. At present these points seem to be justified by the evidence, but if better evidence in the future disproves or modifies them, we must accept that evidence and change our interpretation accordingly.

After this critical analysis, we should at least not begin future research on this period of American history with the illusion that the Beard thesis of the Constitution is valid. If historians insist on accepting the Beard thesis in spite of this analysis, however, they must do so with the full knowledge that their acceptance is founded on "an act of faith," not an analysis of historical method, and that they were indulging in a "noble dream," not history.

 /diclerico10

Internet Resources
Visit our Web site at www.mhhe.com/diclerico10 for links and resources relating to the Constitution.

 chapter 3

Federalism

Unfunded Mandates

*T*he Tenth Amendment to the U.S. Constitution states: "The powers not delegated to the United States by the Constitution, nor prohibited by it to the States, are reserved to the States respectively, or to the people." Although this brief amendment, containing just slightly more than twenty-five words, seems simple and uncomplicated, it has constituted the basis for one of the more protracted debates in U.S. history—namely, the extent to which the national and state governments may encroach on each other's powers and prerogatives.

A modern manifestation of this debate is to be found in the controversy over "unfunded federal mandates." Unfunded mandates are those laws passed by Congress that require states to carry out national regulations without federal government funding. Examples are the Clean Water Act of 1972, the Americans with Disabilities Act of 1990, and the National Voter Registration Act of 1993. Although noble in purpose, these acts have frequently been criticized as interfering with the powers and financial responsibilities of the states in violation of the spirit, if not the letter, of the constitutional division of powers between the national government and the states.

In 1995, Congress attempted to curb both the number and scope of unfunded mandates by passing the Unfunded Federal Mandates Reform Act. This act required Congress, when passing laws mandating states to carry out federal law, to determine the costs of mandates and to provide sufficient funding for them, or, in the worst case scenario, to reconsider the desirability of the mandate, once costs are known. In the ten or so years since the passage of the act, the issue of federal mandates has remained highly contentious, as revealed by the two selections that follow.

In the first, U.S. Representative George Miller, Democrat from California, makes the case for mandates, both funded and unfunded. In a speech on the floor of the House of Representatives at the time the Unfunded Federal Mandates Reform Act was being debated, he argues xthat mandates, despite their critics, have actually improved the quality of life in America and addressed problems that states have been unable or unwilling to deal with adequately on their own.

In the second selection, U.S. Senator Lamar Alexander, Republican from Tennessee, protests the continued use of mandates to force states into taking actions they would not otherwise favor. To Senator Alexander, the Unfunded Federal Mandates Reform Act of 1995 simply has not worked the way the original sponsors thought, and Congress should now take steps to ensure that it does, restoring once again the rightful place of the states in the federal system.

Unfunded Mandates
Laws That Bind Us Together
George Miller

Mr. Chairman [The Federal Unfunded Mandates Reform Act] strikes at the very heart of the body of laws that bind us together as a progressive society, and with the highest standard of living in the world; the body of law that ensures that no matter where you live in this country, you can enjoy clean water: that no matter where you live in this country, local government and the private sector are working every day to improve the air that you breathe, so we no longer have to send our children indoors because it is too smoggy out. We no longer have to tell our senior citizens they cannot go out for a walk because the air quality is too bad, or we cannot drive to work because they do not want the automobiles on the road.

These are the laws that accomplished those successes. These are laws that said "Yes, if you take money from the Federal Government, we are going to put onto you an obligation to educate the handicapped children of this Nation," because before that was the law, the handicapped children of this Nation could not get an education in the public school systems run by the States and localities that we now say are so ready to do the job.

But for that law, tens of thousands of handicapped children, because they have cerebral palsy, because they have Down's syndrome, would not be allowed in our public schools, but that is a Federal mandate. Yes, we pay part of the freight, but this law would say "Unless the Federal Government presents 100 percent of it, no school district would be required to educate that handicapped child. Unless the Federal Government spends 100 percent of the money to clean up the local water supply, the local sewage treatment, the city would have no obligation."

What happens along the Mississippi River in Indiana or Minnesota if they choose, or in Ohio, if they choose not to clean up the municipal sewage because the Federal Government will not pay 100 percent? That means the people in Mississippi and Louisiana have to inherit that sewage.

An unfunded mandate upstream is untreated sewage downstream. What does that mean to the fishermen, to the commercial enterprises, and to the tourist industry in those States? It means they suffer. That is why we have national laws.

George Miller is a Democratic U.S. Representative from the state of California. Excerpted from a speech delivered in the U.S. House of Representatives, Congressional Record, *Proceedings and Debates of the 104th Congress, 1st Session, House of Representatives,* January 19, 1996, *vol. 141, No. 11, H355–H356.*

When I was a young man you could smell San Francisco Bay before you could see it, but now we require all of the cities, not just the town that I live in, not just the oil industry, not just the chemical industry, but the cities upstream and downstream [to clean up]. Some of them, we had to take them to court to tell them to clean it up. Today San Francisco Bay is a tourist attraction. Commercial fishing is back. People can use it for recreation.

That is what these mandates have done. Yes, we have not paid 100 percent, but we have put billions and billions and billions of dollars into helping local communities make airports safe so they could become international airports, so people would have confidence in going to those cities. We have cleaned up their water and air. We have made it safe to drink. That is what this legislation is an assault on.

Mr. Chairman, the proponents of this legislation would have us believe this is a simple and straightforward initiative: Congress should mandate the States and local governments to do nothing that Congress is not willing to pay for in its entirety.

In fact, this legislation strikes at the very heart of the entire concept on which our Government is based. Government does not have the responsibility to require that those in our societies—private individuals, businesses, and State and local governments—meet certain responsibilities.

Even the drafters of this legislation recognize that some mandates need not be paid for. They are ideologues of convenience. They do not require we pay for compliance with civil rights and disability laws. But they would compel funding for actions relating to public health and safety, protection of the environment, education of children, medical services to our elderly, safeguards to our workers.

And they would require that we pay only when that burden is imposed on entities of government. Private industry, many of which compete with State and local government in the provision of services, is accorded no relief. And those who work for Government, performing exactly the same services as those in the private sector, are potentially denied such basic protections as minimum wages, worker right to know about hazardous substances, and OSHA protections.

Never mind that the same State and local governments to whose aid we are rushing impose precisely the same unfunded mandates on lower levels of government.

So, I think this clearly demonstrates what is going on here: this is not about unfunded mandates: It is about undermining this Nation's environmental, education, health and labor laws, and wrapping the attack in the flag of unfunded mandates.

The last time we tried this deceptive tactic—cutting away at the basic role of Government in the name of cost savings—we tripled the national debt in 8 years.

But let me take issue with the very name of this concept—unfunded mandates. Unfunded? Really?

We have spent tens of billions of dollars helping States and local communities meet these mandates by improving water systems, upgrading drinking water supplies, building and improving transportation systems, improving education programs, and on and on.

Have we funded every mandate fully? No. Should the Federal Government have to pay States and local communities to protect their employees, their environment and their public health and safety? Because let's remember: A lot of them were not protecting those people and those resources before the Federal mandates came along.

No, we haven't funded every dollar. But have we covered 50, 75, 90 percent of the cost of many of these projects? Time and time again.

And have we provided these same State and local governments with hundreds of billions of dollars to build, expand and improve highways, rapid transit and harbors and to respond to disasters—even when there was no Federal responsibility to provide a dollar? Have we provided money to assure that communities are safe from nuclear power plants and hazardous waste sites? Have we provided money to educate the handicapped, to train the jobless, and to house tens of millions of Americans?

I have little doubt that those who champion this legislation fully expect that its passage would have no effect on our willingness to fund their future actions in these areas. They are very wrong. Every State and community should be aware that the appetite of the Congress for funding local projects and programs that fail to meet a Federal standard of quality and protection and performance is going to be very minimal, particularly in light of the coming effort for a balanced budget amendment that would slash Federal spending radically.

So I think we should proceed with some caution here. If the States and local communities don't want the mandates, don't expect the Federal dollars either.

I find it somewhat ironic that in my own State of California, for example, the Governor [Republican Governor Pete Wilson—*Editors*] has failed to come up with his promise of matching funds for the $5 billion in Federal disaster aid following [the] Northridge earthquake. Now he wants more Federal money for earthquake assistance; and he will want more still for the flooding, and he'll probably throw in a few billion dollars' worth of dams and other infrastructure from Federal taxpayers.

Yet he is one of the biggest proponents of this unfunded mandates legislation—and at the same time that he forces unfunded mandates down the throat of every county and city in California.

We see that kind of hypocrisy in the legislation before us today.

In case you didn't read the fine print, this mandate ban neglects to include the dozens of new unfunded Federal mandates contained in the Republicans' Contract With America. Just the mandates in the welfare bill alone could bring the States to their knees. But all those new mandates are exempted, even though none of them have yet been enacted into law. So much for being honest with the American people.

Let's be very clear what this legislation is going to do to some of the most important laws this Congress has passed and has spent billions of dollars helping States and local communities implement.

Safe drinking water. We have upgraded the water supply across this Nation, virtually eliminating disease, contamination and danger. Much of that has been paid for by Federal dollars. Which local community would like to have taken on that task without Federal assistance? Which Americans want to put the future and the consistency of our safe drinking water at risk through this legislation?

Clean water. You used to be able to smell San Francisco Bay before you could see it. You used to need a battery of shots if you stuck your toe in the Potomac River. The sewage and waste water of 80 million Americans from a score of States flows out of the mouth of the Mississippi River, and for years contaminated the commercial fishing areas. A few years before the Clean Water Act was passed, the Cuyahoga River in Cleveland was burning. Want to go back to those days? You tell me which financially strapped city and State will take on that burden without Federal assistance?

Nuclear safety. Should nuclear power plants and generators of radioactive wastes—which exist in every large city and many small ones—be able to ignore Federal safety standards for operations and waste disposal?

Deadbeat parents. We are collecting hundreds of millions of dollars a year from parents who have ignored their financial responsibilities to their children, thanks to Federal law. Should we just abandon that program? . . .

Of course we should examine whether Federal funding of mandates has been adequate. In fact, that process was begun last year. . . .

But let us not . . . pass a deeply flawed, confusing, and deceptive bill . . . that misrepresents not only the need for mandates, but ignores the billions of dollars we have given to States and communities to help meet those mandates.

The Federal Unfunded Mandates Reform Act

"Lost in the Weeds"
Lamar Alexander

. . . March 15, 2005, is the 10th birthday of The Federal Unfunded Mandates Reform Act, affectionately known in Washington, D.C., as UMRA.

UMRA was supposed to stop or slow down the one thing that made me maddest as governor—some congressman coming up with a big idea, passing a law, holding a press conference, bragging about it and then sending the bill back to Tennessee for me and the legislature to pay. And then the next weekend, that same congressman would usually be back in Tennessee making a speech about local control.

Lamar Alexander is a United States Senator from Tennessee. Excerpted from a speech given by Senator Alexander before the National League of Cities Congressional City Conference, March 14, 2005.

UMRA was supposed to discourage that—to discourage the imposition of new laws and new rules on state and local governments without paying for them. . . . [I]t was the right policy and a great accomplishment, and it undoubtedly discouraged some action. But it hasn't done nearly as much as we might have hoped.

Just look around you:

- Cities are raising taxes to pay for new EPA storm water run-off rules;
- School boards are still taking money out of one classroom and putting it in another to meet federal requirements for children with disabilities;
- The National Council of State Legislatures has identified $29 billion in federal cost shifts to states in transportation, health care, education, environment, homeland security, election laws and in other areas.
- And just last year . . . in the name of lowering Internet access taxes, Congress tried to take away from state and local officials local control over how to pay for governmental services;

And that's not all.

- The U.S. House of Representatives recently passed legislation that would turn 190 million state drivers' licenses into national ID cards with the states paying most of the cost;
- [In March 2005] governors of both parties met with the president and they asked him how they could reduce the growth of Medicaid spending when federal laws dictate eligibility standards, when federal bureaucrats limit state flexibility and federal courts just say no. . . .

And then the federal courts have piled on—using outdated federal court consent decrees to run Medicaid in Tennessee, to run foster care in Utah, to run transportation in Los Angeles and to decide how to teach English to children in New York City.

During these last 10 years, in my view, about the only part of the federal government that has recognized the importance of strong state and local governments in our federal system is the United States Supreme Court, which has rediscovered that the 10th Amendment to the United States Constitution reserves the states' powers that are not expressly granted to the central government.

So here is what I see is the picture of federalism in Washington, D.C., today— Democrats, still stuck in the New Deal, are reflexively searching for national solutions to local problems; Republicans, having found ourselves in charge, have decided it is more blessed to impose our views rather than to liberate Americans from Washington; and, across America, federal judges have discovered the joys of acting like governors and mayors without having to run for office.

Meanwhile in the states and cities, federal funds make up as much as half of state and local budgets, bringing with them more and more rules that direct and limit what mayors and governors are able to do with revenues raised from state and local taxes.

So as a result, the job of mayor and governor is becoming more and more like the job of university president, which I also used to be: it looks like you're in charge, but you're really not.

That is why to celebrate this 10th birthday of UMRA I propose three steps to give mayors and governors, legislators and local councils more authority to do what they were elected to do.

First, amend UMRA to increase to 60 the number of Senate votes it takes to enact legislation that imposes unfunded federal mandates. . . . For the last 10 years the number has been 50, and it hasn't been used once as a budget point of order. It's a penalty flag that hasn't been thrown.

Second, make it easier for governors and mayors to change or vacate outdated federal court consent decrees and harder for courts and plaintiffs' lawyers to run the government. I have introduced legislation with Senator Mark Pryor of Arkansas and Senator Ben Nelson of Nebraska. They're both Democrats. One was an attorney general of his state, and one was a governor of his state. This legislation would put term limits on consent decrees, shift to plaintiffs the burden of proving that the decrees need to be continued and require that courts draw decrees narrowly with the objective of moving responsibility back into the hands of elected officials as soon as possible.

In Tennessee, for example, we have a governor of the other party who ran to fix what we call our TennCare system, it's our Medicaid system. He's come up with a plan to do it. He's concerned, as I am in looking at it from a distance, that because of the unbridled growth of healthcare spending that we don't have the money for education spending and we need to make some adjustment of that. But he finds himself restricted by four federal court consent decrees entered into by his predecessors over the past 25 years, so he's not able to do what he was elected to do. The people of our state believe that if we have an important policy decision—not a rights decision, but a policy decision—that elected officials ought to be able to make that decision.

Finally, the third thing we should do is to not allow any new federal statute to preempt a local law unless the new federal law specifically states that there is a direct conflict between state and local law.

Now after all this pessimistic talk about ominous trends, let me conclude with an optimistic word about our federal system.

I am optimistic because I believe that excessive centralization of government runs against the grain of what it means to be an American. To ignore that I believe is political dynamite.

Americans do expect Washington, D.C., to take care of war, welfare, social security, health care and debt.

Americans do not want Washington, D.C., running schools, colleges, law enforcement, city parks and most roads. . . .

I recall in October of 1994, Representative Newt Gingrich stood with 300 Republican candidates for Congress on the Capitol steps offering a "Contract with America" promising no more unfunded federal mandates. "If we break our promise," said my fellow Republicans, "throw us out."

Mindful of that promise, new United States Senate Majority Leader Bob Dole in 1995 designated the Federal Unfunded Mandate Reform Act as S.1—the birthday that we celebrate tomorrow, the day of its passage—he made it the first order of business of the new Republican Senate. Senator Dole then campaigned for president across the country pulling a copy of the constitution from his pocket and reading the 10th Amendment to his audiences. . . .

One of the most important reasons to come to Washington to serve is to remind those already here that a plane ticket to Washington doesn't make you any smarter.

That parents and teachers of 50 million students in 15,000 school districts can usually do more to improve a child's education than some national school board can.

That if Washington makes you spend more for Medicaid then you'll probably have less to spend for preschool education—and at least someone elected, who is closer to the problem, needs to decide that issue.

In some countries, which are smaller and in which people are more ethnically alike than we are, it might be possible to have a national school board, a state church and a central government that calls most of the shots.

But we know that doesn't stand a prayer of working in the United States of America. Alexis de Tocqueville in his early writings about America observed that our country works community by community by community. We are so big, we have so many different views, and we come from so many different backgrounds that we need many places to work things out in many different ways. Put too many one-size-fits-all jackets on Americans and this country will explode.

And in America, such an explosion occurs at election time.

That is why most candidates for president run against Washington, D.C.

That is why senators from Washington, D.C., are almost never elected president, and governors from outside Washington, D.C., often are.

That is one reason why Americans elected a Republican Congress in 1994. . . .

So as a good Republican, I am using this birthday celebration of the Unfunded Federal Mandate Act to remind my Republican colleagues that we promised to the American people in 1994: no more unfunded mandates. "If we break our promise, throw us out." I am certain that if we don't remember our promise, our Democratic friends will.

Most of our policy debates in Congress involve conflicting principles of which most of us agree. The principle of federalism should not always be the trump card. There are other important principles to weigh: liberty, equal opportunity, laissez faire, individualism and the rule of law, for example.

But the federalism that the Republican Congress was elected to protect in 1994 has gotten lost in the weeds. It is time to find it and to put it back up front where it belongs. And the first three steps should be to take the Unfunded Mandate Reform Act and increase to 60 the number of votes it takes to enact an unfunded mandate, to put term limits on federal court consent decrees, and to require Congress to specify, announce and admit whenever it decides to preempt a state or local law.

If Congress were to do those three things, then maybe on UMRA's 20th birthday, 10 years from now, we can celebrate an American federal system that has the kind of respect for mayors, governors, legislators and city council members that the founders of this great republic envisioned.

Gay Marriage: A Matter for the States or the Federal Government?

*O*ne of the newest controversies surrounding the proper roles of the federal and state governments in the federal system is the issue of gay marriage. Marriage has traditionally been a matter handled primarily by the states, although Congress has from time to time legislated in this area, as in the case of polygamy, outlawed by Congress and upheld by the U.S. Supreme Court in 1878.

Gay marriage as a recent issue in the federal system has arisen because some states, supported in part by court decisions, have acted to permit marriages between gay and lesbian couples. In response to these developments, President George W. Bush and a group of congressional leaders have proposed an amendment to the U.S. Constitution allowing marriage only between a man and woman. Passage of such an amendment would effectively remove from the states the power to determine what constitutes a marriage.

In the selections that follow, pro and anti-constitutional amendment positions are staked out, oddly enough, by two defenders of "states rights." In the first selection, Adam White, a member of the states' rights advocacy group, The Federalist Society, argues that a constitutional amendment defining marriage is an appropriate exercise of national authority, if only because such an action seems inevitable, given the reality of what is happening in the states and in the courts. Another member of the same Federalist Society, John Yoo, argues the opposite. Yoo's position is one commonly put forth by states' rights advocates—namely, gay marriage is a policy area that is best left to states. States, it is argued, function as "laboratories of democracy," in which the people of each state are better able to decide for themselves what is appropriate public policy rather than to have the national government determine it for them. The fact that both White and Yoo, members of the same traditionally states rights group, take opposite sides on this issue reveals once again how complicated and complex policy making is in our federal system of government.

'States, Right?' Not in the Gay Marriage Debate

Adam White

"The President, who believes so strongly in states' rights in other contexts, should let the states do their jobs and work out their marriage laws before resorting to a constitutional amendment." With those words, the editors of *The New York Times* (Feb. 25, 2004) summed up one prong of the public criticism of the President's proposed Defense of Marriage Amendment.

President Bush is not exactly a poster-boy for "states' rights," but to the extent that he points to Justices Thomas and Scalia as his ideal jurists, the question is a good one: to what extent is a Federal Marriage Amendment compatible with Federalism?

This Federalist's answer, in short: They fit quite well.

The Left seems to have discovered "states' rights" this year, and many point to hypocrisy of those Federalists who do not support a "states' rights" solution to the gay marriage issue.

But "Federalism" is not synonymous with "states rights." Federalism is an ideological commitment to the appropriate division of power between Federal and state governments. Where the Constitution does not pre-ordain the solution, Federalism calls for a pragmatic apportionment of power, not knee-jerk endorsement of "states' rights."

For the marriage question, a Federal solution is not just pragmatically appropriate. It's also inevitable. And, for those who've forgotten, it's *long* been a federal issue.

The baseline form of marriage—be it "one man—one woman," "two people," or "more than one person"—is most pragmatically regulated at the national level. Most obviously, our national legal and financial systems have already integrated marriage into their basic structures. Insurance, tax, federal criminal law (e.g., spousal privilege), and countless other legal/financial matters depend on marriage. Inconsistency among the states severely hampers commerce, a core Federal concern under Federalist principles.

Moreover, the federal government has a strong interest in family structure. The last century's system of social programs (predominantly erected by liberals)

Adam J. White graduated from Harvard Law School in 2004. He served as Editorial Page Editor of the Harvard Law Record. He later clerked for Judge David B. Sentelle at the U.S. Court of Appeals for the District of Columbia and is now an attorney in Washington D.C. *From The Record,* the independent newspaper of Harvard Law School. Reprinted with author's permission.

are greatly affected by marital status. Will the federal government's social programs draw lines between similarly situated "marriages" simply because of the marriage laws of the several States? Will gay couples in Georgia stand pat while gay couples in California collect Federal benefits? Should they?

Finally, the Federal government has a strong interest in the protection of children. . . . In a nation where freedom of movement is not only a constitutional value but also an increasing reality for mobile families, how will children fare when their family's legal structure changes depending on the state in which they currently move? Custody battles will become all the more ugly when same-sex "parents" can try to game the system by fleeing the state, kids in tow. And hospital visitation rights should not vary wildly on the state in which a family's vacation takes a tragic turn.

The above pragmatic concerns strongly suggest that a federal resolution of the marriage question is appropriate. But that justification aside, a national solution strikes this Federalist as a appropriate if only because a national solution seems *inevitable*.

The Federal courts may enforce a national norm on the states. In *Romer* and *Lawrence** the court has grown increasingly eager to force pro-homosexuality positions through the states. Justices may have disclaimed gay marriage in *Lawrence*, but that is hard to swallow from a legal institution that has grown bolder every year in taking sides in these culture wars. The logic of *Lawrence* and *Romer* destroys the foundation of any laws that might preempt someone making his own decisions about the sweet mystery of sexual life.

The Court has made it increasingly clear that in matters of sexual liberation, the life of the law is not logic, but experiment. The Court's own doctrines leave it with no principled opposition to gay marriage (or polygamy, or any other form of "marriage"). Should we simply assume that they'll suddenly discover restraint—and, in waiting, allow Liberal states to spend years building up inertia by handing out thousands of gay-marriage licenses? Those horses won't return to the barn; to wait for the Courts is to enact gay marriage by default.

Liberals are also lining up to challenge Full Faith and Credit defenses of states; why else would gay couples flood San Francisco and return home? Certainly not to watch their marital benefits vanish. They've picked California as the epicenter, not outer limits, of the gay marriage battle.

The Left has declared national war on marriage. There is no reason why Federalists should handcuff themselves in a state-by-state resolution in this case. Given that gay marriage will be decided at the federal level in a matter that will likely pre-empt states that wish to dissent from gay marriage, this Federalist sees no shame in fighting back at the federal level. And at least the Right seeks to do it through an original Constitutional tool—Article V—instead of through a Court-centered social policy power-grab wholly foreign to the Framers.

---

*In *Romer* v. *Evans* (1996), the U.S. Supreme Court invalidated a Colorado constitutional amendment prohibiting state and local governments from outlawing discrimination on the basis of sexual orientation. In *Lawrence* v. *Texas* (2003), the Supreme Court invalidated a law making same-sex sodomy a crime—*Editors*.

Finally, let us not ignore the obvious: the form of marriage—one man and one woman—has long been a federal issue. The basic structure of marriage has never differed from state to state (in 1789, who could have dreamed of "alternative" marriages?), and the federal government has vigorously enforced its notion of marriage on the states before. The Union refused to accept not only Utah, but also Arizona, New Mexico, and Oklahoma, until each renounced polygamy. The federal norm of marriage—one man, one woman—was enforced there. Likewise, the federal courts enforced their colorblind notion of marriage on the states.

Charges of "states' rights" hypocrisy, at least those directed at Federalists, simply don't hold water. "Federalism" only requires deference to states where the Constitution requires it or, where the Constitution is silent, where pragmatism requires—in short, not here. The Left's new fondness for "states' rights" is an amusing development but an empty rallying cry.

Rules of Law
Let States Decide
John Yoo

President Bush has called on Congress to support a constitutional amendment to ban gay marriages by defining marriage as only between a man and a woman. "Some activist judges and local officials have made an aggressive attempt to redefine marriage," he said in justifying the need for this extraordinary step.

Election-year politics aside, surely the administration is correct that this revolutionary change in social norms is being unwisely engineered by a small set of officials: the Supreme Court, Massachusetts judges and legislators, and the mayor of San Francisco. A constitutional amendment would serve as a national plebiscite on the question of gay marriage. In demanding that the amendment define marriage as between a man and a woman, however, President Bush has adopted the wrong constitutional strategy.

John Yoo, a former law clerk to Justice Clarence Thomas, served from 2001 to 2003 as a deputy assistant attorney general in the Office of Legal Counsel at the U.S. Department of Justice. Yoo is currently a professor at UC Berkeley's Boalt Hall School of Law and an American Enterprise Institue scholar. This opinion piece by Yoo was first published by *The Wall Street Journal.* http://www.berkeley.edu/news/media/releases/2004/03/01_yoo.shtml

The purpose of a constitutional amendment should be to restore the status quo ante that existed before the activism of these officials upended the social order in Massachusetts and San Francisco. An amendment in keeping with our federal system would be one that preserved the definition of marriage to each state to decide for itself, just as our constitutional system permitted for the first two centuries of its existence. Conservatives who have criticized the Supreme Court's nationalization of abortion in *Roe v. Wade* should support a more modest amendment that would prevent one state, such as Massachusetts, from deciding the policy on gay marriage for all other states.

The Bush administration should resist the urge to engage in unnecessary changes to the Constitution. The Framers designed the founding document to be difficult to amend. Article V requires that two-thirds of the House and Senate propose the text, which must then receive the approval of three-quarters of the state legislatures. (Another process, never used, allows for two-thirds of the state legislatures to call a constitutional convention.) As James Madison explained in the Federalist No. 43, this process allows for the correction of errors in the Constitution without allowing it to become as flexible as an ordinary piece of legislation. "It guards equally against that extreme facility, which would render the Constitution too mutable; and that extreme difficulty, which might perpetuate its discovered faults." In addition, wrote Madison, the amendment process worked a valuable role in maintaining the balance of powers between the federal and state governments. It "equally enables the general and the State governments to originate the amendment of errors, as they may be pointed out by the experience on one side, or on the other."

It should not be surprising that this hurdle has led to relatively few amendments. Since 1791, when the Bill of Rights added the first 10 amendments to the Constitution, the nation has approved only 17 more over the course of the following 213 years. Many of these changes have focused on modernizing the workings of our democracy, such as expanding the electorate to include African-Americans, women and 18-year-olds, providing for the direct election of senators, limiting presidents to two terms, and specifying the order of presidential selection and succession. Almost all of the amendments have the purpose of either organizing or limiting the powers of the federal or state governments, such as the Equal Protection and Due Process Clauses requirement of equal and fair treatment by the government. The most notable effort to regulate purely private conduct—the 18th Amendment's establishment of Prohibition—failed miserably and led to the rise of organized crime.

An amendment that merely restored state control over marriage also would better allow democracy to function. Federalism is a decentralized decision-making system that allows states to compete for residents and businesses by offering different mixes of economic and social policies. As in a market, citizens can satisfy their preferences by deciding to live in states that provide the tax, education, welfare or family policies that they agree with. Some states, such as Massachusetts, can choose to permit gay marriage, while others such as California might choose to define marriage as between a man and woman, and Americans can choose to live in either state depending on what policy they support. The administration's current plans would prevent our states from allowing their own democratic systems to respond to their citizens in deciding this important question of family law.

A pro-federalism approach also makes sense as a matter of public policy. Advocates on both sides of this emotional debate are floating a variety of arguments about the effects of gay marriage. Supporters claim that it leads to the stability of relationships and extends the positive benefits of marriage to homosexual couples. Opponents argue that it undermines the institution of marriage and could lead to higher divorce and lower marriage rates.

All sides should admit that the sample size for making these judgments is far too small—there simply are not enough jurisdictions that have permitted gay marriage. Allowing each of the 50 states to choose a different policy on gay marriage would provide that diversity of experience that would allow us to see whether gay marriage indeed causes negative effects on society or the opposite.

This would truly take advantage of Justice Brandeis' famous description of the states as "laboratories of democracy." As he observed, "It is one of the happy incidents of the federal system that a single courageous state may, if its citizens choose, serve as a laboratory; and try novel social and economic experiments without risk to the rest of the country." The Bush administration's sweeping amendment would short-circuit the diversity and experimentation in policy that is one of the great benefits of our federal system.

Finally, it is worth asking whether a federalization of marriage would produce more political instability than it would stop. Critics of *Roe v. Wade*, conservatives chief among them, have argued that the Supreme Court's decision to nationalize the regulation of abortion led to the intensification of political conflict over abortion. Rather than allowing the 50 states to decide abortion policy for themselves, we now have the spectacle of Supreme Court abortion decisions every few years, repeated efforts at congressional regulation, annual protests, and the emergence of abortion as a divisive issue in our national politics.

An effort to nationalize marriage could produce the same long-term negative effects, in which candidates of both parties must make pledges on gay marriage and the issue dominates our appointments to the federal courts. Perhaps the blame for this lies squarely with the Supreme Court, which chose in last year's sodomy case to provide constitutional protections for gay rights, but the answer is not to play the game of nationalization, but to respond by restoring our federal system's trust in the states.

Internet Resources

Visit our Web site at www.mhhe.com/diclerico10 for links and resources relating to Federalism.

c h a p t e r   4

Public Opinion

At a time when a substantial number of Americans see government as increasingly remote and excessively influenced by organized interests, it is not surprising that "reformers" are seeking new ways to reconnect the American people to their government. Some reformers have turned to new technology to help provide that connection. Computer enthusiasts, for example, foresee the use of the Internet as a means to energize citizens, to get them to vote, and to get them to express their opinions on a whole range of issues. Thus, in the year 2000, Democratic primary elections in Arizona were held online, and in 2004, Michigan allowed its voters to vote online to select delegates to the Democratic national convention. Moreover, in both 2000 and 2004, candidates for president communicated directly with voters via the Internet, and one Democratic candidate, Howard Dean, in the 2004 primary contest, mobilized thousands of supporters via the Internet. If this trend continues, voting on policy issues will no doubt be online, and the potential for the Internet to provide citizens with information on a whole array of topics will be virtually unlimited.

The two selections that follow present contrasting arguments on the potential for using the new computer technology to improve the public discourse and government decision making. In the first selection, political consultant Dick Morris sees the Internet as revolutionizing politics. An unabashed advocate of the Internet, Morris views the technology of cyberspace as a means to energize the electorate and to connect citizens to their government in a way not possible with any other medium. Indeed, in his judgment politics via the Internet is about as close as one can get to direct democracy, literally allowing millions of Americans to share their opinions one-on-one with representatives and with each other. In the second selection, two Washington, D.C., commentators, Norman Ornstein and Amy Schenkenberg Mitchell, raise very serious questions about the new technology and the role the public should play in our representative system of government. Ornstein and Schenkenberg ask, will "cyberdemocracy" improve our system of representation? Will voters take seriously their responsibilities in this new system of direct participation? Moreover, what controls, if any, will be placed on these new systems? And, most importantly, do we really want a sometimes disinterested and ill-formed public to exert that much control over policy making? These are profound questions that once again cause us to reflect on the proper role of citizens in our still evolving democracy.

Vox Populi in Cyberspace
Dick Morris

Thomas Jefferson would have loved to see the Internet. His utopian vision of a democracy based on town meetings and direct popular participation is about to become a reality. In the era of the Fifth Estate, the massive, uncontrolled, and unregulated interaction of tens of millions of people will be the central political reality. Ideas, opinions, viewpoints, and perspectives will race back and forth over the Internet instantly and continuously, weaving together to create a new national fabric of democracy.

Input from a multiplicity of sources will make it impossible for any organization or agency to control the flow of information or the shaping of opinion. As Matt Drudge, the Internet investigative reporter, puts it, "Everybody will be a publisher, disseminating his views to all who choose to log on to read them." News organizations and opinion leaders will spring up all over in a wonderfully chaotic and anarchic freedom. Limitations imposed by capital, paper, and ink, or the unavailability of bands and frequencies, will no longer screen out the opinions of the less connected and less powerful.

Only a few years ago, the voting records of our elected officials were inaccessible, the identities of large campaign donors were obscured, and the expenditures by government and by campaigns were concealed by layers of bureaucracy. Only by joining one of the few public interest organizations, such as Public Interest Research Group (PIRG) or Common Cause, could we find some of this data. Even then, it was slow to reach us through monthly newsletters, annual reports, or pre-election mailings. All of that is in the past. Now we are able to get instantaneous and comprehensive reports of the activities of political figures. Through a wide array of documents placed on the Internet by organizations, individuals, and the press, we are inundated with the tools of effective citizenship.

The incredible speed and interactivity of the Internet will inevitably return our country to a de facto system of direct democracy by popular referendums. The town-meeting style of government will become a national reality. Eventually the 1990s contrived "town meetings" popularized by Bill Clinton will be obsolete, as voters will reject the idea of specially handpicked, agreeable participants who, in fact, don't reflect our towns. Instead, the real town meetings will occur on the Internet, with real people, and the politicians will have to listen.

Dick Morris is a political consultant, TV commentator for *Fox News Channel*, and newspaper columnist for the *New York Post*. Copyright © 1999 by Dick Morris. From *VOTE.com* by Dick Morris. Reprinted by permission of St. Martin's Press, L.L.C./Renaissance Books.

Ad hoc, nonbinding voting over the Internet is starting to transform our democracy. A proliferation of political Web sites soon will offer voters the chance to be heard at the instant that an issue becomes important. Whether it is in response to a random act of violence such as Columbine, the death of an American icon like John F. Kennedy Jr., or a court decision such as O. J. Simpson's acquittal, American voters are already finding an outlet for their emotions and political views that has never before been available.

Through interactive political and news Web sites, people will be able to vote on any issue they wish. We will all be more like the citizens in California and other states where voters can take matters into their own hands through direct referendums and initiatives in each year's balloting. Internet referendums will not, in the beginning, have any legally binding effect, but they will be politically binding. As the number of people participating in these votes grows from the thousands well into the millions, they will acquire a political force that will compel our elected representatives, anxious to keep their jobs, to heed their message. No congressman, senator, or president would dare fly in the face of so massive an expression of public sentiment.

In all likelihood these Internet referendums will be staged without the slightest government participation. Private Web sites like Vote.com will provide the ballot boxes. Financed by advertising, these nongovernmental means of expressing voter opinion, in effect, mean the end of a government monopoly on the process of registration and voting.

When will voters be consulted on important issues? Whenever they want to be. Anytime enough Internet users want to have a referendum they will simply have one. There will likely be hundreds of referendums each year. Of course only a few will attract the attention of enough voters to matter politically, but, by the self-correcting increase or decrease in turnout, voters will indicate how important they feel a given issue to be. Some issues will arouse sufficient public attention to generate a huge outpouring of public opinion and tens of millions of votes. These referendums, on the key issues of the day, will have an enormous impact on governmental decisionmaking at all levels. Others will, undoubtedly, be flaky or unimportant. Then few will vote or participate and they will be ignored.

Elections will still be run by government bureaucracies. We'll still choose our president and Congress by the old election system, but the influence the public can bring to bear will make it far less important whom we elect. It is the public's will, not theirs, that will most often be controlling.

Is this a good thing? Our legislators and leaders, with their addiction to special-interest money and power, have forfeited their right to our trust. A little direct democracy might dilute the power of these self-interested and well-funded organizations and restore a measure of popular sovereignty. The insider system, with its focus on partisan combat and subservience to powerful lobbyists, could use a bit of fresh air now and then. Thomas Jefferson recommended a revolution every twenty years to "refresh . . . the tree of liberty." As revolutions go, this one is likely to be both more pacific and more constructive than most.

Of course voters make mistakes and are often turned from good sense by racism, bigotry, and prejudice. Demagogues make a good living off the gullible.

Ultimately our experience with direct democracy will lead voters to see the wisdom of ceding back to those who are more experienced a measure of the power the Internet has given the general public. Eventually, chastened and humbled, our elected leaders may find the pendulum swinging back in their direction. But not anytime soon.

Whether direct Internet democracy is good or bad is, however, quite beside the point. It is inevitable. It is coming and we had better make our peace with it. We have to better educate ourselves so that we can make good decisions. Restricting the power of the people is no longer a viable option. The Internet made it obsolete.

People are yearning for some way to express their views on political issues, beyond talking back to an unresponsive television screen or muttering into their coffee over the morning newspaper. (As we shall see, this frustration with the limited opportunities for political self-expression is a basic reason for the popularity of talk radio's call-in format.)

How popular would Internet referendums become? An April 1999 survey by Dresner, Wickers and Associates, taken for the Vote.com Web site, predicts that upwards of 40 percent of people over sixteen years of age would be interested in participating. The survey asked respondents on which issues they would like to vote. The answer is that significant numbers would like to vote on practically anything.

Interest in Voting on the Internet

Topic	% of Internet Users Who Are Interested		
	Very	Somewhat	Total
General interest in participating in referendums	25	19	44
. . . In presidential primaries	35	19	54
How should budget surplus be spent?	48	20	68
Should Hillary run for the Senate?	20	9	29
Should the U.S. grant more trade concessions to China?	20	14	34
Should sales over the Internet be taxed?	24	12	36

Source: Dresner, Wickers and Associates Survey, April 1999. 1,000 Internet users.

How are we to reconcile this predicted quantum leap in voter interest with the depressing spectacle of annually dropping election-day turnout? While turnout has indeed decreased, the falloff is more illusory than real. As political consultant Richard Dresner puts it, the drop in voter turnout is "more a generational thing than anything else." Dresner notes that turnout among those reared during the Depression and amid World War II has always been very high, higher than that of any other generation. "Much of the drop in turnout," Dresner says, "is due to this generation dying out. Turnout among all other generations has been roughly the same over the past twenty or thirty years." The sole exception, he notes, is that there is a very low turnout among young adults who have not been to college.

As turnout drops, how will participation through the Internet rise? Will the X Generation, skilled in the Internet but indifferent to politics, remain online but continue to ignore the ballot box? Probably this is exactly what will happen.

Participation is a simple matter of logging on. There is no trip through the rain to the polling place. No authority-figure inspectors are there to look up your name in the Doomsday Book to verify your status as a legal voter.

Internet users may not elect public officials, but they will tell those officials what to do. Indeed, referendum voting over the Internet will likely become as habitual as reading a newspaper or using e-mail. Instantly the voter will see his or her vote counted and can log on to follow the progress of the referendum. Those who vote will soon learn how their representative in Congress, the state legislature, or the city council voted on the issue at hand. Feedback will be instantaneous and responsive.

Will the resulting vote-count truly mirror the opinions of those who will really vote to select their senators and congressmen on election day? At first, probably not. But in a society where only about half of voting-age adults actually participates in presidential elections, and only about 40 percent in off-year congressional contests, why should this national canvass of opinion exclude the other half to two-thirds? Indeed, as nonvoters get used to voting over the Internet, they will find themselves more involved in the political process and may well become interested enough to make the journey to the polls on election day.

* * *

Internet use is disproportionately concentrated among those under fifty, but contrary to popular wisdom, its use among minorities is extensive. While the proportion of Internet users who are Black or Hispanic is somewhat less than that of the general population, it does approximate their proportion of those who actually vote. The following table compares the proportion of Internet users from each age and race group with their percentage of the general population.

Internet Use by Age and Race

Age or Racial Group	% of Net Users	% of Population over 16
16–30	39	27
31–50	46	40
51–65	11	17
Over 65	4	16
Black	11	12
Hispanic	5	11

Only Hispanics and those over sixty-five are grossly underrepresented on the Internet. The former is likely due, in part, to linguistic problems, which will be overcome as the years pass. As Internet use grows, the participation of Americans over sixty-five is certain to increase. The Internet population is more and more likely to be a reflection of America.

Obviously, a fair number of people under the age of eighteen will also vote in Internet referendums. While these young people would not be able to vote in actual elections, they will likely still want to use the Internet to send messages to the adult leadership of their country. As teen habits go, voting is relatively less pernicious than smoking, drinking, or drug use, so why not encourage it? The Internet will redefine citizenship.

Will Internet voting be subject to fraud or abuse? Technology can, or soon will, likely be able to stop multiple voting. Every once in a while, a dedicated hacker will be up to the challenge of invading the system and recording multiple votes, but systems can be put in place to prevent any substantial abuse of the process. The validity of an Internet referendum will depend mainly on the verification system of the Web site.

As Internet voting becomes widespread and the turnout for Internet referendum mounts, the energies of our political system will flow into the Internet and further increase its impact. Candidates will campaign over the Internet. Lobbying groups will use Internet voting to animate their positions. Special-interest organizations will adapt themselves to using Internet referendums to make their political points. A new arena will be created that will absorb more and more of the kinetic energy of our political process.

The Promise and Perils of Cyberdemocracy
Norman Ornstein and Amy Schenkenberg Mitchell

In 1992, Ross Perot promised that if elected president he would use electronic town hall meetings to guide national decisions. Perot lost the election (and never made clear how those meetings would operate), but the idea of "cyberdemocracy" aroused much interest and is spreading quickly as technology advances. Every U.S. senator and 190 representatives currently have World Wide Web pages, as do all . . . major . . . presidential contenders. In 1995, the Library of Congress, under the leadership of Newt Gingrich, established an online system offering all legislation considered and passed by Congress.

Norman Ornstein is a resident scholar and Amy Schenkenberg Mitchell is a former research associate at the American Enterprise Institute, a government and public policy research organization in Washington, D.C. Reprinted from Norman Ornstein and Amy Schenkenberg Mitchell, "The Promise & Perils of Cyberdemocracy," *American Enterprise* (March/April 1996): 53–54. Reprinted with the permission of The American Enterprise Institute for Public Policy Research, Washington, D.C.

On the local level, the city government of Colorado Springs has a non-commercial electronic bulletin board called Citylink. Established in 1990 to allow citizens to communicate with city managers and city council members, it's available free of charge. In 1994, the Minnesota Electronic Democracy Project conducted online debates among candidates in the gubernatorial and senate races.

States have begun fashioning their governmental processes around this direct-democracy ideal. Twenty-four states permit citizen initiatives that place legislation or constitutional amendments on the ballot. Oregon has held local vote-by-mail elections since 1981, and in 1995 initiated its first state-wide mail ballot to replace Senator Bob Packwood. North Dakota's 1996 presidential primary [was conducted] by mail ballot.

All this may be just the beginning. As new technologies emerge, many futurists paint rosy scenarios of more direct roles for individuals in law-making. Some prophesy that legislators will vote and debate from their home state through computers and televisions, eliminating the need for the actual houses of Congress in Washington. Lawrence Grossman, former president of PBS and NBC, imagines Congress evolving into a body that discusses issues and disseminates information, but only makes decisions after being instructed by the public. Futurist Christine Slaton questions the need for elected legislators at all. She envisions using technology to create a participatory democracy where representatives are selected by lot and rotated regularly. Alvin and Heidi Toffler of "third wave" fame predict that today's political parties will disappear, replaced by fluid coalitions that vary according to changing legislative interests. The Tofflers also envision representatives chosen by lot, or at a minimum, elected officials casting 50 percent of a vote and a random sampling of the public casting the other 50 percent. In this scenario, individuals will not only vote on more things than they do now, they'll vote on more complex questions, as simple yes/no votes are replaced by if-then referenda. Nor will voters have to inconvenience themselves by traveling to the local polling station. They probably won't even have to lick a stamp. Instead, voters will simply punch in their vote from their TV remote control, never leaving the house, never having to speak with another individual, not even having to spend more than a few seconds thinking about their choice.

Enchanting as these innovations may sound to Americans grown weary of Washington ways, several questions arise: Would cyberdemocracy in fact be more representative? Would voters take seriously their new responsibilities? Would they even be interested? Who will determine the exact questions the public will decide? And most importantly, what sort of deliberation, if any, will exist under this new regime?

A cyberdemocracy based on personal computers and upscale television systems will not be equally open to all citizens. Twenty-two percent of college graduates go online at least weekly, while only 1 percent of those with a high school diploma do, a recent Times Mirror survey reports. Men are twice as likely as women to be daily online users. Twenty-seven percent of families with incomes of $50,000 or greater have gone on-line, but only 6 percent of those with incomes under $20,000 have. Indeed, the Colorado Springs information systems manager reported that in 1995 there were only 250 active Citylink users in a city of over 300,000. No doubt the popularity of comparable information systems will increase substantially over time, and costs will come down, but a skew toward the highly educated and well-to-do is inevitable.

Even if the technology were made available to everyone equally, how would interest be sustained? Lloyd Morrisett, president of the Markle Foundation, recently wrote that he envisions the early fascination with cyberdemocracy ebbing until cybervoting falls into the same predicament as current voting rights: treasured but not necessarily used. Studying California's experience with referenda, Morrisett found that "the ballot has become so loaded with complex initiatives that it seems to discourage people from going to the polls, rather than motivating them to express their judgment." If the average voter tuned out complex items flashing across his screen, "voting" would be much less representative than it is today.

Cyberdemocracy's greatest danger lies in the way it would diminish deliberation in government. Everyone applauds technology's capacity to inform voters and to improve communications between them and their representatives. But we must also recall that the Founders expressly rejected "pure" democracies where citizens "assemble and administer the government in person," because they usually end in the tyranny of the majority. The Constitution instead establishes a republic where voters select representatives to make and execute the laws. The Founders designed this process to produce a public *judgment*, enlarging upon and refining popular opinions. That judgment, as opposed to public emotions, can only arise through deliberation. In the slow process of debate, give-and-take, and face-to-face contact among representatives, all perspectives and interests can be considered. The need to persuade an informed group of representatives with diverse concerns should, the Founders thought, result in decisions that are more just and more likely to meet the test of time with citizens.

Deliberation even figures in our political campaigns. Over weeks and months, campaigns provide a larger deliberative canvas, an opportunity for voters to consider issues, governing philosophies, and questions of leadership, resulting in a great appreciation of the choices that will face Congress and the President. Of course, our governing system does not always live up to the challenges of serious deliberation, but it still remains our foundation.

What happens to deliberation with the ascent of cyberdemocracy? Consider elections. For all the understandable criticism of never-ending campaigns, negative advertising, and demagoguery, campaigns still work, at least sometimes, as deliberative processes. Voters' initial inclination, not to mention their priorities on issues, often change as they receive more information. Early polls rarely reflect the actual voting. Citizens striving for informed judgments usually make them in the final, most intense days of a campaign. Instantaneous electronic voting would destroy whatever is left of this deliberative process. In Oregon most voters return their mail ballots within five days, casting their votes well before the final days (or even weeks) of intense campaigning.

Mail or electronic balloting also removes the symbolic quality of voting as an act where voters make a private judgment in a public place, surrounded by their fellow citizens, acknowledging simultaneously our individuality and our collective responsibility and common purpose. Compare standing in line at a polling place, going into a private booth, and making individual choices with the alternative of vote-by-mail—the political equivalent of filling out a Publishers Clearing House ballot—or electronic voting, where elections would resemble the Home Shopping Network.

Voting by mail or electronically is only one challenge cyberpolitics presents to deliberative democracy. Consider the difference between laws passed by referenda and laws passed in legislatures. Legislative deliberation encourages informed debate among somewhat-informed individuals with different interests. It allows a proposal to change, often dramatically, as it goes through the gantlet of hearings, floor debate, and amendment in both houses of Congress.

To be sure, some debate can occur during a state referendum campaign, through ads and media analysis, but that is no substitute for face-to-face debate involving not just two sides, but sometimes dozens or hundreds, reflected in representatives from various areas and constituencies. Mail or electronic balloting would short-circuit campaigns even further. And referenda have no amendment process, no matter how complex the issue. Their outcome relies on voters who have many other things to do besides study the issues, much less read the bills or provisions.

Could electronic town meetings provide a popular equivalent to traditional legislating? Theoretically, a broad mass of voters could be part of a different deliberative process. That's the thesis of political scientist James Fishkin, whose "deliberative poll" brought a random sample of 600 citizens together in late January [1996] at considerable expense for three days of expert-guided discussion in Austin, Texas. Even if the Fishkin experiment were scrupulously fair, such enterprises generally seem susceptible to undemocratic manipulation by "experts" and agenda-setters. And "deliberative polls" are unlikely to win out over the allure of a quick, trigger-like vote on the TV or computer. Cyberdemocratic meetings would likely turn into fancier versions of "Talk Back Live." And most deliberation would be reduced—as now in California and other initiative-prone states—to high-tech public relations campaigns by powerful interests with the resources to put their issues on the ballot—making for more special interest influence, not more democracy.

Cyberspace offers wonderful possibilities for citizens to discuss issues. New electronic alliances based on similar interests can be enjoyed. And every day, citizens and legislators can download more information. But the combination of cynical distrust of political institutions, a rising tide of populism glorifying "pure" democracy, and the increased speed of information technology, is a highly dangerous one. While Newt Gingrich has benefited from the political cynicism and populism that drove voters in 1994, he knows the dangers facing deliberative democracy. As he told one of his college classes, "Direct democracy says, Okay, how do we feel this week? We all raise our hand. Let's rush off and do it. The concept of republican representation, which is very clear in the

Founding Fathers, is you hire somebody who you send to a central place. . . . They, by definition, learn things you don't learn, because you don't want to— you want to be able to live your life. They are supposed to use their judgment to represent you. . . . [The Founders] feared the passion of the moment."

Newt is right. But preserving the Founders' vision as the "third wave" of cybertechnology approaches won't be easy.

 /diclerico10

Internet Resources
Visit our Web site at www.mhhe.com/diclerico10 for links and resources relating to Public Opinion.

c h a p t e r 5

Voting

Despite the fact that our population is better educated and faces fewer procedural impediments to voting than ever before, a significant portion of the American electorate does not participate in elections. Indeed, from 1960 through 1996 voting turnout in presidential elections declined some fourteen percentage points, and the turnout figure of just over forty-nine percent in 1996 was the lowest in seventy-two years. The turnout rate edged up to 51.27 percent in 2000 and, of course, took a considerable jump in 2004—between five and ten percent, depending upon how it is calculated. To many observers, however, the turnout rate is still shockingly low. Low voter turnout, it is argued, is just one more sign of a general deterioration in the quality of political life in the United States as citizens increasingly opt out of the political system.

Should we be alarmed by the decline in voting? In the following selections, three distinguished political commentators address this question. In the first selection, Martin Wattenberg, a professor of political science at the University of California, Irvine, takes a look at the jump in turnout in 2004 and concludes that there really isn't that much to crow about. Turnout, he argues, though improved, is still below what it was at its peak in 1960, and the rate in 2004 is not likely to be any more than a "blip" in the history of turnout in America. According to Wattenberg, voting turnout is still primarily a function of political interest and whereas interest was high in 2004, it might not be so high in 2008 and beyond. Although not optimistic about permanently improving voting turnout, Wattenberg does have one suggestion for improving turnout: Make the election day a national holiday like most other countries in the world.

In the second article, Arend Lijphart, a former president of the American Political Science Association, argues that low voter turnout is indeed a serious problem about which citizens ought to be concerned, for the level of voter participation has important implications for the legitimacy of government, as well as its policies. Indeed, so concerned is Lijphart about low voter turnout in the United States that he proposes what some might regard as a radical solution—compulsory voting.

Finally, the author of the last article, political scientist Austin Ranney, argues that we need not fear the fact that many persons choose not to vote. Ranney bases his argument on two main propositions. First, he contends that because voters and nonvoters do not differ significantly in policy and candidate preferences, no great harm is done to our system of representation if a sizable percentage of people do not vote; and second, nonvoting does not offend any basic democratic principle, for the right not to vote is every bit as precious as the right to vote.

Turnout in the 2004 Presidential Election
Martin P. Wattenberg

One of the major stories of the 2004 presidential election was the increase in voter turnout from 2000. There is no doubt that there was heightened interest in the 2004 campaign and that rates of voter participation increased most everywhere in the United States. All Americans should be pleased with this aspect of the contest between Bush and Kerry. Yet, this good news needs to be tempered once one puts political interest and turnout in 2004 into historical perspective. Journalists who wrote of "unprecedented interest" in the 2004 race for the White House were clearly exaggerating. And anyone who wrote of "record turnout" among voters could only justify such a claim by focusing on the sheer number of voters who cast ballots—not on the percentage of eligible persons. . . .

TURNOUT OF THE VOTING AGE POPULATION IN 2004

The widely reported figure of 122 million voters who participated in the 2004 presidential election was a record-shattering number in terms of raw number of votes, far exceeding the previous mark of 105 million in 2000. Of course, if what is most important in voter turnout is the number of people who vote, then India would win hands down as the world's greatest democracy. One has to take into account the size of the adult population in order to evaluate turnout in any election. Although the American media seemed fascinated with the statistic of 122 million voters, the denominator for calculating turnout was rarely mentioned. The traditionally used measure in the United States, where registration is far from automatic and tens of millions of eligible people do not bother to register, is the Census Bureau's estimate of the voting age population. As of July 2003, the Census estimate of the American population over 18 years of age was 217.8 million. Assuming that the population continued to increase at the recent rate yields an estimate of 221.3 million for voting age population in November 2004. Thus, the turnout rate among Americans who were at least 18 years of age was about 55 percent. Although this represents a 4 percent

Mark P. Wattenberg is professor of political science at the University of California, Irvine. He is the author of Where Have All the Voters Gone? and The Decline of American Political Parties, 1952–1996. *Elections: Turnout in the 2004 Presidential Elections* from Presidential Studies Quarterly 35, no. 1 (March) © 2005 Center for the Study of the Presidency. Reprinted by permission of Blackwell Publishing.

increase over turnout of voting age population in 2000, it is exactly equal to the 55 percent turnout the nation experienced in 1992 and well short of the modern high of 63 percent in 1960. . . .

TURNOUT OF THE CITIZEN VOTING AGE POPULATION IN 2004

It should be noted that all of the turnout percentages presented above are based on a denominator that includes everyone over the age of 18 residing in the United States, including non-citizens, felons, and other individuals who are not actually eligible to vote due to a variety of state laws. McDonald and Popkin argue that turnout decline is a "myth" because the voting age population has increasingly contained more people ineligible to vote due to rising immigration and crime rates.[1] Although they have a reasonable point, adjusting the voting age population for non-citizens does not greatly change the pattern since 1960, as displayed in Table 1. When non-citizens are removed from the calculations, one finds that only about 61 percent of people in the non-South voted in 2004 as compared to 71 percent in 1960; in the South a significant increase can again be seen from 41 to 57 percent. It would be hard to see how a change of this magnitude outside the South can be seen as a myth. And taking into account changes in the percentage of the population that is disenfranchised due to felony convictions (currently about 1.6 percent) is scarcely likely to change the pattern noticeably either.

Substantively, it is my view that the fact that non-citizens and convicted felons are not voting is of importance, and that such information should not be ignored by removing them from the national calculations. Many of these people pay taxes and potentially stand to benefit from government programs as well. Whether it is right or wrong to exclude them from voting is not self-evident, as demonstrated by the varying franchise rules that have been applied throughout U.S. political history[2] and which currently are in place around the world.[3] In his last message to Congress, President Clinton recommended restoring voting rights to felons after they have served their sentences, a proposal which was subsequently endorsed by the National Commission on Federal Election Reform.[4] On the citizenship question, many leaders in the Latino community believe that those who are on the road to becoming citizens

TABLE 1 Voter Turnout Rates in 2004 and 1960 by Region

	2004	1960
Voting age population		
Non-South	56	70
South	52	40
Citizen voting age population		
Non-South	61	71
South	57	41

should be allowed to vote.[5] And in any event, non-citizens are counted in the Census, which means that apportionment of political districts includes them. (In fact, there are districts in the Los Angeles area where the majority of adults are resident aliens. These people are probably receiving de facto representation, even though they can't vote for the people who represent their interests.) In sum, we need to take into account that such people are not voting today, just as the fact that people who were effectively disenfranchised by Jim Crow laws was taken into account in 1960.

STATE PATTERNS OF VOTER TURNOUT

. . . Turnout rates of citizens varied quite widely from state to state in 2004, with a difference of nearly 30 percent between the states with the highest and lowest percentages. Yet, a common pattern is evident among high-, medium-, and low-turnout states alike—namely that the percentage of citizens participating in choosing the president increased from 2000 to 2004. The only clear source of variation is that turnout tended to go up the most in the battleground states, where the candidates focused the vast majority of their time and resources in the final week of the 2004 campaign. In the eleven battleground states (shown in italics in Table 2) the mean increase in turnout was 6.6 percent. In contrast, the typical increase in voter participation in the other states was just 4.2 percent. Thus, greater interest in the presidential campaign nationwide can be estimated to have pushed turnout up about 4 percent. And in the relatively few places where there was extraordinary activity to get out the vote, the rate of increased participation was even greater.

The importance of intense political competition in getting people out to vote can also be seen in the instance of one hard-fought Senate campaign. The race between Democratic Senate leader Tom Daschle and Republican challenger John Thune in South Dakota probably attracted more attention than any other statewide race in 2004. Interestingly, turnout in South Dakota went up 10 percent over the state's 2000 rate, more than any other state. Given that there was never any doubt that Bush would win South Dakota's electoral votes, it is readily apparent that the major force in driving turnout up must have been the heated Senate contest. In fact, South Dakota was the only state in 2004 that recorded more votes for a statewide race (391,092 votes for the Senate contest) than for the presidency (388,156 votes).[6]

Another factor that almost certainly accounts for some of the increase in turnout in 2004 involves technological improvements in voting machines in many states. Because not every state reports the number of people who actually cast ballots, analysts are forced to rely on the total number of votes cast for president as the numerator in calculating turnout. But as the nation learned during the 2000 Florida recount controversy, not everyone who votes has a presidential choice recorded, either because they fail to mark a choice or because of technical problems with their votes. A national study by Caltech and MIT estimated that this percentage was approximately 2.3 percent of all voters in 2000[7]. As a

TABLE 2 Turnout of Citizens of Voting Age by State in 2004, and Changes from 2000 and 1960

State	Turnout of Citizens in 2004	Change from 2000	Change from 1960
Minnesota	77	+5	−1
Wisconsin	74	+6	0
Maine	72	+4	−1
Oregon	71	+6	−2
New Hampshire	70	+6	−10
Iowa	69	+5	−8
Alaska	69	0	+24
South Dakota	68	+10	−10
Colorado	67	+7	−3
Michigan	66	+7	−8
Ohio	66	+10	−5
North Dakota	65	+4	−14
Vermont	65	0	−9
Washington	65	+4	−8
Massachusetts	65	+4	−13
Missouri	64	+6	−8
Florida	64	+7	+14
Montana	64	+2	−7
Wyoming	63	+2	−10
Delaware	63	+5	−10
Connecticut	63	+2	−15
Pennsylvania	62	+7	−9
Nebraska	62	+4	−9
Maryland	62	+7	+4
New Jersey	62	+6	−11
Kansas	61	+5	−9
Idaho	60	+4	−20
Virginia	60	+5	+27
Illinois	60	+4	−17
Louisiana	59	+4	+14
Kentucky	57	+4	0
California	57	+5	−10
New Mexico	57	+7	−5
North Carolina	57	+5	+4
New York	57	0	−12
Rhode Island	56	−1	−21
Oklahoma	56	+6	−7
Tennessee	56	+7	+6
Alabama	56	+5	+25
D.C.	56	+2	—
Utah	55	+4	−20
Arizona	55	+7	+1
Nevada	54	+6	−5
Indiana	54	+4	−23
Mississippi	54	+5	+29
West Virginia	53	+7	−25
Georgia	53	+7	+24
Texas	52	+5	+10
Arkansas	52	+3	+11
South Carolina	52	+5	+22
Hawaii	48	+4	−4

Note: States in *italics* were battleground states in the final week of the 2004 campaign.

result of the Florida fiasco, a number of states undertook major efforts to reduce the percentage of lost votes. These efforts appear to have succeeded splendidly.

Florida itself decertified punch-card machines, which were widely blamed for the high rate of invalid votes in Palm Beach, Miami-Dade, and Broward Counties in 2000. As a result of improved voting machinery between 2000 and 2004, the proportion of invalid votes for president fell from 6.4 to 0.5 percent in Palm Beach, from 4.4 to 0.5 percent in Miami-Dade, and from 2.5 to 0.4 percent in Broward. These numbers clearly played a part in boosting the proportion of Florida's citizens casting a vote for president from 57 percent in 2000 to 64 percent in 2004.

Similarly, Georgia took action to adopt touch-screen voting throughout the state after its secretary of state reported that 3.5 percent of Georgians who showed up at the polls in 2000 had no valid choice for president. Invalid votes were particularly a problem in large counties using punch-card equipment such as Fulton and DeKalb, which had rates of invalid votes of 6.3 and 3.7 percent, respectively; in 2004, both counties reported undervotes were reduced to a mere 0.3 percent. As was the case in Florida, Georgia also experienced a turnout increase, of 7 percent from 2000 to 2004. But unlike Florida, Georgia was never considered to be anything but a Bush state and an easy Senate pickup for the GOP, thereby making it a particularly clear case of turnout being driven up by more efficient voting machinery.

It might be thought that the introduction of punch-card machines in the 1960s played a role in the fall of turnout rates that became apparent soon afterward. However, *The American Voter* estimated in 1960 that 2 percent of votes cast were invalid[8]—a percentage virtually identical to the MIT/Caltech study conducted just after the 2000 election. Thus, if anything, technological changes in vote recording have probably had a favorable impact on turnout rates between 1960 and 2004.

Nevertheless, as can be seen in the right-hand column of Table 2, many non-southern states still have a long way to go to get their rate of citizen turnout up to what it was in 1960. Declines of 15 percentage points or more are found in seven states, and another nine states have experienced declines of at least 10 percentage points. These state-level data demonstrate just how serious the waning of turnout is in some parts of the United States, even with the increase in participation rates from 2000 to 2004. Notably, a fairly steep decline in turnout is quite evident in some of the states that permit Election Day registration, such as Idaho and Wyoming, as well as North Dakota, which does not require registration at all. And those who believe that the decline of turnout is overblown due to the increase of non-citizens in recent years should particularly note that these numbers reflect citizens only.

CONCLUSION: THE START OF A RECOVERY OR JUST A BLIP?

Although the increase in turnout rates from 2000 to 2004 is surely good news, the prospects for this being the start of an extended upward trend are less sanguine. The prospects for interest in the 2008 campaign even equaling that of

2004 are not so good. One only has to briefly reflect on the extraordinary events from the disputed outcome of the 2000 race, to the tragedy of September 11th, to the invasions of Afghanistan and Iraq to realize that the period leading up to Election Day 2004 was no ordinary time. As the old Chinese curse goes: "May you live in interesting times." Were this level of interest in presidential campaigns to be continued through 2008 it would probably not be a good sign for the United States.

Like the substantial increase in turnout which occurred between 1988 and 1992, this most recent increase may well prove to be just a short-lived blip. It is noteworthy that turnout fell off sharply after 1992 even though the newly elected president worked with the Congress to take historic action to make voter registration easier. The National Voter Registration Act of 1993 (widely known as the "Motor Voter Act") succeeded in increasing the percentage of the public that was registered to vote, but this positive development was more than offset by declining interest in the subsequent two presidential elections. Unlike the situation in 1992, in the aftermath of the 2004 campaign the president and the Congress show no apparent interest in further legislation to boost America's still anemic rate of voter turnout.

The lack of momentum in Congress for legislation that might increase turnout is not due to a lack of good ideas on this subject. After the 2000 election, the National Commission on Federal Electoral Reform led by former Presidents Ford and Carter recommended that Congress make Election Day a national holiday—a proposal that was also endorsed by President Clinton. Based on data collected shortly after the 2004 election, there is good reason to suspect that turnout would have been even higher had Election Day been a holiday. A post-election survey by Harvard's Vanishing Voter project found that 24 percent of non-voters said that they didn't vote because they were so busy they didn't have time to go to the polls. Of course, some of these people just used time pressures as an easy excuse, but it does seem reasonable that in today's busy world that many of them would have voted had they had the day off from work or school. According to the Pew Center's post-election poll, 42 percent of voters who went to the polls on Election Day 2004 had to wait in line. Of these voters who faced lines, over 40 percent reported waiting at least half an hour. It does not take much of a leap of faith to infer that some people may have been discouraged by the prospect of waiting in long lines on a workday.

To those who question whether an Election Day holiday would really make a positive difference, I would simply ask them to consider whether they would recommend that Iraq or Afghanistan hold their elections on Tuesday like we do. It is doubtful that any American elections expert would recommend that these countries emulate our example in this respect. So if Americans wouldn't recommend Tuesday elections to other countries, why should the United States continue this practice? By joining the modern world and voting on a leisure day, it is likely that American turnout would increase.

NOTES

1. Michael P. McDonald and Samuel L. Popkin, "The Myth of the Vanishing Voter," *American Political Science Review* 95(2001): 963–74.
2. See Alexander Keyssar, *The Right to Vote: The Contested History of Democracy in the United States* (New York: Basic Books, 2000).
3. See André Blais, Louis Massicotte, and Antoine Yoshinaka, "Deciding Who Has the Right to Vote: A Comparative Analysis of Election Laws," *Electoral Studies* 20(2001): 41–62.
4. See President William Jefferson Clinton, "The Unfinished Work of Building One America," Message to Congress, January 15, 2001; and the National Commission on Federal Election Reform, "To Assure Pride and Confidence in the Electoral Process," August 2001.
5. See Louis DeSipio, *Counting on the Latino Vote: Latinos as a New Electorate* (Charlottesville VA: University of Virginia Press, 1996), 131.
6. South Dakota is the exception that proves the rule, however. When a variety of indicators of competitiveness of Senate and gubernatorial elections were tested in a multivariate model predicting turnout change, they consistently failed to show any significant impact.
7. The Caltech/MIT Voting Project, "Residual Votes Attributable to Technology: An Assessment of the Reliability of Existing Voting Equipment," Version 2, March 30, 2001, p. 7.
8. Angus Campbell, Philip E. Converse, Warren E. Miller, and Donald E. Stokes, *The American Voter* (Chicago: University of Chicago Press, 1960), 95.

Compulsory Voting Is the Best Way to Keep Democracy Strong
Arend Lijphart

Voting is the commonest and most basic way of participating in a democracy, but far too many citizens do not exercise their right to vote, especially in the United States. In the 1988 and 1992 Presidential elections, the turnout of registered voters was only 50 and 55 percent, respectively, and in the midterm Congressional elections in 1990 and 1994, it was only 33 and 36 percent. Four years later, the turnout in the Presidential election was 49 percent, while for the 1998 off-year Congressional election it was 36 percent.*

This is a serious problem for two reasons. One is democratic legitimacy: Can a government that has gained power in a low-turnout election really claim to be a representative government? For instance, some Americans questioned President Clinton's mandate because he received only 43 percent of the votes cast and because only 55 percent of those registered to vote actually did so—which meant that he received the support of fewer than 25 percent of all eligible voters in 1992. The other, even more serious problem is that low turnout almost inevitably means that certain groups vote in greater numbers than other groups and hence gain disproportionate influence on the government and its policies.

The only way to solve these problems is to maximize turnout. It may not be realistic to expect everyone to vote, but a turnout of, say, 90 percent is a feasible goal, as the experience of quite a few democracies shows.

On the basis of studies ranging from the 1920s work of Harold F. Gosnell at the University of Chicago to the 1990s research of Robert W. Jackman of the University of California at Davis and Mark N. Franklin of the University of Houston, we know a great deal about the institutional mechanisms that can increase turnout. They include voter-friendly registration procedures; voting on the weekend instead of during the week; easy access to absentee ballots; proportional representation, with multiple lawmakers representing electoral districts instead of the current U.S. system of winner-takes-all elections; and scheduling as many elections as possible—national, state, and local—on the same day.

Arend Lijphart is a professor of political science at the University of California at San Diego and a former president of the American Political Science Association. From "Compulsory Voting Is the Best Way to Keep Democracy Strong," *The Chronicle of Higher Education* (October 18, 1996): B3–4. Reprinted by permission.

*The 2000 presidential election turnout was 51.2 percent; the 2002 congressional election turnout was 39.3 percent; the 2004 presidential election turnout was 60.7 percent—*Editors.*

The evidence suggests that using all of these measures together can produce a voter turnout of around 90 percent. But adopting all of them is a tall order. Only a handful of states have even managed to introduce the minor reform of allowing citizens to register to vote on the same day as the election.

Fortunately, one other reform, by itself, can maximize turnout as effectively as all of the other methods combined: compulsory voting. In Australia, Belgium, Brazil, Greece, Italy, Venezuela, and several other Latin American democracies, mandatory voting has produced near-universal voter turnout.

It is somewhat surprising that making voting compulsory is so effective, because the penalties for failing to vote are typically minor, usually involving a fine roughly equal to that for a parking violation. Moreover, enforcement tends to be very lax; because of the large numbers of people involved, compulsory voting simply cannot be strictly enforced. (Parking rules tend to be enforced much more strictly.)

For instance, with 10 million eligible voters in Australia, even a typical turnout of 95 percent means that half a million people did not vote, and it obviously is not practical to issue such a large number of fines. Australia is actually among the strictest enforcers of compulsory voting, but even there, only about 4 percent of nonvoters end up having to pay the small fines. In Belgium, fewer than one-fourth of 1 percent of nonvoters are fined.

Mandatory-voting requirements produce large turnouts, however, even though a government technically cannot compel an actual vote. A government can require citizens to show up at the polls, or even to accept a ballot and then drop it into the ballot box, but it cannot require its citizens to cast a valid vote; secret ballots mean that nobody can be prevented from casting an invalid or blank one.

It is worth emphasizing why low voter turnout is such a serious problem for democracies—one that deserves our attention. Low turnout typically means that privileged citizens (those with better education and greater wealth) vote in significantly larger numbers than less-privileged citizens. This introduces a systematic bias in favor of well-off citizens, because, as the old adage has it, "If you don't vote, you don't count." The already-privileged citizens who vote are further rewarded with government policies favoring their interests.

The socio-economic bias in voter turnout is an especially strong pattern in the United States, where turnout is extremely low. In Presidential elections from 1952 to 1988, turnout among the college-educated was 26 percentage points higher than that among the population as a whole; the turnout for people without a high-school diploma was 16 percentage points lower. Unless turnout is very high—about 90 percent—socio-economic biases in voting tend to be a major problem. For instance, low and unequal voter turnout is a major reason why politicians find it so much easier to reduce government aid to the poor than to cut entitlement programs that chiefly benefit the middle class.

The low levels of voter turnout in the United States are often contrasted with turnouts as high as 95 percent in a few other countries. But when we measure turnout in other democracies in the way we usually measure it in the

United States—as a percentage of the *voting-age population*, rather than as a percentage of *the registered electorate*—we find very few countries with turnouts above 90 percent, and most of those nations have compulsory voting. According to a study by G. Bingham Powell of the University of Rochester, half of the world's democracies have turnout levels below about 75 percent of the voting-age population. This half includes most of the larger democracies; not only the United States, but also Britain, France, Japan, and India, none of which require citizens to vote.

Even these figures cast turnouts in a deceptively favorable light, because they measure voting in what political scientists call first-order elections—that is, national-level parliamentary or presidential elections. But the vast majority of elections are second-order elections—for lesser posts—which attract less attention from citizens and lower turnouts. In the United States, only Presidential elections produce turnouts of more than 50 percent of the voting-age population; turnout in midterm Congressional elections has been only about 35 percent in recent years, and in local elections is closer to 25 percent.

Low turnout is typical for second-order elections in other countries, too. For local elections in Britain, it is only about 40 percent. Even in Australia, it is only about 35 percent, because voting at the local level is not mandatory, as it is for national elections. In the 1994 elections for the European Parliament, another example of a second-order contest, the average turnout in the 12 nations of the European Union was 58 percent. The power of mandatory voting is highlighted by the fact that when it is applied to local elections—as it is in all nations with compulsory voting except Australia—turnout levels are almost the same as those for presidential and parliamentary contests.

It is time that we paid more attention to the issue of voter turnout, because the already low levels of voting in many countries around the world are declining even more. In the United States, voting in Presidential elections has fallen to 50 to 55 percent of the voting-age population in the 1980s and '90s, from 60 to 65 percent during the 1950s and '60s. . . .

The biggest advantage of compulsory voting is that, by enhancing voter turnout, it equalizes participation and removes much of the bias against less-privileged citizens. It also has two other significant advantages. One is that mandatory voting can reduce the role of money in politics, since it does away with the need for candidates and political parties to spend large sums on getting voters to the polls. Second, it reduces the incentives for negative advertising.

As the political scientists Stephen Ansolabehere of the Massachusetts Institute of Technology and Shanto Iyengar of the University of California at Los Angeles have shown in *Going Negative: How Attack Ads Shrink and Polarize the Electorate* (Free Press, 1995), attack ads work—indeed, they work all too well. They are effective not because they persuade people to vote for the candidate making the attack and *against* the candidate attacked in the ads, but because they raise enough doubts in voters' minds that they decide not to vote at all. So the candidate making the attack has lowered his or her opponent's total vote.

Moreover, attack ads breed general distrust of politicians and cynicism about politics and government. Under mandatory voting, it would be so much harder for attack ads to depress turnout that I believe they would no longer be worth the effort.

The main objection to compulsory voting is that it violates the individual's freedom—the freedom not to vote. This was the main reason it was abolished in the Netherlands in 1970, for example. It is unlikely, however, that the Dutch would have made this decision had they foreseen the disastrous plunge in their voter turnouts, from about 90 percent in all elections to only 50 percent and 36 percent, respectively, in the most recent elections for provincial offices and for seats in the European Parliament.

In any case, the individual-freedom argument is extremely weak, because—as I've noted—compulsory voting does not actually require a citizen to cast a valid ballot. Besides, mandatory voting entails an extremely small decrease in freedom compared with many other, more onerous tasks that democracies require their citizens to perform, such as serving on juries, paying taxes, and serving in the military.

Some scholars argue that U.S. courts might rule compulsory voting unconstitutional because it restricts individual freedom. Richard L. Hasen, of the Chicago-Kent College of Law at the Illinois Institute of Technology, . . . has argued, in "Voting Without Law?" (*University of Pennsylvania Law Review,* May 1996), that the only plausible ground for such a ruling would be the First Amendment's guarantee of freedom of speech. But the Supreme Court has explicitly rejected the notion that voting can be regarded as a form of speech. For instance, in 1992, in *Burdick* v. *Takushi,* the Court upheld Hawaii's ban on write-in votes, ruling against a voter's claim that the ban deprived him of the right to cast a protest vote for Donald Duck. The Court said an election is about choosing representatives, not about expressing oneself. Of course, even if mandatory voting were to be found unconstitutional, a constitutional amendment permitting it could be adopted—a difficult, but not impossible, prospect.

Probably the most important practical obstacle to compulsory voting in countries that do not have it is the opposition of conservative parties, like the Republican Party in the United States. High turnout is clearly not in their partisan self-interest, because unequal turnout favors privileged voters, who tend to be conservative. But conservative parties generally were also opposed to universal suffrage, which eventually was accepted by all democracies, because it was recognized to be a basic democratic principle. Compulsory voting should be seen as an extension of universal suffrage—which we now all take for granted.

Nonvoting Is Not a Social Disease
Austin Ranney

In 1980 only 53 percent of the voting-age population in the United States voted for president, and in 1982 only 38 percent voted for members of the House.* As the statistics are usually presented, this rate is, on the average, from 10 to 40 points lower than in the democratic nations of Western Europe, Scandinavia, and the British Commonwealth—although such numbers involve major technical problems of which we should be aware.[1] We also know that the level of voter participation has [declined] since the early 1960s.

All forms of *in*voluntary nonvoting—caused by either legal or extralegal impediments—are violations of the most basic principles of democracy and fairness. Clearly it is a bad thing if citizens who want to vote are prevented from doing so by law or intimidation. But what about *voluntary* nonvoters—the 30 percent or so of our adult citizens who *could* vote if they were willing to make the (usually minimal) effort, but who rarely or never do so? What does it matter if millions of Americans who could vote choose not to?

We should begin by acknowledging that suffrage and voting laws, extralegal force, and intimidation account for almost none of the nonvoting. A number of constitutional amendments, acts of Congress, and court decisions since the 1870s—particularly since the mid-1960s—have outlawed all legal and extralegal denial of the franchise to African-Americans, women, Hispanics, people over the age of 18, and other groups formerly excluded. Moreover, since the mid-1960s most states have changed their registration and voting laws to make casting ballots a good deal easier. Many states, to be sure, still demand a somewhat greater effort to register than is required by other democratic countries. But the best estimates are that even if we made our voting procedures as undemanding as those in other democracies, we would raise our average turnouts by only nine or so percentage points. That would still leave our voter participation level well below that of all but a handful of the world's democracies, and far below what many people think is the proper level for a healthy democracy.

Austin Ranney is professor emeritus of political science at the University of California–Berkeley and a former president of the American Political Science Association. This selection was adapted from a paper delivered to the ABC/Harvard Symposium on Voter Participation on October 1, 1983. From Austin Ranney, "Nonvoting Is Not a Social Disease," *Public Opinion* (October/November 1983): pp. 16–19. Reprinted with permission of The American Enterprise Institute for Public Policy Research, Washington, DC.

*The 2000 presidential election turnout was 51.2 percent; the 2002 congressional election turnout was 39.3 percent; the 2004 presidential election turnout was 60.7 percent—*Editors.*

Throughout our history, but especially in recent years, many American scholars, public officials, journalists, civic reformers, and other people of good will have pondered our low level of voting participation and have produced a multitude of studies, articles, books, pamphlets, manifestoes, and speeches stating their conclusions. On one point they agree: All start from the premise that voluntary, as well as involuntary, nonvoting is a bad thing for the country and seek ways to discourage it. Yet, despite the critical importance of the question, few ask *why* voluntary nonvoting is a bad thing.

Voluntary nonvoting's bad name stems from one or a combination of three types of arguments or assumptions. Let us consider these arguments in turn.

WHAT HARM DOES IT DO?

One of the most often-heard charges against nonvoting is that it produces unrepresentative bodies of public officials. After all, the argument runs, if most of the middle-class WASPs vote and most of the African-Americans, Hispanics, and poor people do not, then there will be significantly lower proportions of African-Americans, Hispanics, and poor people in public office than in the general population. Why is that bad? For two reasons. First, it makes the public officials, in political theorist Hanna Pitkin's term, "descriptively unrepresentative." And while not everyone would argue that the interests of African-Americans are best represented by African-American officials, the interests of women by women officials, and so on, many people believe that the policy preferences of the underrepresented groups will get short shrift from the government. Second, this not only harms the underrepresented groups but weakens the whole polity, for the underrepresented are likely to feel that the government cares nothing for them and they owe no loyalty to it. Hence it contributes greatly to the underclasses' feelings of alienation from the system and to the lawlessness that grows from such alienation.

This argument seems plausible enough, but a number of empirical studies comparing voters with nonvoters do not support it. They find that the distributions of policy preferences among nonvoters are approximately the same as those among voters, and therefore the pressures on public officials by constituents for certain policies and against others are about the same as they would be if everyone, WASPs and minorities, voted at the same rate.

Moreover, other studies have shown that the level of cynicism about the government's honesty, competence, and responsiveness is about the same among nonvoters as among voters, and an increased level of nonvoting does not signify an increased level of alienation or lawlessness. We can carry the argument a step further by asking if levels of civic virtue are clearly higher and levels of lawlessness lower in Venezuela (94 percent average voting turnout), Austria (94 percent), and Italy (93 percent) than in the United States (58 percent), Switzerland (64 percent), and Canada (76 percent). If the answer is no, as surely it is, then at least we have to conclude that there is no clear or strong relationship between high levels of voting turnout and high levels of civic virtue.

Another argument concerns future danger rather than present harm to the Republic. Journalist Arthur Hadley asserts that our great and growing number of "refrainers" (his term for voluntary nonvoters) constitutes a major threat to the future stability of our political system. In his words:

> These growing numbers of refrainers hang over the democratic process like a bomb, ready to explode and change the course of our history as they have twice in our past. . . . Both times in our history when there have been large numbers of refrainers, sudden radical shifts of power have occurred. As long as the present gigantic mass of refrainers sits outside of our political system, neither we nor our allies can be certain of even the normally uncertain future. This is why creating voters, bringing the refrainers to the booth, is important.

Hadley's argument assumes that if millions of the present nonvoters suddenly voted in some future election, they would vote for persons, parties, and policies radically different from those chosen by the regular voters. He asserts that that is what happened in 1828 and again in 1932, and it could happen again any time. Of course, some might feel that a sudden rush to the polls that produces another Andrew Jackson or Franklin Roosevelt is something to be longed for, not feared, but in any case his assumption is highly dubious. We have already noted that the policy preferences of nonvoters do not differ greatly from those of voters, and much the same is true of their candidate preferences. For example, a leading study of the 1980 presidential election found that the five lowest voting groups were African-Americans, Hispanics, whites with family incomes below $5,000 a year, whites with less than high school educations, and working-class white Catholics. The study concluded that if all five groups had voted at the same rate as the electorate as a whole, they would have added only about one-and-a-half percentage points to Carter's share of the vote, and Reagan would still have been elected with a considerable margin. So Hadley's fear seems, at the least, highly exaggerated.

WHAT SOCIAL SICKNESS DOES NONVOTING MANIFEST?

Some writers take the position that, while a high level of voluntary nonvoting may not in itself do harm to the nation's well-being, it is certainly a symptom of poor civic health. Perhaps they take their inspiration from Pericles, who, in his great funeral oration on the dead of Marathon, said:

> . . . Our ordinary citizens, though occupied with the pursuits of industry, are still fair judges of public matters; for, unlike any other nation, regarding him who takes no part in these duties not as unambitious but as useless. . . .

One who holds a 20th-century version of that view is likely to believe that our present level of voluntary nonvoting is a clear sign that millions of Americans are civically useless—that they are too lazy, too obsessed with their own selfish affairs and interests, and too indifferent to the welfare of their country and the quality of their government to make even the minimum effort required to vote. A modern Pericles might ask, How can such a nation hope to defend itself in war and advance the public welfare in peace? Are not the lassitude and indifference manifested by our high level of nonvoting the root cause of our country's declining military strength and economic productivity as well as the growing corruption and bungling of our government?

Perhaps so, perhaps not. Yet the recent studies of nonvoters have shown that they do not differ significantly from voters in the proportions who believe that citizens have a civic duty to vote or in the proportions who believe that ordinary people have a real say in what government does. It may be that nonvoters are significantly less patriotic citizens, poorer soldiers, and less productive workers than voters, but there is no evidence to support such charges. And do we accept the proposition that the much higher turnout rates for the Austrians, the French, and the Irish show that they are significantly better on any or all of these counts than the Americans? If not, then clearly there is no compelling reason to believe that a high level of nonvoting is, by itself, a symptom of sickness in American society.

WHAT BASIC PRINCIPLES DOES IT OFFEND?

I have asked friends and colleagues whether they think that the high level of voluntary nonvoting in America really matters. Almost all of them believe that it does, and when I ask them why they usually reply not so much in terms of some harm it does or some social illness it manifests but rather in terms of their conviction that the United States of America is or should be a democracy, and that a high level of voluntary nonvoting offends some basic principles of democracy.

Their reasoning goes something like this: The essential principle of democratic government is government by the people, government that derives its "just powers from the consent of the governed." The basic institution for ensuring truly democratic government is the regular holding of free elections at which the legitimate authority of public officials to govern is renewed or terminated by the sovereign people. Accordingly, the right to vote is the basic right of every citizen in a democracy, and the exercise of that right is the most basic duty of every democratic citizen.

Many have made this argument. For example, in 1963 President John F. Kennedy appointed an 11-member Commission on Registration and Voting Participation. Its report, delivered after his death, began:

> Voting in the United States is the fundamental act of self-government. It provides the citizen in our free society the right to make a judgment, to state a choice, to participate in the running of his government. . . . The ballot box is the medium for the expression of the consent of the governed.

In the same vein the British political philosopher Sir Isaiah Berlin declares, "Participation in self-government is, like justice, a basic human requirement, *an end in itself.*"

If these views are correct, then any nominal citizen of a democracy who does not exercise this basic right and fulfill this basic duty is not a full citizen, and the larger the proportion of such less-than-full citizens in a polity that aspires to democracy, the greater the gap between the polity's low realities and democracy's high ideals.

Not everyone feels this way, of course. The late Senator Sam Ervin, for example, argues:

> I'm not going to shed any real or political or crocodile tears if people don't care enough to vote. I don't believe in making it easy for apathetic, lazy people. I'd be extremely happy if nobody in the United States voted except for the people who thought about the issues and made up their own minds and wanted to vote. No one else who votes is going to contribute anything but statistics, and I don't care that much for statistics.

The issues between these two positions are posed most starkly when we consider proposals for compulsory voting. After all, if we are truly convinced that voluntary nonvoting is a violation of basic democratic principles, and a major social ill, then why not follow the lead of Australia, Belgium, Italy, and Venezuela and enact laws *requiring* people to vote and penalizing them if they do not?

The logic seems faultless, and yet most people I know, including me, are against compulsory voting laws for the United States. All of us want to eradicate all vestiges of involuntary nonvoting, and many are disturbed by the high level of voluntary nonvoting. Yet many of us also feel that the right to abstain is just as precious as the right to vote, and the idea of legally compelling all citizens to vote whether they want to or not is at least as disturbing as the large numbers of Americans who now and in the future probably will not vote without some compulsion.

THE BRIGHT SIDE

In the light of the foregoing considerations, then, how much should we worry about the high level of voluntary nonvoting in our country? At the end of his magisterial survey of voting turnout in different democratic nations, Ivor Crewe asks this question and answers, "There are . . . reason[s] for not worrying—too much."

I agree. While we Americans can and probably should liberalize our registration and voting laws and mount register-and-vote drives sponsored by political parties, civic organizations, schools of government, and broadcasting companies, the most we can realistically hope for from such efforts is a modest increase of 10 or so percentage points in our average turnouts. As a college professor and political activist for 40 years, I can testify that even the best reasoned and most attractively presented exhortations to people to behave like good democratic citizens can have only limited effects on their behavior, and most get-out-the-vote drives by well-intentioned civic groups in the past have had disappointingly modest results.

An even more powerful reason not to worry, in my judgment, is that we are likely to see a major increase in our voting turnouts to, say, the 70 or 80 percent levels, only if most of the people in our major nonvoting groups—

African-Americans, Hispanics, and poor people—come to believe that voting is a powerful instrument for getting the government to do what they want it to do. The . . . register-and-vote drives by the NAACP and other African-American-mobilization organizations have already had significant success in getting formerly inactive African-American citizens to the polls. . . . Organizations like the Southern Voter Registration Education Project have had some success with Hispanic nonvoters in Texas and New Mexico and may have more. Jesse Helms and Jerry Falwell may also have success in their . . . efforts to urge more conservatives to register and vote. But hard evidence that voting brings real benefits, not exhortations to be good citizens, will be the basis of whatever success any of these groups enjoy.

If we Americans stamp out the last vestiges of institutions and practices that produce *in*voluntary nonvoting, and if we liberalize our registration and voting laws and procedures to make voting here as easy as it is in other democracies, and if the group-mobilization movements succeed, then perhaps our level of voting participation may become much more like that of Canada or Great Britain. (It is unlikely ever to match the levels in the countries with compulsory voting or even those in West Germany or the Scandinavian countries.)

But even if that does not happen, we need not fear that our low voting turnouts are doing any serious harm to our politics or our country, or that they deprive us of the right to call ourselves a democracy.

NOTE

1. European and American measures of voting and nonvoting differ significantly. In all countries the numerator for the formula is the total number of votes cast in national elections. In most countries the denominator is the total number of persons on the electoral rolls—that is, people we would call "registered voters"—which includes almost all people legally eligible to vote. In the United States, on the other hand, the denominator is the "voting-age population," which is the estimate by the Bureau of the Census of the number of people in the country who are 18 or older at the time of the election. That figure, unlike its European counterpart, includes aliens and inmates of prisons and mental hospitals as well as persons not registered to vote. One eminent election analyst, Richard M. Scammon, estimates that if voting turnout in the United States were computed by the same formula as that used for European countries, our average figures would rise by 8 to 10 percentage points, a level that would exceed Switzerland's and closely approach those of Canada, Ireland, Japan, and the United Kingdom.

 /diclerico10

Internet Resources

Visit our Web site at www.mhhe.com/diclerico10 for links and resources relating to Voting.

c h a p t e r   6

Campaigns and the Media

*P*robably nothing has so revolutionized American politics as the emergence of television as the principal means of communicating with voters. What used to be the experience of only a few people—hearing and seeing a candidate at a campaign rally, for example— is now an experience shared by many millions of Americans. Because television enables political candidates to be seen and heard in every living room of the country, it is no wonder that politicians devote so much time and resources to producing television advertisements and other political programming.

The advent of TV advertising also has led to shorter and shorter campaign spots, in which candidates in thirty-second or shorter sound and picture bites "bash" their opponents or attempt to communicate key word messages to the sometimes uninformed, unsuspecting, and undecided voters. These political advertisements are most often referred to as "negative ads," though exactly what constitutes a negative ad is often in dispute.

The thirty-second or less campaign TV spots, particularly those deemed "negative," are roundly criticized by "good government" advocates. Critics claim that such ads do not simply present a negative view of specific candidates for office, but also damage the political system itself. Such a view is taken by the author of the first selection in this chapter—Fred Wertheimer—who argues that the effect of negative ads is to breed public distrust of the political process. According to Wertheimer, the damage done by negative ads makes it very difficult to govern in a world increasingly beset with public cynicism and distrust, that cynicism being fed by negative campaigning. To remedy this, Wertheimer suggests a number of reforms to make those who sponsor negative ads more accountable.

There are those, however, who defend TV spots, be they negative or not, arguing that political ads actually are highly beneficial. Such a point of view is presented by the authors of our second selection—Stephen Bates and Edwin Diamond. Bates and Diamond, while recognizing that TV spots have their negative aspects, are not convinced that such spots are as bad as the critics allege. Indeed, they see such ads as contributing greatly to political "discourse," leaving the voter better informed than would otherwise be the case. To Bates and Diamond, then, reforming TV campaign spots is like trying to remove politics from campaigns. TV is the modern medium of politics; it cannot and should not be "turned off" for the sake of satisfying the critics.

TV Ad Wars

How to Cut Advertising Costs in Political Campaigns
Fred Wertheimer

[Television,] like the colossus of the ancient world, stands astride our political system, demanding tribute from every candidate for major public office, incumbent or challenger. Its appetite is insatiable, and its impact is unique.
—SENATOR EDWARD KENNEDY, SENATE COMMITTEE ON
COMMERCE, HEARINGS, 92ND CONGRESS, 1971

. . . Television advertising is the principal means by which candidates publicly define for the voters their opponents and themselves and the government in which they serve or hope to serve. Television advertising is characterized in the public's mind by one word: negative.

Every two years during the fall, and much earlier in presidential election years, a focused, intense, negative message goes out to the American people over the airwaves about how bad the candidates are, how dangerous their ideas are, how their programs don't work, how problems cannot be solved. Obviously, discussing and disagreeing with your opponent's record and views is a normal and necessary part of our political process. It is a key part of informing and educating voters on the choice they have to make. However, our political TV ad campaigns go far beyond traditional comparative advertising.

Although many candidates have some positive things to say in their TV ads, these messages are overwhelmed by the negative attack ads that set the tone and dominate the debate. Because television appeals to our emotions and magnifies and intensifies what it communicates, the impact of the negative message is much more powerful and damaging on television than if the same message were being communicated through print.

Most politicians and their media handlers focus their TV advertising exclusively on one goal: winning on election day. If winning on election day means undermining your own credibility or damaging your ability to govern or breeding public distrust and cynicism or turning large segments of the public away from voting, so be it. Thus we end up with the perverse result that many

Fred Wertheimer is President of *Democracy 21* and served as President of Common Cause from 1981 to 1995. "TV Ad Wars: How to Cut Advertising Costs in Political Campaigns," by Fred Wertheimer from *The Harvard International Journal of Press/Politics 2* (Summer 1997), pp. 93–101. © 1997. Reprinted by permission of Sage Publications, Inc.

politicians use TV advertising in their campaigns in ways that ultimately do as much damage to their own credibility as they do to their opponents'.

Regardless of what politicians may believe about negative advertising "working" in their campaigns, it certainly does not work when it comes to doing their jobs and serving the American people as effective and credible representatives. As Stephen Ansolabehere and Shanto Iyengar find in their book, *Going Negative*, "Negative advertising demoralizes the electorate . . . eats away at the individual's sense of civic duty . . . and contribute[s] to the general antipathy towards politicians and parties and the high rates of disapproval and distrust of political institutions" (1996).

Although the candidates bear the principal responsibility for this happening, we cannot underestimate how important the role played by media consultants is in bringing about these enormously damaging results. As a result of the perceived need for consultant expertise to design and produce TV ad campaigns, many candidates abdicate much of the power to define themselves and their opponents to their media consultants. The media consultants have only one objective—winning the election—and this is often equated with negative attack ads. The carnage that is left after the election is over and it is time to govern is someone else's problem.

Media consultants, furthermore, normally receive as part of their fee a percentage of the amount spent to purchase TV advertising time for the campaign, such as 15 percent. This can involve hundreds of thousands of dollars—sometimes even millions of dollars—in fees. It also means that media consultants have a strong personal economic incentive to spend as much money as they can to conduct the negative TV ad campaigns they devise.

Although the thirty-second negative ad has a preeminent role in U.S. politics today, it hasn't always been this way, in terms of either the length or the content of our political ads. During the first twenty years of presidential ads, for example, sixty-second spots were the dominant form of TV advertising. In the 1970s, ads of four minutes and twenty seconds played the dominant role, and starting in the 1980s, the thirty-second spot became dominant in presidential campaigns. Presidential ads also went through a transition, over time, from positive to negative. According to one study, for example, from 1960 to 1988, ads in presidential campaigns were 72 percent positive and 29 percent negative. In 1992, 63 percent of Bill Clinton's ads and 56 percent of George Bush's ads were negative, representing a high-water mark, as of that time, in negative ad emphasis in a presidential campaign (Kaid and Holtz-Bacha, 1995).

A PROPOSED SOLUTION

A number of proposals have been offered to challenge and break out of the grip of the thirty-second negative attack ad. The most radical proposal would bar all political advertising on TV. Other proposals include requiring that candidates appear on screen the whole time in their campaign TV ads, that whenever a negative charge is made in a campaign TV ad that it be made on screen by the candidate, that all campaign TV ads be five minutes or more in length, and that candidates take greater personal responsibility for their campaign ads.

The issues and choices involved here are very difficult. On the one hand, there is great value to our political process and our democracy in moving away from the political culture embedded in the thirty-second attack ad. On the other hand, regulating, through mandatory requirements, the use and content of political ads raises fundamental First Amendment and policy concerns regarding the ability of citizens to exercise free speech in presenting their candidacies to the American people.

Although TV ad campaigns are causing deep problems for our political system today, it is also important to keep in mind how valuable communicating on TV can be. TV campaign ads allow candidates to communicate their views to mass audiences and to do so unfiltered by any intermediaries, such as the media. Ansolabehere and Iyengar point out the real problem: "It's not the pervasiveness of broadcast advertising that spawns public cynicism; it is instead the tone of the advertising campaign. If campaigns were to become more positive, people would be less embittered about politics as usual and more willing to vote" (1996).

Congress should require that candidates appear on screen at the end of their political ads and state they are responsible for the ads. This would provide clearer public accountability for candidates regarding the messages they present to voters on TV. By having to take personal responsibility for their ads, visually, candidates may become less interested in and less likely to run the kinds of negative attack ads that are common practice today.

Congress should also require TV stations to provide a designated amount of free TV time to political parties for use either by their candidates for their campaigns or by party officials to present party views. The free TV time to the parties could be conditioned on the candidates and party officials appearing on screen to present their messages. Broadcasters could be provided financial relief for this free TV time through tax credits or deductions. (Most democracies provide free TV time for campaigns, and since most of these countries involve parliamentary systems, the free time is given to the political parties.) This would strengthen the role of political parties, providing them with new clean campaign resources to use to support their candidates or present their views. It would also provide the parties with the opportunity to focus new resources on underfinanced challengers, to the extent the parties are willing to assist them as opposed to their incumbent candidates.

CONCLUSION

There *are* ways to reduce the financial and social costs of TV advertising in U.S. campaigns. The policy changes proposed here would greatly reduce the current financial costs to federal candidates of communicating through TV. The changes would also challenge the basic premise that currently drives TV political ad campaigns. Through a combination of incentives and requirements, they would help move us away from the thirty-second negative attack ad without intruding on the candidates' First Amendment free-speech rights.

Changing the culture of American political campaigns is no easy task, needless to say. Citizens, however, are rightly fed up with the current system. The stakes involved here for our politics, our governance, and our country are enormous. Now is the time to begin changing our TV ways.

REFERENCES

Ansolabehere, Stephen, and Shanto Iyengar. 1996. *Going Negative: How Political Advertisements Shrink and Polarize the Electorate*. New York: Free Press.
Kaid, Lynda Lee, and Christiana Holtz-Bacha, eds. 1995. *Political Advertising in Western Democracies: Parties and Candidates on Television*. London: Sage.

Damned Spots
A Defense of Thirty-Second Campaign Ads
Stephen Bates and Edwin Diamond

. . . [E]veryone denounc[es] 30-second spots as demeaning, manipulative, and responsible for all that's wrong with American politics. David Broder, the mandarin of the op-ed page, admits he's "a crank on the subject." Otherwise staunch First Amendment champions, including *Washington Monthly* and, yes, *The New Republic*, want Congress to restrict the content of political ads. In fact, such commercials are good for the campaign, the voter, and the republic.

To cite the most common complaints:

1. ***TV Spots Make Campaigns Too Expensive.***   The problem is nearly as old as television itself. William Benton, an ad-agency founder and a U.S. senator from Connecticut, talked of the "terrifying" cost of TV back in 1952. Campaign spending has risen sharply since then, and television advertising has contributed disproportionately. Whereas total political spending,

Stephen Bates is a Senior Fellow with the Annenberg Washington Program in Communication Policy Studies, Washington, D.C. Edwin Diamond is professor of journalism at New York University and a media columnist for *The New Yorker* magazine. From "Damned Spots," New Republic (September 7 and 14, 1992): pp. 14–18. Reprinted by permission of the New Republic, © 1992, The New Republic, LLC.

adjusted for inflation, has tripled since 1952, the amount spent on television has increased at least fivefold. In some races, nine out of ten campaign dollars go to TV.

The important question is what candidates get in return. Quite a lot: a dollar spent on TV advertising may reach as many voters as $3 worth of newspaper ads or $50 worth of direct mail. Banning spots would probably *increase* campaign spending, by diverting candidates to less efficient forms of communication. In addition, spots reach supporters, opponents, and fence-sitters alike. This mass auditing imposes a measure of accountability that other media, particularly direct mail, lack.

2. *A Candidate Can't Say Anything Substantive in 30 Seconds.* Referring to sound bites as well as spots, Michael Dukakis* sourly concluded that the 1988 campaign was about "phraseology," not ideology. But a lot can be said in thirty seconds. John Lindsay's 1972 presidential campaign broadcast a 30-second spot in Florida that gave the candidate's positions on, among other issues, gun control (for), abortion rights (for), and school prayer (against). Lindsay's media manager, David Garth, later joked that the spot "probably lost the entire population of Florida."

A candidate can even make his point in 10 seconds. In California's 1992 Republican primary for U.S. Senate, one spot said simply: "I'm Bruce Herschensohn. My opponent, Tom Campbell, was the only Republican congressman opposing the 1990 anti-crime bill. He's liberal and wrong." Campbell replied in kind: "Bruce Herschensohn is lying, Tom Campbell voted to extend the death penalty to twenty-seven crimes, and was named Legislator of the Year by the California Fraternal Order of Police."

Though hardly encyclopedic, these spots reveal something about the candidates' priorities. They assert facts that can be checked and conclusions that can be challenged. If nothing else, they improve on what may have been the first ten-second spot, broadcast in 1954: "Minnesota needs a wide-awake governor! Vote for Orville Freeman and bring wide-awake action to Minnesota's problems!"

Brief ads do have one shortcoming. In 30 seconds, a candidate cannot hope to answer a half-true attack spot. In Bush's [Willie Horton] "revolving door" prison ad of 1988,[†] for instance, the voice-over says that Dukakis "gave weekend furloughs to first-degree murderers not eligible for parole," while the text on the screen tells viewers that "268 escaped" and "many are still at large." But as reporters discovered, only 4 of the 268 escapees were first-degree murderers, and only three escapees—none of them a murderer—were still at large. The Willie Horton example was an aberration.

---

*Dukakis was 1988 Democratic candidate for president—*Editors.*

†The "revolving door" ad became associated with convicted murderer Willie Horton, who, under a Massachusetts furlough program, was released from prison in 1986 for 48 hours, but never returned. He subsequently assaulted and raped a woman in Maryland, for which he was convicted and sentenced to prison in 1987—*Editors.*

This point might have been hard for the Dukakis team to convey in 30 seconds. What kept them from responding to Hortonism, however, was not the constraints of brevity; it was their decision to try to get public attention off the furlough program—a subject that, even without the Bush campaign's factual finagling, was bound to cost them votes. No sensible candidate will defend himself by saying he's only half as bad as his opponent charges.

Just as short spots aren't invariably shallow, long telecasts aren't invariably thoughtful. The 1960 John F. Kennedy campaign aired a two-minute spot with a bouncy jingle; it conveyed youth and vitality, but scarcely any information (except for a musical reference to Kennedy's Catholicism: "Can you deny to any man/The right he's guaranteed/To be elected president/No matter what his creed?"). As Ross Perot demonstrated, a candidate determined to be evasive can do so in a 30-second spot or in a two-hour live Q&A session.

3. ***Political Ads Are Responsible for the Low-Down-and-Dirty State of Political Discourse.*** According to Arthur Schlesinger Jr., television is "draining content out of campaigns." But that assertion romanticizes the past. In the 1890s James Bryce, a Briton, decried American political campaigns in 1990s terms. Campaigns devote less attention to issues, he fretted, than to "questions of personal fitness," such as any "irregularity" in the candidate's relations with women. These issueless campaigns diminish the "confidence of the country in the honor of its public men."

Sleazy ads hardly raise the level of political discourse, but they aren't the superweapon that critics claim. "When a client of ours is attacked," boasts Democratic consultant Bob Squier, "the people of that state are going to get some kind of response the next day." These responses are invariably revealing. In a 1988 Dukakis ad, the candidate watches a TV set showing a Bush ad. "I'm fed up with it," Dukakis says. "Never seen anything like it in twenty-five years of public life—George Bush's negative television ads, distorting my record. . . ." But instead of presenting a sharp reply, Dukakis only turns off the set—a metaphor for his entire campaign.

4. ***TV Ads Keep the Potatoes on the Couch.*** Barely half of eligible citizens voted in 1988, the lowest turnout in 40 years.* In fact, turnout has declined steadily since 1960. During the same period campaign-TV expenditures have tripled in constant dollars. Many of the TV dollars have been diverted from doorbell pushing, rallies, and other activities that involve citizens in politics. And, according to critics, simplistic, unfair spots discourage people from voting.

It is nearly impossible to untangle the factors that influence voter turnout. Some consultants, like Republican Eddie Mahe, argue that the decline in voting is a passing consequence of demographics. In the 1960s and 1970s the baby-boom generation reached voting age and lowered voting figures (so did the 26th Amendment, which changed the voting age

---

*Turnout in 1996 was even lower—49 percent—*Editors.*

from 21 to 18). No surprises there: Turnout is traditionally lower among the young. So, as the boomer generation ages, turnout will increase.

As for how spots affect turnout in particular elections, the evidence goes both ways. In the 1990 race for U.S. Senate in North Carolina, early polls showed blue-collar whites inclined to stay home. But many of them turned out to vote for Jesse Helms after his anti-quotas spot received heavy air play and news coverage.

Are spots, then, blameless for the parlous state of voter participation? Well, no. Even if they don't cloud the mind, they may in some sense sap the political will. To the extent that spots resemble lifestyle commercials—It's Miller Time, It's Morning in America—they may be taken no more seriously than other TV advertising. This is especially so when no other campaign is visible to the viewer. Today's political rally, as Democratic consultant Robert Shrum has said, consists of three people around the TV set.

But the doomsayers' solution—to try to divorce politics from TV—won't work. Since the 1950s the voting classes have increasingly stayed home to be entertained, a trend encouraged by demographics (the suburban migration), by new at-home options (cable, VCRs), and at least partly by fear (crime in the streets). Banning political spots, as some cranks in the press and Congress would do, wouldn't bring voters outdoors. It would deprive the couch-potato/citizen of a sometimes abused but ultimately unmatched source of electoral information. As Dukakis discovered, melodramatically turning off the TV resolves nothing.

 /diclerico10

Internet Resources

Visit our Web site at www.mhhe.com/diclerico10 for links and resources relating to Campaigns and the Media.

chapter 7

Elections

The Nominating Process

In the "old days" (pre-1972), the crucially important decision on who would be the presidential nominees of our political parties was made by party bosses in the infamous "smoke-filled room." Presidential candidates, if they entered any primaries at all, did so only to convince the party bosses of their vote-getting ability. Primaries were typically not an important consideration in winning the nomination, in part because there were not very many of them, and partly because most were "beauty contests"; that is, primaries where voters expressed a presidential preference but the results had no impact on how a state's delegates to the national party conventions were allocated. Most of the delegates were chosen in caucuses (similar to Iowa's system) or appointed—both methods controlled by the party bosses.

In the 1970s, both parties were swept by reform movements that opened the presidential nominating process to greater participation. The caucus method of selecting delegates was made more democratic and less subject to manipulation by the party bosses, and the number of delegates who could be appointed by the party bosses was greatly reduced. Although the reformers did not require that states select their delegates by primary, more and more states began to switch to this method. To the extent that primaries provided an opportunity for more participation by the party rank and file, they were seen as consistent with the spirit of the reform movement. In addition, states saw a greater economic payoff by switching to a primary because it seemed to attract more media attention than a caucus and required a greater expenditure of funds by the candidates. Although a number of states continue to select their delegates by caucus—Iowa being the most notable example—the nominating process is now dominated by primaries.

How well the does this seemingly more open and democratic nominating process work? Not very, according to the first article, written by Robert E. DiClerico. As he sees it, the way we choose nominees for the most important political office in the world does a disservice to the candidates, the voters, and the political parties. The authors of the second and third selections, while not disputing DiClerico's general assessment, differ on how to correct what's wrong. John Armor favors getting rid of all the primaries and caucuses and replacing them with a single day national primary—a change, he believes, that would not only be fairer to the candidates and the voters, but would invigorate the political parties as well. Thomas Gangale, on the other hand, sees no need to abandon individual state primaries. In his view, the problems that plague the presidential nominating process can instead be solved by simply changing the order in which the primaries occur.

Choosing Our Choices 2004
Robert E. DiClerico

In July and September of 2004 the two major political parties assembled at their respective national conventions and once again decided who would carry their standards into the November general election. Our presidential nominating process, unique among the democracies of the world, is also the most crucial stage in the presidential selection process, structuring as it does the choices we will confront on election day. This point was not lost on William "Boss" Tweed, the notorious leader of Tammany Hall, who was fond of reminding his compatriots, "I don't care who does the electin', so long as I do the nominatin'."

The only party with a contested nomination in 2004, the Democrats settled on their nominee with remarkable alacrity. Indeed, John Kerry, speaking to supporters in Charleston, West Virginia, in mid-March minutes after his win in the Illinois primary, declared that he now had won the Democratic nomination—this coming just seven weeks after the opening contest in Iowa. Unfortunately, neither Democrats in West Virginia nor any of the other seventeen states and territories with contests yet to be held played any role in the making of that decision.

Actually, the Democratic Party nomination was for all practical purposes decided back in January following John Kerry's decisive victories in both Iowa and New Hampshire, enabling him to build up a head of steam that was nearly impossible to stop. The Iowa win suddenly moved him from a stagnating third place standing in the New Hampshire polls into first place, and his commanding finish there made him the poll leader in all seven of the state contests coming a week later, where he had scarcely campaigned.[1] By the time Super Tuesday was concluded on March 2nd, the most John Edwards had been able to manage was a single victory in his native state; Dean, a win in his home state; and Clark, a first place showing in a state to which he had directed a disproportionate share of his time and money.

Losses in both Iowa and New Hampshire doom a presidential candidacy except when one of their own is running and wins, in which case the results are largely discounted. If you win or exceed expectations in one or the other state, your candidacy is advanced to the next round. Victories in both, however, generate a bandwagon effect that appears unstoppable, as Jimmy Carter demonstrated in 1976 and now John Kerry in 2004. The ability of these two opening

An earlier version of this article appeared in *Arts & Sciences* (Eberly College of Arts and Sciences, West Virginia University, Summer 2004), pp. 23–25.

contests to decide who will be the nominee and, more often, who will not be has caused more and more states to move their contests up to the front end of the nominating process lest they be left out of the action completely. The net effect of this "front-loading," which has been steadily growing in the last four presidential elections, has been to accelerate the decision on a presidential nominee.[2] Thus, whereas Jimmy Carter and Gerald Ford in the 1976 race had not accumulated enough delegates to win until June and August, respectively, Clinton and Dole (1996) and G.W. Bush and Al Gore (2000), had done so by March.[3]

The slingshot effect of Iowa and New Hampshire was particularly robust in 2004 because the Democratic Party quite by design allowed states to hold their contests as early as one week after the Granite State, unlike 2000, when five weeks intervened between New Hampshire and the starting dates for subsequent Democratic Party contests. The motive behind configuring the primary calendar in this way was to deny Republican primaries the monopoly on media attention, which they enjoyed during this five-week period in 2000, and second, to settle on a nominee quickly, thereby minimizing internal divisions and sending the party into the general election united.[4]

Although an accelerated decision might be good for party unity, it is not entirely clear that this rush to judgment, and the prominent role of Iowa and New Hampshire in it, is best for the voters and the political system. We are, after all, selecting an individual who may go on to occupy the most consequential elective office in the world. Those seeking this office deserve to be tested and vetted longer in the rough and tumble of the primary process, and the public given more time to take their measure, particularly since most voters don't even start to focus on the candidates until the primaries begin. A Pew Research poll, for example, found that late in September of 2004, with the informal campaign well under way and after one presidential debate had already been held, only 39 percent of Americans could name *one* of the ten announced candidates![5] And just three days before the Super Tuesday primaries, the National Annenberg Election Survey reported that two-thirds of registered voters polled felt they lacked enough information to make a choice.[6]

Much was made of the high turnout in the 2004 primaries but, in fact, only New Hampshire set a record. According to the Committee for the Study of the American Electorate, the overall turnout for all the primaries held through Super Tuesday was the lowest ever for a contested Democratic nomination race.[7] This should occasion no great surprise, for many voters, seeing that the die was cast following Kerry's victories in Iowa and New Hampshire, were decidedly less motivated to go to the polls. Nor is it surprising that in the states holding primaries following John Kerry's March victory announcement, the average turnout was a modest 9.56 percent.[8] An accelerated nomination decision may be good for party unity, but not for participation by party rank and file.

As the presidential nominating process has grown shorter, so the general election campaign has become longer, leaving presidential nominees of the outparty in a potentially disadvantageous position. They now find themselves scrambling to stay in the news since they no longer enjoy the automatic and free media attention that comes with coverage of the primaries. Moreover, if they opt to finance their nomination campaigns with matching public funds, *and* the mandatory spending limits that come with them, they are likely to find themselves, as Robert Dole did in 1996, with little or no money to tide them over from the end of March until the conventions—their money having all been spent at the front end of the primary process. The incumbent president, meanwhile, assuming he faces no serious challenger for his renomination, has an abundant supply of funds (whether public or privately raised) and command of the microphone, both of which he can now direct at his opponent as Bill Clinton did to Republican nominee Robert Dole in 1996 and George W. Bush to John Kerry in 2004. It is for precisely this reason that both John Kerry and Howard Dean declined to accept public funding of their nomination campaigns, fearing that the mandated spending limits ($43 million in 2004) would leave them with no money to answer the pounding being directed at them by the opposition in what has become a much longer post-nomination period.

The 2004 nomination contest, incidentally, marked the first time since the landmark campaign finance reform legislation was passed (1974) that at least one candidate in both parties declined public financing of their nomination campaigns. The decision by George W. Bush and John Kerry to raise their money exclusively from private sources no doubt provided the former with an unprecedented war chest ($170 million) with which to go after his opponent in this post-nomination period, and the latter with some ability to respond, but for those concerned about the influence of money in elections, it is scarcely a welcome development.

Finally, whether Iowa and New Hampshire ought to enjoy the privileged position of going first, thereby shaping the dynamics of what follows, is open to serious question. They are relatively small states and send modest numbers of delegates to their national conventions. Nor are there grounds for believing that their voters are any more discerning than the inhabitants of the other forty-eight states or D.C. For the Democrats especially, New Hampshire seems an inappropriate choice as the first primary, for it has few urban areas, low union membership, and scarcely any blacks or Hispanics within its borders. Defenders argue that the relatively small size of Iowa and New Hampshire allows individuals less known and of limited funds to compete more effectively, and voters the opportunity to observe the candidates "up close and personal." True enough, but other states (e.g., Vermont, Maryland, West Virginia, South Carolina) could serve this purpose as well.

There has been no shortage of proposals on how to improve the way presidential candidates are nominated. One such plan, a one-day national primary, predates the problem of front-loading and has long been advocated by majorities of Americans. It calls for a campaign running from January through May, or thereabouts, at which time voters in each party would select a candidate to serve as their nominee.

The National Association of Secretaries of State has offered a plan of its own, this one organized around the concept of regional primaries commencing in rotation with the East, followed by the South, Midwest, and West. Beginning with the first grouping in March, each region would be separated by one month. Iowa and New Hampshire, however, would still be allowed to go ahead of any region.

Most intriguing is a reform advanced by the Brock Commission, a group created in 2000 by the Republican Party to recommend changes in the primary system. It proposes that primaries occur in waves, each separated by one month, starting with the small states and gradually working up to the most heavily populated. The percentage of delegates chosen in each wave would be as follows: March (12 percent), April (18 percent), May (23 percent), and June (47 percent).

Whether any of these proposals gains traction remains to be seen. One thing seems clear, however. If no changes are made in how the current nominating process operates, we can expect more states to advance the dates of their contests, producing further compression at the front end of the process, and leaving us with candidates insufficiently tested, voters inadequately informed, and nominees the parties may come to regret.

NOTES

1. *Roll Call,* February 5, 2004, p. 6.
2. William G. Mayer and Andrew E. Busch, The *Front-Loading Problem in Presidential Nomination* (Washington, DC: Brookings Institution, 2004), p. 7.
3. *Ibid.,* p. 50.
4. James A Barnes. "Democrats Compressing 2004 Calendar," *National Journal,* December 1, 2001, p. 3699.
5. Dana Milbank, "Lost in Cyberspace: Playing Catch-Up @ Meetup," *Washington Post,* September 28, 2003, p. A5.
6. *The New York Times,* March 3, 2004, p. A16.
7. *The New York Times,* March 10, 2004, p. A17; *Washington Post,* March 10, 2004, p. A6.
8. Primary turnout figures were kindly supplied to the author by Curtis Gans, Director of the Committee for the Study of the American Electorate.

The National Primary: An Excellent Idea
John Armor

TIME TO TALK ABOUT THE 2008 ELECTION

. . . A gentleman named James Talley happened to tell me about a letter he had published in *USA Today* in January. I told him there was a story there, and I'd write it. Here are his first two paragraphs:

"The time has come for this archaic process we call election primary—a long drawn out process state by state—to be abolished and replaced by a true national primary. The year 2004 should be the last year for this old system.

"In our present ancient process by the time the first three or four states have voted, and the news media have declared the trends and the effective result, the party moguls have the stage set for their guy or gal. This disenfranchises the voters. Every registered American citizen deserves the opportunity to enter the voting booth and to express a choice totally uninfluenced by exit polls and media rhetoric."

And Jim went on to suggest a date for this national primary: the Tuesday nearest to the 4th of July. In 2008 that would be July 1.

In any proposal for major change in a long-established system, a necessary question is "How can this be accomplished?" It's like the story about belling the cat. The mice might be in total agreement that a bell on the cat would be a safety measure. But the question immediately arises as to who will get that bell on that cat. There are two theoretical ways to accomplish what Jim suggests. One method would never succeed for pragmatic political reasons. But the other one could work, if properly approached, so it's doable. And we can talk about whether it makes sense.

If you look over the history of national political conventions, beginning with the Anti-Masonic and National Republican Conventions in Baltimore in 1831, most of them have been reasonably exciting and have had actual tasks to perform. They have either chosen nominees in contested elections, or written platforms on contested issues.

In the span of American history, 2004 was an exceptionally dull year for conventions. Both candidates were known months in advance of their conventions. (I'm speaking here of the only parties with a chance to win in this year, the Republicans and the Democrats.) Both campaigns controlled their

John Armor is a graduate of Yale University and Maryland Law School. He has 30 year First Amendment practice in the U.S. Supreme Court. This opinion piece was first published on Chronwatch.com. http://www.chronwatch.com/content/contentDisplay.asp?aid=9649&catcode=13

conventions—who would speak, what they would speak about, what the party platforms would say.

Whenever one party has a one-term occupant in the White House, its convention is almost guaranteed to be "thoroughly scripted." That's because no incumbent president has ever been denied renomination if he sought that. Yes, I see your hands waving. No, Lyndon Johnson was not defeated for renomination. He was not even defeated in New Hampshire by Gene McCarthy. McCarthy did run nearly even with Johnson, and demonstrated Johnson's vulnerability. Johnson then announced that he would not run again. The result was the 1968 Chicago Convention, one of the most violent and fractious in history.

Presidential nominations now begin with the Iowa Caucuses, followed by the New Hampshire Primary. Both states defend their turf by threatening to move their caucuses or primaries to an even earlier date, if any other state proposes a law to move its primary into January. Even though these two small states are hardly typical of the United States as a whole, the press and pundits put great stock by the candidates who win in those states, plus a small number of the others who "did better than expected."

So almost anyone who wants to be president has to spend at least a year prior to the election year preparing for a solid showing in Iowa and New Hampshire. Unless that changes, 2008 will be a repeat of 2004. Everyone seeking the presidency will be at it for two years, and as citizens our TVs will be cluttered with both the ads and the sound bites from all those people for two years.

Then as the process continues, it's possible that one candidate will outlast the others and force them out of the race (I'm not referring to the "tick" candidates like Al Sharpton and Dennis Kucinich, who burrowed in and claimed to be still in the race after it was over). When the contests on both sides are over early in the year, as now, states with later primary dates find themselves spending serious money to conduct meaningless primaries in which no one campaigns and few people vote.

There are two ways to defang the early overemphasis on Iowa and New Hampshire. One appears in the U.S. Constitution. Article I, Section 4, of the Constitution gives the control of election laws first to the "State Legislatures," but then adds, "Congress may at any time by Law alter such regulations . . ." So if Congress decided that a national primary was desirable, it could pass a law and require that result. This is theory only. The leaders of Congress have all grown up in the current system of nominations. They know how to play this game, not the new game which would result with this change. Discount to zero the chance that Congress would act on this idea before 2008.

Fortunately, that does not foreclose the change. What if two-thirds of the state legislatures decided that a national primary was a good idea? What if those legislators agreed that July 1, 2008, was a good time to conduct this primary and did so by law?

First, the excessive focus on Iowa and New Hampshire would disappear. Every candidate would justly say that for anyone to win a majority of the delegates to his/her convention, that must include a strong win in many states on July 1. The primaries on other dates could not, mathematically, foreclose the nominations at the conventions.

The first obvious result is that all states holding their primaries on July 1, 2008, would be guaranteed to have contested and relevant elections. All candidates would have an incentive to go to all such states—in person, on TV, by Internet—because all such voting would matter.

The second obvious factor is this: It would be far less likely for any one candidate to take a mathematical majority in the July 1 Primary. All candidates would be "in the race" through July 1. None of them would be likely to be "scraped off," like Indiana Jones falling from the outside of a speeding German truck. It isn't just the press focus on the horse race aspects, but the federal election law's provisions concerning federal matching funds, that destroys candidacies early under the present process.

It's more likely that a national primary would produce just leading candidates for the Republican and Democratic nominations, rather than absolute winners. It's common sense that the leading candidates would negotiate with the trailing candidates that they generally agreed with. Perhaps that would result in a committed majority (and ticket) in either or both parties before their 2008 conventions.

But there's a far greater chance under this process than under the present one, that there would NOT be a final, mathematical victory in either or both of the Republican and Democratic Conventions in 2008 as there was in 2004. Are there public benefits to this difference?

Some Democrats are already having buyer's remorse about their selection of John Kerry in 2004. The wrong time to find out about major defects in your candidate for president is after your party has selected that person. The whole point of primary elections is to test candidates against each other, including a comparison of their defects as well as their assets.

If the proposed National Primary did not produce nominees for both parties, that would guarantee that the public and press review of the candidates continued until the conventions. That would allow a maximum opportunity for sound decisions on nominees and minimum risk of buyer's remorse. "Marry in haste, repent in leisure," is attributed to Ben Franklin. Committing to a candidate is a form of political marriage. The observation applies, though Franklin may have borrowed it.

Another public advantage concerns issues. If the candidates are not buttoned up before the conventions, then the issues and party platforms are probably not buttoned up either. When was the last time you recall seeing a debate on any platform point at a convention? And yet, choosing between policy choices on subjects from war and peace to social security are the very essence of modern American politics.

Why should the presidential nominating process continue to be rigged the way it is today, so that the conversations Americans routinely have around water coolers and at kitchen tables are prevented at the party conventions? A National Primary offers the best chance of conventions that have real work to do—candidates to choose, issues to decide.

And if the conventions offer more than pre-scripted content, the press is more likely to offer more coverage. Danger attracts the press. Would anyone cover NASCAR races if there was a written guarantee in advance of no car crashes? Think of the plot theory behind all movies and television shows. If there's no conflict, there's no story.

Of course, the purpose of the leading candidates is always to go over the top. Close out debate on issues. Line up supporting speakers, and conduct a unified convention. But what's good for the individual candidate isn't necessarily healthy for either the whole party, or the whole nation.

The Graduated Random Presidential Primary System
Thomas Gangale

THE RUSH TO JUDGMENT

The traditional presidential primary schedule that had long existed by custom was successively battered down in the 1990s as more states began scheduling their presidential primaries earlier in the year in an attempt to exert greater influence over the presidential campaign process. The presidential primary schedule has now become so front-loaded that the anointed "front-runner" in each of the major parties, i.e., he who has the most money, is the *de facto* nominee. The primaries are becoming mere pageantry, as the national conventions have been for several decades. . . .

Front-loading extravaganzas such as Super Tuesday and Mega Tuesday are the weapons of mass destruction in presidential politics. They kill candidacies by the score. In the last three contested Republican presidential nominations—1988, 1996, and 2000—the campaign season began with six, ten, and twelve candidates, respectively. In each case the race was conceded to the front-runner by the Ides of Mach. . . .

THE BEST THAT MONEY CAN BUY

Not only does front-loading disenfranchise millions of voters by presenting them with a nomination that is already a *fait accompli* by the time they get the opportunity to vote, it also cheapens the value of the votes that are cast by the fortunate few at the front of the process, because many of the starting candidates are forced out of the race before the first vote is even cast. During the twelve months leading up to the first actual selection of delegates, candidates contend not for votes, but for dollars. The year before the primary season has become known as the "money primary." In 1996, two Republican candidates bowed out of the race before the first delegate was selected. In 2000, six Republican candidates—half of the total field of twelve—dropped out of the race during the money primary, more than three months before the first voter cast a ballot that counted for purposes of delegate selection. . . .

THE RISE AND FALL OF THE DELAWARE PLAN

While a number of ideas for reforming the presidential nomination process have been put forward, none has come as close to being implemented as the Delaware Plan, developed by Delaware Republican Committee member Richard A. Forsten and state chairman Basil Battaglia. Under the Delaware Plan, the states would be grouped into four "pods" according to population, as determined by the decennial census. The smallest twelve states, plus federal territories, would go first, followed by the next smallest thirteen states, then the thirteen medium-sized states, and finally the twelve largest states.

The advantage of the plan is that it delays costly, high stakes campaigns in large states until later in the season, with the intent of allowing a wide field of candidates to run inexpensive campaigns in small states in early contests. In theory, this should open the political process to more candidates, a fuller debate of the issues of the day, and a more competitive nomination process. The plan was adopted on May 4, 2000, by the Advisory Commission on the Presidential Nominating Process, headed by former Republican National Committee (RNC) chairman Bill Brock.

However, a major criticism of the Delaware Plan is that states are locked into the same schedule in every quadrennial cycle. The larger the state, the later it is always scheduled. This is inherently unfair to voters in large states. At the Republican National Convention in July 2000, Haley Barbour (former RNC chairman, member of the Brock Commission, and advisor to George W. Bush's presidential campaign) said that the Delaware Plan is a "sincere" but "impractical" effort to fix the system. Barbour objected to a system that would allow a candidate to lock up the nomination before being tested in a big state like New York, Pennsylvania, California, Texas or Florida. . . .

THE CALIFORNIA PLAN

The Graduated Random Presidential Primary System, or California Plan, is designed to begin with contests in small-population states, where candidates do not need tens of millions of dollars in order to compete. A wide field of presidential hopefuls will be competitive in the early going. A "minor candidate's" surprise successes in the early rounds, based more on the merit of the message than on massive amounts of money, will tend to attract money from larger numbers of small contributors for the campaign to spend in later rounds of primaries. Thus there should be more longevity of candidacy, and more credible challengers to the "front-runners." However, as the campaign proceeds, the aggregate value of contested states becomes successively larger, requiring the expenditure of larger amounts of money in order to campaign effectively. A gradual weeding-out process occurs, as less-successful candidates drop out of the race. The goal is for the process to produce a clear winner in the end, but only after all voices have had a chance to be heard.

Within the proposed system's static structure of escalating stakes, the scheduling of presidential primary elections in specific states is random and dynamic from one quadrennial cycle to the next. Thus Iowa and New Hampshire are not always first. The presidential campaign might instead kick off in Alaska, Colorado, South Carolina, or other small-population states. No state would receive preferential treatment as Iowa and New Hampshire do at present.

This system features a schedule consisting of ten two-week intervals, during which randomly selected states may hold their primaries. This twenty-week schedule is the approximate length of the traditional presidential primary season. The schedule is weighted as an ascending scale based on the number of congressional districts. The actual number of delegates for each state would be set by the political parties themselves, as they always have been. The District of Columbia, Guam, Puerto Rico, and the Virgin Islands, which also send delegates to both national conventions, are each counted as one district in this system, although they in fact have no voting representatives in Congress.

In the first interval, a randomly determined combination of states with a combined total of eight congressional districts would hold their primaries, caucuses, or conventions. This is approximately equal to the total number of congressional districts in Iowa (5) and New Hampshire (2), thus preserving the door-to-door "retail politicking." However, these two particular states would not necessarily comprise the first round. Any state or combination of states amounting to a total of eight congressional districts could be in the first round of primaries and caucuses. This could include such ethnically diverse jurisdictions as American Samoa, the District of Columbia, Guam, Puerto Rico, the Virgin Islands, Alaska, Hawaii, New Mexico, Arkansas, Mississippi, Oklahoma, South Carolina, Alabama, Louisiana, Arizona, and Maryland. These jurisdictions have large proportions of people of color such as Asians, Pacific Islanders, Hispanics, Native Americans, and African Americans, and seventeen of thirty-eight jurisdictions have poverty rates above the national average. Opening the first contests to this field of jurisdictions would empower demographic groups that the current system marginalizes.

In the second period—two weeks later—the eligibility number would increase to sixteen (8 × 2). In the baseline design of the California Plan, every two weeks, the combined size of the contests would grow by eight congressional districts, until a combination of states totaling eighty congressional seats (8 × 10)—nearly one-fifth of the total—would be up for grabs in the tenth and last interval toward the end of June. As the political stakes increased every two weeks, a steady weeding-out process would occur, as less successful campaigns reached the point at which they were no longer competitive in these larger contests. The widest possible political debate would be fostered by this system, commensurate with the need to resolve the debate to one or two viable candidacies at the end of the primary process. . . .

Small states like Iowa and New Hampshire would be eligible for the entire primary season. They might luck out and be first, get stuck with the last interval, or end up somewhere in the middle. Not every state would have a chance to go first, but every state would have an opportunity to be last. No one region of the country would consistently have an advantage over all the others, while there would be equal advantage in being a large, small, or medium-size state.

The unique and innovative design of the California Plan achieves the goal of preserving "retail politicking" in small, early venues without imposing an unacceptable handicap on large-population states. For instance, Virginia could vote as early as the second of ten intervals, whereas under the Delaware Plan it would always vote in the very last round. In the California Plan, the four most populous states are eligible to vote in the fourth of ten rounds. Since only eleven percent of the American electorate votes in the first three intervals, these large states can figure early enough in the delegate selection process to have as meaningful an input as any state. In fact, the California Plan treats all states with surprising evenhandedness; on average, the smallest states are scheduled at random to vote after 32.5 percent of the country has voted, but for the largest states this figure is no higher than 45.5 percent, a spread of only 13 points. . . .

The Graduated Random Presidential Primary System, or California Plan, is at the same time both random in composition, yet predictable in structure. The composition of the schedule favors no one state or one region. Meanwhile, the structure of the system enables the widest possible political debate in the early stages of the presidential primary schedule, yet provides a gradual winnowing process as the price of staying in the game increases with each successive round. A successful candidate need not start out well-heeled, but will cross the finish line fully vetted. He or she need not hail from any particular region of the country, but must appeal to the whole nation. America deserves such a president, and America deserves a rational, systematic presidential nomination process for the twenty-first century.

The Electoral College

*N*o *feature of our Constitution has been the subject of more constitutional amendments than the Electoral College. The primary impetus behind these proposals has been to correct what is widely regarded as the most fundamental flaw in the Electoral College—the possibility that presidents can be elected with fewer votes than their opponents. This outcome has in fact been visited upon us three times (excluding the 1824 election decided by the House) in American history. The most recent, of course, was the 2000 presidential election in which Vice President Al Gore outran George W. Bush by more than half a million votes nationwide, while losing to Bush by five votes (271–266) in the Electoral College.*

It should come as no surprise that this latest "misfiring" of the Electoral College has renewed the debate over what to do about it. In the first selection, historian Arthur Schlesinger Jr. minces no words, arguing that the Electoral College as it currently functions is simply incompatible with the theory of democracy. Although insisting that change is imperative, he rejects as inadequate a number of alternatives, including direct election, which, while guaranteeing victory to the candidate with the most votes, could be harmful to the political process in other ways. The solution, he suggests, is a simple and workable proposal advanced in 1978 by the Twentieth Century Fund Task Force on Reform of the Presidential Election Process. Known as the "national bonus" plan, it retains the Electoral College arrangement while at the same time insuring that the candidate with the most popular votes wins.

Political scientist Robert Weissberg is little moved by Schlesinger's call for action. Not only does he question exactly what "majority" Schlesinger has in mind for presidential elections, but he also finds the historian to be highly selective in his concern for majority rule. Although readily acknowledging that the Electoral College is a flawed institution, Weissberg also cautions us against expecting too much from attempts to reform the system. Any changes will, after all, be fashioned by human beings, all having their own agendas, which may well result in substituting one set of biases for another, or even more likely—deadlock. And as for the particular fix advanced by Schlesinger, Weissberg is dismissive, insisting that the purpose behind the national bonus plan can easily be corrupted and make much worse some of the problems that already attend our electoral process.

Not the People's Choice
How to Democratize American Democracy
Arthur M. Schlesinger Jr.

The true significance of the disputed 2000 election has thus far escaped public attention. This was an election that made the loser of the popular vote the president of the United States. But that astounding fact has been obscured: first by the flood of electoral complaints about deceptive ballots, hanging chads, and so on in Florida; then by the political astuteness of the court-appointed president in behaving as if he had won the White House by a landslide; and now by the effect of September 11 in presidentializing George W. Bush and giving him commanding popularity in the polls.

"The fundamental maxim of republican government," observed Alexander Hamilton in the 22d *Federalist*, "requires that the sense of the majority should prevail." A reasonable deduction from Hamilton's premise is that the presidential candidate who wins the most votes in an election should also win the election. That quite the opposite can happen is surely the great anomaly in the American democratic order.

Yet the National Commission on Federal Election Reform, a body appointed in the wake of the 2000 election and co-chaired (honorarily) by former Presidents Gerald Ford and Jimmy Carter, virtually ignored it. [In] August 2001, in a report optimistically entitled *To Assure Pride and Confidence in the Electoral Process*, the commission concluded that it had satisfactorily addressed "most of the problems that came into national view" in 2000. But nothing in the ponderous 80-page document addressed the most fundamental problem that came into national view: the constitutional anomaly that permits the people's choice to be refused the presidency.

Little consumed more time during our nation's Constitutional Convention than debate over the mode of choosing the chief executive. The framers, determined to ensure the separation of powers, rejected the proposal that Congress elect the president. Both James Madison and James Wilson, the "fathers" of the Constitution, argued for direct election by the people, but the convention, fearing the parochialism of uninformed voters, also rejected that plan. In the end,

Arthur M. Schlesinger, Jr. is a former special assistant to President John F. Kennedy and the recipient of two Pulitzer Prizes. This article is adapted from his contribution to "A Badly Flawed Election," edited by Ronald Dworkin (New Press 2002). Reprinted with permission from Arthur M. Schlesinger, Jr., "Not the People's Choice," *The American Prospect*, Volume 13, Number 6: March 25, 2002. The American Prospect, 11 Beacon St., Suite 1120, Boston, MA 02108. All rights reserved.

the framers agreed on the novel device of an electoral college. Each state would appoint electors equal in number to its representation in Congress. The electors would then vote for two persons. The one receiving a majority of electoral votes would then become president; the runner-up, vice president. And in a key sentence, the Constitution stipulated that of these two persons at least one should not be from the same state as the electors. . . .

"The mode of appointment of the Chief Magistrate [President] of the United States," wrote Hamilton in the 68th Federalist, "is almost the only part of the system, of any consequence, which has escaped without severe censure." This may have been true when Hamilton wrote in 1788; it was definitely not true thereafter. According to the Congressional Research Service, legislators since the First Congress have offered more than a thousand proposals to alter the mode of choosing presidents.

No legislator has advocated the election of the president by Congress. Some have advocated modifications in the electoral college—to change the electoral units from states to congressional districts, for example, or to require a proportional division of electoral votes. In the 1950s, the latter approach received considerable congressional favor in a plan proposed by Senator Henry Cabot Lodge, Jr., and Representative Ed Gossett. The Lodge-Gossett amendment would have ended the winner-take-all electoral system and divided each state's electoral vote according to the popular vote. In 1950 the Senate endorsed the amendment, but the House turned it down. Five years later, Senator Estes Kefauver revived the Lodge-Gossett plan and won the backing of the Senate Judiciary Committee. A thoughtful debate ensued, with Senators John F. Kennedy and Paul H. Douglas leading the opposition and defeating the amendment.

Neither the district plan nor the proportionate plan would prevent a popular-vote loser from winning the White House. To correct this great anomaly of the Constitution, many have advocated the abolition of the electoral college and its replacement by direct popular elections. . . .

The most recent president to propose a direct-election amendment was Jimmy Carter in 1977. The amendment, he said, would "ensure that the candidate chosen by the votes actually becomes President. Under the Electoral College, it is always possible that the winner of the popular vote will not be elected." This had already happened, Carter said, in 1824, 1876, and 1888. . . .

Over the last half-century, many other eminent politicos and organizations have also advocated direct popular elections: Presidents Richard Nixon and Gerald Ford; Vice Presidents Alben Barkley and Hubert Humphrey; Senators Robert A. Taft, Mike Mansfield, Edward Kennedy, Henry Jackson, Robert Dole, Howard Baker, and Everett Dirksen; the American Bar Association, the League of Women Voters, the AFL-CIO, and the U.S. Chamber of Commerce. Polls have shown overwhelming public support for direct elections.

In the late 1960s, the drive for a direct-election amendment achieved a certain momentum. Led by Senator Birch Bayh of Indiana, an inveterate and persuasive constitutional reformer, the campaign was fueled by the fear that Governor George Wallace of Alabama might win enough electoral votes in 1968 to throw the election into the House of Representatives. In May 1968, a Gallup poll recorded 66 percent of the U.S. public in favor of direct election—and in November of that year, an astonishing 80 percent. But Wallace's 46 electoral votes in 1968 were not enough to deny Nixon a majority, and complacency soon took over. "The decline in one-party states," a Brookings Institution study concluded in 1970, "has made it far less likely today that the runner-up in popular votes will be elected President."

Because the danger of electoral-college misfire seemed academic, abolition of the electoral college again became a low-priority issue. Each state retained the constitutional right to appoint its electors "in such manner as the legislature thereof directs." And all but two states, Maine and Nebraska, kept the unit rule.

Then came the election of 2000. For the fourth time in American history, the winner of the popular vote was refused the presidency. And Albert Gore, Jr., had won the popular vote not by Grover Cleveland's dubious 100,000 but by more than half a million. Another nearly three million votes had gone to the third-party candidate Ralph Nader, making the victor, George W. Bush, more than ever a minority president.

Nor was Bush's victory in the electoral college unclouded by doubt. The electoral vote turned on a single state, Florida. Five members of the Supreme Court, forsaking their usual deference to state sovereignty, stopped the Florida recount and thereby made Bush president. Critics wondered: If the facts had been the same but the candidates reversed, with Bush winning the popular vote (as indeed observers had rather expected) and Gore hoping to win the electoral vote, would the gang of five have found the same legal arguments to elect Gore that they used to elect Bush?

I expected an explosion of public outrage over the rejection of the people's choice. But there was surprisingly little in the way of outcry. It is hard to imagine such acquiescence in a popular-vote-loser presidency if the popular-vote winner had been, say, Adlai Stevenson or John F. Kennedy or Ronald Reagan. Such leaders attracted do-or-die supporters, voters who cared intensely about them and who not only would have questioned the result but would have been ardent in pursuit of fundamental reform. After a disappointing campaign, Vice President Gore simply did not excite the same impassioned commitment.

Yet surely the 2000 election put the Republic in an intolerable predicament—intolerable because the result contravened the theory of democracy. Many expected that the election would resurrect the movement for direct election of presidents. Since direct elections have obvious democratic plausibility and since few Americans understand the electoral college anyway, its abolition seems a logical remedy.

The resurrection has not taken place. Constitutional reformers seem intimidated by the argument that a direct-election amendment would antagonize small-population states and therefore could not be ratified. It would necessarily eliminate the special advantage conferred on small states by the two electoral votes handed to all states regardless of population. Small-state opposition, it is claimed, would make it impossible to collect the two-thirds of Congress and the three-fourths of the states required for ratification.

This is an odd argument, because most political analysts are convinced that the electoral college in fact benefits large states, not small ones. Far from being hurt by direct elections, small states, they say, would benefit from them. The idea that "the present electoral-college preserves the power of the small states," write Lawrence D. Longley and Alan G. Braun in *The Politics of Electoral Reform*, ". . . simply is not the case." The electoral-college system "benefits large states, urban interests, white minorities, and/or black voters." So, too, a Brookings Institution report: "For several decades liberal, urban Democrats and progressive, urban-suburban Republicans have tended to dominate presidential politics; they would lose influence under the direct-vote plan."

Racial minorities holding the balance of power in large states agree. "Take away the electoral college," said Vernon Jordan as president of the Urban League, "and the importance of being black melts away. Blacks, instead of being crucial to victory in major states, simply become 10 percent of the electorate, with reduced impact."

The debate over whom direct elections would benefit has been long, wearisome, contradictory, and inconclusive. Even computer calculations are of limited use, since they assume a static political culture. They do not take into account, nor can they predict, the changes wrought in voter dynamics by candidates, issues, and events.

As Senator John Kennedy said during the Lodge-Gossett debate: "It is not only the unit vote for the Presidency we are talking about, but a whole solar system of governmental power. If it is proposed to change the balance of power of one of the elements of the solar system," Kennedy observed, "it is necessary to consider all the others. . . . What the effects of these various changes will be on the Federal system, the two-party system, the popular plurality system and the large-State-small-State checks and balances system, no one knows."

Direct elections do, however, have the merit of correcting the great anomaly of the Constitution and providing an escape from the intolerable predicament. "The electoral college method of electing a President of the United States," said the American Bar Association when an amendment was last seriously considered, "is archaic, undemocratic, complex, ambiguous, indirect, and dangerous." In contrast, as Birch Bayh put it, "direct popular election of the president is the only system that is truly democratic, truly equitable, and can truly reflect the will of the people."

The direct-election plan meets the moral criteria of a democracy. It would elect the people's choice. It would ensure equal treatment of all votes. It would reduce the power of sectionalism in politics. It would reinvigorate party competition and combat voter apathy by giving parties the incentive to get out their votes in states that they have no hope of carrying.

The arguments for abolishing the electoral college are indeed powerful. But direct elections raise troubling problems of their own—especially their impact on the two-party system and on JFK's "solar system of governmental power." . . .

The two-party system has been a source of stability; FDR called it "one of the greatest methods of unification and of teaching people to think in common terms." The alternative is a slow, agonized descent into an era of what Walter Dean Burnham has termed "politics without parties." Political adventurers might roam the countryside like Chinese warlords, building personal armies equipped with electronic technologies, conducting hostilities against various rival warlords, forming alliances with others, and, if they win elections, striving to govern through ad hoc coalitions. Accountability would fade away. Without the stabilizing influences of parties, American politics would grow angrier, wilder, and more irresponsible.

There are compelling reasons to believe that the abolition of state-by-state, winner-take-all electoral votes would hasten the disintegration of the party system. Minor parties have a dim future in the electoral college. Unless third parties have a solid regional base, like the Populists of 1892 or the Dixiecrats of 1948, they cannot hope to win electoral votes. Millard Fillmore, the Know-Nothing candidate in 1856, won 21.6 percent of the popular vote and only 2 percent of the electoral vote. In 1912, when Theodore Roosevelt's candidacy turned the Republicans into a third party, William Howard Taft carried 23 percent of the popular vote and only 1.5 percent of the electoral votes.

But direct elections, by enabling minor parties to accumulate votes from state to state—impossible in the electoral-college system—would give them a new role and a new influence. Direct-election advocates recognize that the proliferation of minor candidates and parties would drain votes away from the major parties. Most direct-election amendments therefore provide that if no candidate receives 40 percent of the vote the two top candidates would fight it out in a runoff election.

This procedure would offer potent incentives for radical zealots (Ralph Nader, for example), freelance media adventurers (Pat Buchanan), eccentric billionaires (Ross Perot), and flamboyant characters (Jesse Ventura) to jump into presidential contests; incentives, too, to "green" parties, senior-citizen parties, nativist parties, right-to-life parties, pro-choice parties, anti-gun-control parties, homosexual parties, prohibition parties, and so on down the single-issue line.

Splinter parties would multiply not because they expected to win elections but because their accumulated vote would increase their bargaining power in the runoff. Their multiplication might well make runoffs the rule rather than the exception. And think of the finagling that would take place between the first and second rounds of a presidential election! Like J. Q. Adams in 1824, the victors would very likely find that they are a new target for "corrupt bargains."

Direct election would very likely bring to the White House candidates who do not get anywhere near a majority of the popular votes. The prospect would be a succession of 41 percent presidents or else a succession of double national elections. Moreover, the winner in the first round might often be beaten in the second round, depending on the deals the runoff candidates made with the splinter parties. This result would hardly strengthen the sense of legitimacy that the presidential election is supposed to provide. And I have yet to mention the problem, in close elections, of organizing a nationwide recount.

In short, direct elections promise a murky political future. They would further weaken the party system and further destabilize American politics.

They would cure the intolerable predicament—but the cure might be worse than the disease.

Are we therefore stuck with the great anomaly of the Constitution? Is no remedy possible?

There is a simple and effective way to avoid the troubles promised by the direct-election plan and at the same time to prevent the popular-vote loser from being the electoral-vote winner: Keep the electoral college but award the popular-vote winner a bonus of electoral votes. This is the "national bonus" plan proposed in 1978 by the Twentieth Century Fund Task Force on Reform of the Presidential Election Process. . . .

Under the bonus plan, a national pool of 102 new electoral votes—two for each state and the District of Columbia—would be awarded to the winner of the popular vote. This national bonus would balance the existing state bonus—the two electoral votes already conferred by the Constitution on each state regardless of population. This reform would virtually guarantee that the popular-vote winner would also be the electoral-vote winner.

At the same time, by retaining state electoral votes and the unit rule, the plan would preserve both the constitutional and the practical role of the states in presidential elections. By insulating recounts, it would simplify the consequences of close elections. By discouraging multiplication of parties and candidates, the plan would protect the two-party system. By encouraging parties to maximize their vote in states that they have no chance of winning, it would reinvigorate state parties, stimulate turnout, and enhance voter equality. The national-bonus plan combines the advantages in the historic system with the assurance that the winner of the popular vote will win the election, and it would thus contribute to the vitality of federalism.

The national-bonus plan is a basic but contained reform. It would fit comfortably into the historic structure. It would vindicate "the fundamental maxim of republican government . . . that the sense of the majority should prevail." It would make the American democracy live up to its democratic pretensions.

How many popular-vote losers will we have to send to the White House before we finally democratize American democracy?

The Electoral College Didn't Do It
Robert Weissberg

That Al Gore out-polled George W. Bush in the 2000 presidential election is incontestable. That many Gore supporters, notably Professor Arthur Schlesinger, feel that Gore was robbed of a deserved victory is equally indisputable. And, as typical when a serious crime is alleged, the question is, "Who did it?" The likely suspects include malicious Florida election officials, cunning GOP lawyers, and "the gang" of five conservative Supreme Court Justices. But, at least for Professor Schlesinger, this compilation omits the Arch Foe, the Mother of All tribulations: the Electoral College. In legal language, these other miscreants were merely willing accomplices. The rickety old anti-democratic Electoral College was the true mastermind perpetrating the most heinous crime—subverting a genuine popular majority. Worse, the troublemaker is still at large, and who knows when it will strike again. Surely the good democratic town folk must act swiftly, abolish this Evil, and replace it with an electoral system that will honor majority rule. Anything less, it appears, denies the very legitimacy of American democracy.

This is nonsense, a view better understood as sour grapes that comes when an immense, just-within-reach victory is denied by a disputed few hundred votes. That the popular vote winner and the Electoral College vote victor are different people does not constitute smoking gun evidence that this presidential selection system is antithetical to majority rule and should therefore be abolished. The equivalent is to insist that Oakland "really" won the 2003 Super Bowl against Tampa Bay since the rules (somehow) gave Tampa Bay an unfair advantage and the rulebook needs a major overhaul. Fantasizing about improved outcomes under alternative rules is a therapeutic exercise, not a method for implementing reform.

A MAJORITY OF WHOM?

Let's begin simply. Even had Gore prevailed in 2000, he could not properly have claimed a popular majority verdict. Since only about half of all those eligible actually voted, this "mandate" arrives from about only a little more than a quarter of all those permitted to vote, and voters typically differ from non-voters. Who knows, these stay-at-homes might have loved Bush. And even

Robert Weissberg is a professor of political science at the University of Illinois—Urbana. This article was written especially for *Points of View* in 2003.

this "eligible voter" category does not comprise "the people." The list of those excluded from this "people" is substantial: non-citizens, felons, the mentally incompetent, and countless others legally denied access. Significantly, those who insist that a majority of "the people" elect the president are oddly silent about the banished outsiders, all of whom can be incorporated via simple statute, not a Constitutional amendment. If a "real" majority is so vital, why the silence regarding compulsory voting, same day registration, Sunday elections, polling places in malls, and all the other mechanisms readily available to boost turnout? Surely these enhancements are as relevant as junking an antique, difficult-to-change system. The hush on these expansion possibilities suggests that achieving "real" popular majorities may not be that pressing.

In reality, uncovering a Platonically true popular majority is a hopeless task, save in dictatorial regimes favoring compulsory voting (and hanging chads are seldom a problem there). Taking a cue from those wanting to replace census enumerations with random sampling, why not use an opinion poll to elect the president? And do we really want "all the people" taking part? Certainly some people should be disqualified, so incompleteness is not a lethal defect. What about the millions of permanent foreign residents who are virtually identical to those permitted to vote save their allegiance to overseas governments? Or temporary, even illegal, foreign workers? In actual practice, *no* rendered collective judgment will be a "real" popular majority. Each alleged definitive mechanism inevitably yields contradictory outcomes depending on minor details except when the division is lopsided. To insist upon this lofty standard is fantasy, a tactic more useful for damning the sturdy status quo than achieving perfection.

Moreover, if a *bona fide* popular majority (regardless of how "the people" are defined) is the non-negotiable gold standard, where was Professor Schlesinger when Bill Clinton was "undemocratically" elected in 1992 and 1996 with less than a popular majority? What was wrong with the Electoral College back then? Did he complain in 1992 when Bush senior was the real victor and Clinton was the usurper since, quite reasonably, most Perot voters would have chosen Bush in a two-way contest? Did Clinton represent, as Alexander Hamilton intoned in *Federalist 22*, "the sense of the majority"? Would our fretful professor argue that Lincoln, Truman, Kennedy were similarly illegitimate since each failed to gain popular majorities? Maybe the Confederacy was right about Lincoln being a false claimant since a majority *clearly* opposed him. Perhaps for Professor Schlesinger only Richard Nixon's victory in 1968 contravened the "will of the people" and therefore subverted democratic governance. Judgments here are obviously flavored by who wins and loses, grandiloquence aside.

Let's put this all into a broader context. We admit that the Electoral College is flawed, prone to what may appear anti-majority outcomes, and what transpired in 2000 is only minor compared to what might happen eventually—for example, the U.S. House of Representatives selecting the third-place finisher to avoid deadlock. Garbling the enigmatic "public will" is not, however, a death sentence that requires returning to the drawing boards. *Every* electoral system is blemished when the standard is faithfully translating votes into political power.

For decades proponents of proportional representation (PR)—which awards legislative seats according to votes for party lists—have tinkered with mechanisms to eliminate disproportional outcomes, but to no avail. Connoisseurs of PR know all too well that slight administrative details—for example, assembling "wasted" votes when calculating final seat awards—can be critical, and PR-created coalition governments result from elite negotiations, not mechanically implementing voting totals. Those who have labored for this elusive perfection usually embrace some system of multiple, cumulative voting having zero to do with the Electoral College (these add second and third choices to the official tally to achieve a broad consensus). Runoff systems designed to force majorities to emerge are notorious for undesirable outcomes—two conservatives in a field of six candidates where everyone else is a liberal can easily be the final choices, though clear majorities oppose both. Runoffs have also been attacked for de facto disenfranchising of racial minorities. Demonstrating "unpopular" outcomes of every conceivable election arrangement, complete with concrete examples, is a well-established scholarly industry.

The upshot of this inescapable bias is that every proposed reform is assessed not as gradually moving toward democratic perfection, but in terms of electoral advantage. To imagine Congress reflecting on Electoral College alternatives as disinterested Philosopher Kings displays a remarkable disconnect from grubby real world politics. Without question, each party would microscopically scan alternatives, and recommendations would surely seek to maximize subsequent electoral advantage under the guise of "making democracy work." The relevant parallel is periodic redistricting. Though the Supreme Court has seemingly provided strict criteria (e.g., compactness, equal population) partisans have become boundary-making geniuses to exploit the smallest gain.

THE NATIONAL BONUS SYSTEM

Subverting the professor's "national bonus" system to "guarantee" a popular presidential majority would be a snap and may make matters worse. Since it puts a premium on total votes, regardless of where secured, it differs not one iota from the potentially troublesome direct election proposal for choosing presidents. It adds nothing new in the way of safeguards or disincentives to prevent skullduggery. It will surely encourage each party to mobilize—by hook or crook—its supports while immobilizing foes. Predicting the likely outcomes is not rocket science. Savvy Republicans and Democrats will keep third parties off the ballot in their strongholds while encouraging them in their enemy's backyard. Envision Democrats faced with Republicans quietly funding a Black Nationalist party in California while fundamentalist Christian parties "mysteriously" arise in Texas. Multiple voting, voting by non-citizens, ballot box tampering, and all the other well-practiced scurrilous tricks will become a national epidemic, not just limited to a few corrupt localities.

Democratic elections comprise more than simple majorities. A manufactured statistical majority cannot, in and of itself, bestow democratic legitimacy if the outcome is widely perceived as being rigged, and rigging may entail opportunistically manipulating the rules in addition to securing bogus votes. Legitimacy comes from heeding long established conventions—even rules putting one at a disadvantage—not merely achieving 50% plus one. Better to win fair and square with a popular minority than manufacture a counterfeit margin with make-it-up-as-you-go-along laws. That the 2000 outcome *was* judged legitimate by nearly everyone should not be forgotten. A newfangled system may not be so lucky.

At best, this "national bonus" plan is uncertain in its impact, a stellar instance of the "perfect is the enemy of the good" adage. This is no small liability given the horrendous political obstacles awaiting constitutional ratification. It is preposterous to assume that once "tinkering with the Electoral College" is put into play, this particular reform—of the dozens of available options—will prevail. Much depends on who dominates when reform is afloat, and any successful plan must garner multiple super-majorities, a difficult task in the face of nervous minorities intent on exercising veto power. If Las Vegas betting parlors were to put odds on this amendment enterprise, the safest bet would probably be "no change." This is certainly consistent with past countless failed efforts to "improve" the Electoral College or abolish it altogether. Inertia is not catastrophic—partisans can still play politics with clear-cut rules, even if these rules are archaic.

Is this a defense of preserving the Electoral College against all critiques? Hardly, though compared to what often transpires elsewhere, the arrangement seems sturdy enough. Multiple, differing electoral arrangements perform admirably in other democracies, and, conceivably, modifications or outright abandonment might improve matters, though it is not clear what, precisely, would bring net improvement. Our point is more modest—beware of those hawking novel contrivances to "rescue" democracy. Changing the rules means shifting the odds on likely winners, and this is the likely aim here. Had Gore prevailed by a razor thin plurality (when taking into account minor party votes), and captured the Electoral vote, today's disgruntled Democrats would have probably celebrated the Electoral College's power to diminish divisive nation-wide recounts. Bush won, and he did not gain the presidency by administrative accident. The Electoral College is not guilty of subverting the popular will.

mhhe
●*com* ▶/diclerico10   **Internet Resources**
Visit our Web site at www.mhhe.com/diclerico10 for
links and resources relating to Elections.

chapter 8

Political Parties

*O*ver the course of our nation's history, the political process has periodically experienced the equivalent of a political earthquake, whereby the reigning majority party in the electorate is replaced by a newly dominant party. This party then runs with the ball until finally losing its appeal, only to return the other party to power. Referred to as "political realignments," such events occurred in 1800, 1828, 1860, 1896, and 1932, suggesting to some that they were likely to happen every thirty-two to thirty-six years.

In a much discussed book (The Emerging Republican Majority), *political writer Kevin Phillips predicted in 1969 that the New Deal Democratic party coalition, which had dominated American politics since 1932, was breaking down and about to be replaced by a new Republican Party majority. Despite some significant Republican gains, that prediction has never been fully realized, leaving political observers to speculate on when the next, long overdue, political realignment will occur. Karl Rove, one such observer, and key political advisor to President George W. Bush, has argued that his boss's ascension to the presidency would lead to just such a realignment, thereby cementing the Republican Party's grip on a majority of Americans.*

In the first article that follows, Darrell West contends that Karl Rove is well on the road to becoming right. Political realignments are fundamentally determined by issues, and according to West, George W. Bush in 2004 succeeded in redefining the national agenda away from issues that play to the strengths of the Democratic Party, toward concerns that benefit the Republicans. There were other signs in the 2004 election as well, including Republican electoral success below the presidential level, John Kerry's inability to do any better than Al Gore with traditional Democratic constituencies, and the fact that critical groups in the Republican coalition appear to have been more easily mobilized to vote than those of the Democrats.

Not so fast, say John Judis and Ruy Teixeira, authors of the second selection. Political realignments have always resulted from a candidate's ability to create a new majority coalition of voters. George W. Bush, they insist, has so far failed at that task. The Democrats, on the other hand, continue to show strength among groups that are growing in numbers. And, Judis and West are convinced, those emerging Democratic majorities that twice elected Bill Clinton to office would have further solidified in 2004 and provided their party with yet another win, had it not been for the events of September 11, 2001, and a less than formidable challenger.

Do Cultural + Security Issues = National Republican Era?

An Assessment of Election 2004
Darrell M. West

In 1896, Republican William McKinley defeated William Jennings Bryan and ushered in a Republican hold on political power that would last 30 years—until Herbert Hoover and the Great Depression. Is it possible that Republican strategist Karl Rove is helping history repeat itself?

President George W. Bush's re-election victory over Democrat John Kerry plus the GOP pickup of five seats in the U.S. Senate and one seat in the U.S. House signals that Karl Rove's vision of a Republican era is a big step closer to realization. Combined with the 11-state affirmation of a ban on same-sex marriages, the 2004 election offers tantalizing hints about how cultural and security issues are reshaping the national political landscape.

For several years, GOP strategist Karl Rove has speculated that the current political era is similar to elections of the late 19th century. According to his theory, there was a series of very close elections between the end of the Civil War and 1896. The parties were very closely divided and the country experienced some of its most tightly contested and controversial outcomes as it struggled to deal with race, regional politics, and the aftermath of the Civil War.

The victory of Republican presidential candidate William McKinley over populist William Jennings Bryan in 1896 resolved this stalemate in favor of the GOP, and Republicans went on to dominate the politics and policy choices of the next 30 years. It was not until Herbert Hoover's terrible performance in response to the Great Depression that Democrats were able to regain ascendancy and dominate the following decades.

Rove has made no secret of his goal for elections in the opening years of the 21st century to return to this pattern. His hope is that Republicans will emerge as a majority party in firm control of the presidency, Congress, and the courts. The $64,000 question is whether the elections of 2000, 2002, and 2004 represent fulfillment of the Rove vision.

Bush's victory in 2004 rests on several factors. He successfully turned his election into a referendum on terrorism. National polls demonstrate that Bush

Darrell M. West is professor of political science at Brown University. This opinion was first published at http://www.brown.edu/Administration/News_Bureau/2004-50/04-049.html.

won 85 percent of the votes of those who cited terrorism as their most important issue, compared to 15 percent for Kerry. Seventy-eight percent of those naming moral values as the most important consideration in the election cast ballots for Bush, compared to 19 percent who did so for Kerry. In contrast, Kerry's top issues were the economy and jobs (he received 81 percent of the vote of individuals saying this was their most important issue), education (76 percent of their vote), and Iraq (75 percent).

These results suggest how potent a combination cultural values and security concerns have become. While American elections traditionally have focused more on domestic economic concerns, Bush successfully redefined the national agenda away from the economy, education, and health care to cultural and security issues. In so doing, he took advantage of voter anxiety in the post-September 11 world and repositioned his party as the one that would best defend America against both foreign and domestic threats.

It may be no coincidence that in each of the 11 states where voters were asked to express preferences on the issue of same-sex marriages traditional, conservative values prevailed. The issue played to the Rove strategy of distinguishing the two parties on cultural wedge issues and GOP arguments that Democrats (not Republicans) were out of touch with mainstream values.

Evidence of Republican success in building its coalition can be found in demographic trends in the 2004 elections. Kerry ran well among African-Americans (receiving 90 percent of that vote), Hispanics (56 percent), women (54 percent), and union households (61 percent).

However, despite Democratic anger over Bush's policies, many of these numbers are no better than Al Gore's showing in 2000. For example, Gore received 54 percent of the women's vote, 90 percent of the African-American vote, and 62 percent of the Hispanic vote. With the extreme voter polarization and clear Democratic dissatisfaction over the Bush administration, one would have expected Kerry to do better among these traditional Democratic constituencies.

It is noteworthy that Bush received 37 percent of the union vote in 2004, 76 percent of the evangelical vote, 59 percent of the votes of gun-owners (who comprise 41 percent of the overall electorate), 43 percent of first-time voters, 21 percent of the gay vote, 41 percent of Hispanics, and 55 percent of the support of military veterans. In essence, Bush lost no ground between 2000 and 2004 with traditional Democratic audiences and energized his conservative cultural, economic, and security base.

One of the most important results in 2004 was voter turnout. Before the election, experts predicted that somewhere between 117 and 121 million voters would cast ballots (up from 106 million in 2000). If this vote had materialized, it would have broken a 30-year record for voter turnout and probably propelled Kerry to victory. Among first-time voters, Kerry won a 55 to 43 percent margin over Bush.

However, these optimistic projections of a big turnout did not materialize. Turnout did increase to around 113 million, but not to the 121 million level anticipated by some observers. This helps explain why Bush won a popular vote victory nationwide by 3.5 million ballots.

It was not just angry women, minorities, and liberals coming out, but Republicans were able to mobilize first-time evangelicals, gun-owners, small business owners, and cultural conservatives. The idea that a bigger turnout would aid Kerry was somewhat correct, but not nearly to the extent anticipated before the election.

Bush's victory is impressive not just at the presidential level, but in the U.S. Senate. In that chamber, Republicans picked up four seats, giving them a 55 to 44 advantage over Democrats, with one Senator being an Independent who often votes with Democrats.

Democratic Minority Leader Tom Daschle was defeated, and Republicans won all five of the Southern state vacancies left by retiring Democrats (North Carolina, South Carolina, Georgia, Florida, and Louisiana). This reinforces the emerging pattern of the South moving solidly Republican. It is becoming increasingly difficult for Democrats to run strongly in the South. The big Republican advantage in the South moves the GOP closer to a veto-proof and filibuster-proof Senate. It also marginalizes moderate Republicans.

Republicans . . . picked up one seat in the U.S. House. This gives them a 13-seat advantage in that chamber. With ironclad discipline and straight party voting on most controversial subjects, this outcome insures that many of the Bush policies will not be rolled back. In addition, combined with GOP gains in the Senate, Republicans will be in a stronger position to pursue their agenda of an "ownership society" in the United States.

With clear-cut control of the presidency, the U.S. Senate, the U.S. House, and many governorships around the country, Republicans are tantalizingly close to fulfilling Karl Rove's vision of a national GOP era. Similar to 1896, Bush ran a campaign that crystallized differences between the two parties and took a clear stance on several important issues. By triumphing in many (albeit close) races, Republicans have institutional control of government that will allow them to cement their hold on power and to follow through on their agenda.

The risk for any party in control of government is that it misunderstands its mandate and overreaches its own political support. Although Republicans are in control of government, their presidential victory was razor-thin and several of the congressional and gubernatorial victories were by tiny margins.

There is a distinct possibility that Republicans will misinterpret their party victory as a policy victory. Although the GOP triumph in 2004 is impressive in purely political terms, Republicans should not conclude Americans have endorsed their agenda.

It is clear from national polls that on many domestic issues such as education and health care that Kerry did very well with voters who thought those issues were the most important ones facing the country. Republicans should not confuse electoral victories with agreement on every policy issue.

Democrats face some difficult soul-searching following their losses at the presidential and congressional levels. Some will criticize Kerry for having centered this election on foreign policy as opposed to the traditional domestic issues of the economy, health care, and education that generally undergird Democratic presidential victories. Critics will say he should have not talked so much about his Vietnam experience and should not have devoted so much effort to contesting Bush's foreign policy but should have confronted Republicans on issues where Democrats often have an edge with voters, such as education, health care, and the economy.

Others will complain about the quality of the campaign run by Kerry. The charge will be that his message was not clearly focused and his campaign was slow to react to GOP attacks. Rather than let Bush criticize him as a liberal, he should have pointed out that Republicans are out of the political mainstream on several key issues. Critics will say that if he had run a better campaign, Democrats could have won.

However, that critique ignores the fact that Democrats lost not only the presidential race, but also suffered losses in the Senate, House, and governorships. The Republican victory was not just a reflection of Kerry's deficiencies as a candidate, but of a successful GOP strategy to focus the agenda on issues such as cultural values and security issues where they were seen as the party better equipped to handle those concerns.

The biggest risk for Democrats is that the party will splinter between forces who wanted the party to confront Bush on all fronts (the Howard Dean wing of the party) and centrists who wanted to blur differences in some areas and confront Bush on selected topics that might have been advantageous to Democrats.

If this happens, Karl Rove's vision becomes a reality. Republicans will divide and conquer the Democrats as easily as Sherman marched through Georgia. Republicans will cement their hold on the levers of government and be in a strong position to dominate succeeding elections around the country. Democrats will have to think very carefully about what happened in 2004 and what it means for future races.

Movement Interruptus
John B. Judis and Ruy Teixeira

There were certainly reasons to despair after the 2004 election—chiefly, the awful thought that George W. Bush and a Republican Congress could find the means to exceed the egregious irresponsibility, the xenophobia, the sheer partisan pettiness, and the callous disregard for life and law of Bush's first term.

Reprinted with permission from John B. Judis and Ruy Teixeira, "Movement Interruptus," *The American Prospect*, Volume 16, Number 1: January 04, 2005. The American Prospect, 11 Beacon St., Suite 1120, Boston, MA 02108. All rights reserved.

But the election itself, and Bush's margin of victory over Democrat John Kerry, were not reasons to despair. Bush won re-election by a smaller margin than Bill Clinton, Ronald Reagan, Richard Nixon, or Dwight Eisenhower—and against a deeply flawed Democratic opponent.

And there was little sign of a party realignment. In the great realigning elections of 1932 and '36, and '80 and '84, Franklin Delano Roosevelt and Ronald Reagan, respectively, created majorities by winning over new blocs of voters from their opponents. In the 2000 and 2004 elections, Bush and the Republicans had to patch together what remained of Reagan's older coalition— without those states and voters that had earlier begun moving toward the Democrats. Bush's victory in 2004 didn't represent the onset of a new majority but the survival of an older one.

The Democrats surely showed weaknesses in the election, particularly in the Deep South and among white working-class voters, but they also displayed continuing strength among constituencies that will command a growing share of the electorate in years to come. These include minorities, single men and women, and college-educated voters. The Democrats also demonstrated surprising strength among younger voters—partly, to be sure, because of the Iraq War, but also because these voters are in tune with the cosmopolitan sensibility that the Democrats represent. And in this election, the Democrats benefited from a new Internet-based popular movement that could do for this era's Democratic Party what the labor movement did for the old party and what the religious right has done for the Reagan Republicans.

REVIVING REAGANISM

In 1980, Reagan won a new majority that combined long-standing Republican support among upscale voters, farmers, and businesspeople with new levels of support from white working-class Democrats in the South and the North. He fused a traditional Republican attack on high taxes with militant anti-communism, opposition to racial preference, and support for a cultural conservatism rooted in church and family. With this appeal, Reagan not only carried the South and the Plains but, drawing on the suburban vote, states like California, Illinois, and New Jersey. In the '90s, Republicans maintained their support in the South and the Plains, but the Democrats under Clinton won over a new generation of upscale suburbanites and city dwellers who lived in postindustrial metropolitan areas. By winning back a modest share of the white working class and maintaining Democratic support among minorities, Clinton obtained a plurality of votes in '92 and '96. He also turned California, Illinois, and New Jersey into Democratic enclaves. And in 2000, Al Gore won the popular vote. On the basis of these trends, we foresaw, in our 2002 book, the emergence of a new Democratic majority by the end of this decade. But the movement toward a Democratic majority was interrupted by the September 11 terrorist attacks. By responding dramatically to al-Qaeda, Bush was able to revive the Republicans' reputation as the party of national security. In the 2002 election, Bush was able to exploit his success on that score—and to amplify it through carefully timed "terror" alerts and wild exaggeration of the Iraqi threat—to override his failures in managing the economy. In the 2004 election, he used virtually the same formula, and it worked. For substantial parts of the spring and early summer, Kerry actually held the lead in opinion polls. Voters didn't know him, but they knew Bush and were wary of the war in Iraq, which had turned into a quagmire, and the sputtering economy, which had never fully recovered from the recession. Yet after the Republican convention, which was almost entirely devoted to promoting the president as the commander in chief in the war against terrorism, Bush moved ahead in the polls, and, except for the week after his dismal performance in the first debate, never relinquished his advantage.

Bush combined a public campaign as commander in chief and tax cutter with a more targeted campaign aimed at spurring turnout among white evangelicals and winning over observant Catholics (including Hispanics) and Jews who backed Israel's Ariel Sharon. Unless you lived in a small town in a battleground state—say, Lakeland, Florida—you would not have been aware, for instance, of Bush's pitch for evangelical votes, which was often conducted on Christian radio stations, in churches, and on billboards reading "One Nation Under God—Bush/Cheney."

Bush's targeting was successful. He picked off Democratic constituencies in battleground states, including culturally conservative Hispanics in New Mexico, evangelicals and some Jews in Florida, and observant Catholics in Ohio. In the national exit poll, Catholics who attended church weekly voted for Bush by 53 percent to 45 percent, very close to the president's margin among this group in 2000, but in Ohio, Bush won 62 percent of the observant Catholic vote, up from 55 percent in 2000. These were significant tactical successes, but they didn't add up nationally to a new coalition.

Bush failed to capture any of the northeastern or Pacific Coast states that Reagan had won easily in 1980 and '84, and he failed to make dramatic gains nationally among the voting groups that had moved into the Democratic Party in the 1990s. Rather, the key to Bush's victory was reviving Reagan's support among the white working class. According to the post-election survey by Greenberg Quinlan Rosner for Democracy Corps/Institute for America's Future, Bush enjoyed a whopping 24 percent edge among non-college-educated whites, compared with a 19 percent advantage in 2000. (Clinton had actually carried this group by a point in each of his election victories.) Insofar as whites still make up 77 percent of the electorate and non-college-educated whites represent a majority of the white vote, that increase alone accounts for most— perhaps 70 percent—of Bush's improved performance in 2004.

This increase came primarily among white working-class women, a group that has shown particular sensitivity to issues surrounding terrorism. One mid-October poll of women voters by comScore, a marketing firm, showed that terrorism was the top issue for women voters, ahead of the Iraq War, the economy or health care. Of the quarter of women voters who selected terrorism as the top issue, more than three-fourths favored Bush. And according to the Greenberg Quinlan Rosner post-election poll, white working-class women voters, in particular, chose terrorism and security (35 percent, up from 28 percent in late September) over the economy/jobs (25 percent, down from 39 percent in late September), the Iraq War (25 percent), and health care (9 percent) as their most important voting issue.

KERRY AND THE WAR

. . . To have won in November, a Democratic candidate would either have had to match Bush's credibility on the war on terrorism or make the failure of Iraq, rather than the war on terrorism, the focus of voters' anxieties. Kerry was unable to accomplish either objective. In August he would declare, astonishingly, that even if he had known there were no weapons of mass destruction in Iraq, he would still have voted for the war. Even in October, after he had developed a clearer position, voters could still detect little difference in what he planned to do if elected and what Bush might do. The main difference was in the steadfastness of their approaches.

To make matters worse, Kerry was also incapable of articulating a clear economic message. According to exit polls, while just 49 percent of voters said they trusted Bush to handle the economy, only 45 percent trusted Kerry with the job. Kerry's health care program was incomprehensible except to policy wonks. And he embodied an austere, upper-class New England liberalism that turned off many voters. He lacked a popular touch.

Kerry's failure as a candidate was evident to us in two visits we made to Martinsburg, a small, blue-collar town in West Virginia. We first visited Martinsburg in July, before the Democratic and Republican conventions. At that time, knocking on doors in a working-class neighborhood, we discovered considerable dissatisfaction with Bush over the war in Iraq and the economy. Few people knew Kerry, but they said they were considering voting for him. Visiting Martinsburg two days before the election, we discovered that most of these voters had decided to support Bush. They often mentioned gay marriage and "family values"—the area is dotted with churches—and feeling "safer" under Bush. They also thought Kerry was too "liberal," a comment about his "values" rather than his program.

Most of these voters were registered Democrats who had voted for Clinton in '92 and '96. And many of them told us, and Democratic canvassers, that they would have voted for Clinton this time, too. Typically, one voter, who faulted Kerry for being "too liberal" on "family values," said Clinton had been "dishonest," but that he was "an excellent president." When these voters talked about the economy, they were clearly closer to the Democrats than Republicans, but they expressed confusion at what Kerry wanted to do. One older voter said, "Of all the countries today, we are the only one that doesn't have any sort of health care plan." That sounded like a line from a Democratic ad, but the voter added that he couldn't figure out how Kerry's health plan worked.

In battleground states where there was also a closely contested state race, Kerry usually ran behind the other Democrats on the ticket. In Washington,

Patti Murray's margin in the Senate race was 6 points better than Kerry's; in Wisconsin, Russ Feingold's margin was 11 points wider; in Arkansas, Blanche Lincoln won and Kerry lost; and in Colorado, Ken Salazar won and Kerry lost. If Bush's victory represented a maximization of opportunity, Kerry's totals represented a bare minimum. Yet this bloc of anti-Bush voters who supported Kerry was extremely large—Kerry garnered the most voters ever for a Democratic candidate—and could be the basis for future Democratic victories.

THE TWO COALITIONS

In the wake of the election, some commentators argued that Bush had dramatically altered the electoral map of the last two decades, but as the corrected exit polls and other post-election surveys have appeared, it has become clear that Bush's successes were primarily tactical. He didn't make fundamental or decisive inroads into the Hispanic vote except perhaps in New Mexico. Overall, Bush probably increased his support among Hispanics by no more than 4 percent or 5 percent—only slightly more than among voters overall. In Florida, Kerry actually appears to have done better among Hispanics than Gore did.

Much was also made of Bush's support in exurban and rural areas. The president did increase his support in these areas, but that is part of a trend that began in 1980. It did not decide the 2004 election. Only 13 percent of Bush's gain in overall vote could be attributed to his increased support in the fringe or ex-urban counties of large metropolitan areas. And this support is unlikely to prove decisive in the future. Despite the fact that ex-urban areas have been growing fairly rapidly, they start from such a small base that their share of all voters has increased only modestly over the last 20 years, from 3 percent to 5 percent. Together with rural counties, which have been declining in population, these areas have stalled at 25 percent of the vote between 1984 and 2004. Exurbia and rural America don't make for much of a political growth stock. They help make Republicans competitive, but they don't give them a new and enduring majority.

The Democrats, on the other hand, continue to show support among groups that are steadily growing as a percentage of the electorate. Among minorities (now up to 23 percent of the electorate), Kerry increased his margin among Asian Americans. His margin among African Americans was slightly smaller than Gore's in 2000—no doubt a product of his patrician aloofness—but higher than that of Clinton in '92 or '96. While Kerry got drubbed among white working-class women, he and the Democrats continued to show strength among single and college-educated women. Single women, whose vote he carried by 25 percent, increased their share of the electorate from 19 percent to 22 percent; college-educated women, whom Kerry won by 10 percent, increased their share from 21 percent to 22 percent.

Kerry actually did better than Gore did among professionals, a key group in the transformation of the suburban vote. He carried voters with a post-graduate education by 11 percent, 3 percent better than Gore had done. Like Gore, Kerry split college-educated voters overall with Bush, but he increased

Democratic support among college-educated men, going from a 57 percent to 39 percent deficit in 2000 to a 53 percent to 45 percent deficit this year.

Kerry also did exceptionally well in '04 among the new generation of voters, winning 18-to-29-year-old voters by 54 percent to 45 percent, compared with a narrow 48 percent to 46 percent margin for Gore in 2000. He even won young male voters by a 51 percent to 47 percent margin, a big change from 2000, when Gore lost these voters 51 percent to 41 percent. In 2000, youth were only 2 points more Democratic than all voters. In this election, youth were 12 points more Democratic. By its nature, the youth vote is transient. But Kerry's and the Democrats' success among these voters could have lasting results. Young voters, like suburban professionals, seem to be turning Democratic because of the Republicans' identification with the cultural right. If so, this trend is likely to continue. Young voters also tend to preserve their loyalties as they get older. Many of the voters who turned 18 during the Reagan years are still voting Republican; many of the current younger voters will continue to vote Democratic as they get older.

The Republicans got their most impressive results in the South, where they won five Senate seats vacated by Democrats and increased their congressional delegation. Kerry's percentage was even less than Gore's was in every state of the old Confederacy except Virginia and the Carolinas (where Kerry managed only to match Gore's poor performance). If the Democrats get shut out in Deep South states like Alabama and Georgia (except in majority black congressional districts), their political infrastructure will deteriorate and they will become less able to field competitive candidates, even when the opportunity for success might arise. That will make it more difficult for Democrats to win back Congress, and may also hamper them in presidential races.

Outside the Deep South, however, the Democrats made inroads. In Arkansas and Colorado, they won impressive Senate victories. Democrats also continued to dominate the nation's postindustrial metropolitan areas, or "ideopolises," increasing the pro-Democratic bias of these areas relative to the rest of the country by a point (three quarters of Bush's net-vote gains, in fact, came outside of ideopolis areas). Kerry predictably racked up large margins in Illinois' Cook County and California's Bay Area, but he also increased the Democrats' margin in Texas' Travis County (from a 5-point deficit to a 14-point lead), North Carolina's Mecklenburg County (from a 3-point deficit to a 4-point lead), and northern Virginia's Fairfax County (from a 1-point deficit to a 6-point lead). It is voters in these ideopolis areas of the solid red states (those Bush carried by 6 points or more in 2000) that are increasing their share of the nation's vote, while the non-ideopolis areas of these states, where Bush made big gains in 2004 (more than two-fifths of his overall increase in vote margin), remain stagnant.

THE NEW CENTER-LEFT

In this . . . election, the Democratic coalition was strengthened by the emergence of new political organizations. Some of these, like America Coming Together (ACT), grew out of the older alliances among labor and public-interest groups in Washington. Others, like MoveOn.org, came out of the virtual community that the Internet has created. . . .

These new groups—and particularly those like MoveOn that are based on the Internet—are most clearly expressions of the growing importance of professionals and college-educated women in the Democratic Party. Many were founded by high-tech professionals, and their members are drawn primarily from the college-educated workforce that has been turning Democratic. In fall 2003, when MoveOn surveyed those of its million-plus members who had voted in its Democratic primary, it found that the single largest group was college-educated women—a perfect match with the profile of the new Democratic Party.

. . . [T]he outlook of these new, primarily upscale and highly educated activists is Clintonite and center-left rather than left wing. These people support environmental regulation and women's rights, vehemently reject the social strictures and anti-scientific attitudes of the religious right, and favor tolerance and fairness in social policy. But, like many college-educated liberals, they are also fiscal conservatives. When MoveOn held a poll in January 2004 on what ad the organization should run on the week of Bush's State of the Union address, its members chose one attacking the Bush administration's budget deficits. . . .

THE CONTINGENCIES

But elections aren't won simply by demographic changes. They are won by candidates, and the results often depend on unanticipated events like 9-11. In Congress, Democrats will have a difficult time winning back either the House or the Senate in 2006. In 2002, the Democrats had an extremely good chance to increase their hold over the Senate; instead, they lost it because of 9-11. In 2004, they couldn't overcome retirements in the South, and in 2006, they will face an unfavorable set of contests, although retirements can always alter this. . . . Barring the unforeseen, the Democrats' next chance of winning back the Senate will probably be in 2008.

Meanwhile, the Democrats' best chance of winning back the House (as well as the Senate) is to do what the Reagan Republicans did: oust or convert likeminded members of the opposite party. The Republicans won the southern seats that were held by conservative Democrats; similarly, the Democrats need to take over the seats outside the Deep South that are now held by moderate Republicans. There are about 50 to 60 such Republicans in the House, well enough to tilt the majority back to the Democrats. But this could take several election cycles, as it did in the case of the Republicans and the South. Popular Republicans will have to retire or lose some of their support in redistricting, as Maryland Republican Connie Morella did. Of course, this process could be accelerated if the conservative Republican leadership in Congress runs roughshod over such moderates as Rhode Island Senator Lincoln Chafee and Delaware Representative Mike Castle.

As for events in the world, Democrats—and Americans in general—have to worry about a darker scenario. Much of the election in 2004 was decided on whether the electorate focused on 9-11 or the war in Iraq. If voters worried about the former, they backed Bush; if they worried about the latter, they backed Kerry. Many Democrats pointed out that Bush has increased the threat of terrorism by invading Iraq, but Bush was able to convince enough voters that the war on terrorism is a seamless web that has to be combated, whether in Afghanistan or Iraq, and he actually used the mobilization of Islamic radicals in Iraq as grounds to *support* his candidacy.

A dynamic like that could be set up in the future as well. If Bush were to continue on his present course in the Middle East—launching, for instance, a preemptive strike against Iran or encouraging the Israelis to do it—he would succeed in even further enflaming this region and making it even more likely that Islamic terrorism would blow back into western Europe and the United States. Bush and the Republicans could then argue that this spread of terrorism rendered their tenure in office even more necessary. Nobody knows whether American voters would buy this argument the second time around, but it is certainly possible that they would.

Barring that, though, the Republicans' "Reagan-lite" coalition does not appear to have broad enough support to dominate American politics for the rest of the decade. That should open the door to the Democrats and their new coalition—especially if they can find a way to both mobilize their new center-left *and* nominate candidates with some comfort level among white working-class voters. The results of the 2004 election suggest that's the right formula. If Democrats want to win and bring their majority into being by the end of the decade, they should adopt it.

Internet resources
Visit our Web site at http://www.mhhe.com/diclerico10 for links and resources relating to Political Parties.

chapter 9

Interest Groups

At the time the new Constitution was being debated in 1789, James Madison, the "Father of the Constitution," argued in the Federalist Papers (No. 10), that one of the advantages of the proposed new government was that it would allow for the "control of factions" (in modern-day language, "interest groups"). He argues "Factions," derived as they were mostly from economic interests, had tended to advance their own interests to the detriment of the common interest. It was Madison's idea that the best way to deal with these factions was to incorporate them into the operations of the government, but in such a way as to minimize the possibility of any single faction exercising excessive power. Hence, the new Constitution provided for separation of powers, checks and balances, divided government, staggered elections, overlapping terms of office, and a scheme of governance that emphasized competition for power and influence among an array of interest groups and actors.

Since Madison's day, two views have emerged as to who actually has power in America. The first, the "power elite" view, holds that power is concentrated in the hands of a relatively few corporate elites, specifically, those holding positions in the nation's major corporations. These economically powerful individuals, according to the theory, control not only what happens in the economy, but also what happens in government.

A second view, and one closer to Madison's original idea, is that power is shared, checked, and dispersed among multiple interests and political actors, all of whom compete with each other. According to this so-called "pluralist" perspective, no interest gets all it might want, but all (and by inference, the general public) get some of what they want.

The articles selected for this chapter speak to these divergent views on who exercises power in America. The first article, written by G. William Domhoff, advances the argument that power in America rests in the hands of the economically powerful. According to Domhoff, there is indeed a ruling class in America consisting of a group of wealthy individuals, drawn from the upper classes, who control the economy, and, in turn, because of their great economic power, determine what the government does or does not do. In the end, according to Domhoff, working-class America is largely left out of the mix as corporate America gets its way.

In the second article, Jeff Birnbaum, a Washington Post reporter and longtime observer of lobbyists in Washington, contends that the "power elite" view is a popular myth. He argues that power in Washington depends not on the actions of a corporate few, but on the steady mobilization of interests over time. This places Birnbaum in the "pluralist" camp, but it is pluralism with a twist—namely, that those policy interests in Washington that are able to get their issues on the agenda for consideration by the nation's political leaders are those with a well-organized, financed, enduring, and persistent campaign to persuade the government to do what they want. To Birnbaum, that is the key to their success.

Power in America
Who Has the Power?
G. William Domhoff

Who has predominant power in the United States? The short answer, from 1776 to the present, is: Those who have the money have the power. George Washington was one of the biggest landowners of his day; presidents in the late 19th century were close to the railroad interests; for George W. Bush, it is oil and other natural resources, agribusiness, and finance. But to be more exact, those who own income-producing property—corporations, real estate, and agribusinesses—set the rules within which policy battles are waged.

While this may seem simple and/or obvious, the reasons behind it are complex. They involve an understanding of social classes, the role of experts, the two-party system, and the history of the country. . . . In terms of the big world-historical picture . . . money rules in America because there are no rival networks that grew up over a long and complex history:

- No big church, as in many countries in Europe
- No big government, as it took to survive as a nation-state in Europe
- No big military until after 1940 (which is not very long ago) to threaten to take over the government

So, the only power network of any consequence in the history of the United States has been the economic one, which under capitalism generates a business-owning class that hires workers and a working class, along with small businesses and skilled artisans who are self-employed, and a relatively small number of independent professionals like physicians. . . .

Domination by the few does not mean complete control, but rather the ability to set the terms under which other groups and classes must operate. Highly trained professionals with an interest in environmental and consumer issues have been able to couple their technical information and their understanding of the legislative process with timely publicity to win governmental restrictions on some corporate practices. Wage and salary workers, when they are organized or disruptive, sometimes have been able to gain concessions on wages, hours, and working conditions.

Most of all, there is free speech and the right to vote. While voting does not necessarily make government responsive to the will of the majority, under

G. William Domhoff is a research professor at the University of Santa Clara. This essay was originally published online at http://sociology.ucsc.edu/whorulesamerica/power/who.html. Reprinted with permission.

certain circumstances the electorate has been able to place restraints on the actions of the wealthy elites, or to decide which elites will have the greatest influence on policy. This is especially a possibility when there are disagreements within the higher circles of wealth and influence. . . .

POWER AND POWER INDICATORS

. . . By "power" I mean "the capacity of some persons to produce intended and foreseen effects on others" (Wrong, 1995). This is a very general definition that allows for the many forms of power that can be changed from one to another, such as economic power, political power, military power, ideological power, and intellectual power (i.e., knowledge, expertise). . . .

There are three primary indicators of power, which can be summarized as (1) who benefits? (2) who governs? and (3) who wins? In every society there are experiences and material objects that are highly valued. If it is assumed that everyone in the society would like to have as great a share as possible of these experiences and objects, then the distribution of values in that society can be utilized as a power indicator. Those who benefit the most, by inference, are powerful. In American society, wealth and well-being are highly valued. People seek to own property, earn high incomes, to have interesting and safe jobs, and to live long and healthy lives. All of these "values" are unequally distributed, and all may be utilized as power indicators.

Power also can be inferred from studies of who occupies important institutional positions and takes part in important decision-making groups. If a group or class is highly over-represented in relation to its proportion of the population, it can be inferred that the group is powerful. If, for example, a group makes up 10% of the population but has 50% of the seats in the main governing institutions, then it has five times more people in governing positions than would be expected by chance, and there is thus reason to believe that the group is a powerful one.

There are many policy issues over which groups or classes disagree. In the United States different policies are suggested by opposing groups in such "issue-areas" as foreign policy, taxation, welfare, and the environment. Power can be inferred from these issue conflicts by determining who successfully initiates, modifies, or vetoes policy alternatives. . . .

THE SOCIAL UPPER CLASS

One good starting point for the study of power in the United States, and the one I have preferred as a sociologist (especially in the 1960s and 1970s, when there was far less readily available information than there is now) is a careful consideration of the small social upper class at the top of the wealth, income, and status ladders. . . .

The upper class probably makes up only a few tenths of 1% of the population. For research purposes, I use the conservative estimate that it includes 0.5% to 1% of the population for determining the over-representation of its members in corporations, nonprofit organizations, and the government. Members of the upper class live in exclusive suburban neighborhoods, expensive downtown co-ops, and large country estates. They often have faraway summer and winter homes as well. They attend a system of private schools that extends from pre-school to the university level; the best known of these schools are the "day" and "boarding" prep schools that take the place of public high schools in the education of most upper-class teenagers. Adult members of the upper class socialize in expensive country clubs, downtown luncheon clubs, hunting clubs, and garden clubs. Young women of the upper class are "introduced" to high society each year through an elaborate series of debutante teas, parties, and balls. Women of the upper class gain experience as "volunteers" through a nationwide organization known as the Junior League, and then go on to serve as directors of cultural organizations, family service associa-tions, and hospitals (see Kendall, 2002, for a good account of women of the upper class by a sociologist who was also a participant in upper-class organizations). . . .

For research purposes, the important thing about these social institutions is that they provide us with a starting point for systematic studies of power. For example, these class "indicators" allow us to determine which economic and political leaders are and are not members of the upper class. Put another way, class indicators allow us to trace members of the upper class into the economic, political, and ideological power systems of the society. . . .

Cautions aside, there is no doubt that there is a nationwide upper class in the United States with its own distinctive social institutions, lifestyle, and outlook. There is also no doubt that most of these people are active in business or the pro-fessions, and that all of them are very wealthy. Their great wealth is obvious, of course, from the large sums that it takes to maintain their homes and their style of life, but systematic studies also show that the wealthiest families are part of the social institutions of the upper class. Combining our studies with findings by econ-omists on the wealth and income distributions, it is possible to say that the upper class, comprising 0.5% to 1% of the population, owns 35–40% of all privately held wealth in the United States and receives 12–15% of total yearly income. In short, the upper class scores very high on the "who benefits" power indicator.

The wealth and income of members of the upper class certainly imply that the upper class is powerful, but they do not demonstrate how power operates. It is therefore necessary to turn to studies of the economy to gain further under-standing of the American power structure.

THE CORPORATE COMMUNITY

Major economic power in the United States is concentrated in an organizational and legal form known as the corporation, and has been since the last several decades of the 19th century. No one doubts that individual corporations have great power in the society at large. For example, they can hire and fire workers, decide where to invest their resources, and use their income in a variety of tax-deductible ways to influence schools, charities, and governments. The argu-ment begins over whether the large corporations are united enough to exert a common social power, and then moves to the question of whether they are still controlled by members of the upper class.

The unity of the corporations can be demonstrated in a number of ways. They share a common interest in making profits. They are often owned by the same families or financial institutions. Their executives have very similar educational and work experiences. It is also important for their sense of unity that corporate leaders see themselves as sharing common opponents in organized labor, environmentalists, consumer advocates, and government officials. A sense of togetherness is created as well by their use of the same few legal, accounting, and consulting firms.

However, the best way to demonstrate the unity among corporations is through the study of what are called "interlocking directors," meaning those individuals who sit on two or more of the boards of directors that are in charge of the overall direction of the corporation. Boards of directors usually include major owners, top executives from similar corporations or corporations located in the same area, financial and legal advisors, and the three or four officers who run the corporation on a daily basis. Several studies show that those 15–20% of corporate directors who sit on two or more boards, who are called the "inner circle" of the corporate directorate, unite 80–90% of the largest corporations in the United States into a *well-connected "corporate community."* . . .

. . . More generally, members of the upper class own roughly half of all corporate stock. Then too, upper-class control of corporations can be seen in its overrepresentation on boards of directors. Several past studies show that members of the upper class sit on boards far more than would be expected by chance. They are especially likely to be part of the "inner circle" that has two or more directorships. According to the "who governs" power indicator, the upper class still controls the corporate community. Thus, we can conclude that the upper class is rooted in the ownership and control of the corporations that comprise the corporate community. We can say that members of the upper class are for the most part a "corporate rich" who continue to be involved in the business world as investors, venture capitalists, bankers, corporate lawyers, and top executives.

True enough, there are many top corporate executives who did not grow up in the upper class. Most CEOs of major corporations do not come from the upper class. However, they are gradually socialized into the upper class and its values as they move up the corporate ladder; indeed, they are advanced on the basis of their ability to fulfill upper-class goals of corporate expansion and profitability. In return, these rising managers are given the opportunity to buy corporate stock at below-market prices, paid very high salaries, and given other "perks" that make it possible for them to join the upper class economically as well as socially. The end result is a strengthening of the power of the upper class, not a diminution of it.

HOW GOVERNMENT POLICY IS SHAPED FROM OUTSIDE GOVERNMENT

The upper class and the closely related corporate community do not stand alone at the top of the power structure. They are supplemented by a wide range of nonprofit organizations that play an important role in framing debates over public policy and in shaping public opinion. . . .

Upper-class and corporate dominance of the major nonprofit organizations can be seen in their founding by wealthy members of the upper class and in their reliance on large corporations for their funding. However, dominance is once again most readily demonstrated through studies of boards of directors, which have ultimate control of the organizations, including the ability to hire and fire top executives. These studies show that (1) members of the upper class are greatly over-represented on the boards of these organizations, and (2) that nonprofit organizations share a large number of directors in common with the corporate community, particularly directors who are part of the "inner circle." In effect, most large nonprofit organizations are part of the corporate community.

All the organizations in the nonprofit sector have a hand in creating the framework of the society in one way or another, and hence in helping to shape the political climate. The cultural and civic organizations set the standard for what is beautiful, important, and "classy." The elite universities play a big part in determining what is important to teach, learn, and research, and they train most of the professionals and experts in the country. However, it is the foundations, think tanks, and policy-discussion organizations that have the most direct and important influences. Their ideas, criticisms, and policy suggestions go out to the general public through a wide array of avenues, including pamphlets, books, local discussion groups, mass media, and not least, the public relations departments of major corporations. . . .

Tax-free foundations receive their money from wealthy families and corporations. Their primary purpose is to provide money for education, research, and policy discussion. They thus have the power to encourage those ideas and researchers they find compatible with their values and goals, and to withhold funds from others. . . .

The role of the think tanks is to suggest new policies to deal with the problems facing the economy and government. Using money from wealthy donors, corporations, and foundations, think tanks hire the experts produced by the graduate departments of the elite universities. The ideas and proposals developed by the experts are disseminated through pamphlets, books, articles in major magazines and newspapers, and, most importantly, through the participation of the experts themselves in the various forums provided by the policy-discussion organizations.

The policy-discussion organizations are the hub of the policy-planning network. They bring together wealthy individuals, corporate executives, experts, and government officials for lectures, forums, meetings, and group discussions of issues that range from the local to the international, and from the economic to the political to the cultural. New ideas are tried out in weekly or monthly discussion groups, and differences of opinion are aired and compromised. . . .

The many discussion groups that take place within the several policy-discussion organizations have several functions that do not readily meet the eye. . . . First, these organizations help to familiarize busy corporate leaders with policy options outside the purview of their day-to-day business concerns.

This gives these executives the ability to influence public opinion through the mass media and other outlets, to argue with and influence experts, and to accept appointments for government service. Second, the policy-discussion organizations give members of the upper class and corporate community the opportunity to see which of their colleagues seem to be the best natural leaders through watching them in the give and take of the discussion groups. . . .

Third, these organizations legitimate their participants to the media and interested public as knowledgeable leaders who deserve to be tapped for public service because they have used their free time to acquaint themselves with the issues in nonpartisan forums. The organizations thereby help make wealthy individuals and corporate executives into "national leaders" and "statesmen." Finally, these organizations provide a forum wherein members of the upper class and corporate community can come to know policy experts. This gives them a pool of people from which they can draw advisors if they are asked to serve in government. It also gives them a basis for recommending experts to politicians for government service. . . .

THE POWER ELITE

Now that the upper class, corporate community, and policy-planning network have been defined and described, it is possible to discuss the leadership group that I call the "power elite." I define the power elite as the leadership group of the upper class. It consists of active-working members of the upper class and high-level employees in profit and nonprofit institutions controlled by members of the upper class through stock ownership, financial support, or involvement on the board of directors. . . .

Conversely, not all those involved in the power elite are members of the upper class. They are sons and daughters of the middle class, and occasionally, the blue-collar working class, who do well at any one of several hundred private and state universities, and then go to grad school, MBA school, or law school at one of a handful of elite universities—e.g., Harvard, Yale, Princeton, Columbia, MIT, Johns Hopkins, University of Chicago, and Stanford. From there they go to work for a major corporation, law firm, foundation, think tank, or university, and slowly work their way to the top. . . .

THE POWER ELITE AND GOVERNMENT

Members of the power elite directly involve themselves in the federal government through three basic processes, each of which has a slightly different role in ensuring "access" to the White House, Congress, and specific agencies, departments, and committees in the executive branch. Although some of the same people are involved in all three processes, most leaders specialize in one or two of the three processes. These three processes are:

1. The special-interest process, through which specific families, corporations, and industrial sectors are able to realize their narrow and short-run interests

on taxes, subsidies, and regulation in their dealings with congressional committees, regulatory bodies, and executive departments;
2. The policy-making process, through which the policies developed in the
   policy-planning network described earlier are brought to the White House
   and Congress;
3. The candidate selection process, through which members of the power elite
   influence electoral campaigns by means of campaign donations to political
   candidates.

Power elite domination of the federal government can be seen most directly
in the workings of the corporate lobbyists, backroom super-lawyers, and industry-
wide trade associations that represent the interests of specific corporations or business sectors. This special-interest process is based in varying combinations of
information, gifts, insider dealing, friendship, and, not least, promises of lucrative
private jobs in the future for compliant government officials. This is the aspect of
business-government relations described by journalists and social scientists in
their case studies. While these studies show that the special interests usually get
their way, the conflict that sometimes erupts within this process, occasionally pit-
ting one corporate sector against another, reinforces the image of widely shared
and fragmented power in America, including the image of a divided corporate
community. Moreover, there are some defeats suffered by the corporate rich in the
special-interest process. For example, laws that improved auto safety standards
were passed over automobile industry objections in the 1970s, as were standards
of water cleanliness opposed by the paper and chemical industries.

Policies of concern to the corporate community as a whole are not the
province of the special-interest process. Instead, such policies come from the
network of foundations, think tanks, and policy-discussion organizations
discussed in an earlier section. The plans developed in the organizations of the
policy-planning network reach the federal government in a variety of ways.
On the most general level, their reports, news releases, and interviews are read
by elected officials and their staffs, either in pamphlet form or in summary
articles in the *Washington Post, New York Times*, and *Wall Street Journal*. Members
of the policy-planning network also testify before congressional committees
and subcommittees that are writing legislation or preparing budget proposals.
More directly, leaders from these organizations are regular members of the
dozens of little-known committees that advise specific departments of the
executive branch on general policies, making them in effect unpaid temporary
members of the government. They are also very prominent on the extremely
important presidential commissions that are appointed to make recommendations on a wide range of issues from foreign policy to highway construction.
They also serve on the *little-known federal advisory committees* that are part of
just about every department of the executive branch.

Finally, and crucially, they are appointed to government positions with a
frequency far beyond what would be expected by chance. Several different
studies show that top cabinet positions in both Republican and Democratic
administrations are held by members of the upper class and corporate executives who are leaders in policy-discussion organizations.

The general picture that emerges from the findings on the overrepresentation of members of the power elite in appointed governmental positions is that the highest levels of the executive branch are interlocked constantly with the upper class and corporate community through the movement of executives and lawyers in and out of government. Although the same person is not in governmental and corporate positions at the same time, there is enough continuity for the relationship to be described as one of "revolving interlocks." Corporate leaders resign their numerous directorships in profit and nonprofit organizations to serve in government for two or three years, then return to the corporate community or policy-planning network. . . .

As important as the special-interest and policy-planning processes are for the power elite, they could not operate successfully if there were not sympathetic, business-oriented elected officials in government. That leads us to the third process through which members of the power elite dominate the federal government, the candidate-selection process. It operates through the two major political parties. . . .

Contrary to what many believe, . . . American political parties are not very responsive to voter preferences. Their candidates are fairly free to say one thing to get elected and to do another once in office. This contributes to confusion and apathy in the electorate. It leads to campaigns where there are no "issues" except "images" and "personalities" even when polls show that voters are extremely concerned about certain policy issues. You don't raise unnecessary issues during a campaign, one successful presidential candidate once said.

It is precisely because the candidate-selection process is so personalized, and therefore dependent on name recognition, images, and emotional symbolism, that it can be in good part dominated by members of the power elite through the relatively simple and direct means of large campaign contributions. Playing the role of donors and money raisers, the same people who direct corporations and take part in the policy-planning network have a crucial place in the careers of most politicians who advance beyond the local level or state legislatures in states with large populations. Their support is especially important in party primaries, where money is an even larger factor than in general elections.

The two-party system therefore results in elected officials who are relatively issueless and willing to go along with the policies advocated by those members of the power elite who work in the special-interest and policy-planning processes. They are motivated by personal ambition far more than they are by political conviction. . . .

In summary, the special-interest process, policy-planning process, and campaign finance make it possible for the power elite to win far more often than it loses on the policy issues that come before the federal government. The power elite is also greatly over-represented in appointed positions, presidential blue-ribbon commissions, and advisory committees within the government. In terms of both the "who wins" and "who governs" power indicators, the power elite dominates the federal government.

However, this domination does not mean control on each and every issue, or lack of opposition, and it does not rest upon government involvement alone. Involvement in government is only the final and most visible aspect of power elite domination, which has its roots in the class structure, the nature of the economy, and the functioning of the policy-planning network. If government officials did not have to wait on corporate leaders to decide where and when they will invest, and if government officials were not further limited by the acceptance of the current economic arrangements by the large majority of the population, then power elite involvement in elections and government would count for a lot less than it does under present conditions.

REFERENCES

Kendall, D. (2002). *The Power of Good Deeds: Privileged Women and the Social Reproduction of Class.* Lanham, MD: Rowman and Littlefield.

Wrong, D. (1995). *Power: Its Forms, Bases, and Uses* (2nd ed.). New Brunswick: Transaction Publishers.

The Forces That Set the Agenda
Jeffrey H. Birnbaum

In the grand scheme of things, Social Security isn't the nation's biggest fiscal problem. That's not my view. That's the assessment of Douglas Holtz-Eakin, a Bush political appointee before he became head of the nonpartisan Congressional Budget Office, who says that looming financial calamities in Medicare and Medicaid are larger and more immediate worries in a strictly budgetary sense.

As economic calamities go, more significant crises confront the states, which are responsible for our kids' education; the nation's hospitals, which bear the brunt of an overburdened health care system; and international institutions, which have to deal with famine, poverty and HIV/AIDS.

With all these pressing woes, how did Social Security, Terri Schiavo's end-of-life fight and judicial nominations make it to the top of the Washington agenda? [It was] not merely because the White House or the party in power

Jeffrey Birnbaum is a Post reporter whose K Street Confidential column on the intersection of business and politics appears on alternate Mondays in the Business section of *The Washington Post.* He has four books on Washington, including *The Money Men: The Real Story of Fund-raising's Influence on Political Power in America* (Crown). From: *The Washington Post,* April 24, 2005, B-1, 5. © 2005, *The Washington Post.* Reprinted with permission.

[wanted] them to be there. [It was] because deep-rooted, well-heeled organizations [had] been targeting those issues for years. What seems like serendipity to the public—why *is* Congress talking about trial lawyers again?—is more often the result of an interest group's advance work combining with the right circumstances to send an issue hurtling into the limelight.

Like it or not, we increasingly live in a stage-managed democracy where highly orchestrated interests filter our priorities. These groups don't have absolute power, of course. In the nation's capital, home to 30,000 registered lobbyists, hundreds of politicians, thousands of journalists and untold numbers of entrenched bureaucrats, no one's in charge. But long-established entities like the AARP, the Family Research Council and the U.S. Chamber of Commerce mold our collective thinking and regularly dictate the language and tenor of our civic debates.

This notion runs counter to an abiding myth—that political leaders actually lead. That's true sometimes, of course, but more often than not, the ideas and movements that get on the government's to-do list come from the broad middle and not from the top.

A case in point: More than a decade ago, the National Federation of Independent Business, the country's premier small-business lobby, began to methodically contact its half-million members by phone and mail to categorize them by political leanings and their willingness to contact federal lawmakers. The lobby group trained its most eager members at local seminars and sent staffers door-to-door during elections in critical congressional districts. Regular "grassroots" outpourings from this made-to-order machine vaulted NFIB-championed issues onto center stage—especially when the Republicans it favored took control of the White House and Congress. In particular, the inheritance tax (which NFIB loyalists redubbed the "death tax" for marketing purposes) was repealed (temporarily so far, but Congress is now considering whether to make the repeal permanent). This was the organization's No. 1 priority.

The process is a lot like surfing. Interest groups float along, waiting for the perfect wave of public sentiment or official fiat to carry their issues to victory. They can't create the wave, but they can be ready for the moment when it comes. The key is to be prepared for that moment: Not every issue has an organization with the wealth and staying power to be in that position. Those that do have a shot at winning.

"Lobbying is subtle and complicated," says John W. Kingdon, a professor emeritus of political science at the University of Michigan who studies interest groups. But the most important attribute of a successful lobbying campaign, he says, is persistence—something that only entrenched organizations possess.

"It takes a sustained organization, mobilized followers and an immense amount of power to get onto a legislative agenda," agrees Theodore J. Lowi, a professor of government at Cornell University.

In many ways, interest groups have replaced political parties as the real influence brokers. Candidates for office rely on these groups for campaign cash, for campaign workers and, increasingly, for campaign issues—all of which had once been the domain of the Republican and Democratic national committees.

Republican ground troops come from such diverse groups as the NFIB, the U.S. Chamber of Commerce, the Family Research Council and the National Rifle

Association. Democratic soldiers are recruited from places like labor unions, the trial bar and Moveon.org. "The standard distinction between interest groups and parties used to be that parties were committed to winning elections and that pressure groups let elections happen and then tried to influence the people who got elected," Lowi said. "Now interest groups through their PACs and a variety of other methods are very much involved in the pre-policy arena."

Such involvement has become a prime factor in agenda-setting. Take Social Security. Few federal programs attract as much scrutiny. AARP, the nation's largest lobbying organization, is dedicated to keeping Social Security alive and well, as are groups such as the National Committee to Preserve Social Security and Medicare. The reason: Large portions of their membership depend on Social Security checks to survive in old age. AARP has taught a million and a half of its 35 million members how to hammer elected officials by mail, phone and in person, primarily about Social Security.

But AARP has learned that it needs to be careful what it wishes for. Its obsession with the issue has made Social Security a front-of-the-mind topic and, therefore, a perennial contender to shoot to Washington's upper tier. Ideological opponents of the current Social Security system have also been active, raising the issue's profile even higher. Free market think tanks such as the Cato Institute and anti-tax-increase lobbies have been churning out position papers for a quarter-century promoting partial privatization of Social Security as a way to undercut what they see as "big government." One appreciator of that work: George W. Bush.

So when the president went looking for a problem to solve that could guarantee him a lasting legacy—and, perhaps, realign party domination—he went for that old chestnut Social Security. He also embraced a proposal that AARP dislikes—the creation of private accounts. That notion has fallen flat largely because of more than $15 million worth of AARP advertising against it. When the process moves to another phase and compromises are explored, AARP is likely to become an important negotiator and perhaps the key indicator of whether the effort will succeed or fail.

The same high-stakes maneuvering couldn't have happened with, say, Medicaid, the health care program for the poor, even though it's in more dire financial straits. Medicaid doesn't have similarly situated citizens' groups beating the bushes on its behalf. So while saving Social Security is the watchword of the day, Medicaid's fate will be to languish and occasionally fend off budget cuts until its finances reach an emergency.

Terri Schiavo is another example of interest-group politics at work. The 41-year-old brain-damaged woman was in many ways not out of the ordinary. She was one of thousands of people whose families annually struggle with the question of when a relative's life has ended. But skilled marketers on the well-established, pro-life side of the abortion debate seized on her situation. The National Right to Life Committee, Operation Rescue, Priests for Life, the Family Research Council and others set up Web sites, held news conferences and raised lots of money for lawyers and for themselves.

Their pleas touched a chord with millions of Americans and made Schiavo's plight a cause celebre. The omnipresence of her situation in direct-mail communications from those groups and on talk radio made her synonymous with the battle over life and death issues of all kinds—from the womb to the grave. By the time Schiavo's parents had finally exhausted their legal options and her feeding tube was about to be removed permanently, the public policy pump had been thoroughly primed. Republican leaders sympathetic to the cause brought Congress back for an extraordinary weekend session. Only later did it appear, based on various polls, that the majority of Americans did not see Schiavo's case the way the Republican leadership did.

As a result, the starvation of a solitary middle-class woman in Florida riveted government for a couple of weeks while similar—and more severe— situations went almost unnoticed. Mass starvation in Sudan, for instance, was a legislative footnote by comparison. Why? It's not only that Sudan is far away and hard to solve. Help for the Sudan catastrophe lacks the backing of as many obsessively focused and widely dispersed interest groups.

The brewing battle in the Senate over a mere seven judicial nominees is another telling example. Groups on the political left and right are making the coming confrontation seem like World War III. (Witness the use of the word "nuclear" to describe the Republicans' effort to force a vote.) In fact, the debate is a warm-up for the more consequential conflict over filling the next Supreme Court vacancy as well as a stand-in for other divisive issues, such as gay rights, abortion rights and affirmative action.

Why such tumult and passion? Organizations with wide and longstanding interest have been on the prowl for supporters on these matters for years. On the anti-Bush side are the Alliance for Justice, the Leadership Conference on Civil Rights and People for the American Way, which was instrumental in derailing Robert Bork's nomination to the Supreme Court in 1987. The president's allies include groups such as the Committee for Justice, Focus on the Family, the Federalist Society, Americans for Tax Reform and Freedom Works, which have not only raised millions for the purpose but coordinate their activities in conference calls among their leaders.

In an odd way, all this attention to Washington ways is heartening. The common view is that elites run the show and sheep-like citizens allow them to. In fact, organized interests able to motivate blocs of voters really can make a difference, as long as they can stick around for a while.

Unfortunately, not every vital issue has a group or groups that are clever or rich enough to generate unrelenting support from back home. That leaves out of the mix too many people with worthy woes: the unemployed, the uninsured, the unaligned.

There's probably an opportunity there for yet another powerful interest.

 /diclerico10

Internet resources
Visit our Web site at http://www.mhhe.com/diclerico10 for links and resources relating to Interest Groups.

c h a p t e r   1 0

Congress

Representation: Redistricting

*T*he Constitution requires that membership in the U.S. House of Representatives be apportioned on the basis of population every ten years. As a matter of law and practice, state legislatures have the responsibility of redrawing congressional districts after apportionment has been completed. Historically, the drawing of district lines has been a very political process, often involving partisanship, racial politics, regional interests, and intraparty factionalism.

In recent years, redistricting has taken on a whole new dimension as political parties have sought to consolidate their power. In an effort to protect partisan interests, many state legislatures have redrawn districts so as to render them noncompetitive. Indeed, it is estimated that today ninety percent or more of congressional districts are "safe districts," meaning that one party or the other is virtually guaranteed election.

The lack of competitive districts, and hence, competitive elections, has become such a problem that two members of the House of Representatives—one Democrat and one Republican—have suggested that reform of the process is absolutely essential for the health of our democracy. According to these congressmen, Earl Blumenauer and Jim Leach, it is time to take the redistricting process out of state legislatures and turn it over to special commissions in the states.

Reform efforts to the contrary, the author of the second article, Bill Bishop, argues that any reform might be doomed from the very beginning since it is not the redistricting process that is at fault. Rather, according to Bishop, no amount of tinkering with the current system will be able to overcome what is happening demographically in America, namely, that people are simply choosing to live with like-minded people, thereby making any attempt to reform redistricting meaningless.

Redistricting, a Bipartisan Sport
Earl Blumenauer and Jim Leach

Congressional redistricting is about as interesting as someone else's genealogy. But occasionally the subject produces headlines, as it did in [2003] when Democratic members of the Texas Legislature fled to Oklahoma to avoid creating a quorum to address the issue. Their desperate maneuver failed. . . .

Despite the public perception that the drawing of legislative maps is an insider's game of no particular relevance, the health of American democracy hinges on how state officials approach the issue. If competitive elections matter—and to much of the world they are what America stands for—then redistricting also matters.

Using redistricting to gain advantage over one's opponents has been going on almost since America was founded. "Gerrymandering," the term to describe the process of creating strangely shaped legislative districts, dates back to 1812 or so, when Elbridge Gerry devised a legislative map in Massachusetts to benefit his political party's interests.

The courts have occasionally waded into this legislative thicket, principally to protect the one-person, one-vote principle but also to ensure compliance with the Voting Rights Act. But redistricting simply for partisan advantage—so long as it doesn't result in less minority representation and isn't too geographically egregious—is not generally considered grounds for court interference.

It is, however, a matter of profound importance to our system of government. A few partisans should not be allowed to manipulate the landscape of state and national politics by legislative line-drawing. But that's exactly what has happened.

Gerrymandering has become a bipartisan pastime. California Democrats produced a plan that turned a closely divided Congressional delegation (22–21) into a 28–17 Democratic advantage after the 1980 reapportionment. After the 1990 reapportionment, Georgia Republicans were able to turn a 9–1 disadvantage into an eventual 8–3 majority. In fact, Republican control of the House, won in 1994 for the first time in 40 years, was probably due more to shrewd redistricting than to the much-publicized "Contract with America."

In the wake of the 2000 census, candidates for governor and even obscure state legislators who would have a hand in drawing new legislative boundaries received unprecedented attention. In an unusual role reversal, some members

Earl Blumenaur, Democrat of Oregon, and Jim Leach, Republican of Iowa, are members of the House of Representatives. From *The New York Times,* July 8, 2003, A27.

of Congress even contributed money to state campaigns and hired their own lobbyists to represent their interests in state capitols.

The effort paid off. In big states that Republicans came to control, they were able to make gains. In Michigan, incumbent Democrats were forced into races against each other. In Pennsylvania, Democratic-leaning districts were eliminated altogether. And though the 2000 presidential election made clear that Florida is evenly divided on party preferences, it sends 18 Republicans to Congress and only 7 Democrats.

Democrats, meanwhile, did their own manipulating where they could, picking up seats in Georgia, North Carolina and Maryland. . . .

More than either political party, however, the real winners in the redistricting games are incumbents. Nationwide, in 2002 only eight incumbents were defeated in the general election—and four of those lost to other incumbents. On average . . . Congressional incumbents won with more than two-thirds of the vote.

One response to all this, of course, could be indifference. Political manipulation is to be expected. . . .

But the consequences of entrenched incumbency should concern us all. Without meaningful competition in 90 percent of all races in the House, representatives become less accountable to voters and citizens lose interest in democracy.

More subtle consequences also unfold. When control of Congress rests on the results of those 20 to 30 races that are potentially competitive, the political dialogue in these campaigns, and legislative strategies in the House, become skewed. The few competitive races become playgrounds for power brokers who specialize in expensive, divisive and manipulative campaign techniques.

In Washington, legislative initiatives are frequently distorted in an effort to keep the vulnerable few in the political cross hairs. Bills on issues like farm policy or free trade are often framed to force members to choose between constituencies—farmers and unions, for example. Bills on health care may force members to choose between doctors and lawyers.

There is also a profound problem that is not subtle at all. Primary elections in districts that are overwhelmingly Republican produce candidates generally to the right of the average Republican, while more liberal Democrats usually emerge from primaries in districts that are overwhelmingly Democratic. The political center—where most Americans are most comfortable—gets the least representation in Congress.

In short, the current system produces a House that is both more liberal and more conservative than the country at large. Members are less inclined to talk and cooperate, much less compromise. The legislative agenda is shaped more to energize the political base than to advance the common good.

It doesn't have to be this way. Iowa, which has about 1 percent of the United States population and only five representatives in the House, saw as many competitive races in the last election as California, New York and Illinois combined. (For the record, those three states account for 101 seats in the House.) Iowa is so competitive largely because it has an independent redistricting commission that is prohibited from considering where incumbents live when it draws new legislative maps.

What works for Iowa could work for the nation. The formula for avoiding inequities, undue partisan advantage and political dysfunction is the creation of independent redistricting commissions. Arizona recently followed Iowa's example, and such a commission has been proposed in Texas.

These commissions offer the best hope for taking partisanship out of the redistricting process. The public should insist that candidates for governor and state legislatures favor the development of strong nonpartisan redistricting plans.

Competitive elections are essential to the American system of government. Just as antitrust laws are necessary for a strong economy, so redistricting reform is critical for a healthy democracy.[1]

You Can't Compete with Voters' Feet
Bill Bishop

When not a single California congressional or state legislative seat changed political party in last year's election, Republican Gov. Arnold Schwarzenegger reacted with his signature bluntness. "What kind of democracy is that?" he demanded. Blaming the lack of competitiveness in all the races on state legislators who in 2000 created voting districts guaranteed to preserve their own seats and their respective parties' dominance, Schwarzenegger has proposed taking control of redistricting away from partisan politicians and entrusting it to a panel of retired judges.

On the virtues of this plan, the unconventional governor has a lot of conventional company. Many see independent redistricting, free from the possibility of gerrymandering—the practice of drawing a voting district to one party's advantage—as the route to resurrecting competitive elections and resuscitating democracy.

But the paucity of competitive elections isn't simply something created by diabolical legislators or nerdy mapmakers. It has been, in large measure, an inside job, the result of citizens who, given the choice, would prefer to live among those most like themselves. Taking redistricting away from the politicians may do something about the appearance of partisanship in the legislature, but it can't change the actual partisanship that resides in our communities.

Schwarzenegger has a point, of course. Most legislative races *aren't* competitive. In U.S. House races in 2004, only seven of 401 incumbents lost. Only 22 races were decided by a margin of less than 10 percentage points.

Bill Bishop is a reporter with the *Austin American-Statesman* (Texas), where a version of this article previously appeared.

But when the early-19th-century Massachusetts politician Elbridge Gerry redrew a state Senate seat to his party's advantage in a shape that looked like a salamander—thus enshrining the "gerrymander" forevermore—was he contributing to the demise of democracy in the 21st century? Several political scientists who study congressional elections don't think so.

Alan Abramowitz, a professor of political science at Emory University in Atlanta, measured the "competitiveness" of congressional districts in a recent study. He used presidential election returns to get a sense of whether congressional districts vote more Republican or Democratic than the nation as a whole. Abramowitz found that over the past 30 years, there have been fewer and fewer districts where Republicans and Democrats are evenly mixed. But redistricting doesn't seem to be the cause.

Abramowitz reasoned that if partisan redistricting were causing the decline in competitive House races, then there should be a jump in non-competitive districts—defined as districts that are 10 percentage points more Republican or Democratic than the nation as a whole—right after legislative redistricting, which by law must occur after the new census every 10 years. But Abramowitz found no discernible increase after the new districts were drawn. Instead, districts grew most lopsided *in between* redistricting years. So other factors must be at work.

Yes, legislatures can still gerrymander to get rid of incumbents. The Texas legislature did that in 2003, under House Majority Leader Tom DeLay's tutelage, when it drew congressional districts in a way that led to the defeat of four incumbent Democrats last November. But Abramowitz contends that the unusual mid-decade redistricting simply recognized the growing partisanship in Texas.

"I keep hearing Democrats saying that Republicans basically stole those seats by redistricting again," said Abramowitz, who describes himself as a liberal Democrat. "The fact is, that's a minor issue. The underlying reality is that states like Texas and Georgia have been trending Republican. Sooner or later, more likely sooner, that was going to translate into a Republican takeover of the congressional delegation."

This is also true nationally. More people are choosing where to live based on demographic factors that now align with a political party. In effect, voters themselves are largely responsible for tipping the balance in many districts by moving to where they can find neighbors of like mind.

Vanderbilt University professor Bruce Oppenheimer has a simple way of testing whether gerrymandering is increasing partisanship in congressional districts. He recently studied the seven states that have only one representative in the House—Alaska, Delaware, Montana, North and South Dakota, Vermont and Wyoming—to compare their behavior in the 1960 and 2000 presidential elections. Since their borders are unchanging, whatever has happened in the past four decades can't be the result of redistricting.

The national vote in both the 1960 and 2000 presidential elections was evenly split.

But over the 40 years between those two elections, these seven single-district states grew more partisan than the average congressional district. In 1960, the winning candidate for president (whether Republican or Democrat) in these seven states received an average 53.1 percent of the vote. In 2000, however, the winning candidate received an average 62.9 percent of the vote.

"A lot of this has to do with self-selection," Oppenheimer said. "Democrats tend to live next to Democrats. Republicans tend to live next to Republicans."

That is indeed happening. Last year, I helped prepare a series of articles for my newspaper showing that from 1976 to 2004, most U.S. counties became increasingly lopsided politically. The paper's statistical consultant, former University of Texas sociologist Robert Cushing, found that by 2004, in one of the closest elections in U.S. history, nearly half of the country's voters lived in communities where the winning presidential candidate had won by at least a 20 percentage point margin. Over seven presidential elections, Cushing's measurements of Republican and Democratic residential segregation increased by 50 percent.

Another reason why incumbents are winning at increasing rates is that oldest of political advantages: money. Regardless of party, incumbents are raising far more money than opponents, even in districts where Republicans and Democrats live in a near electoral balance, said Abramowitz. From the early 1990s to 2002, the median spending by incumbents in these competitive districts increased from $596,000 to $910,000. Median spending by challengers in these same districts fell from $229,000 to $198,000.

During the 1970s, Abramowitz found, winning congressional candidates spent 69 percent of the amount spent by all candidates in their races. From 1998 through 2002, however, the winning candidates accounted for an average of 82 percent of the total campaign spending.

So if money and demography are mostly to blame for less competitive elections, then what good would it do to turn redistricting over to some retired judges, as Schwarzenegger has suggested? Not much, probably. In most states, regions have become so resolutely partisan that it would be nearly impossible to draw competitive districts, says Nathaniel Persily, a University of Pennsylvania law professor who has worked on redistricting cases in New York, California, Georgia and Maryland.

"That's been my experience every time I've been drawn into these redistricting cases," Persily said. "It's incredibly difficult to draw competitive districts. The only way you can do it is to turn cities into pizzas, where you have districts that go from the inner cities out into the suburbs."

Or barber poles. In the San Francisco area, Schwarzenegger's nonpartisan panels would have to draw legislative districts in stripes connecting the Democratic coast to the Republican inland, says Abramowitz.

This would require some new thinking. The opposite of the gerrymandered district is a compact legislative region encompassing a community of interest. That's the goal of most redistricting reforms. But as communities themselves become politically like-minded, these good government definitions may have to be abandoned in pursuit of competitiveness. Creating competitive districts in the age of political segregation, in short, might require more cunning than that of an Elbridge Gerry—or an action hero turned governor—and more shapes than the simple salamander.

Representation: Legislative Role

*T*he three selections in this section are illustrative of a long-standing debate among political theorists and elected officials alike: namely, whose views should prevail on a given issue—the constituents' or the representatives'? In the first selection, taken from an early debate in the General Assembly of Virginia, the argument is made that legislators are obliged to act as instructed delegates—that is, they must vote in accordance with the will of their constituents. In the second selection, former Massachusetts Senator and President John F. Kennedy, writing in 1956, argues that legislators should act as trustees, voting according to their own conscience, regardless of whether their choices reflect the sentiments of their constituents. Finally, George Galloway, a former staff assistant in Congress, contends that on some occasions legislators must follow public opinion, while on others they are obliged to vote according to their own conscience. This view, which combines both the delegate and the trustee approach, is characterized as the politico role.

The Legislator as Delegate
General Assembly of Virginia

There can be no doubt that the scheme of a representative republic was derived to our forefathers from the constitution of the English House of Commons; and that that branch of the English government . . . was in its origin, and in theory always has been, purely republican. It is certain, too, that the statesmen of America, in assuming that as the model of our own institutions, designed to adopt it here in its purest form, and with its strictest republican tenets and principles. It becomes, therefore, an inquiry of yet greater utility than curiosity, to ascertain the sound doctrines of the constitution of the English House of Commons in regard to this right of the constituent to instruct the representative. For the position may safely be assumed that the wise and virtuous men who framed our constitutions deigned, that, in the United States, the constituent should have at least as much, if not a great deal more, influence over the representative than was known to have existed from time immemorial in England. Let us then interrogate the history of the British nation; let us consult the opinions of their wise men.

Instances abound in parliamentary history of formal instructions from the constituent to the representative, of which . . . the following may suffice: In 1640, the knights of the shire for Dorset and Kent informed the commons *that they had in charge from their constituents* seven articles of grievances, which they accordingly laid before the House, where they were received and acted on. In the 33rd year of Charles II, the citizens of London instructed their members to insist on the bill for excluding the Duke of York (afterward King James II) from the succession to the throne; and their representative said "that his *duty* to his electors *obliged* him to vote the bill." At a subsequent election, in 1681, in many places, formal instructions were given to the members returned, to insist on the same exclusion bill; we know, from history, how uniformly and faithfully those instructions were obeyed. . . . In 1741, the citizens of London instructed their members to vote against standing armies, excise laws, the septennial bill, and a long train of evil measures, already felt, or anticipated; and expressly affirm their right of instruction—"We think it" (say they) "our *duty,* as it is *our undoubted right,* to acquaint you, with *what we desire and expect from you, in discharge*

From Commonwealth of Virginia, General Assembly, *Journal of the Senate,* 1812, pp. 82–89. In some instances, spelling and punctuation have been altered from the original in order to achieve greater clarity.

of the great trust we repose in you, and what we take to be *your duty as our representative,* etc." In the same year, instructions of a similar character were sent from all parts of England. In 1742, the cities of London, Bristol, Edinburgh, York, and many others, instructed their members in parliament to seek redress against certain individuals suspected to have betrayed and deserted the cause of the people. . . .

Instances also are on record of the deliberate formal knowledgement of the right of instruction by the House of Commons itself, especially in old times. Thus the commons hesitated to grant supplies to King Edward III *till they had the consent of their constituents,* and desired that a new parliament might be summoned, which might be *prepared with authority from their constituents.* . . .

"Instructions" (says a member of the House of Commons) "ought to be *followed implicitly,*" after the member has respectfully given his constituents *his opinion* of them: *"Far be it from me to oppose my judgment to that of 6000 of my fellow citizens."* "The practice" (says another) "of consulting our constituents was good. I wish it was continued. *We can discharge our duty no better, than in the direction of those who sent us hither. What the people choose is right, because they choose it."* . . .

Without referring to the minor political authors . . . who have maintained these positions (quoted from one of them)—"that the people have a right to instruct their representatives; that no man ought to be chosen that will not receive instructions; that the people understand enough of the interests of the country to give general instructions; that it was the custom formerly to instruct all the members; and the nature of deputation shows that the custom was well grounded"—it is proper to mention that the great constitutional lawyer Coke . . . says, "It is the *custom of parliament,* when any new device is moved for on the king's behalf, for his aid and the like, that the commons may answer, *they dare not agree to it without conference with their counties."* And Sydney . . . maintains "that members derive their power from those that choose them; that those who give power do not give an unreserved power; that many members, in all ages, and sometimes the whole body of the commons have refused to vote until they consulted with those who sent them; that the houses have often adjourned to give them time to do so and if this were done more frequently, or if cities, towns and counties had on some occasions given instructions to their deputies, matters would probably have gone better in parliament than they have done." . . . The celebrated Edmund Burke, a man, it must be admitted, of profound knowledge, deep foresight, and transcendent abilities, disobeyed the instructions of his constituents; yet, by placing his excuse on the ground that the instructions were but the clamour of the day, he seems to admit the authority of instructions soberly and deliberately given; for he agrees, "he ought to look to their opinions" (which he explains to mean their permanent settled opinions) "but not the flash of the day"; and he says elsewhere, that he could not bear to show himself "a representative, whose face did not reflect the face of his constituents—a face that did not joy in their joys and sorrow in their sorrows." It is remarkable that, notwithstanding a most splendid display of warm and touching eloquence, the people of Bristol would not reelect Mr. Burke, for this very offense of disobeying instructions. . . .

It appears, therefore, that the right of the constituent to instruct the representative, is firmly established in England, on the broad basis of the nature of representation. The existence of that right, there, has been demonstrated by the only practicable evidence, by which the principles of an unwritten constitution can be ascertained—history and precedent.

To view the subject upon principle, the right of the constituent to instruct the representative, seems to result, clearly and conclusively, from the very nature of the representative system. Through means of that noble institution, the largest nation may, almost as conveniently as the smallest, enjoy all the advantages of a government by the people, without any of the evils of democracy—precipitation, confusion, turbulence, distraction from the ordinary and useful pursuits of industry. And it is only to avoid those and the like mischiefs, that representation is substituted for the direct suffrage of the people in the office of legislation. The representative, therefore, must in the nature of things, represent his own particular constituents only. He must, indeed, look to the general good of the nation, but he must look also, and especially to the interests of his particular constituents as concerned in the commonweal; because the general good is but the aggregate of individual happiness. He must legislate for the whole nation; but laws are expressions of the general will; and the general will is only the result of individual wills fairly collected and compared. In order . . . to express the general will . . . it is plain that the representative must express the will and speak the opinions of the constituents that depute him.

It cannot be pretended that a representative is to be the organ of his own will alone; for then, he would be so far despotic. *He must be the organ of others—*of whom? Not of the nation, for the nation deputes him not; but of his constituents, who alone know, alone have trusted, and can alone displace him. And if it be his province and his duty, in general, to express the will of his constituents, to the best of his knowledge, without being particularly informed thereof, it seems impossible to contend that he is not bound to do so when he is so especially informed and instructed.

The right of the constituent to instruct the representative, therefore, is an essential principle of the representative system. It may be remarked that wherever representation has been introduced, however unfavorable the circumstances under which it existed, however short its duration, however unimportant its functions, however dimly understood, the right of instruction has always been regarded as inseparably incidental to it. . . .

A representative has indeed a wide field of discretion left to him; and great is the confidence reposed in his integrity, fidelity, wisdom, zeal; but neither is the field of discretion boundless, nor the extent of confidence infinite; and the very discretion allowed him, and the very confidence he enjoys, is grounded on the supposition that he is charged with the will, acquainted with the opinions, and devoted to the interests of his constituents. . . .

Various objections have been urged to this claim of the constituent, of a right to instruct the representative, on which it may be proper to bestow some attention.

The first objection that comes to be considered . . . is grounded on the supposed impossibility of fairly ascertaining the sense of the constituent body. The *impossibility* is denied. It may often be a matter of great *difficulty;* but then the duty of obedience resolves itself into a question, not of principle, but of fact: whether the right of instruction has been exercised or not. The representative cannot be bound by an instruction that is not given; but that is no objection to the obligation of an instruction *actually given.* . . .

It has been urged that the representatives are not bound to obey the instructions of their constituents because the constituents do not hear the debates, and therefore, cannot be supposed judges of the matter to be voted. If this objection has force enough to defeat the right of instruction, it ought to take away, also, the right of rejecting the representative at the subsequent election. For it might be equally urged on that occasion, as against the right of instruction, that the people heard not the debate that enlightened the representative's mind—the reasons that convinced his judgment and governed his conduct. . . . In other words, the principle that mankind is competent to self-government should be renounced. The truth is, that our institutions suppose that although the representative ought to be, and generally will be, selected for superior virtue and intelligence, yet a greater mass of wisdom and virtue still reside in the constituent body than the utmost portion allotted to any individual. . . .

Finally, it has been objected, that the instructions of the constituent are not obligatory on the representative because the obligation insisted on is fortified with no sanction—the representative cannot be punished for his disobedience, and his vote is valid notwithstanding his disobedience. It is true that there is no mode of legal punishment provided for this . . . default of duty and that the act of disobedience will not invalidate the vote. It is true, too, that a representative may perversely advocate a measure which he knows to be ruinous to his country; and that neither his vote will be invalidated by his depravity, nor can he be punished by law for his crime, heinous as it surely is. But it does not follow that the one representative is *not bound to obey the instructions* of his constituents any more than that the other is not bound to obey the dictates of his conscience. Both duties stand upon the same foundation, with almost all the great political and moral obligations. The noblest duties of man are without any legal sanction: the great mass of social duties . . . , our duties to our parents, to our children, to our wives, to our families, to our neighbor, to our country, our duties to God, are, for the most part, without legal sanction, yet surely not without the strongest obligation. The duty of the *representative* to obey the instructions of the *constituent* body cannot be placed on higher ground.

Such are the opinions of the General Assembly of Virginia, on the subject of this great right of instruction, and such the general reasons on which those opinions are founded. . . .

The Legislator as Trustee
John F. Kennedy

The primary responsibility of a senator, most people assume, is to represent the views of his state. Ours is a federal system—a union of relatively sovereign states whose needs differ greatly—and my constitutional obligations as senator would thus appear to require me to represent the interests of my state. Who will speak for Massachusetts if her own senators do not? Her rights and even her identity become submerged. Her equal representation in Congress is lost. Her aspirations, however much they may from time to time be in the minority, are denied that equal opportunity to be heard to which all minority views are entitled.

Any senator need not look very long to realize that his colleagues are representing *their* local interests. And if such interests are ever to be abandoned in favor of the national good, let the constituents—not the senator—decide when and to what extent. For he is their agent in Washington, the protector of their rights, recognized by the vice president in the Senate Chamber as "the senator from Massachusetts" or "the senator from Texas."

But when all of this is said and admitted, we have not yet told the full story. For in Washington we are "United States senators" and members of the Senate of the United States as well as senators from Massachusetts and Texas. Our oath of office is administered by the vice president, not by the governors of our respective states; and we come to Washington, to paraphrase Edmund Burke, not as hostile ambassadors or special pleaders for our state or section, in opposition to advocates and agents of other areas, but as members of the deliberative assembly of one nation with one interest. Of course, we should not ignore the needs of our area—nor could we easily as products of that area—but none could be found to look out for the national interest if local interests wholly dominated the role of each of us.

There are other obligations in addition to those of state and region—the obligations of the party. . . . Even if I can disregard those pressures, do I not have an obligation to go along with the party that placed me in office? We believe in this country in the principle of party responsibility, and we recognize

John F. Kennedy, 35th President of the United States, was a Democratic member of the U.S. Senate from the state of Massachusetts from 1952 to 1960 and a member of the U.S. House of Representatives from 1947 to 1952. Selected excerpts from pp. 33–39 from *Profiles in Courage* by John F. Kennedy. Copyright © 1955, 1956, 1961 by John F. Kennedy. Copyright renewed © 1983, 1984, 1989 by Jacqueline Kennedy Onassis. Foreword copyright © 1964 by Robert F. Kennedy. Reprinted by permission of HarperCollins Publishers, Inc.

the necessity of adhering to party platforms—if the party label is to mean anything to the voters. Only in this way can our basically two-party nation avoid the pitfalls of multiple splinter parties, whose purity and rigidity of principle, I might add—if I may suggest a sort of Gresham's Law of politics—increase inversely with the size of their membership.

And yet we cannot permit the pressures of party responsibility to sub-merge on every issue the call of personal responsibility. For the party which, in its drive for unity, discipline and success, ever decides to exclude new ideas, independent conduct or insurgent members, is in danger. . . .

Of course, both major parties today seek to serve the national interest. They would do so in order to obtain the broadest base of support, if for no nobler rea-son. But when party and officeholder differ as to how the national interest is to be served, we must place first the responsibility we owe not to our party or even to our constituents but to our individual consciences.

But it is a little easier to dismiss one's obligations to local interests and party ties to face squarely the problem of one's responsibility to the will of his constituents. A senator who avoids this responsibility would appear to be accountable to no one, and the basic safeguards of our democratic system would thus have vanished. He is no longer representative in the true sense, he has violated his public trust, he has betrayed the confidence demonstrated by those who voted for him to carry out their views. "Is the creature," as John Tyler asked the House of Representatives in his maiden speech, "to set him-self in opposition to his Creator? Is the servant to disobey the wishes of his master?"

> How can he be regarded as representing the people when he speaks, not their language, but his own? He ceases to be their representative when he does so, and represents himself alone.

In short, according to this school of thought, if I am to be properly respon-sive to the will of my constituents, it is my duty to place their principles, not mine, above all else. This may not always be easy, but it nevertheless is the essence of democracy, faith in the wisdom of the people and their views. To be sure, the people will make mistakes—they will get no better government than they deserve—but that is far better than the representative of the people arro-gating for himself the right to say he knows better than they what is good for them. Is he not chosen, the argument closes, to vote as they would vote were they in his place?

It is difficult to accept such a narrow view of the role of a United States senator—a view that assumes the people of Massachusetts sent me to Washington to serve merely as a seismograph to record shifts in popular opin-ion. I reject this view not because I lack faith in the "wisdom of the people," but because this concept of democracy actually puts too little faith in the people. Those who would deny the obligation of the representative to be bound by every impulse of the electorate—regardless of the conclusions his own deliberations direct—do trust in the wisdom of the people. They have faith in their ultimate sense of justice, faith in their ability to honor courage and respect judgment, and faith that in the long run they will act unselfishly for the good of the nation. It is that kind of faith on which democracy is based, not simply the often frustrated hope that public opinion will at all times under all circumstances promptly identify itself with the public interest.

The voters selected us, in short, because they had confidence in our judgment and our ability to exercise that judgment from a position where we could determine what were their own best interests, as a part of the nation's interests. This may mean that we must on occasion lead, inform, correct and sometimes even ignore constituent opinion, if we are to exercise fully that judgment for which we were elected. But acting without selfish motive or private bias, those who follow the dictates of an intelligent conscience are not aristocrats, demagogues, eccentrics, or callous politicians insensitive to the feelings of the public. They expect—and not without considerable trepidation—their constituents to be the final judges of the wisdom of their course; but they have faith that those constituents—today, tomorrow, or even in another generation—will at least respect the principles that motivated their independent stand.

If their careers are temporarily or even permanently buried under an avalanche of abusive editorials, poison-pen letters, and opposition votes at the polls—as they sometimes are, for that is the risk they take—they await the future with hope and confidence, aware of the fact that the voting public frequently suffers from what ex-Congressman T. V. Smith called the lag "between our way of thought and our way of life." . . .

Moreover, I question whether any senator, before we vote on a measure, can state with certainty exactly how the majority of his constituents feel on the issue as it is presented to the Senate. All of us in the Senate live in an iron lung—the iron lung of politics, and it is no easy task to emerge from that rarefied atmosphere in order to breathe the same fresh air our constituents breathe. It is difficult, too, to see in person an appreciable number of voters besides those professional hangers-on and vocal elements who gather about the politician on a trip home. In Washington I frequently find myself believing that forty or fifty letters, six visits from professional politicians and lobbyists, and three editorials in Massachusetts newspapers constitute public opinion on a given issue. Yet in truth I rarely know how the great majority of the voters feel, or even how much they know of the issues that seem so burning in Washington.

Today the challenge of political courage looms larger than ever before. For our everyday life is becoming so saturated with the tremendous power of mass communications that any unpopular or unorthodox course arouses a storm of protests. . . . Our political life is becoming so expensive, so mechanized, and so dominated by professional politicians and public relations men that the idealist who dreams of independent statesmanship is rudely awakened by the necessities of election and accomplishment. . . .

And thus, in the days ahead, only the very courageous will be able to take the hard and unpopular decisions necessary for our survival. . . .

The Legislator as Politico
George B. Galloway

One question which the conscientious congressman must often ask himself, especially when conflicts arise between local or regional attitudes and interests and the national welfare, is this: "As a member of Congress, am I merely a delegate from my district or state, restricted to act and vote as the majority which elected me desire, bound by the instructions of my constituents and subservient to their will? Or am I, once elected, a representative of the people of the United States, free to act as I think best for the country generally?"

In a country as large as the United States, with such diverse interests and such a heterogeneous population, the economic interests and social prejudices of particular states and regions often clash with those of other sections and with conceptions of the general interest of the whole nation. The perennial demand of the silver-mining and wool interests in certain western states for purchase and protection, the struggle over slavery, and the . . . filibuster of southern senators against the attempt to outlaw racial discrimination in employment are familiar examples of recurring conflicts between local interests and prejudices and the common welfare. These political quarrels are rooted in the varying stages of cultural development attained by the different parts of the country. It is the peculiar task of the politician to compose these differences, to reconcile conflicting national and local attitudes, and to determine when public opinion is ripe for legislative action. Some conflicts will yield in time to political adjustment; others must wait for their legal sanction upon the gradual evolution of the conscience of society. No act of Congress can abolish unemployment or barking dogs or racial prejudices. . . .

TYPES OF PRESSURES ON CONGRESS

One can sympathize with the plight of the conscientious congressman who is the focal point of all these competing pressures. The district or state he represents may need and want certain roads, post offices, courthouses, or schools. Irrigation dams or projects may be needed for the development of the area's resources. If the representative is to prove himself successful in the eyes of the

George B. Galloway (1898–1967) formerly was senior specialist in American government with the Legislative Reference Service of the Library of Congress. Selected excerpts are from pp. 284–85, 301, and 319–22 from *Congress at the Crossroads* by George B. Galloway. Copyright 1946 by George B. Galloway. Reprinted by permission of HarperCollins Publishers, Inc.

people back home, he must be able to show, at least occasionally, some visible and concrete results of his congressional activity. Or else he must be able to give good reasons why he has not been able to carry out his pledges. The local residence rule for congressmen multiplies the pressures that impinge upon him. Faithful party workers who have helped elect him will expect the congressman to pay his political debts by getting them jobs in the federal service. Constituents affected by proposed legislation may send him an avalanche of letters, telegrams, and petitions which must be acknowledged and followed up. The region from which he comes will expect him to protect and advance its interests in Washington. All the various organized groups will press their claims upon him and threaten him if he does not jump when they crack the whip. Party leaders may urge a congressman to support or oppose the administration program or to "trade" votes for the sake of party harmony or various sectional interests. He is also under pressure from his own conscience as to what he should do both to help the people who have elected him and to advance the best interests of the nation. Besieged by all these competing pressures, a congressman is often faced with the choice of compromising between various pressures, of trading votes, of resisting special interests of one sort or another, of staying off the floor when a vote is taken on some measure he prefers not to take a stand on, of getting support here and at the same time running the risk of losing support there. Dealing with pressure blocs is a problem in political psychology which involves a careful calculation of the power of the blocs, the reaction of the voters on election day, and the long-haul interests of the district, state, and nation. . . .

SHOULD CONGRESS LEAD OR FOLLOW PUBLIC OPINION?

It is axiomatic to say that in a democracy public opinion is the source of law. Unless legislation is sanctioned by the sense of right of the people, it becomes a dead letter on the statute books, like Prohibition and the Hatch Act. But public opinion is a mercurial force; now quiescent, now vociferous, it has various moods and qualities. It reacts to events and is often vague and hard to weigh.

Nor is public opinion infallible. Most people are naturally preoccupied with their personal problems and daily affairs; national problems and legislative decisions seem complex and remote to them, despite press and radio and occasional Capitol tours. Comparatively few adults understand the technicalities of foreign loans or reciprocal trade treaties, although congressional action on these aspects of our foreign economic policy may have far-reaching effects upon our standard of living. . . .

In practice, a congressman both leads and follows public opinion. The desires of his constituents, of his party, and of this or that pressure group all enter into his decisions on matters of major importance. The influence of these factors varies from member to member and measure to measure. Some congressmen consider it their duty to follow closely what they think is the majority opinion of their constituents, especially just before an election. Others feel that they should make their decisions without regard to their constituents' wishes in the first place, and then try to educate and convert them afterward. Some members are strong party men and follow more or less blindly the program of the party leaders. Except when they are very powerful in the home district, the pressure groups are more of a nuisance than a deciding influence on the average member. When a legislator is caught between the conflicting pressures of his constituents and his colleagues, he perforce compromises between them and follows his own judgment.

The average legislator discovers early in his career that certain interests or prejudices of his constituents are dangerous to trifle with. Some of these prejudices may not be of fundamental importance to the welfare of the nation, in which case he is justified in humoring them, even though he may disapprove. The difficult case occurs where the prejudice concerns some fundamental policy affecting the national welfare. A sound sense of values, the ability to discriminate between that which is of fundamental importance and that which is only superficial, is an indispensable qualification of a good legislator.

Senator Fulbright* gives an interesting example of this distinction in his stand on the poll-tax issue and isolationism. "Regardless of how persuasive my colleagues or the national press may be about the evils of the poll tax, I do not see its fundamental importance, and I shall follow the views of the people of my state. Although it may be symbolic of conditions which many deplore, it is exceedingly doubtful that its abolition will cure any of our major problems. On the other hand, regardless of how strongly opposed my constituents may prove to be to the creation of, and participation in, an ever stronger United Nations Organization, I could not follow such a policy in that field unless it becomes clearly hopeless."[1]

A TWO-WAY JOB

As believers in democracy, probably most Americans would agree that it is the duty of congressmen to follow public opinion insofar as it expresses the desires, wants, needs, aspirations, and ideals of the people. Most Americans probably would also consider it essential for their representatives to make as careful an appraisal of these needs and desires as they can, and to consider, in connection with such an appraisal, the ways and means of accomplishing them. Legislators have at hand more information about legal structures, economic problems, productive capacities, manpower possibilities, and the like, than the average citizen they represent. They can draw upon that information to inform and lead the people—by showing the extent to which their desires can be realized.

In other words, a true representative of the people would follow the people's desires and at the same time lead the people in formulating ways of accomplishing those desires. He would lead the people in the sense of calling

*At the time this article was written, J. William Fulbright was a U.S. senator from Arkansas—*Editors.*

to their attention the difficulties of achieving those aims and the ways to overcome the difficulties. This means also that, where necessary, he would show special interest groups or even majorities how, according to his own interpretation and his own conscience, their desires need to be tempered in the common interest or for the future good of the nation.

Thus the job of a congressman is a two-way one. He represents his local area and interests in the national capital, and he also informs the people back home of the problems arising at the seat of government and how these problems affect them. It is in the nature of the congressman's job that he should determine, as far as he can, public opinion in his own constituency and in the whole nation, analyze it, measure it in terms of the practicability of turning it into public policy, and consider it in the light of his own knowledge, conscience, and convictions. Occasionally he may be obliged to go against public opinion, with the consequent task of educating or reeducating the people along lines that seem to him more sound. And finally, since he is a human being eager to succeed at his important job of statesmanship and politics, he is realistic enough to keep his eyes on the voters in terms of the next election. But he understands that a mere weather-vane following of majority public opinion is not always the path to reelection. . . .

NOTE

1. In an address on "The Legislator" delivered at the University of Chicago on February 19, 1946. *Vital Speeches,* May 15, 1946, pp. 468–72.

Legislative Process: The Filibuster

*T*he legislative process in Congress requires the building of coalitions among its members over and over again until all legislative hurdles have been overcome. Thus, successful legislators are those who are able to shepherd legislation through various committees in both houses, then to the floors of the House and Senate, then to the conference committees, and back to the floors. If the legislation requires an appropriation, then the whole process is repeated with different committees.

Although there is much that is the same legislatively in the House of Representatives and the Senate, there are some critical differences that, in the end, make the passage of legislation very difficult. One such difference is the filibuster in the Senate.

In the House of Representatives, the majority party leadership (i.e., the speaker of the house, the majority leader, and others) control the flow of legislation. In the Senate that control is ultimately in the hands of senators themselves. Typically, if the speaker of the house wants something, he or she can get it. In the Senate, however, a group of senators determined to block action can do so through the filibuster.

The filibuster is a legislative device to prevent action on a bill. It grows out of the necessity, under Senate custom and rules, for the Senate as a whole to determine when debate shall end on a bill. Under the current rule, a three-fifths vote is required to end debate. This "supermajority"—sixty senators—is extremely difficult to achieve.

For much of the twentieth century, the filibuster was used sparingly, and usually on the most critical of issues, such as civil rights bills. In recent years, however, the filibuster has been elevated to a new level, with senators from both parties either threatening or carrying out a filibuster almost as a matter of course on any manner of bills. Indeed, there have been more than thirty filibusters a year since 1993. In 2005, the minority Democrats used the filibuster to block nominees to the federal courts, thus causing the majority Republicans to threaten to take away the filibuster altogether in cases involving judicial nominations.

The central issue surrounding the filibuster is the extent to which a minority of senators should be able to block the will of the majority. Some argue, as does Senator Tom Harkin (D-Iowa) in the first selection, that whatever validity the filibuster had in history (and he thinks it was very little), it should not be allowed to continue unchanged today. The filibuster, he argues, only leads to gridlock in the legislative process, contributing to even greater cynicism and frustration among the American people.

In the second selection, a former member of the House of Representatives, Bill Frenzel (R-Minn.), makes the case for keeping the filibuster. Frenzel argues that the filibuster fits into the general scheme of limited government fashioned by the framers of the Constitution and should not be cast aside merely because it is viewed today as a major impediment to majority rule. According to Frenzel, if a majority of the people truly want the government to act, the Congress, including the Senate, will act. In the meantime, the filibuster is a useful device to filter out unneeded or unwise legislation.

It's Time to Change the Filibuster
Tom Harkin

Mr. Harkin. Mr. President, for the benefit of the Senators who are here and watching on the monitors, we now have before us an amendment by myself, Senator Lieberman, Senator Pell, and Senator Robb that would amend rule XXII, the so-called filibuster rule of the U.S. Senate. . . .

This amendment would change the way this Senate operates more fundamentally than anything that has been proposed thus far this year. It would fundamentally change the way we do business by changing the filibuster rule as it currently stands.

Mr. President, the last Congress showed us the destructive impact filibusters can have on the legislative process, provoking gridlock after gridlock, frustration, anger, and despondency among the American people, wondering whether we can get anything done at all here in Washington. The pattern of filibusters and delays that we saw in the last Congress is part of the rising tide of filibusters that have overwhelmed our legislative process.

While some may gloat and glory in the frustration and anger that the American people felt toward our institution which resulted in the tidal wave of dissatisfaction that struck the majority in Congress, I believe in the long run that it will harm the Senate and our Nation for this pattern to continue. . . . Mr. President, there has . . . been a rising tide in the use of the filibuster. In the last two Congresses, in 1987 to 1990, and 1991 to 1994, there have been twice as many filibusters per year as there were the last time the Republicans controlled the Senate, from 1981 to 1986, and 10 times as many as occurred between 1917 and 1960. Between 1917 and 1960, there were an average of 1.3 per session. However, in the last Congress, there were 10 times that many. This is not healthy for our legislative process and it is not healthy for our country.

I have [also] compare[d] filibusters in the entire 19th century and in the last Congress. We had twice as many filibusters in the 103d Congress as we had in the entire 100 years of the 19th century.

Clearly, this is a process that is out of control. We need to change the rules. We need to change the rules, however, without harming the longstanding Senate tradition of extended debate and deliberation, and slowing things down.

I have here [also] the issues that were subject to filibusters in the last Congress. Some of these were merely delayed by filibusters. Others were killed

Tom Harkin is a Democratic U.S. Senator from the state of Iowa. Excerpted from a speech delivered in the U.S. Senate, *Congressional Record,* Proceedings and Debates of the 104th Congress. First Session, Senate, January 4, 1995, vol. 141, No. 1, 530–33, and January 5, 1995, vol. 141, No. 2, 5431.

outright, despite having the majority of both bodies and the President in favor of them. That is right. Some of these measures had a majority of support in the Senate and in the House, and by the President. Yet, they never saw the light of day. Others simply were perfunctory housekeeping types of issues.

For example, one might understand why someone would filibuster the Brady Handgun Act. There were people that felt very strongly opposed to that. I can understand that being slowed down, and having extended debate on it. Can you say that about the J. Larry Lawrence nomination? I happen to be a personal friend of Mr. Lawrence. He is now our Ambassador to Switzerland, an important post. He was nominated to be Ambassador there, and he came through the committee fine. Yet, his nomination was the subject of a filibuster. Or there was the Edward P. Berry, Jr., nomination. There was the Claude Bolton nomination. You get my point.

We had nominations that were filibustered. This was almost unheard of in our past. We filibustered the nomination of a person that actually came through the committee process and was approved by the committee, and it was filibustered here on the Senate floor.

Actually, Senators use these nominations as a lever for power. If one Senator has an issue where he or she wants something done, it is very easy. All a Senator needs to do is filibuster a nomination. Then the majority leader or the minority leader has to come to the Senator and say, "Would you release your hold on that, give up your filibuster on that?"

"OK," the Senator will reply. "What do you want in return?"

Then the deals are struck.

It is used, Mr. President, as blackmail for one Senator to get his or her way on something that they could not rightfully win through the normal processes. I am not accusing any one party of this. It happens on both sides of the aisle.

Mr. President, I believe each Senator needs to give up a little of our pride, a little of our prerogatives, and a little of our power for the good of this Senate and for the good of this country. Let me repeat that: Each Senator, I believe, has to give up a little of our pride, a little of our prerogatives, and a little of our power for the better functioning of this body and for the good of our country.

I think the voters of this country were turned off by the constant bickering, the arguing back and forth that goes on in this Senate Chamber, the gridlock that ensued here, and the pointing of fingers of blame.

Sometimes, in the fog of debate, like the fog of war, it is hard to determine who is responsible for slowing something down. It is like the shifting sand. People hide behind the filibuster. I think it is time to let the voters know that we heard their message in the last election. They did not send us here to bicker and to argue, to point fingers. They want us to get things done to address the concerns facing this country. They want us to reform this place. They want this place to operate a little better, a little more openly, and a little more decisively.

Mr. President, I believe this Senate should embrace the vision of this body that our Founding Fathers had. There is a story—I am not certain whether it is true or not, but it is a nice story—that Thomas Jefferson returned from France, where he had learned that the Constitutional Convention had set up a separate body called the U.S. Senate, with its Members appointed by the legislatures and not subject to a popular vote. Jefferson was quite upset about this. He asked George Washington why this was done. Evidently, they were sitting at a breakfast table. Washington said to him, "Well, why did you pour your coffee in the saucer?" And Jefferson replied, "Why, to cool it, of course." Washington replied, "Just so: We created the Senate to cool down the legislation that may come from the House."

I think General Washington was very wise. I think our Founding Fathers were very wise to create this body.

They had seen what had happened in Europe—violent changes, rapid changes, mob rule—so they wanted the process to slow things down, to deliberate a little more, and that is why the Senate was set up.

But George Washington did not compare the Senate to throwing the coffee pot out the window. It is just to cool it down, and slow it down.

I think that is what the Founding Fathers envisioned, and I think that is what the American people expect. That is what we ought to and should provide. The Senate should carefully consider legislation, whether it originates here, or whether it streams in like water from a fire hose from the House of Representatives, we must provide ample time for Members to speak on issues. We should not move to the limited debate that characterizes the House of Representatives. I am not suggesting that we do that. But in the end, the people of our country are entitled to know where we stand and how we vote on the merits of a bill or an amendment.

Some argue that any supermajority requirement is unconstitutional, other than those specified in the Constitution itself. I find much in this theory to agree with—and I think we should treat all the rules that would limit the ability of a majority to rule with skepticism. I think that this theory is one that we ought to examine more fully, and that is the idea that the Constitution of the United States sets up certain specified instances in which a supermajority is needed to pass the bill, and in all other cases it is silent. In fact, the Constitution provides that the President of the Senate, the Vice President of the United States, can only vote to break a tie vote—by implication, meaning that the Senate should pass legislation by a majority vote, except in those instances in which the Constitution specifically says that we need a supermajority.

The distinguished constitutional expert, Lloyd Cutler, a distinguished lawyer, has been a leading proponent of this view. I have not made up my mind on this theory, but I do believe it is something we ought to further examine. I find a lot that I agree with in that theory.

But what we are getting at here is a different procedure and process, whereby we can have the Senate as the Founding Fathers envisioned—a place to cool down, slow down, deliberate and discuss, but not as a place where a handful— yes, maybe even one Senator—can totally stop legislation or a nomination.

Over the last couple of years, I have spent a great deal of time reading the history of this cloture process. Two years ago, about this time, I first proposed this to my fellow Democratic colleagues at a retreat we had in Williamsburg, VA. In May of that year, I proposed this to the Joint Committee on Congressional Reform.

Some people said to me at that time: Senator Harkin, of course you are proposing it, you are in the majority, you want to get rid of the filibuster. Well, now I am in the minority and I am still proposing it because I think it is the right thing to do.

Let me take some time to discuss the history of cloture and the limitations on debate in the Senate. Prior to 1917 there was no mechanism to shut off debate in the Senate. There was an early version in 1789 of what was called the "previous question." It was used more like a tabling motion than as a method to close debate.

In the 19th century, Mr. President, elections were held in November and Congress met in December. This Congress was always a lame duck session, which ended in March of the next year. The newly elected members did not take office until the following December, almost 13 months later. During the entire 19th century, there were filibusters. But most of these were aimed at delaying congressional action at the end of the short session that ended March 4. A filibuster during the 19th century was used at the end of a session when the majority would try to ram something through at the end, over the objections of the minority. Extended debate was used to extend debate to March 4, when under the law at that time, it automatically died.

If the majority tried to ram something through in the closing hours, the minority would discuss it and hold it up until March 4, and that was the end of it. That process was changed. Rather than going into an automatic lame-duck session in December, we now convene a new Congress in January with the new Members. I think this is illustrative that the filibuster used in the 19th century was entirely different in concept and in form than what we now experience here in the U.S. Senate.

So those who argue that the filibuster in the U.S. Senate today is a time-honored tradition of the U.S. Senate going clear back to 1789 are mistaken, because the use of the filibuster in the 19th century was entirely different than what it is being used for today, and it was used in a different set of laws and circumstances under which Congress met.

So that brings us up to the 20th century. In 1917, the first cloture rule was introduced in response to a filibuster, again, at the end of a session that triggered a special session. This cloture rule provided for two-thirds of Members present and voting to cut off debate. It was the first time since the first Congress met that the Senate adopted a cloture rule in 1917. However, this cloture rule was found to be ineffective and was rarely used. Why? Because rulings of the chair said that the cloture rule did not apply to procedural matters. So, if someone wanted to engage in a filibuster, they could simply bring up a procedural matter and filibuster that, and the two-thirds vote did not even apply to that. For a number of years, from 1917 until 1949, we had that situation.

In 1949 an attempt was made to make the cloture motion more effective. The 1949 rule applied the cloture rule to procedural matters. It closed that loophole but did not apply to rules changes. It also raised the needed vote from two-thirds present and voting to two-thirds of the whole Senate, which at that time meant 64 votes. That rule existed for 10 years.

In 1959, Lyndon Johnson pushed through a rules change to change the needed vote back to two-thirds of those present and voting, and which also applied cloture to rules changes.

There were many attempts after that to change the filibuster. In 1975, after several years of debate here in the Senate, the current rule was adopted, as a compromise proposed by Senator Byrd of West Virginia. The present cloture rule allows cloture to be invoked by three-fifths of Senators chosen and sworn, or 60 votes, except in the case of rules changes, which still require two-thirds of those present and voting.

This change in the rule reducing the proportion of votes needed for cloture for the first time since 1917, was the culmination of many years of efforts by reformers' numerous proposals between 1959 and 1975.

Two of the proposals that were made in those intervening years I found particularly interesting. One was by Senator Hubert Humphrey in 1963, which provided for majority cloture in two stages. The other proposal I found interesting was one by Senator Dole in 1971 that moved from the then current two-thirds present and voting down to three-fifths present and voting, reducing the number of votes by one with each successive cloture vote.

We drew upon Senator Dole's proposal in developing our own proposal. Our proposal would reduce the number of votes needed to invoke cloture gradually, allowing time for debate, allowing us to slow things down, but ultimately allowing the Senate to get to the merits of a vote.

Under our proposal, the amendment now before the Senate, Senators still have to get 16 signatures to offer a cloture motion. The motion would still have to lay over 2 days. The first vote to invoke cloture would require 60 votes. If that vote did not succeed, they could file another cloture motion needing 16 signatures. They would have to wait at least 2 further days. On the next vote, they would need 57 votes to invoke cloture. If you did not get that, well, you would have to get 16 signatures, file another cloture motion, wait another couple days, and then you would have to have 54 votes. Finally, the same procedure could be repeated, and move to a cloture vote of 51. Finally, a simple majority vote could close debate, to get to the merits of the issue.

By allowing this slow ratchet down, the minority would have the opportunity to debate, focus public attention on a bill, and communicate their case to the public. In the end, though, the majority could bring the measure to a final vote, as it generally should in a democracy.

Mr. President, in the 19th century as I mentioned before, filibusters were used to delay action on a measure until the automatic expiration of the session.

Senators would then leave to go back to their States, or Congressmen back to their districts, and tell people about the legislation the majority was trying to ram through. They could get the public aroused about it, to put pressure on Senators not to support that measure or legislation.

Keep in mind that in those days, there was no television, there was no radio, and scant few newspapers. Many people could not read or write and the best means of communication was when a Senator went out and spoke directly with his constituents. So it was necessary to have several months where a

Senator could alert the public as to what the majority was trying to do, to protect the rights and interests of the minority.

That is not the case today. Every word we say here is instantaneously beamed out on C-SPAN, watched all over the United States, and picked up on news broadcasts. We have the print media sitting up in the gallery. So the public is well aware and well informed of what is happening here in the Senate on a daily basis. We do have a need to slow the process down, but we do not need the several months that was needed in the 19th century.

So as a Member of the new minority here in the Senate, I come to this issue as a clear matter of good public policy. I am pleased to say that it is a change that enjoys overwhelming support among the American people.

A recent poll conducted by Action Not Gridlock . . . found that 80 percent of Independents, 84 percent of Democrats, and 79 percent of Republicans believe that once all Senators have been able to express their views, the Senate should be permitted to vote for or against a bill. . . .

. . . [S]laying the filibuster dinosaur—and that is what I call it, a dinosaur, a relic of the ancient past—slaying the filibuster dinosaur has also been endorsed by papers around the country, including the *New York Times, USA Today,* and the *Washington Post.* . . .

* * *

But I will close my opening remarks, with this quote:

> It is one thing to provide protection against majoritarian absolutism; it is another thing again to enable a vexatious or unreasoning minority to paralyze the Senate and America's legislative process along with it.

I could not have said it better, and it was said by Senator Robert Dole, February 10, 1971.

If Senator Dole thought the filibuster was bad in 1971, certainly when we are down here, the filibuster has increased at least threefold on an annual basis since then. So it is time to get rid of this dinosaur. It is time to move ahead with the people's business in a productive manner.

Defending the Dinosaur
The Case for Not Fixing the Filibuster
Bill Frenzel

Defending the filibuster may not be quite as nasty as taking candy from a baby, but neither is it a good route to popular acclaim. Few kind words are ever spoken in defense of filibusters. Conventional wisdom and political correctness have pronounced them to be pernicious. The very word is pejorative, evoking ugly images of antidemocratic activities.

During the last biennium, filibusters became so unlovable that a group, including former senators, formed "Action, Not Gridlock!" to try to stamp them out. The public, which had tested both gridlock and action, seemed to prefer the former. The organization disappeared.

As that public reaction suggests, political correctness is a sometime thing and conventional wisdom oft goes astray. The American public may not be rushing to embrace the filibuster, but neither has it shown any inclination to root it out. The Senate's overwhelming vote . . . against changing the filibuster means that the practice won't go away soon, so it is worth examining. Despite its bad press, the story of the modern filibuster is not one-sided.

FILIBUSTERS, THE CONSTITUTION, AND THE FRAMERS

Filibuster haters claim they are contrary to the spirit of the Constitution because they require extraordinary majorities. The rationale is that the Framers, who created a majority system and rejected supermajorities, would be horrified by filibusters. Perhaps, but don't be too sure. Remember that no one has dug up a Framer lately to testify to the accuracy of this theory.

The Framers created our system based on their profound distrust of government. They loaded the system with checks and balances to make it work very slowly and with great difficulty. Their intention was to prevent swift enactment of laws and to avoid satisfying the popular whimsy of each willful majority. Maybe they would trade popular election for a filibuster rule.

Without any live Framers, we can only speculate about their feelings. However, it is hard to believe that, having designed an extremely balky system,

Bill Frenzel is a former Republican U.S. Representative from the State of Minnesota (1971–1991). From Bill Frenzel, "Defending the Dinosaur: The Case for Not Fixing the Filibuster," *The Brookings Review* (Summer 1995): 47–49. Reprinted by permission.

they would want to speed it up today. More likely, they would merely remind us that for more than 200 years major American policymaking has been based on "concurrent majorities" anyway.

PARLIAMENTARY COMPARISONS

Most of the parliaments of the world are copies, or variants, of Westminster [England]. With only one strong house and no separated executive branch, they can usually deliver laws swiftly. But when their actions affront public opinion, there is a political price to be paid, often very quickly. The government that offends the people soon becomes the opposition.

In our regional system, our majorities, assisted by a wide range of taxpayer-paid perks, do not usually pay any price. Our members of Congress are unbeatable (even in the earthquake of 1994, more than 90 percent of them who sought reelection were reelected). Our majorities are not eternal, but they are long-lived, unlike the Westminster forms.

It might make sense to consider trading the filibuster for congressional mortality (perhaps through term limits), but it is probably unwise to accept the blockbuster majority power of the Westminster system without accepting its balance of political turnover in return.

Actually, filibusters are not unique to the United States. Other parliaments are finding new opportunities for dilatory practices. The Japanese upper house recently presented its "ox-step," and an appointed majority in the Canadian Senate frustrated the intentions of the prime minister and his government on the ratification of the U.S.–Canada Free Trade Agreement. The strokes are different for different folks, but we are not alone. Delay is a time-honored political exercise that transcends political boundaries.

THE FILIBUSTER AND THE POPULAR WILL

The filibuster has been often indicted for denying the popular will, but over recent history, that point is hard to demonstrate. In the first place, it is not easy to get, and hold, 41 votes in the Senate under any circumstances. It is practically impossible to do so against a popular proposal. Filibusters simply do not succeed *unless* they have popular support or unless there is a lack of enthusiasm for the proposal being filibustered.

In 1993 Senator Bob Dole (R-KS) led a filibuster against the Clinton Emergency Spending Bill. It succeeded because the public liked the filibuster better than the spending. In the Bush years, Senator George Mitchell (D-ME) stopped a capital gains proposal by threat of filibuster. Senator Mitchell succeeded because the people saw no urgency in the proposal. In both cases, political reality prevailed.

If the public wants a vote, it tells its representatives. In 1994 Senate Republicans tried to filibuster the Crime Bill. Based on hot flashes from home, more than 60 senators perceived that the bill was popular, so the filibuster was broken quickly. The same thing happened to the Motor Voter Bill, the National Service Bill, and five out of six presidential appointments. If any proposal has substantial public support, a couple of cloture votes will kill the filibuster. The political reality is: frivolous filibusters do not succeed. The modern filibuster can gridlock ideas that are not popular, but it has not gridlocked the people.

THE BICAMERAL SYSTEM

In our unique system, the two houses of Congress have developed similar, but not identical, personalities and processes. The House of Representatives, with 440 orators, is harder to manage and has therefore created a set of rules to limit debate. In recent years, its majority has handled bills under rules that permitted few, if any, amendments and only an hour or two of debate.

The Senate, with only 100 orators, has stayed with free debate and an open amendment system. That is not a bad division of process. One house has been too closed, the other too open. The House operates with the relentlessness of Westminster majority, and the Senate has more time to examine, to delay, to amend, and, if necessary, to kill. All are vital functions of any legislature. . . .

There is still a relatively open pipeline for bills flowing from the House. . . . Following the Framers' wisdom, it is prudent to have a sieve in the Senate to compete with that open pipe in the House. At least some of the worst legislative lumps may be smoothed out in the finer mesh. . . .

KEY TO COMPROMISE

Many filibusters are not filibusters at all, but merely threats. Most are undertaken to notify the managers of the proposal that problems exist. They are a signal from a minority to a majority that negotiations are in order. Sometimes the majority tries a cloture vote or two before negotiating. Sometimes it negotiates. Sometimes it does not.

Most of these procedures end in a modified bill, not a dead bill. The Crime Bill noted above passed. The Dole filibuster of emergency spending did not prevent passage of many of its bits of pork in regular appropriations bills. . . .

The filibuster surely gives a minority a little more clout, but it does not prevent a majority from passing reasonably popular proposals. It gives a minority the opportunity to negotiate what it believes is an intolerable proposal into one it can live with. That compromise may serve the needs of the majority tolerably well too.

NO NEED FOR A HEAVY HAND

One political reality test for the filibuster is the congressional ingenuity in finding ways to avoid it when necessary. Trade and Reconciliation bills are considered under laws that obviate filibusters. When there is a good reason to finesse the filibuster, the Senate always seems to get the job done.

Many other Senate rules, only dimly understood by common folks, reduce the legislative pace. I do not mean to bless multiple efforts to filibuster the same proposal. Once on the bill and once on the conference report is enough. Unlimited amendment after cloture is also too much opportunity for mischief.

Former Senate Majority Leader Mitchell has left constructive proposals to speed the work of the Senate without damaging the filibuster. They ought to be considered. The minority needs rights for protection. The majority needs the ability to move its program. Both needs can be well served by the modern 60-vote cloture rule. It should not be changed.

KEEP THE FILIBUSTER

The test of the filibuster ought to be whether it is fair, appropriate, and constructive. It may have been a killer in the old days, when it slew civil rights bills, but under the new 60-vote system, it is difficult to recall a filibustered proposition that stayed dead if it was popular.

Most antifilibuster noise comes from advocates of ideas that were going to fail anyway. It is not essential for every idea that comes bouncing up or down Pennsylvania Avenue to become law. The filibuster is a useful legislative tool, consistent with the goals of the Framers, that keeps whimsical, immature, and ultimately unpopular bills out of the statute books. . . .

 /diclerico10

Internet Resources
Visit our Web site at www.mhhe.com/diclerico10 for links and resources relating to Congress.

chapter 11

The Presidency

In 1973, the noted historian Arthur Schlesinger, Jr., published his influential book titled The Imperial Presidency *in which he argued that the powers and prerogatives of the office had grown so extensive over the course of the twentieth century that our cherished principle of balanced government was in jeopardy. Richard Nixon, whose abuses of power would ultimately force his resignation from office, represented for Schlesinger the farthest extension of that trend.*

Even before Nixon's departure, scholars, politicians, and political observers alike were calling upon Congress to rein in the power of the "imperial presidency." Legislators responded to that call, moving on both the domestic and foreign policy fronts to limit and render more accountable the exercise of presidential power. As a number of presidential scholars see it, the Congress succeeded all too well—leaving the presidency a shadow of its former self.

In the first selection, however, Donald R. Wolfensberger dissents from this assessment. Writing from the perspective of someone who worked on Capitol Hill for nearly twenty years, he contends that congressional efforts to defang presidential power have met with very limited success, as presidents have managed to artfully maneuver around such restrictions. Moreover, he observes that if some of the statements and actions by President George W. Bush are any indication, the events of September 11, 2001, have provided fertile soil for the reassertion of an imperial presidency.

Eric Posner, on the other hand, writes in the second article that the charges of an imperial presidency now being leveled at George W. Bush are nothing new in American history. Nor, judging by the historical record, should we be particularly alarmed by them.

The Return of the Imperial Presidency?
Donald R. Wolfensberger

Moments after President George W. Bush finished his stirring antiterrorism speech before Congress last September, presidential historian Michael Beschloss enthusiastically declared on national television that "the imperial presidency is back. We just saw it."

As someone who began his career as a Republican congressional staff aide during the turbulence of Vietnam and Watergate in the late 1960s and early 1970s, I was startled by the buoyant tone of Beschloss's pronouncement. To me, "imperial presidency" carries a pejorative connotation closely tied to those twin nightmares. Indeed, *Webster's Unabridged Dictionary* bluntly defines *imperial presidency* as "a U.S. presidency that is characterized by greater power than the Constitution allows."

Was Beschloss suggesting that President Bush was already operating outside the Constitution in prosecuting the war against terrorism, or did he have a more benign definition in mind? Apparently it was the latter. As Beschloss went on to explain, during World War II and the Cold War, Congress deferred to presidents, not just on questions of foreign policy and defense, but on domestic issues as well. Whether it was President Dwight D. Eisenhower asking for an interstate highway system or President John F. Kennedy pledging to land a man on the moon, Congress said, "If you ask us, we will." Without such a galvanizing crisis, the president would not be able to define the national interest so completely. "Now," continued Beschloss, "George Bush is at the center of the American solar system; that was not true 10 days ago." In fact, just nine months earlier Beschloss had described Bush as "the first post-imperial president" because, for the first time since the Great Depression, "we were not electing a president under the shadow of an international emergency like the Cold War or World War II or an economic crisis." Then came September 11.

Still, it's hard to join in such a warm welcome for the return of an idea that was heavily burdened just a generation ago with negative associations and cautionary experiences. Presidential scholars understandably become admirers of strong presidents and their presidencies. But a focus on executive power can become so narrow as to cause one to lose sight of the larger governmental system,

From *The Wilson Quarterly.* Spring 2002. pp. 36–41. © 2002 by the Woodrow Wilson International Center for Scholars in Washington, DC. Reprinted with permission.

with its checks and balances. To invest the idea of the imperial presidency with an aura of legitimacy and approbation would be a serious blow to America's constitutional design and the intent of the Framers.

It was historian Arthur M. Schlesinger, Jr., who popularized the term *imperial presidency* in his 1973 book by that title. Schlesinger, who had earlier chronicled the strong presidencies of Andrew Jackson and Franklin D. Roosevelt in admiring terms, admits in *The Imperial Presidency* his own culpability in perpetuating over the years "an exalted conception of presidential power":

> American historians and political scientists, this writer among them, labored to give the expansive theory of the Presidency historical sanction. Overgeneralizing from the [pre-World War II] contrast between a President who was right and a Congress which was wrong, scholars developed an uncritical cult of the activist Presidency.

The view of the presidency as "the great engine of democracy" and the "American people's one authentic trumpet," writes Schlesinger, passed into the textbooks and helped shape the national outlook after 1945. This faith of the American people in the presidency, coupled with their doubts about the ability of democracy to respond adequately to the totalitarian challenge abroad, are what gave the postwar presidency its pretensions and powers.

"By the early 1970s," Schlesinger writes, "the American President had become on issues of war and peace the most absolute monarch (with the possible exception of Mao Tse Tung of China) among the great powers of the world." Moreover, "the claims of unilateral authority in foreign policy soon began to pervade and embolden the domestic presidency."

The growth of the imperial presidency was gradual, and occurred "usually under the demand or pretext of an emergency," Schlesinger observes. Further, "it was as much a matter of congressional abdication as of presidential usurpation." The seeds of the imperial presidency were sown early. Schlesinger cites as examples Abraham Lincoln's 1861 imposition of martial law and his suspension of habeas corpus, and William McKinley's decision to send 5,000 American troops to China to help suppress the Boxer Rebellion of 1900. It is a measure of how much things have changed that Theodore Roosevelt's 1907 decision to dispatch America's Great White Fleet on a tour around the world was controversial because he failed to seek congressional approval. Then came Woodrow Wilson's forays into revolutionary Mexico, FDR's unilateral declaration of an "unlimited national emergency" six months before Pearl Harbor, and Harry Truman's commitment of U.S. troops to the Korean War in 1950, without congressional authorization, and his 1952 seizure of strike-threatened steel mills.

In 1973, the year *The Imperial Presidency* was published, Congress moved to reassert its war-making prerogatives during non-declared wars by enacting the War Powers Resolution over President Nixon's veto. The following year, prior to Nixon's resignation under the imminent threat of impeachment, Congress enacted two more laws aimed at clipping the wings of the imperial presidency and restoring the balance of power between the two branches. The Congressional

Budget and Impoundment Control Act of 1974 was designed to enable Congress to set its own spending priorities and prohibit the president from impounding funds it had appropriated. The Federal Election Campaign Act of 1974 was supposed to eliminate the taint of big money from presidential politics. Subsequent years witnessed a spate of other statutes designed to right the balance between the branches. The National Emergencies Act (1976) abolished scores of existing presidential emergency powers. The Ethics in Government Act (1978) authorized, among other things, the appointment of special prosecutors to investigate high-ranking executive branch officials. The Senate, in 1976, and the House, in 1977, established intelligence committees in the wake of hearings in 1975 revealing widespread abuses; and in 1980 the Intelligence Oversight Act increased Congress's monitoring demands on intelligence agencies and their covert operations.

Since those Watergate-era enactments, presidential scholars have decried the way Congress has emasculated the presidency. As recently as January of last year, political scientist Richard E. Neustadt, author of the classic *Presidential Power* (1964), lamented that "the U.S. presidency has been progressively weakened over the past three decades to the point where it is probably weaker today than at almost any time in the preceding century." Neustadt cited congressional actions as one of several causes of the decline.

As one who worked in the House of Representatives from 1969 to 1997, I have long been puzzled by such complaints. They have never rung true. What I witnessed during those years was the continuing decline of the legislative branch, not its ascendancy. Even Congress's post-Watergate efforts to reassert its authority look rather feeble in the harsh light of reality. The War Powers Resolution has been all but ignored by every president since Nixon as unconstitutional. They have abided by its reporting requirements, but presidential military forays abroad without explicit congressional authority continue unabated. Bosnia, Kosovo, Haiti, Somalia, and Serbia come readily to mind.

The congressional budget act has been used by every president since Ronald Reagan to leverage the administration's priorities by using budget summits with Congress to negotiate the terms of massive reconciliation bills on taxes and entitlements. The independent counsel act has been allowed to expire twice— though, in light of the unbridled power it gives counsels and the potential for abuse, this may have been wise. Federal funding of presidential campaigns has not stopped campaign finance abuses. And congressional oversight of perceived executive abuses has met with mixed results at best.

In the meantime, presidents have been relying more heavily than before on executive agreements to avoid the treaty ratification process, and on executive orders (or memorandums) of dubious statutory grounding in other areas. Administrations have defied Congress's requests for information with increasing frequency, dismissing the requests as politically motivated. And they have often invoked executive privilege in areas not previously sanctioned by judicial judgments.

The most recent example is Vice President Richard Cheney's refusal, on grounds of executive privilege, to turn over to the General Accounting Office

(GAO), an arm of Congress, information about meetings between the president's energy task force and energy executives. The controversy took on added interest with the collapse of Enron, one of the energy companies that provided advice to the task force. Vice President Cheney, who served as President Gerald R. Ford's White House chief of staff, said his action was aimed at reversing "an erosion of the powers" of the presidency over the last 30 to 35 years resulting from "unwise compromises" made by past Administrations. President Bush backed Cheney's claim of executive privilege, citing the need to maintain confidentiality in the advice given to a president.

It is revealing in this case that the congressional requests for information came not through formal committee action or subpoenas but more indirectly from the GAO, at the prompting of two ranking minority committee Democrats in the House, even though their Senate party counterparts are committee chairmen with authority to force a vote on subpoenas. The committee system, which should be the bulwark of congressional policy-making and oversight of the executive branch, has been in steady decline since the mid-1970s. Not the least of the causes is the weakening of committee prerogatives and powers by Congress itself, as a response to members' demands for a more participatory policy process than the traditional committee system allowed. Party leaders eventually replaced committee leaders as the locus of power in the House, a shift that was not altered by the change in party control of Congress in 1995.

Another contributing factor has been the shift in the Republican Party's base of power to the South and West, which has given a more populist and pro-presidential cast to the GOP membership on Capitol Hill.

Even with recent promises by Speaker of the House Dennis Hastert (R-Ill.) and Senate Majority Leader Tom Daschle (D-S.D.) to "return to the regular order" by giving committees greater flexibility and discretion in agenda setting and bill drafting, Congress is hamstrung by self-inflicted staff cuts and three-day legislative workweeks that make deliberative law-making and careful oversight nearly impossible. The "permanent campaign" has spilled over into governing, diminishing the value members see in committee work and encouraging partisan position taking and posturing. (It also makes members eager to get back to their districts for the serious work of campaigning, which explains the three-day workweek in Washington.) It is easier to take a popular campaign stand on an unresolved issue than make a painful policy choice and explain it to the voters.

Is it any wonder that even before the current emergency the executive was in a stronger position than Congress? Such power alone is not necessarily a sign of an imperial presidency. But testing the limits of power seems to be an inborn trait of political man, and presidents are no exception. Even presidential power proponent Richard Neustadt, who sees the presidency at the beginning of this 21st century as the weakest it's been in three decades, concedes that none of the formal limits on presidential powers by Congress or the courts have managed to eliminate those powers of greatest consequence, including the "plentitude of prerogative power" (a Lockean concept of acting outside the constitutional box to save the nation) that Lincoln assumed during the Civil War.

Both presidents George H. W. Bush and George W. Bush, to their credit, sought authorization from Congress for the use of force against Iraq and international terrorists, respectively, before committing troops to combat. Yet both also claimed they had inherent powers as president to do so to protect the national interest. (The younger Bush was on firmer ground since even the Framers explicitly agreed that the president has authority to repel foreign invasions and respond to direct attacks on the United States.)

The presidency is at its strongest at the outset of a national crisis or war. Just as President Franklin D. Roosevelt was encountering public and congressional wariness over his depression-era policies in the late 1930s, along came World War II and a whole new lease on the throne. Presidential power tends to increase at the expense of Congress. Alexander Hamilton put it succinctly in *The Federalist* 8: "It is of the nature of war to increase the executive at the expense of the legislative authority."

One way to gauge this balance of power is to look at the extent to which Congress deliberates over policy matters and the extent to which it gives the president most of what he requests with minimal resistance. Two weeks after Congress passed a $40 billion emergency spending bill and a resolution authorizing the president to use force against those behind the World Trade Center attacks, Senator Robert S. Byrd (D-W.Va.) rose in a nearly empty Senate chamber to remind his colleagues of their deliberative responsibilities. "In the heat of the moment, in the crush of recent events," Byrd observed, "I fear we may be losing sight of the larger obligations of the Senate."

> Our responsibility as Senators is to carefully consider and fully debate major policy matters, to air all sides of a given issue, and to act after full deliberation. Yes, we want to respond quickly to urgent needs, but a speedy response should not be used as an excuse to trample full and free debate.

Byrd was concerned in part about the way in which language relating to the controversy over adhering to the 1972 antiballistic missile treaty had been jettisoned from a pending defense authorization bill in the interest of "unity" after the terrorist attacks. But he was also disturbed by the haste with which the Senate had approved the use-of-force resolution "to avoid the specter of acrimonious debate at a time of national crisis." Byrd added that he was not advocating unlimited debate, but why, he asked, "do we have to put a zipper on our lips and have no debate at all?" Because of the "paucity of debate" in both houses, Byrd added, there was no discussion laying a foundation for the resolution, and in the future "it would be difficult to glean from the record the specific intent of Congress."

A review of the *Congressional Record* supports Byrd's complaint. Only Majority Leader Daschle and Minority Leader Trent Lott (R-Miss.) spoke briefly before the Senate passed the emergency spending bill and the use-of-force resolution. The discussion was truncated chiefly because buses were waiting to take senators and House members to a memorial service at the National Cathedral.

The House, to its credit, did return after the service for five hours of debate on the resolution, which it passed 420 to 1. Some 200 members spoke for about a minute each—hardly the stuff of a great debate. At no time did any member raise a question about the breadth, scope, or duration of the authority granted by the resolution. The closest some came were passing references to the way in which President Lyndon B. Johnson had used the language of the 1964 Gulf of Tonkin Resolution as authority to broaden U.S. involvement in Vietnam.

To the credit of Congress, a small, bipartisan leadership group had earlier negotiated a compromise with the White House to confine the resolution's scope to "those nations, organizations or persons" implicated in the September 11 attacks. The original White House proposal was much broader, extending the president's authority "to deter and pre-empt any future acts of terrorism or aggression against the United States." The language change is significant. If President Bush cannot demonstrate that Iraq was somehow involved in the September 11 attacks but decides to take military action against it, he will have to decide whether to seek additional authority from Congress or act without it, as President Bill Clinton did before him.

In times of war or national emergency, presidents have always acted in what they thought to be the national interest. That is not to say that Congress simply becomes a presidential lap dog. While it tends to defer to the commander in chief on military matters once troops have been committed to combat, it continues to exercise oversight and independence on matters not directly affecting the war's outcome. For example, President Bush was forced to make drastic alternations in his economic stimulus package by Senate Democrats who disagreed with his tax relief and spending priorities. And even in the midst of the war on terrorism, the House and Senate intelligence committees launched a joint inquiry into why our intelligence services were not able to detect or thwart the September 11 terrorist plot. In the coming months, moreover, Congress is sure to have its own ideas on how the federal budget can best be allocated to meet the competing demands for defense, homeland security, and domestic social-welfare programs.

Is the imperial presidency back? While at this writing the White House has not overtly exercised any extraconstitutional powers, the imperial presidency has been with us since World War II, and it is most likely to be re-energized during times of national crisis. Every president tends to test the limits of his power during such periods in order to do what he deems necessary to protect national security. To the extent that Congress does not push back and the public does not protest, the armor of the imperial presidency is further fortified by precedent and popular support against future attacks.

What is the danger in a set of powers that have, after all, evolved over several decades into a widely recognized reality without calamitous consequences for the Republic? As James Madison put in *The Federalist* 51, "The separate and distinct exercise of the different powers of government . . . is admitted on all hands to be essential to the preservation of liberty." The "great security against a gradual concentration of power in the same department," he went on, is to provide each department with the "necessary constitutional means and personal motives to resist. . . . Ambition must be made to counteract ambition."

The Constitution's system of separated powers and checks and balances is not a self-regulating machine. Arthur M. Schlesinger, Jr., observed in *The Imperial Presidency*, that what kept a strong presidency constitutional, in addition to the president's own appreciation of the Framers' wisdom, was the vigilance of the nation. "If the people had come to an unconscious acceptance of the imperial presidency," he wrote, "the Constitution could not hold the nation to ideals it was determined to betray." The only deterrent to the imperial presidency is for the great institutions of our society—Congress, the courts, the press, public opinion, the universities, "to reclaim their own dignity and meet their own responsibilities."

All Hail . . . King George?
Eric A. Posner

Some say President Bush acts like an autocrat. Then again, so have most of America's greatest presidents.

President George W. Bush draws fire from many quarters. That's hardly surprising: Presidents who surround themselves with pomp and ceremony, or who claim new or controversial powers, always provoke strong criticism. But the intensity of the criticism directed at Bush is explained in part by its roots—a fear that the president sometimes exhibits monarchial or imperial tendencies. The lavish fanfare surrounding Bush's January inauguration sparked howls of protest, as did the revelation that Bush's lawyers believed that the president could, as commander in chief, unilaterally suspend U.S. treaty obligations and statutes, including one banning torture. John Dean, once a lawyer in the famously power-hungry Richard Nixon administration, has derisively said Bush's reign "may be the most imperial Presidency our history has yet seen." Bush is not, however, the

Eric A. Posner, a professor of law at the University of Chicago, is author of *Law and Social Norms*, and coauthor of the *Limits of International Law*. Reproduced with permission from www.ForeignPolicy.com (March 2005). © 2003 Carnegie Endowment for International Peace.

first U.S. president to aggressively expand the authority of the Oval Office. Charges of presidential lawlessness date back to the first presidency.

George Washington and his contemporaries faced the vital question of how the Constitution's vague provisions on executive powers should be interpreted. James Madison argued that the president's powers were limited to those enumerated in the Constitution and those delegated to him by Congress. These enumerated powers included the powers of commander in chief, the power to enter into treaties (with the Senate's consent), the power to receive ambassadors, and little else. Alexander Hamilton argued that the president, as chief executive, had all the powers that an executive in those days had—and executives in those days were kings—except where the Constitution said otherwise. Although the Constitution gave some significant powers to Congress, including the power to appropriate funds and to declare war, Hamilton's formulation ensured that the president had dominant authority over foreign affairs.

Washington exercised Cincinnatus-like restraint throughout his career; nonetheless, as president he sided with Hamilton. As a result, he was not just the first president, but also the first strong president—and the first to be accused of usurping the powers of Congress. He was also the first great president. And there have been several other great presidents who also claimed (and exercised) expansive presidential powers, and were called usurpers by their critics. Abraham Lincoln won the Civil War and freed the slaves, but he also suspended the writ of habeas corpus. Theodore Roosevelt introduced the United States to the world stage, but he also asserted new presidential powers to use force and negotiate treaties without congressional involvement, especially in Panama and elsewhere in Latin America. Franklin D. Roosevelt led the United States through the Great Depression and World War II, but he also tried to pack the Supreme Court with his own nominees and broke the norm that confined presidents to two terms in office. By contrast, a dozen or more milquetoast presidents both abjured imperial power and exercised what power they acknowledged in as undistinguished a manner as possible.

So should we welcome or fear the imperial presidency? To answer this question, I conducted a very unscientific empirical study. First, I used presidential ratings compiled by Prof. James Lindgren of Northwestern Law School. I used the mean scores assigned to the presidents by a politically balanced group of political scientists, historians, and law professors, with 1 going to the worst and 5 to the best.

Second, I classified all of the presidents as either "imperial" or "republican" according to whether they, in word or deed, adopted an expansive or limited view of presidential power. (To classify presidents as imperial or republican, I focus on whether the president strained against existing constitutional understandings, and I do not try to use an absolute measure.) To minimize my own biases, I used a standard textbook on the presidency, Sidney M. Milkis and Michael Nelson's *The American Presidency*, and relied on the authors' conclusions about whether a particular president sought to expand his power, or seemed satisfied with what he had. For example, I classify Dwight D. Eisenhower as republican because he was uninterested in expanding presidential power; and I classify

Andrew Johnson as imperial, even though he was perhaps the weakest president ever, because he fought hard against the efforts of an ambitious congress to curtail the powers of the presidency.

The Power and Quality of U.S. Presidents

View of Power	Low Quality (1–2)	Medium Quality (3)	High Quality (4–5)
Republican (acknowledges limited powers)	Warren Harding Franklin Pierce James Buchanan Zachary Taylor Millard Fillmore Ulysses S. Grant Jimmy Carter	James Madison Gerald Ford John Quincy Adams Bill Clinton Herbert Hoover Calvin Coolidge James Monroe William Taft Benjamin Harrison Martin Van Buren Chester Arthur John Adams George H.W. Bush	Dwight D. Eisenhower
Imperial (claims expansive powers)	Andrew Johnson John Tyler Richard Nixon	John F. Kennedy Grover Cleveland Rutherford B. Hayes William McKinley Lyndon B. Johnson Thomas Jefferson	Andrew Jackson Harry S. Truman Teddy Roosevelt Woodrow Wilson Ronald Reagan Franklin D. Roosevelt Abraham Lincoln George Washington

The table demonstrates the pattern. Imperial presidents perform better than limited-power republican presidents. Average presidents are found in both categories, but within the extremes—the great and the terrible—there are only two modern exceptions. Eisenhower was a good president who did not try to expand his power, and Nixon was a bad president who did. Indeed, Nixon alone is probably responsible for the modern view that the imperial presidency is the worst kind of presidency. But if a constitutionally weak presidency prevents another Nixon, it also prevents another FDR or Lincoln. Although once in a while an Eisenhower could come along, most of the time we would have to make do with a Jimmy Carter, a Gerald Ford, or a Millard Fillmore. Such a state of affairs would hardly be appealing.

This argument, of course, is open to several objections. First, the character of the president might explain more than the power of the presidency. Lincoln and FDR might have been great presidents even if they couldn't have exercised as much power as they did. But it seems just as likely that a limited office, with limited powers, would not have attracted a person with a powerful character; or else, such a person would have overreached and been blocked by other institutions such as Congress and the courts.

Second, the ratings themselves may reflect the scholars' emphasis on heroic traits rather than actual contributions to the welfare of the nation. A weak presidency implies more power is invested in institutions such as Congress, state governments, and courts. However, it's hard to find a single historical example in which these institutions produced great achievements during a weak presidency. In contrast, the most ambitious and successful legislation—including the Social Security Act of 1935 and the Civil Rights Act of 1964—has almost always been propelled by an imperial president.

Finally, many are concerned that the great imperial presidents set the stage for the awful ones. The familiar argument is that FDR established precedents that would be used by Nixon. But FDR also established precedents that would be used by Truman, Eisenhower, and Reagan.

None of this is to say that presidents should be unconstrained. They would then be dictators. Popular elections, a two-term limit, congressional participation in ordinary legislation, and judicial limitations are all good and necessary, and no one today would object to them. But much of the structure of the presidency—especially in foreign affairs—is hampered by 18th century restrictions that were motivated by fears of monarchy. By pushing against these restrictions, Bush is not bolstering a dangerous and all-powerful executive as much as he is further modernizing the office of the presidency and preparing it for the challenges ahead. Bush's critics should argue with the way the president is using his powers, not the fact that he is expanding them.

 /diclerico10

Internet Resources
Visit our Web site at www.mhhe.com/diclerico10 for links and resources relating to the Presidency.

c h a p t e r 1 2

Bureaucracy

*T*he Pendleton Act, a landmark piece of legislation passed in 1883, created a system *whereby certain federal employees would be hired and rewarded on the basis of merit rather than political connections. Although the purpose behind this civil service system was a noble one—to protect us from unqualified political hacks placed in the permanent government by the old "spoils system"—Philip Howard, author of the first selection, maintains it has become overburdened with rules and regulations that protect the incompetent, demoralize the capable, frustrate accountability, and discourage change. Believing that these pathologies will paralyze the critical mission of the newly created Department of Homeland Security, Howard enthusiastically endorses the successful efforts of the Bush Administration to gain greater control over the career civil servants housed in that department.*

In the accompanying selection, Gerald Pops, while readily acknowledging the faults of the merit system, also maintains that these faults are not principally rooted in a maze of deadening rules, as Howard claims, but rather lie elsewhere. Moreover, the "management flexibility" built into the new Department of Homeland Security, so earnestly sought by the president and strongly endorsed by Howard, may well, according to Pops, reintroduce the very problems the merit system was designed to correct. Pops also predicts that the ability of this new department to deliver security to the American people is destined to be compromised, not by anything having to do with the civil service system, but rather by its unwieldy size and decision-making structure.

Civil Service Rules: A Drag on Our National Security
Philip K. Howard

A Department of Homeland Security is essential, both political parties agree, to avoid a repeat of the failures of coordination and intelligence that allowed terrorists to slip into the country and clues to be dropped. But the new department was temporarily stalled over the application of civil service rules for its employees. The Democratic majority in the Senate said the proposal did not "protect the rights of federal workers." President Bush said he wouldn't sign a bill without "management flexibility."

On the surface, this looked like just a petty political dispute over obscure administrative details—bullying Republicans against bleeding-heart Democrats. In fact, the fight goes to the heart of why government is too often ineffective. Warren Rudman and Lee Hamilton, co-chairmen of the U.S. Commission on National Security/21st Century, could not be more blunt; they assert that "today's civil service has become a drag on our national security."

Jim King, head of the Office of Personnel Management under President Bill Clinton, once noted that the civil service system looks great in theory but trying to accomplish anything is "like swallowing a 64-pound pill." The layers in internal regulations would be unimaginable to most Americans. At the core of civil service is one assumption that paralyzes daily choices; public employees and their unions can demand a legal hearing whenever there is a disagreement.

For personnel decisions, the civil service rules operate as a kind of legal air bag, allowing a disgruntled worker to force the supervisor to prove the wisdom of an adverse decision, even a negative comment on an evaluation form. The process of dismissing a worker who is incompetent or worse can take years. (The minimum generally is 18 months.) Getting rid of someone who has bad judgment is basically impossible: How would a supervisor prove bad judgment? Last year, according to the Office of Personnel Management, out of an estimated 64,000 federal employees who were designated a poor performers," only 434 were dismissed through the legal hearings. That's seven out of 1,000.

Assigning the best person to a new job is impossible unless you're prepared to prove in a hearing that more senior personnel aren't up to the task. After Sept. 11, 2001, the U.S. Customs Service immediately reassigned its best inspectors

Philip K. Howard is a lawyer and author and chairman of Common Good, a legal reform coalition. From Philip K. Howard, "A Drag on Our National Security," as appeared in *The Washington Post,* October 15, 2002, p. A19. Used by permission.

to better secure our northern border. The union filed a legal proceeding claiming that the reassignments required a nationwide survey of interested civil servants, from which choices should be made on the basis of seniority.

No decision, no matter how important or how trivial, is immune from a legal proceeding alleging that it violates the rights of federal workers. In August, following a directive outlining standard protective measures under each of the homeland security threat levels, the union filed a proceeding to overturn it because it was issued "without first notifying and affording (the union) the opportunity to negotiate." Several years ago a decision that U.S. Border Patrol officers should carry a side-handled club was rejected as not being within their job description.

Imagine being a supervisor in this environment. Do you go through the day thinking about how to stop terrorists, or are you preoccupied with how to negotiate the legal minefield of civil service?

The bureaucratic mind-set may be tolerable in a department processing crop reports, but not where instinct and agility can make the difference between life and death. The public servants guarding our freedom must be alert to subtle clues and suspicions, and be willing to go the extra mile to figure out what's really going on. Some people will be good at it; others will not. Other than our military, which operates with similar flexibility, it's hard to imagine a greater or graver public responsibility.

Bureaucracy inevitably flows from the absence of personal accountability, because the only alternative is *rule* accountability. Having a rule for everything was an idea that fit neatly with early 20th century theories that government could be run like an assembly line, with each person doing his or her delineated task. But that's much like central planning, and it works just as badly, because it suppresses the human instincts needed for success.

What's amazing is that anything gets done. That's a tribute to the fact that most public employees are good and many superb. Instead of defending the system, Congress should take note of the one characteristic that all effective public institutions seem to have in common: an internal culture in which employees basically ignore the rules, focusing instead on getting the job done.

Public employees are the victims, not the villains of this system. Imagine being a dedicated public servant and having to work, day after day, with an incompetent colleague. The destructive effect on morale, as a personnel report to Clinton noted, is "far greater than the number of poor employees." Imagine what it's like to have your instincts of right and wrong suppressed by mind-numbing bureaucracy. Study after study has confirmed the debilitating effects of working in this kind of environment, including higher stress and cardiac disease and as an "institutional neurosis marked by apathy, withdrawal, lack of initiative and spontaneity."

Every administration in memory has tried to overhaul the civic service system. Al Gore's Reinventing Government initiative got beaten back almost at the gate. The Volcker Commission in 1989 concluded that civil service "is legally trammeled and intellectually confused" and "certainly not hiring the most meritorious candidates."

The Carter administration actually succeeded in increasing accountability, but only for the most senior civil servants. The most effective reformer in recent history is Sen. Zell Miller (D-Ga.), who in 1996, when he was governor of Georgia, abolished civil service for all new hires. Almost alone among active political leaders, Miller has been willing to say that this emperor has no clothes: "Despite its name, the merit system is not about merit. It offers no reward to good workers. It only provides cover for bad workers."

No one is advocating a return to the spoils system. Under the proposal supported by the administration, agencies would still be subject to general strictures against patronage hiring and arbitrary dismissals. Probably the one weakness of the proposal in this age of distrust is that it leaves to a later date how to accomplish non-litigation safeguards. But new safety nets are not hard to imagine—for example, a management-labor committee with power to guard against arbitrariness.

What's ultimately needed is a new deal for public servants. The civil service system is broken. The worst flaw—that it suppresses the human element needed to get the job done—is precisely what America cannot afford when ferreting out the terrorists trying to destroy the fabric of our free society.

A Strong Civil Service System Is the Cure, Not the Problem
Gerald Pops

President Bush has gotten what he asked for—a Homeland Security Department with the executive branch authority to strip federal employees of their civil service protection. Comprised of twenty-six former agencies and approximately 170,000 employees, this mammoth new bureaucracy will constitute almost 10 percent of the total federal workforce. With this new department comes executive flexibility to hire, promote, transfer, discipline, fire, and otherwise treat employees without reference to the civil service rules that apply to the other 90 percent of federal workers hired under the civil service system. However, along with this "management flexibility" also comes a dangerous undermining of the system that has undergirded public service, at all levels of

Gerald Pops is professor of public administration at West Virginia University. This article was written especially for *Points of View* in 2003.

government, for more than a century. Furthermore, management flexibility is not likely to lead to greater homeland security.

In gaining his prize, the president argued strenuously that homeland security is too important a function to hamstring with restrictions on hiring, assignment, transfer, discipline, and promotion that characterize the system. Philip K. Howard's argument contains most of a familiar litany that goes like this: The civil service system is broken. American business has the answers to questions such as how to produce at higher levels and how to increase innovation and excellence. Civil servants are overprotected to the point that the "deadwood" are protected as well as the worthy. Civil service promotes more concern with compliance with the rules than it does performance. Efforts to discipline or fire poorly performing employees lead to frustration and failure because of the excessive legal protections associated with tenure. Civil service employees are over-concerned with job security and under-concerned about production. The fact that they are protected by unions makes matters much worse. It is interesting to note, moreover, that neither economic recession nor the shameful and destructive practices of Enron, WorldCom, Arthur Andersen, and their ilk, both signs that all is not well in American business practice, have cooled enthusiasm for the private sector model.

THE MERIT OF THE MERIT SYSTEM

To be an informed critic, it is necessary to have a complete sense of the history of the civil service, why it came into existence, and what type of system or systems might possibly replace it, were it to vanish. Actually, its use has been decreasing and so we have some clear evidence of what is taking its place as well as the dangers of the substitution. As originally conceived in the Civil Service Act of 1883, the civil service was designed to (1) promote the competitive selection of employees; (2) allow employees who prove competent in their jobs to keep them (this was the intent of "tenure rights") in the face of removal for political or personal reasons by managers (most frequently managers who are politically appointed by new administrations); and (3) promote equality by assuring that no person would be turned away from applying for and being selected for a federal job except on the basis that he or she lacked the ability to do it. Non-political selection, continuity of a competent civil service that is able to survive elections, and equal access to public jobs on the basis of merit are the original and essential values of the civil service system. As augmented over the years, civil service jobs were "classified" (specifically described, to include duties, qualifications, and pay associated with each position), and the concept spread to virtually all state and local government employment in America. The system was to function so as to enshrine the basic principle of merit, which can be most simply defined as "the individual's ability to perform the job." Thus, the civil service system came to be known as "the merit system."

CRACKS IN THE MERIT SYSTEM IDEAL

It would be foolish to argue that the merit system always works in a way that promotes the merit principle. Pressures developed over the years that interfered with the merit ideal, a short list of which follows:

1. Public policies favoring the hiring and promotion of veterans (called "veteran preference laws") redirected hiring, promotion, and retention in the event of reduction of positions, on a basis not clearly related to merit.
2. Discrimination on the basis of race, ethnicity, religion, physical appearance, sex and sexual orientation, age, and disability often interfered with hiring, reward, and separation based on merit.
3. Centralization of testing and hiring procedures in the central "personnel agencies" of governments often worked against the interests of the hiring agencies who had a better idea of what kinds of skills and talents they needed.
4. The growing legalities surrounding the tenure/hearing process, although often increasing fairness to individual employees involved, also created obstacles in the firing of incompetent employees.
5. Most importantly, the position classification system became outdated and dysfunctional, causing rigidity and the underutilization of human talents.

Union-related problems, to the extent that they exist, are not a part of this list. Much of the protectionism (job security, keeping incompetent employees, resisting management decisions that may improve operations but reduce the number of employees) that the Bush administration objects to is largely the result of the unionization of the public service. But public unionization is a phenomenon that developed independently and came well after establishment of the civil service (about 80 years!). Unionization, as even its opponents acknowledge, results from bad management—worker resentment builds to the point that public employees do not feel their voice will be carried or understood by management. It is not the result of unhappiness over merit practices. Nor is unionization very far advanced in government—only 30 percent of government employees are unionized! A frequent tactic of civil service opponents is to confuse civil service with unionism, so as to use popular anti-union feeling to reduce support for the civil service. Whatever the arguments for and against unionization, and this is a complex debate that needs to be aired, this subject should be separated from the current discussion over the value of the civil service system.

In light of the problems that have developed over time, it is accurate to argue, as did President Carter when proposing broad reforms to civil service law in 1978, that the merit system does not always serve the merit principle. Unfortunately, Carter's attempts to reform the system did not go far enough to solve the problems. Position classification still dominates with the result that the development and flexible use of people is secondary. Cumbersome legal processes still control in the area of discipline and firing the incompetent.

On the other hand, much decentralization has occurred, innovations have appeared, and the merit system is less impaired by racial and sexual discrimination than it once was.

CIVIL SERVICE REFORM?

With this mixed record of success, is it wise to give up on civil service reform and to sacrifice the effort to sustain and improve a professional and public-spirited workforce more dedicated to service than to making money? Or do we continue to have faith in the original wisdom of the merit concept, recognize that political and economic realities have changed, and try to make reasonable reforms to correct the problems that are clear to most student-scholars of the system? The more reasonable view is that the greatest "inefficiencies" of government employment are rooted in causes other than excessive legalism or failure to adopt the market-driven ideals of the business sector. These inefficiencies are, principally, (1) the conflict and competition among branches of government that are written into the American Constitution and (2) the nature of hierarchical decision making found in bureaucratic structure. As these sources of inefficiency in government service are examined, we will find that the Homeland Security "super-department" approach and greater executive branch control make things worse, not better.

The constitutional system that we have erected in this country intentionally creates conflict among branches of government so as to promote separation of powers with the aim of preventing tyranny. Many of the rules placed upon the operations of public agencies are put there by the Congress to prevent abuse of power by the executive branch. Typically, these constraints are lessened during periods of national emergency and reimposed during more normal times. The purposes of these constraints are many, but they include, importantly, ensuring administrative functioning in line with legislative budget and program authorization, prevention of waste and fraud by executive branch managers, and protection of civil servants from arbitrary and unfair actions of executive branch managers undertaken for political reasons. Thus, many of the rules imbedded in civil service are not "meaningless," as the critics allege.

CIVIL SERVICE AND HOMELAND SECURITY

What stands in the path of abuse of power by the executive branch if the civil service is destroyed? "No one is advocating a return to the spoils system," says Howard, but the growth of an executive-dominated, entrepreneurial system of human resources creates the conditions for just such a result. Without civil service guarantees that protect against political patronage, what obstacle is there to awarding government contracts on the basis of political favoritism or ideological purity? How will management-labor committees emerge during an administration that is admittedly hostile to labor? What will prevent the creation of a professional contract monitoring process in which those government monitors guarding the public interest, usually underpaid relative to their private sector counterparts, must excel in their jobs and themselves enter the kind of legal wars that are supposedly making the civil service system so impossible?

Will "Christian values" be allowed to dictate hiring decisions at the expense of a knowledge of Muslim and Arabic needs and dynamics (imagine the value of enlisting the help of the American-Arab community, stimulating their patriotism and tapping into their knowledge of Arab languages)? Will undue reliance be placed on European and Israeli intelligence to the exclusion of Iranian and Saudi and Turkish intelligence? Will certain response units in the non-profit sector and state and local governments be underutilized because they bear Democratic Party associations or links to group causes like pro-choice or civil liberties? Are we to have homeland security provided by government contractors with Texas or with Massachusetts connections? Will contract recipients more likely be centered in important electoral states that the party in power hopes to influence? While executive leaders may not intend to weaken response networks, political agendas inevitably creep in and displace the original goals. "Government by contracting-out" is already attracting from its critics the label of "the new patronage" because of the tendency of contracts to flow in the direction of political friends and financial supporters.

Finally, the creation of a giant new department, with new levels of command authority and reporting, hugely increases the type of "big bureaucracy" that both parties have recognized as paralyzing to the type of inter-agency cooperation, flexibility, and quick decision making essential to linking information that the administration says it must have. House Democratic Whip Nancy Pelosi, the ranking Democrat on the Select Committee on Homeland Security, issued the following statement as debate ended on H.R. 5005, the Homeland Security Act:

> I had hoped that we could present to the American people a Department of Homeland Security that was lean and of the future, not a monstrous bureaucracy of the 1950s that would have been obsolete even then. I had hoped that this new lean department would, instead of size, have capitalized on the technological revolution in order to increase communication and coordination. I had hoped that the Secretary of Homeland Security could coordinate, rather than have to manage and administer staff.

Unfortunately, of course, Congress took a different course of action. Moreover, the General Accounting Office, which works for the Congress, declared it will take five to ten years for DHS to be up and running, after a startup cost of $4.5 billion.

Briefly put, the major problem that can be foreseen in the managing of homeland security is bureaucracy and hierarchical decision making, *not* civil service. The meaningful interaction among different units of the federal government, state and local government units, and non-governmental organizations (NGOs) such as the American Red Cross and veterans' organizations will be stifled in favor of rigid bureaucratic reporting procedures that cause delays and exclude many of these groups from participating in decision making. The twenty-six old agencies that make up the new department will continue to fight for control and a piece of the decision-making action that will be concentrated at the higher echelons of the DHS hierarchy. Congressional funds will go to the most effective lobbyists, and these will be centered within the DHS and exclude the multitude of state and local police departments, local hospital and emergency response centers, state health units and volunteer units so vital to "first response" who will remain uncoordinated.

The new department, despite its size and resources, still lacks the two agencies critical to real security, the Central Intelligence Agency (CIA) and the Federal Bureau of Investigation (FBI). These two agencies are the key organizations for gathering foreign intelligence and maintaining surveillance of terrorist organizations within the country, respectively. How does the reorganization help to bring these vital functions within a "more rational decision process"?

Although it is true that both political parties cooperated in passing the act, the only debate that occurred centered on civil service protection and unionism, and virtually nothing was said about whether the creation of a huge new bureaucracy, lacking essential components (i.e., CIA, FBI), was a good approach to solving problems of homeland security. Those who make a profession of thinking about these matters favored a "networking" approach to homeland security information collection and decision making, not bureaucracy. Coordination of the activities of all state and local governments and NGOs and decision making through consultation were preferred to hierarchical review. Apparently, neither party was prone to listen to or consider these arguments.

The Department of Homeland Security is not an efficient way to handle the national need for homeland security. It is this mindless approach to organizing through bureaucratization, and not the civil service with its proud tradition of political neutrality and competence, that is at fault. The stakes are high, and the nation is moving in the wrong direction.

 /diclerico10

Internet Resources

Visit our Web site at www.mhhe.com/diclerico10 for links and resources relating to Bureaucracy.

chapter 13

Courts

The Supreme Court and Judicial Review

*W*hile *few would question the Supreme Court's authority to interpret the Constitution, there has long been disagreement over how the nine justices should approach this awesome responsibility. This debate grew in intensity during the Reagan era as the president and his attorney general inveighed against the Supreme Court, charging that justices had all too often substituted their own values and principles for those contained in the Constitution.*

In the first selection, Edwin Meese, U.S. attorney general during part of the Reagan administration, calls upon judges to interpret the Constitution in accordance with the intent of those who wrote and ratified it. Insisting that the Founding Fathers expected as much from the members of the Supreme Court, Meese goes on to suggest how the justices should approach this task. He remains convinced that the application of original intent—undistorted by the personal values of well-meaning judges—will best preserve the principles of democratic government.

The second selection offers a markedly different perspective from someone who has had the responsibility of interpreting our Constitution. Irving Kaufman, formerly chief judge of the United States Court of Appeals for the Second Circuit, maintains that ascertaining the original intent of the Founding Fathers is decidedly more difficult than Edwin Meese would lead us to believe. Nor, for that matter, is the strict application of original intent necessarily desirable in every instance. This is not to say that judges are at liberty to read whatever they choose into the wording of our Constitution, and Kaufman points to several factors that serve to restrain judges from doing so.

A Jurisprudence of Original Intention
Edwin Meese III

. . . Today I would like to discuss further the meaning of constitutional fidelity. In particular, I would like to describe in more detail this administration's approach.

Before doing so, I would like to make a few commonplace observations about the original document itself. . . .

The period surrounding the creation of the Constitution is not a dark and mythical realm. The young America of the 1780s and '90s was a vibrant place, alive with pamphlets, newspapers, and books chronicling and commenting upon the great issues of the day. We know how the Founding Fathers lived, and much of what they read, thought, and believed. The disputes and compromises of the Constitutional Convention were carefully recorded. The minutes of the convention are a matter of public record. Several of the most important participants—including James Madison, the "father" of the Constitution—wrote comprehensive accounts of the convention. Others, Federalists and Anti-Federalists alike, committed their arguments for and against ratification, as well as their understandings of the Constitution, to paper, so that their ideas and conclusions could be widely circulated, read, and understood.

In short, the Constitution is not buried in the mists of time. We know a tremendous amount of the history of its genesis. . . .

With these thoughts in mind, I would like to discuss the administration's approach to constitutional interpretation. . . .

Our approach . . . begins with the document itself. The plain fact is, it exists. It is something that has been written down. Walter Berns of the American Enterprise Institute has noted that the central object of American constitutionalism was "the effort" of the Founders "to express fundamental governmental arrangements in a legal document—to 'get it in writing.'"

Indeed, judicial review has been grounded in the fact that the Constitution is a written, as opposed to an unwritten, document. In *Marbury v. Madison* John Marshall rested his rationale for judicial review on the fact that we have a written constitution with meaning that is binding upon judges. "[I]t is apparent," he wrote, "that the framers of the Constitution contemplated that instrument as a rule for the government of *courts*, as well as of the legislature. Why otherwise does it direct the judges to take an oath to support it?"

Edwin Meese III served as U.S. Attorney General under President Ronald Reagan. Excerpted from a speech by Attorney General Meese before the Washington, D.C., chapter of the Federal Society, Lawyers Division, November 15, 1985, pp. 2–14.

The presumption of a written document is that it conveys meaning. As Thomas Grey of the Stanford Law School has said, it makes "relatively definite and explicit what otherwise would be relatively indefinite and tacit."

We know that those who framed the Constitution chose their words carefully. They debated at great length the most minute points. The language they chose meant something. They proposed, they substituted, they edited, and they carefully revised. Their words were studied with equal care by state ratifying conventions.

This is not to suggest that there was unanimity among the framers and ratifiers on all points. The Constitution and the Bill of Rights, and some of the subsequent amendments, emerged after protracted debate. Nobody got everything they wanted. What's more, the framers were not clairvoyants—they could not foresee every issue that would be submitted for judicial review. Nor could they predict how all foreseeable disputes would be resolved under the Constitution. But the point is, the meaning of the Constitution can be known.

What does this written Constitution mean? In places it is exactingly specific. Where it says that Presidents of the United States must be at least 35 years of age it means exactly that. (I have not heard of any claim that 35 means 30 or 25 or 20.) Where it specifies how the House and Senate are to be organized, it means what it says.

The Constitution also expresses particular principles. One is the right to be free of an unreasonable search or seizure. Another concerns religious liberty. Another is the right to equal protection of the laws.

Those who framed these principles meant something by them. And the meanings can be found. The Constitution itself is also an expression of certain general principles. These principles reflect the deepest purpose of the Constitution—that of establishing a political system through which Americans can best govern themselves consistent with the goal of securing liberty.

The text and structure of the Constitution is instructive. It contains very little in the way of specific political solutions. It speaks volumes on how problems should be approached, and by *whom*. For example, the first three articles set out clearly the scope and limits of three distinct branches of national government. The powers of each being carefully and specifically enumerated. In this scheme it is no accident to find the legislative branch described first, as the framers had fought and sacrificed to secure the right of democratic self-governance. Naturally, this faith in republicanism was not unbounded, as the next two articles make clear.

Yet the Constitution remains a document of powers and principles. And its undergirding premise remains that democratic self government is subject only to the limits of certain constitutional principles. This respect for the political process was made explicit early on. When John Marshall upheld the act of Congress chartering a national bank in *McCulloch v. Maryland* he wrote: "The Constitution [was] intended to endure for ages to come, and, consequently, to be adapted to the various crises of human affairs." But to use McCulloch, as some have tried, as support for the idea that the Constitution is a protean, changeable thing is to stand history on its head. Marshall was keeping faith with the original intention that Congress be free to elaborate and apply constitutional powers and principles. He was not saying that the Court must invent some new constitutional value in order to keep pace with the times. In Walter Berns's words: "Marshall's meaning is not that the Constitution may be adapted to the 'various crises of human affairs,' but that the legislative powers granted by the Constitution are adaptable to meet these crises."

The approach this administration advocates is rooted in the text of the Constitution as illuminated by those who drafted, proposed, and ratified it. In his famous Commentary on the Constitution of the United States Justice Joseph Story explained that:

> The first and fundamental rule in the interpretation of all instruments is, to construe them according to the sense of the terms, and the intention of the parties.

Our approach understands the significance of a written document and seeks to discern the particular and general principles it expresses. It recognizes that there may be debate at times over the application of these principles. But it does not mean these principles cannot be identified.

Constitutional adjudication is obviously not a mechanical process. It requires an appeal to reason and discretion. The text and intention of the Constitution must be understood to constitute the banks within which constitutional interpretation must flow. As James Madison said, if "the sense in which the Constitution was accepted and ratified by the nation . . . be not the guide in expounding it, there can be no security for a consistent and stable, more than for a faithful exercise of its powers."

Thomas Jefferson, so often cited incorrectly as a framer of the Constitution, in fact shared Madison's view: "Our peculiar security is in the possession of a written Constitution. Let us not make it a blank paper by construction."

Jefferson was even more explicit in his personal correspondence:

> On every question of construction [we should] carry ourselves back to the time, when the constitution was adopted; recollect the spirit manifested in the debates; and instead of trying [to find] what meaning may be squeezed out of the text, or invented against it, conform to the probable one, in which it was passed.

In the main a jurisprudence that seeks to be faithful to our Constitution—a jurisprudence of original intention, as I have called it—is not difficult to describe. Where the language of the Constitution is specific, it must be obeyed. Where there is a demonstrable consensus among the framers and ratifiers as to a principle stated or implied by the Constitution, it should be followed. Where there is ambiguity as to the precise meaning or reach of a constitutional provision, it should be interpreted and applied in a manner so as to at least not contradict the text of the Constitution itself.

Sadly, while almost everyone participating in the current constitutional debate would give assent to these propositions, the techniques and conclusions of some of the debaters do violence to them. What is the source of this violence? In large part I believe that it is the misuse of history stemming from the neglect of the idea of a written constitution.

There is a frank proclamation by some judges and commentators that what matters most about the Constitution is not its words but its so-called "spirit." These individuals focus less on the language of specific provisions than on what they describe as the "vision" or "concepts of human dignity" they find embodied in the Constitution. This approach to jurisprudence has led to some remarkable and tragic conclusions.

In the 1850s, the Supreme Court under Chief Justice Roger B. Taney read blacks out of the Constitution in order to invalidate Congress's attempt to limit the spread of slavery. The *Dred Scott* decision, famously described as a judicial "self-inflicted wound," helped bring on civil war.

There is a lesson in this history. There is danger in seeing the Constitution as an empty vessel into which each generation may pour its passion and prejudice.

Our own time has its own fashions and passions. In recent decades many have come to view the Constitution—more accurately, part of the Constitution, provisions of the Bill of Rights and the Fourteenth Amendment—as a charter for judicial activism on behalf of various constituencies. Those who hold this view often have lacked demonstrable textual or historical support for their conclusions. Instead they have "grounded" their rulings in appeals to social theories, to moral philosophies or personal notions of human dignity, or to "penumbras," somehow emanating ghostlike from various provisions—identified and not identified—in the Bill of Rights. The problem with this approach, as John Hart Ely, Dean of the Stanford Law School, has observed with respect to one such decision, is not that it is bad constitutional law, but that it is not constitutional law in any meaningful sense, at all.

Despite this fact, the perceived popularity of some results in particular cases has encouraged some observers to believe that any critique of the methodology of those decisions is an attack on the results. This perception is sufficiently widespread that it deserves an answer. My answer is to look at history.

When the Supreme Court, in *Brown v. Board of Education,* sounded the death knell for official segregation in the country, it earned all the plaudits it received. But the Supreme Court in that case was not giving new life to old words, or adapting a "living," "flexible" Constitution to new reality. It was restoring the original principle of the Constitution to constitutional law. The *Brown* Court was correcting the damage done 50 years earlier, when in *Plessy v. Ferguson* an earlier Supreme Court had disregarded the clear intent of the framers of the Civil War amendments to eliminate the legal degradation of blacks, and had contrived a theory of the Constitution to support the charade of "separate but equal" discrimination.

Similarly, the decisions of the New Deal and beyond that freed Congress to regulate commerce and enact a plethora of social legislation were not judicial adaptations of the Constitution to new realities. They were in fact removals of encrustations of earlier courts that had strayed from the original intent of the framers regarding the power of the legislature to make policy.

It is amazing how so much of what passes for social and political progress is really the undoing of old judicial mistakes.

Mistakes occur when the principles of specific constitutional provisions—such as those contained in the Bill of Rights—are taken by some as invitations to read into the Constitution values that contradict the clear language of other provisions.

Acceptances to this illusory invitation have proliferated in recent decades. One Supreme Court justice identified the proper judicial standard as asking "what's best for this country." Another said it is important to "keep the Court out in front" of the general society. Various academic commentators have poured rhetorical grease on this judicial fire, suggesting that constitutional interpretation appropriately be guided by such standards as whether a public policy "personifies justice" or "comports with the notion of moral evolution" or confers "an identity" upon our society or was consistent with "natural ethical law" or was consistent with some "right of equal citizenship."

Unfortunately, as I've noted, navigation by such lodestars has in the past given us questionable economics, governmental disorder, and racism—all in the guise of constitutional law. Recently one of the distinguished judges of one of our federal appeals courts got it about right when he wrote: "The truth is that the judge who looks outside the Constitution always looks inside himself and nowhere else." Or, as we recently put it before the Supreme Court in an important brief: "The further afield interpretation travels from its point of departure in the text, the greater the danger that constitutional adjudication will be like a picnic to which the framers bring the words and the judges the meaning."

In the *Osborne v. Bank of United States* decision 21 years after *Marbury,* Chief Justice Marshall further elaborated his view of the relationship between the judge and the law, be it statutory or constitutional:

> Judicial power, as contradistinguished from the power of the laws, has no existence. Courts are the mere instruments of the law, and can will nothing. When they are said to exercise a discretion, it is a mere legal discretion, a discretion to be exercised in discerning the course prescribed by law; and, when that is discerned, it is the duty of the Court to follow it.

Any true approach to constitutional interpretation must respect the document in all its parts and be faithful to the Constitution in its entirety.

What must be remembered in the current debate is that interpretation does not imply results. The framers were not trying to anticipate every answer. They were trying to create a tripartite national government, within a federal system, that would have the flexibility to adapt to face new exigencies—as it did, for example, in chartering a national bank. Their great interest was in the distribution of power and responsibility in order to secure the great goal of liberty for all.

A jurisprudence that seeks fidelity to the Constitution—a jurisprudence of original intention—is not a jurisprudence of political results. It is very much concerned with process, and it is a jurisprudence that in our day seeks to depoliticize the law. The great genius of the constitutional blueprint is found in its creation and respect for spheres of authority and the limits it places on governmental power. In this scheme the framers did not see the courts as the exclusive custodians of the Constitution. Indeed, because the document posits so few conclusions it leaves to the more political branches the matter of adapting and vivifying its principles in each generation. It also leaves to the people of the states, in the Tenth Amendment, those responsibilities and rights not committed to federal care. The power to declare acts of Congress and laws of the states null and void is truly awesome. This power must be used when the Constitution clearly speaks. It should not be used when the Constitution does not.

In *Marbury v. Madison,* at the same time he vindicated the concept of judicial review, Marshall wrote that the "principles" of the Constitution "are deemed fundamental and permanent," and except for formal amendment, "unchangeable." If we want a change in our Constitution or in our laws we must seek it through the formal mechanisms presented in that organizing document of our government.

In summary, I would emphasize that what is at issue here is not an agenda of issues or a menu of results. At issue is a way of government. A jurisprudence based on first principles is neither conservative nor liberal, neither right nor left. It is a jurisprudence that cares about committing and limiting to each organ of government the proper ambit of its responsibilities. It is a jurisprudence faithful to our Constitution.

By the same token, an activist jurisprudence, one which anchors the Constitution only in the consciences of jurists, is a chameleon jurisprudence, changing color and form in each era. The same activism hailed today may threaten the capacity for decision through democratic consensus tomorrow, as it has in many yesterdays. Ultimately, as the early democrats wrote into the Massachusetts state constitution, the best defense of our liberties is a government of laws and not men.

On this point it is helpful to recall the words of the late Justice Frankfurter. As he wrote:

> [T]here is not under our Constitution a judicial remedy for every political mischief, for every undesirable exercise of legislative power. The framers carefully and with deliberate forethought refused so to enthrone the judiciary. In this situation, as in others of like nature, appeal for relief does not belong here. Appeal must be to an informed, civically militant electorate. . . .

What Did the Founding Fathers Intend?
Irving R. Kaufman

. . . In the ongoing debate over original intent, almost all federal judges hold to the notion that judicial decisions should be based on the text of the Constitution or the structure it creates. Yet, in requiring judges to be guided solely by the expressed views of the framers, current advocates of original intent seem to call for a narrower concept. Jurists who disregard this interpretation, the argument runs, act lawlessly because they are imposing their own moral standards and political preferences on the community.

As a federal judge, I have found it often difficult to ascertain the "intent of the framers," and even more problematic to try to dispose of a constitutional question by giving great weight to the intent argument. Indeed, even if it were possible to decide hard cases on the basis of a strict interpretation of original intent, or originalism, that methodology would conflict with a judge's duty to apply the Constitution's underlying principles to changing circumstances. Furthermore, by attempting to erode the base for judicial affirmation of the freedoms guaranteed by the Bill of Rights and the 14th Amendment (no state shall "deprive any person of life, liberty, or property without due process of law; nor deny to any person . . . the equal protection of the laws"), the intent theory threatens some of the greatest achievements of the Federal judiciary.

Ultimately, the debate centers on the nature of judicial review, or the power of courts to act as the ultimate arbiters of constitutional meaning. This responsibility has been acknowledged ever since the celebrated 1803 case of *Marbury v. Madison*, in which Chief Justice John Marshall struck down a congressional grant of jurisdiction to the Supreme Court not authorized by Article III of the Constitution. But here again, originalists would accept judicial review only if it adhered to the allegedly neutral principles embalmed in historical intent.

In the course of 36 years on the federal bench, I have had to make many difficult constitutional interpretations. I have had to determine whether a teacher could wear a black armband as a protest against the Vietnam War; whether newspapers have a nonactionable right to report accusatory statements; and whether a school system might be guilty of de facto segregation. Unfortunately, the framers' intentions are not made sufficiently clear to provide easy answers.

Irving R. Kaufman (1910–1992) was a judge of the 2d U.S. Circuit Court of Appeals. From Irving R. Kaufman, "What Did the Founding Fathers Intend?" as it appeared in *The New York Times Magazine*, February 23, 1986, pp. 59–69.

A judge must first determine what the intent was (or would have been)—a notoriously formidable task.

An initial problem is the paucity of materials. Both the official minutes of the Philadelphia Convention of 1787 and James Madison's famous notes of the proceedings, published in 1840, tend toward the terse and cursory, especially in relation to the judiciary. The congressional debates over the proposed Bill of Rights, which became effective in 1791, are scarcely better. Even Justice William Rehnquist, one of the most articulate spokesmen for original intent, admitted in a recent dissent in a case concerning school prayer that the legislative history behind the provision against the establishment of an official religion "does not seem particularly illuminating."

One source deserves special mention. *The Federalist Papers*—the series of essays written by Alexander Hamilton, James Madison and John Jay in 1787 and 1788—have long been esteemed as the earliest constitutional commentary. In 1825, for example, Thomas Jefferson noted that The *Federalist* was regularly appealed to "as evidence of the general opinion of those who framed and of those who accepted the Constitution of the United States."

The *Federalist,* however, did not discuss the Bill of Rights or the Civil War amendments, which were yet to be written. Moreover, the essays were part of a political campaign—the authors wrote them in support of New York's ratification of the Constitution. The essays, therefore, tended to enunciate general democratic theory or rebut anti-Federalist arguments, neither of which offers much help to modern jurists. (In light of the following passage from *The Federalist,* No. 14, I believe Madison would be surprised to find his words of 200 years ago deciding today's cases: "Is it not the glory of the people of America that . . . they have not suffered a blind veneration for antiquity . . . to overrule the suggestions of their own good sense . . . ?")

Another problem with original intent is this: Who were the framers? Generally, they are taken to be the delegates to the Philadelphia Convention and the congressional sponsors of subsequent amendments. All constitutional provisions, however, have been ratified by state conventions or legislatures on behalf of the people they represented. Is the relevant intention, then, that of the drafters, the ratifiers or the general populace?

The elusiveness of the framers' intent leads to another, more telling problem. Originalist doctrine presumes that intent can be discovered by historical sleuthing or psychological rumination. In fact, this is not possible. Judges are constantly required to resolve questions that 18th-century statesmen, no matter how prescient, simply could not or did not foresee and resolve. On most issues, to look for a collective intention held by either drafters or ratifiers is to hunt for a chimera.

A reading of the Constitution highlights this problem. The principles of our great charter are cast in grand, yet cryptic, phrases. Accordingly, judges usually confront what Justice Robert Jackson in the 1940s termed the "majestic generalities" of the Bill of Rights, or the terse commands of "due process of law," or "equal protection" contained in the 14th Amendment. The use of such open-ended provisions would indicate that the framers did not want the

Constitution to become a straitjacket on all events for all times. In contrast, when the framers held a clear intention, they did not mince words. Article II, for example, specifies a minimum Presidential age of 35 years instead of merely requiring "maturity" or "adequate age."

The First Amendment is a good example of a vaguer provision. In guaranteeing freedom of the press, some of our forefathers perhaps had specific thoughts on what publications fell within its purview. Some historians believe, in light of Colonial debates, that the main concern of the framers was to prevent governmental licensing of newspapers. If that were all the First Amendment meant today, then many important decisions protecting the press would have to be overruled. One of them would be the landmark *New York Times v. Sullivan* ruling of 1964, giving the press added protection in libel cases brought by public figures. Another would be *Near v. Minnesota*, a case involving Jay Near, a newspaper publisher who had run afoul of a Minnesota statute outlawing "malicious, scandalous and defamatory" publications. The Supreme Court struck down the statute in 1931, forbidding governmental prior restraints on publication; this ruling was the precursor of the 1971 Pentagon Papers decision.

The Founding Fathers focused not on particularities but on principles, such as the need in a democracy for people to engage in free and robust discourse. James Madison considered a popular government without popular information a "Prologue to a Farce or a Tragedy." Judges, then, must focus on underlying principles when going about their delicate duty of applying the First Amendment's precepts to today's world.

In fact, our nation's first debate over constitutional interpretation centered on grand principles. Angered at John Adams's Federalist Administration, advocates of states' rights in the late 18th century argued that original intent meant that the Constitution, like the Articles of Confederation, should be construed narrowly—as a compact among separate sovereigns. The 1798 Virginia and Kentucky Resolutions, which sought to reserve to the states the power of ultimate constitutional interpretation, were the most extreme expressions of this view. In rejecting this outlook, a nationalistic Supreme Court construed the Constitution more broadly.

The important point here is that neither side of this debate looked to the stated views of the framers to resolve the issue. Because of his leading role at the Philadelphia Convention, Madison's position is especially illuminating. "Whatever veneration might be entertained for the body of men who formed our Constitution," he declaimed on the floor of Congress in 1796, "the sense of that body could never be regarded as the oracular guide in expounding the Constitution."

Yet, I doubt if strict proponents of original intent will be deterred by such considerations. Their goal is not to venerate dead framers but to restrain living judges from imposing their own values. This restraint is most troublesome when it threatens the protection of individual rights against governmental encroachment.

According to current constitutional doctrine, the due process clause of the 14th Amendment incorporates key provisions of the Bill of Rights, which keeps in check only the Federal Government. Unless the due process clause is construed to include the most important parts of the first eight amendments in the Bill of Rights, then the states would be free, in theory, to establish an official church or inflict cruel and unusual punishments. This doctrine is called incorporation.

Aside from the late Justice Hugo Black, few have believed that history alone is a sufficient basis for applying the Bill of Rights to the states. In his Georgetown University address, Justice Brennan noted that the crucial liberties embodied in the Bill of Rights are so central to our national identity that we cannot imagine any definition of "liberty" without them.

In fact, a cramped reading of the Bill of Rights jeopardizes what I regard as the true original intent—the rationale for having a written Constitution at all. The principal reason for a charter was to restrain government. In 1787, the idea of a fundamental law set down in black and white was revolutionary. Hanoverian England in the 18th century did not have a fully written, unified constitution, having long believed in a partially written one, based on ancient custom and grants from the Crown like the Magna Carta. To this day, the British have kept their democracy alive without one. In theory, the "King-in-Parliament" was and is unlimited in sovereign might, and leading political theorists, such as Thomas Hobbes and John Locke, agreed that governments, once established by a social contract, could not then be fettered.

Although not a Bill of Rights, the Magna Carta—King John's concessions to his barons in 1215—was symbolic of the notion that even the Crown was not all-powerful. Moreover, certain judges believed that Parliament, like the king, had to respect the traditions of the common law. This staunch belief in perpetual rights, in turn, was an important spark for the Revolutionary conflagration of 1776.

In gaining independence, Americans formed the bold concept that sovereignty continually resided with the people, who cede power to governments only to achieve certain specific ends. This view dominated the Philadelphia Convention. Instead of merely improving on the Articles of Confederation, as they had been directed to do, the framers devised a government where certain powers—defined and thereby limited—flowed from the people to the Congress, the President and the Federal judiciary.

Alexander Hamilton recognized that the basic tenets of this scheme mandated judicial review. Individual rights, he observed in *The Federalist,* No. 78, "can be preserved in practice no other way than through the medium of courts of justice, whose duty it must be to declare all acts contrary to the manifest tenor of the Constitution void." Through a written constitution and judicial enforcement, the framers intended to preserve the inchoate rights they had lost as Englishmen.

The narrow interpretation of original intent is especially unfortunate because I doubt that many of its proponents are in favor of freeing the states from the constraints of the Bill of Rights. In fact, I believe the concern of many modern "intentionalists" is quite specific: outrage over the right-of-privacy cases, especially *Roe v. Wade,* the 1973 Supreme Court decision recognizing a woman's right to an abortion. (The right of privacy, of course, is not mentioned in the Constitution.) Whether one agrees with this controversial decision or not, I would submit that concern over the outcome of one difficult case is not sufficient cause to embrace a theory that calls for so many changes in existing law. . . .

. . . [I]f original intent is an uncertain guide, does some other, more functional approach to interpreting the Constitution exist?

One suggestion is to emphasize the importance of democratic "process." As John Hart Ely, dean of the Stanford Law School forcefully advocates, this approach would direct the courts to make a distinction between "process" (the rules of the game, so to speak) and "substance" (the results of the game). Laws dealing with process include those affecting voting rights or participation in society; the Supreme Court correctly prohibited segregation, for example, because it imposed on blacks the continuing stigma of slavery. Judges, however, would not have the power to review the substantive decisions of elected officials, such as the distribution of welfare benefits.

Basically, such an approach makes courts the guardians of democracy, but a focus on process affords little help when judges decide between difficult and competing values. Judicial formulation of a democratic vision, for example, requires substantive decision-making. The dignities of human liberty enshrined in the Bill of Rights are not merely a means to an end, even so noble an end as democratic governance. For example, we cherish freedom of speech not only because it is necessary for meaningful elections, but also for its own sake.

The truth is that no litmus test exists by which judges can confidently and consistently measure the constitutionality of their decisions. Notwithstanding the clear need for judicial restraint, judges do not constitute what Prof. Raoul Berger, a retired Harvard Law School fellow, has termed an "imperial judiciary." I would argue that the judicial process itself limits the reach of a jurist's arm.

First, judges do not and cannot deliberately contravene specific constitutional rules or clear indications of original intent. No one would seriously argue or expect, for instance, that the Supreme Court could or would twist the Presidential minimum-age provision into a call for "sufficient maturity," so as to forbid the seating of a 36-year-old.

I doubt, in any event, that federal judges would ever hear such a question. The Constitution limits our power to traditional "cases" and "controversies" capable of judicial resolution. In cases like the hypothetical one regarding the presidential age, the High Court employs doctrines of standing (proving injury) and "political question" to keep citizens from suing merely out of a desire to have the government run a certain way.

Moreover, the issues properly before a judge are not presented on a *tabula rasa.* Even the vaguest constitutional provisions have received the judicial gloss of prior decisions. Precedent alone, of course, should not preserve clearly erroneous decisions; the abhorrent "separate but equal" doctrine survived for more than 50 years before the Warren Court struck it down in 1954.

The conventions of our judicial system also limit a jurist's ability to impose his or her own will. One important restraint, often overlooked, is the tradition that appellate judges issue written opinions. That is, we must support our decisions with reasons instead of whims and indicate how our constitutional rulings relate to the document. A written statement is open to the dissent of colleagues, possible review by a higher court and the judgment, sometimes scathing, of legal scholars.

In addition, the facts of a given case play a pivotal role. Facts delineate the reach of a legal decision and remind us of the "cases and controversies" requirement. Our respect for such ground rules reassures the public that, even in the most controversial case, the outcome is not just a political ruling.

Judges are also mindful that the ultimate justification for their power is public acceptance—acceptance not of every decision, but of the role they play. Without popular support, the power of judicial review would have been eviscerated by political forces long ago.

Lacking the power of the purse or the sword, the courts must rely on the elected branches to enforce their decisions. The school desegregation cases would have been a dead letter unless President Eisenhower had been willing to order out the National Guard—in support of a decision authored by a Chief Justice, Earl Warren, whose appointment the President had called "the biggest damned-fool mistake I ever made."

Instead of achieving the purple of philosopher-kings, an unprincipled judiciary would risk becoming modern King Canutes, with the cold tide of political reality and popular opprobrium lapping at their robes.

My revered predecessor on the Court of Appeals, Judge Learned Hand, remarked in a lecture at Harvard in the late 1950s that he would not want to be ruled by "a bevy of Platonic Guardians." The Constitution balances the danger of judicial abuse against the threat of a temporary majority trampling individual rights. The current debate is a continuation of an age-old, and perhaps endless, struggle to reach a balance between our commitments to democracy and to the rule of law. . . .

Judicial Selection

*T*he *U.S. Constitution empowers presidents of the United States to appoint individu-*
als to serve on the federal courts, provided they secure the consent of the Senate. It
should occasion no surprise that this division of power creates the potential for conflict
between the two branches. Over the course of our history, presidents have in fact had
some of their most bitter fights with the Senate over who should serve on the highest
court in the land. Witness, for example, Ronald Reagan's failed attempt to appoint
Robert Bork to the U.S. Supreme Court in 1987—a confrontation that left a residue of
ill will between the two parties—and George Bush's successful but similarly bruising
battle to place Clarence Thomas there four years later.

With the atmosphere in Washington having grown decidedly more partisan in
recent years, some have voiced concern that senators' votes on federal court nominees
are being determined more and more by political considerations, and less and less by
qualifications for the office. In the first article, John Eastman and Timothy Sandefur
give voice to this concern, charging that liberal senators are employing an ideological
litmus test for prospective court nominees, viewing favorably those who share their
expansive view of the Constitution, while declining to support those espousing a more
conservative and restrictive judicial philosophy. By doing so, Eastman and Sandefur
maintain, these senators are not only violating the expressed intent of the Founding
Fathers, but also seriously compromising the principle of separation of powers.

Erwin Chemerinsky, author of the second selection, totally disagrees. He insists
that presidents and senators have always factored ideology into their decisions on nom-
inees for the courts, and offers a number of reasons why it is wholly appropriate for
them to do so.

The Senate Is Supposed to Advise and Consent, Not Obstruct and Delay
John C. Eastman and Timothy Sandefur

I. THE FRAMERS OF THE CONSTITUTION ASSIGNED TO THE PRESIDENT THE PRE-EMINENT ROLE IN APPOINTING JUDGES

Article II of the Constitution provides that the President "shall nominate, and by and with the Advice and Consent of the Senate, shall appoint . . . Judges of the supreme Court [and such inferior courts as the Congress may from time to time ordain and establish]."[1] As the text of the provision makes explicitly clear, the power to choose nominees—to "nominate"—is vested solely in the President,[2] and the President also has the primary role to "appoint," albeit with the advice and consent of the Senate. The text of the clause itself thus demonstrates that the role envisioned for the Senate was a much more limited one than is currently being claimed.

The lengthy debates over the clause in the Constitutional Convention support this reading. According to Madison's notes, an initial proposal on July 18, 1787, to place the appointment power in the Senate was opposed because, as Massachusetts delegate Nathaniel Ghorum noted, "even that branch [was] too numerous, and too little personally responsible, to ensure a good choice."[3] Ghorum suggested instead that Judges be appointed by the President with the advice and consent of the Senate, as had long been the method successfully followed in his home state. James Wilson and Governeur Morris of Pennsylvania, two of the Convention's leading figures, agreed with Ghorum and moved that judges be appointed by the President.

In contrast, Luther Martin of Maryland and Roger Sherman of Connecticut argued in favor of the initial proposal, contending that the Senate should have the power because, "[b]eing taken fro[m] all the States it [would] be best informed of the characters & most capable of making a fit choice."[4] And

John C. Eastman is an associate professor, Chapman University School of Law, and Director, The Claremont Institute Center for Constitutional Jurisprudence. He formerly served as a law clerk to the Honorable Clarence Thomas, Associate Justice, Supreme Court of the United States. Timothy Sandefur is a contributing editor of *Liberty* magazine and articles editor of *NEXUS*. This article is from John C. Eastman and Timothy Sandefur, "The Senate Is Supposed to Advise and Consent, Not Obstruct and Delay," *NEXUS: A Journal of Opinion*, 7 (2002), pp. 11–25. Notes have been renumbered to correspond to edited text. Reprinted by permission.

Virginia's George Mason argued that the President should not have the power to appoint judges because (among other reasons) the President "would insensibly form local & personal attachments . . . that would deprive equal merit elsewhere, of an equal chance of promotion."[5]

Ghorum replied to Mason's objection by noting that the senators were at least equally likely to "form their attachments."[6] Giving the power to the President would at least mean that he "will be responsible in point of character at least" for his choices, and would therefore "be careful to look through all the States for proper characters." For him, the problem with placing the appointment power in the Senate was that "Public bodies feel no personal responsibility, and give full play to intrigue & cabal,"[7] while if the appointment power were given to the President alone, "the Executive would certainly be more answerable for a good appointment, as the whole blame of a bad one would fall on him alone."[8]

Seeking a compromise, James Madison suggested that the power of appointment be given to the President with the Senate able to veto that choice by a 2/3 vote.[9] Another compromise was suggested by Edmund Randolph, who "thought the advantage of personal responsibility might be gained in the Senate by requiring the respective votes of the members to be entered on the Journal."[10] These compromises were defeated, however, and the vote on Ghorum's motion—that the President nominate and with the advice and consent of the Senate, should appoint—resulted in a 4–4 tie.[11] The discussion was then postponed.

When the appointment power was taken up again on July 21, the delegates returned to their previous arguments. One side argued that the President should be solely responsible for the appointments, because he would be less likely to be swayed by "partisanship"—what Madison's generation called "faction"[12]— than the Senate. The other side opposed vesting the appointment power in the President for a similar reason: he would not know as many qualified candidates as the Senate would, and might still be swayed by personal considerations or nepotism. . . .

In the end, the Convention agreed that the President would make the nominations, and the Senate would have a limited power to withhold confirmation as a check against political patronage or nepotism. Governeur Morris put the decision succinctly: "as the President was to nominate, there would be responsibility, and as the Senate was to concur, there would be security."[13] As the Supreme Court subsequently recognized, "the Framers anticipated that the President would be less vulnerable to interest-group pressure and personal favoritism than would a collective body."[14] No one argued that the Senate's participation in the process should include second-guessing the judicial philosophy of the President's nominees or attempting to mold that philosophy itself. Indeed, such a suggestion was routinely rejected as presenting a dangerous violation of the separation of powers, by allowing the Senate to control the President's choices and, ultimately, intrude upon the judiciary. . . .

In short, by assigning the sole power to nominate (and the primary power to appoint) judges to the President, the Convention specifically rejected a more expansive Senate role; such would undermine the President's responsibility, and far from providing security against improper appointments, would actually lead to the very kind of cabal-like behavior that the Convention delegates feared. . . .

II. THE CURRENT STATE OF THE CONFIRMATION POWER

Despite the original understanding of the Senate's limited role in the confirmation process . . . the Senate today appears bent on using its limited confirmation power to impose ideological litmus on presidential nominees and even to force the President to nominate judges preferred by individual senators, thus arrogating to itself the nomination as well as the confirmation power.

The Senate's expanded use of its confirmation power should perhaps come as no surprise. As a result of the growing role of the judiciary—and of government in general—in the lives of Americans today, the Senate's part in the nomination process has become a powerful political tool, and, like all powerful political tools, it is the subject of a strenuous competition among interest groups every time the President seeks to fill a judicial vacancy. Moreover, it is a tool that poses grave dangers to our constitutional system of government. In its current manifestation, the Senate's ideological use of the confirmation power threatens the separation of powers by undermining the responsibility for appointments given to the President, by demanding of judicial nominees a commitment to a role not appropriate to the courts, and, perhaps most importantly, by threatening the independence of the judiciary.

The reason that some senators are so intent on delving into the judicial philosophy of nominees is deeply connected to their view of the proper role of the judiciary in American government. Viewing the Constitution as a "living document," modern-day liberals see the Court as a place where the Constitution is stretched, shaped, cut, and rewritten in order to put in place so-called "progressive" policies that could never emerge from the legislative process. . . .

Judicial ideology is therefore critically important to modern-day liberals because an honest reading of the Constitution reveals that it is incompatible with their scheme of government. Senator Charles Schumer of New York, for example, has been quite candid in acknowledging that his opposition to President Bush's judicial nominees is based on the fact that they respect and will enforce the Constitution's limitations on the power of Congress. "Elected officials," Sen. Schumer told the press on May 9, 2002,

> should get the benefit of the doubt with respect to policy judgments and courts should not reach out to impose their will over that of elected legislatures. . . . Many of us on our side of the aisle are acutely concerned with the new limits that are now developing on our power to address the problems of those who elect us to serve—these decisions affect, in a fundamental way, our ability to address major national issues like discrimination against the disabled and the aged, protecting the environment, and combating gun violence.[15]

This is not to say that ideology should never play a role in the confirmation process. Some ideologically-based views render it impossible for a nominee who holds them to fulfill his oath of office. Consider, for instance, Judge Harry

Pregerson, who, when he was nominated to the Court of Appeals for the Ninth Circuit by President Carter, was asked whether he would follow his conscience or the law, if the two came into conflict. "I would follow my conscience," he replied.[16] That statement, grounded in Pregerson's own ideology, should easily have been grounds for disqualification, yet Pregerson was not only confirmed to the bench, but roundly praised for this statement, despite the fact that it threatens to undermine the very essence of constitutionalism and the rule of law.[17]

Contrast this with Justice Antonin Scalia, who in a recent speech said that he was glad the Pope had not declared the Catholic Church's opposition to the death penalty a matter of infallible Church doctrine, because if the Pope had done so, Justice Scalia would, as a practicing and committed Catholic, feel compelled to resign, unable to abide by his oath to enforce the law. In his view,

> the choice for the judge who believes the death penalty to be immoral is resignation, rather than simply ignoring duly enacted constitutional laws and sabotaging death penalty cases. He has, after all, taken an oath to apply the laws and has been given no power to supplant them with rules of his own. . . . This dilemma, of course, need not be confronted by a proponent of the "living Constitution," who believes that it means what it ought to mean. If the death penalty is (in his view) immoral, then it is (hey, presto!) automatically unconstitutional, and he can continue to sit while nullifying a sanction that has been imposed, with no suggestion of its unconstitutionality, since the beginning of the Republic. (You can see why the "living Constitution" has such attraction for us judges.)[18]

Ideology understood in this light is of course relevant in selecting a judicial nominee. Broadly understood, "ideology" would encompass a nominee's honor and character, which are necessary to fulfill the oath of office.[19] A nominee who for ideological reasons cannot "support and defend the Constitution of the United States"—say, an agent working for the Taliban—would be unfit for office because he would lack the *qualifications* necessary for the position. In fact, although we tend to take the concept of an oath lightly today, James Madison wrote that under the Constitution, "*the concurrence of the Senate chosen by the State Legislatures, in appointing the Judges, and the oaths and official tenures of these, with the surveillance of public Opinion,* [would be] relied on as *guarantying their impartiality.* . . ."[20] This is very different than demanding of a nominee that he toe the line of leftist jurisprudence.

Today, senators inquire into a nominee's ideology for precisely the opposite reason: to ensure that the nominee will *not* abide by the Constitution— to ensure that he will stretch and bend the Constitution in the directions that the senator prefers.

On top of the danger that this presents to the fair resolution of controversies in Constitutional law, it presents a great danger to another vital principle of American government: separation of powers. In *Federalist* 78, Alexander Hamilton declared the judiciary the "least dangerous branch" of the new federal government. "[T]he general liberty of the people can never be endangered" by the judiciary, he wrote, "so long as the judiciary remains truly distinct from both the legislature and the Executive. . . . [L]iberty can have nothing to fear from the judiciary alone, but would have every thing to fear from its union with either of the other departments," and "all the effects of such a union must ensue from a dependence of the former on the latter, notwithstanding a nominal and apparent separation."[21] The enforcement of political orthodoxy on the bench is creating precisely this dependence, strengthened even more by judicial "deference" to Congressional acts that exceed the limited scope of the federal government's Constitutional powers.

"The complete independence of the courts of justice is peculiarly essential in a limited Constitution," wrote Hamilton. The courts alone could "declare all acts contrary to the manifest tenor of the Constitution void."[22] But the current attempt to block judges who believe in limited government is not motivated by a desire to maintain inviolate the "exceptions to the legislative authority." It is motivated by a desire to ensure that the judiciary will interpret the Constitution in a way most suited to *extend* that legislative authority as far as possible.

What that essentially means is that the current attempt to use the Senate's confirmation power to regulate the ideology of judges is part of an overall trend which is turning the *judiciary* into a second *legislative* branch. The fundamental differences between the legislative and the judicial branch is that in the former, parties lobby, contend, vote, and decide on procedures that may infringe on the private rights of individuals. The courts are supposed to act as a "countermajoritarian" mechanism to ensure that the legislature does not engage in "the invasion of private rights . . . from acts in which the Government is the mere instrument of the major number of the constituents."[23] The very existence of the judiciary is premised on the fact that the majority is not always right. Allowing the Senate—elected by the majority—too great a hand in regulating the federal bench risks eroding the judiciary's power to perform this most crucial task. . . .

CONCLUSION

In June of 2001, President Clinton's White House Counsel, Lloyd Cutler, told the Senate Judiciary Committee that "it would be a tragic development if ideology became an increasingly important consideration in the future. To make ideology an issue in the confirmation process is to suggest that the legal process is and should be a political one. That is not only wrong as a matter of political science; it also serves to weaken public confidence in the courts."[24]

Today the Senate is doing precisely what one delegate to the North Carolina ratification convention warned against: it is taking over the nomination power which the Constitution vested in the President alone. "[T]he President may nominate, but they have a negative upon his nomination, till he has exhausted the number of those he wishes to be appointed: He will be obliged finally to acquiesce in the appointment of those which the Senate shall nominate, or else no appointment will take place."[25] The dangers posed by such a system are as real today as they were to the founding generation. It is time to rid ourselves of all ideological litmus tests save one: "Mr. Nominee, are you prepared to honor your oath to support the Constitution as written and not as you would like it to be, if we confirm you to this important office?"[26] Any nominee who answers that question in the negative deserves to be rejected. Unfortunately, the Senate is today refusing a hearing to several nominees precisely because the current leadership knows that those nominees would honestly answer that question in the affirmative.

NOTES

1. U.S. Const. art. II § 2 cl. 2; art. III § 1.
2. See also *Weiss v. United States,* 510 U.S. 163, 185 n. 1 (1994) (Souter, J., concurring) ("the President was . . . rightly given the sole power to nominate").
3. 2 M. Farrand, Records of the Federal Convention 41 (1911).
4. *Id.*
5. *Id.* at 42. Mason's objections were actually more complicated. He argued that the President should not appoint judges because the judges might try impeachments of the President. This problem was later avoided by having the Senate try impeachments with the Chief Justice of the Supreme Court merely presiding. See U.S. Const. art. I § 3 cl. 6. Governeur Morris, in replying to Mason, argued that impeachments should not be "tried before the Judges."Farrand, *supra* note 6 at 41–42. Mason also worried that "the Seat of Govt must be in some state,"and the President would form personal attachments to people in that state, which might exclude citizens of other states from the federal bench—an understandable objection from an antifederalist like Mason. This problem was at least partly obviated by placing the capital in a federal district which would not be subject to the jurisdiction of any state. See U.S. Const. art. I § 8 cl. 17.
6. Farrand, supra note 6 at 42.
7. *Id.*
8. *Id.* at 43.
9. *Id.* at 42.
10. *Id.* at 43.
11. The Convention voted by state. Georgia abstained from this vote, and Rhode Island never sent a delegate. Other states' delegates were sometimes absent for various reasons—for instance, although the Convention had been under way for more than a month, New Hampshire's delegates had still not arrived. In addition, this debate came during one of the lowest points of the Convention, when the differences between the delegates was at its severest. New York delegates, Robert Yates and John Lansing, had left the Convention on July 10, opposed to all its proceedings. New York's third delegate, Alexander Hamilton, had left ten days earlier. See Catherine Drinker Bowen, *Miracle at Philadelphia* 140 (Book of the Month Club, 1986) (1966). The day Lansing and Yates left the Convention, Washington wrote to Hamilton that he "almost despaired" of the Convention's success. *Id.* at 185–186. (Hamilton returned to the Convention in September and was

New York's only signer.) Thus the vote on July 18 was Massachusetts, Pennsylvania, Maryland and Virginia in favor of Ghorum's motion, and Connecticut, Delaware, North Carolina and South Carolina against.

12. See *The Federalist* Nos. 10 & 51 (C. Rossiter ed. 1961).
13. Farrand, *supra* note 6 at 539.
14. *Edmond v. United States,* 520 U.S. 651, 659 (1997).
15. Statement at Courts Subcommittee hearing, May 9, 2002 (visited May 26, 2002) <http://schumer.senate.gov/SchumerWebsite/pressroom/pressreleases/PR00978.html>.
16. John Johnson, "Judge Harry Pregerson, Choosing between Law and His Conscience," *Los Angeles Times,* May 3, 1992 at B5.
17. In 1992, Judge Pregerson ordered a stay to the execution of the serial killer Robert Alton Harris, the *fourth* such stay that was issued on the night of Harris' scheduled execution. The result was an unprecedented decision from the Supreme Court of the United States, ordering that "no further stays of Robert Alton Harris' execution shall be entered by the federal courts except upon order of this Court." *Vasquez v. Harris,* 503 U.S. 1000 (1992). See further Charles Fried, *Impudence,* 1992 Sup. Ct. Rev. 155, 188–92.
18. Antonin Scalia, "God's Justice and Ours," *First Things,* May 1, 2002 at 17.
19. The oath of office is prescribed in U.S. Const. art. VI § 3.
20. Letter to Thomas Jefferson (June 27, 1798), in Rakove, *supra* note 3 at 801 (emphasis added).
21. *The Federalist* No. 78 at 466 (C. Rossiter ed. 1961).
22. *Id.*
23. Letter from James Madison to Thomas Jefferson (Oct. 17, 1788) in Madison: *Writings* (J. Rakove ed. 1999) at 418, 421.
24. Statement to Administrative Oversight And The Courts Subcommittee (June 26, 2001) 2001 WL 21756493.
25. Samuel Spencer, *Speech at the North Carolina Ratification Convention,* July 28, 1788, reprinted in 2 Bailyn, DEBATE ON THE CONSTITUTION, at 879.
26. In this view, the qualifications of judges are similar to the qualifications of jurors as explained in *Wainwright v. Witt,* 469 U.S. 412 (1985). There the Court held that "the proper standard for determining when a prospective juror may be excluded for cause because of his or her views on capital punishment. That standard is whether the juror's views would 'prevent or substantially impair the performance of his duties as a juror in accordance with his instructions and his oath.'" *Id.* at 424 (*quoting Adams v. Texas,* 448 U.S. 38, 45 (1980)).

Of Course Ideology Should Matter in Judicial Selection
Erwin Chemerinsky

I. IDEOLOGY ALWAYS HAS MATTERED IN JUDICIAL SELECTION

The debate over the place of ideology in the judicial selection process has so far been framed in terms of whether it is appropriate for the United States Senate to consider the views of the prospective judge during the confirmation process. No one seems to deny that it is completely appropriate for the President to consider ideology when making appointments. In fact, they always have done so. Every President has appointed primarily, if not almost exclusively, individuals from the President's political party. Ever since George Washington, Presidents have looked to ideology when making judicial picks. Some Presidents are more ideological than others; not surprisingly, these Presidents focus more on ideology in their judicial nominations. President Franklin Roosevelt, for example, wanted judges who would uphold his "New Deal" programs and President Ronald Reagan emphasized selecting conservative jurists.

Senates always have done the same, using ideology as a basis for evaluating presidential nominees for the federal bench. Early in American history, President George Washington appointed John Rutledge to be the second Chief Justice of the United States.[1] Rutledge was impeccably qualified; he already had been confirmed by the Senate as an Associate Justice (although he never actually sat in that capacity) and had even been a delegate to the Constitutional Convention. But the Senate rejected Rutledge for the position as Chief Justice, because of its disagreement with Rutledge's views on a United States treaty with Great Britain.

During the nineteenth century, the Senate rejected twenty-one presidential nominations for the United States Supreme Court.[2] The vast majority of these individuals were defeated because of Senate disagreement with their ideology.[3] Professor Grover Rees explains that "during the nineteenth century only four Supreme Court Justices were rejected on the ground that they lacked the requisite credentials, whereas seventeen were rejected for political or philosophical reasons."[4]

Erwin Chemerinsky is Sydney M. Irmas Professor of Public Interest Law, Legal Ethics, and Political Science, University of Southern California Law School. This article is from Erwin Chemerinsky, "Of Course Ideology Should Matter in Judicial Selection," *NEXUS: A Journal of Opinion,* 7 (2002), pp. 3–10. Notes have been renumbered to correspond to edited text. Reprinted by permission.

During the twentieth century, too, nominees for the Supreme Court were rejected solely because of their ideology. In 1930, a federal court of appeals judge, John Parker, was denied a seat on the high Court because of his anti-labor, anti-civil rights views.[5] In 1969, the Senate rejected United States Court of Appeals judge Clement Haynsworth largely because of his anti-union views.[6] The Senate then rejected President Nixon's next pick for the Supreme Court, Federal Court of Appeals Judge Harold Carswell.[7]

In 1987, the Senate rejected Robert Bork, even though he had impeccable professional qualifications and unquestioned ability. Bork was rejected because of his unduly restrictive views of Constitutional law, for instance, he rejected constitutional protection for a right to privacy,[8] believed freedom of speech was limited only to political expression,[9] and denied protection for women under the Equal Protection Clause. The defeat of Robert Bork was in line with a tradition as old as the republic itself.[10]

Those who contend that ideology should play no role in judicial selection are arguing for a radical change from how the process has worked from the earliest days of the nation. Never has the selection or confirmation process focused solely on whether the candidate has sufficient professional credentials.

There is a widespread sense that the focus on ideology has increased in recent years. . . . There are several explanations for why there is such intense focus on ideology at this point in American history. First, the demise of the general public's belief in formalism encourages a focus on ideology. People have come to recognize that law is not mechanical, that judges often have great discretion in deciding cases. They realize that how judges rule on questions like abortion, affirmative action, the death penalty, and countless other issues is a reflection of the individual jurist's views. *Bush v. Gore*[11] simply reinforced the widespread belief that judges' political views often determine how they vote in important cases. Thus, Democratic voters want Democratic Senators to block conservative nominees and Republican voters want Republican Senators to block liberal nominees. This creates a political incentive for Senators to do so, and means that they will certainly not risk alienating their core constituency by using ideology in evaluating nominees.

Second, the lack of "party government" in recent years explains the increased focus on ideology. During the last six years of the Clinton presidency, the Senate was controlled by Republicans. During at least the first two years of the current Bush presidency, the Senate has been controlled by Democrats. If the Senate is of the same political party as the President, there will obviously be far fewer fights over judicial nominations. Certainly, confirmation battles are still possible, for instance through filibusters, or if the President lacks support from a faction of his own party. But in general confirmation fights are a product of the Senate and the President being from different political parties.

Finally, confirmation fights occur when there is the perception of deep ideological divisions over issues likely to be decided by the courts. Now, for example, conservatives and liberals deeply disagree over countless issues: the appropriate method of constitutional interpretation; the desirable scope of Congress's power and the judicial role in limiting it; the content of individual

rights, such as privacy. It is widely recognized that the outcome of cases concerning these questions will be determined by who is on the bench. Therefore,
Senators know, and voters recognize, that the confirmation process is enormously important in deciding the content of the law. Interest groups on both
sides of the ideological divide have strong reasons for making judicial confirmation a high priority, because they know what is at stake in who occupies the
federal bench.

II. IDEOLOGY SHOULD BE CONSIDERED IN THE JUDICIAL SELECTION AND CONFIRMATION PROCESS

There are many reasons why ideology should be considered in the judicial
selection process.

First, most simply and most importantly, ideology should be considered
because ideology matters. Judges are not fungible; a person's ideology influences
how he or she will vote on important issues. It is appropriate for an evaluator—
be it the President, the Senate, or the voters in states with judicial elections[12]—
to pay careful attention to the likely consequences of an individual's presence
on the court.

This seems so obvious as to hardly require elaboration. Imagine that the
President appoints someone who turns out to be an active member of the Ku
Klux Klan or the American Nazi Party and repeatedly has expressed racist or
anti-semitic views.[13] Assume that the individual has impeccable professional
qualifications: a degree from a prestigious university, years of experience in
high level legal practice, and a strong record of bar service. Notwithstanding
these credentials, I think virtually everyone would agree that the nominee
should be rejected. If I am correct in this assumption, then everyone agrees that
ideology *should* matter and the only issue is *what* views should be a basis for
excluding a person from holding judicial office.

On the Supreme Court, the decisions in a large proportion of cases are a
product of the judges' views. The federalism decisions of recent years—limiting
the scope of Congress's power under the commerce clause and section five of
the Fourteenth Amendment, reviving the Tenth Amendment as a limit on federal
power, and the expansion of sovereign immunity—have almost all been 5–4
rulings reflecting the ideology of the Justices.[14] Beyond the obviously controversial issues like abortion, affirmative action, and the death penalty, virtually
all cases about individual liberties and civil rights are a product of who sits on
the bench. Criminal procedure cases often require balancing the government's
interests in law enforcement against the rights of individuals; this balancing
will reflect the individual Justice's views. Decisions in statutory cases, too, are
a result of the ideology of the Justices. Frequently in statutory civil rights cases,
the Court is split exactly along ideological lines.[15]

Obviously this is not limited to the Supreme Court. Every case before the
Supreme Court was first decided by the lower federal courts, and ideology
matters there just as much. There may be more cases in the lower courts where

ideology does not matter in determining outcomes—that is, where regardless of ideology any judge would come to the same conclusion—but that does not deny the large number of cases in which the judge's views matter greatly. When I talk to a lawyer who is about to have an argument before a federal court of appeals, the first question I always ask is: *who is your panel*? That is because ideology matters so much in determining the result in so many cases.

Second, the Senate should use ideology precisely because the President uses it. Republicans who today are arguing for the Senate to approve nominations without regard to their views are being disingenuous when the President—from their party—is basing his picks so much on ideology. Under the Constitution, the Senate should not be a rubber-stamp and should not treat judicial selection as a presidential prerogative. The Senate owes no duty of deference to the President and, as explained above, never has shown such deference through American history.

Finally, ideology should be considered because the judicial selection process is the key majoritarian check on an anti-majoritarian institution. Once confirmed, federal judges have life tenure. A crucial democratic check is the process of determining who will hold these appointments. A great deal of constitutional scholarship in the last quarter-century has focused on what Professor Alexander Bickel termed the "counter-majoritarian difficulty"— the exercise of substantial power by unelected judges who can invalidate the decisions of elected officials.[16] The most significant majoritarian check is at the nomination and confirmation stage. Selection by the President and confirmation by the Senate is a legitimate mechanism of majoritarian control over the composition of the federal courts.

Those who oppose the use of ideology in the judicial selection process must sustain one of two arguments: either that an individual's ideology is unlikely to affect his or her decisions on the bench, or that, even if ideology will influence decisions, it should not be examined because the disadvantages to such consideration will outweigh the benefits.

The former argument—that a person's ideology is unlikely to affect performance in office—is impossible to sustain. Unless one believes in truly mechanistic judging,[17] it is clear that judges possess discretion and that the exercise of discretion is strongly influenced by that judge's preexisting ideological beliefs. In cases involving questions of constitutional or statutory interpretation, the language of the document and the intent of the drafters often will be unclear. Judges will have to decide the meaning, and this is going to be a product of their views. Many cases, especially in Constitutional law, require a balancing of interests. The relative weight assigned to the respective claims often turns on the judge's own values. Given the reality of judicial decision making, it is impossible to claim that a judge's ideology will not affect his or her decisions.

So opposition to considering ideology must be based on the latter argument: that even though ideology matters, it is undesirable for the Senate to consider it. One argument is that considering ideology will undermine judicial independence. Professor Stephen Carter makes this argument: "if a nominee's ideas fall within the very broad range of judicial views that are not radical in any non-trivial sense—and Robert Bork has as much right to that middle ground as any other nominee in recent decades—the Senate enacts a terrible threat to the independence of the judiciary if a substantive review of the nominee's legal theories brings about a rejection."[18]

But Professor Carter never explains why judicial independence requires blindness to ideology during the confirmation or selection of a federal judge. Judicial independence means that a judge should feel free to decide cases according to his or her view of the law and not in response to popular pressure. This is why Article III's assurance of life tenure, and its protection against a reduction in salaries, provide independence.[19] Judges are free to decide each case according to their consciences and best judgment; they need not worry that their rulings will cause them to be ousted from office. Professor Carter never justifies why this is insufficient to protect judicial independence. He subtly shifts the definition of independence from autonomy while in office to autonomy from scrutiny before taking office. But he does not explain why the latter, freedom from evaluation before ascending to the bench, is a prerequisite for judicial independence in the former, far more meaningful sense. In fact, the opposite order makes more sense. It is precisely because the framers of the Constitution's protections for judicial independence *understood* that judges would be subject to great ideological pressures, that they saw fit to insulate them from expressions of popular resentment. Judicial independence was therefore created by people who understood that judicial ideology matters.[20]

Another argument against considering ideology is that it will deadlock the selection process, with liberals blocking conservatives and vice versa. The reality is that this is a risk only when the Senate and the President are from different political parties. Even then, every Senate—including the Republican Senate during the Clinton years and the Democratic Senate today—has approved a large number of presidential nominations for the federal bench. There have been times when a number of nominations have been rejected—for instance, the Senate refused to confirm *any* of President John Tyler's picks for the Supreme Court,[21] and rejected two nominations in a row by President Nixon.[22] But in over 200 years of history, deadlocks have been rare.

Most importantly . . . the solution to deadlocks is in the President's hands: nominate individuals who are acceptable to the Senate. Presidents will have to select more moderate individuals than if the Senate was controlled by their political party. President Clinton undoubtedly was forced to select more moderate judges because the Senate was controlled by Republicans for the last six years of his presidency.President Bush would be far more successful in getting his nominations through the Senate if he chose less conservative individuals. The President has the prerogative to pick conservatives like Pickering, McConnell, Kuhl, or Estrada, but he should expect resistance in a Democratic Senate that would not be there if Bush selected more moderate nominees.

Finally, some suggest that using ideology is undesirable because it will encourage judges to base their rulings on ideology. The argument is that ideology must be hidden from the process so as to limit the likelihood that once on the bench judges will base their decisions on ideology. This argument is based on numerous unsupportable assumptions: it assumes that it is possible for judges to decide cases apart from their views and ideology; that judges don't already often decide cases because of their views and ideology; that considering ideology in the selection process will somehow increase this tendency. All of these are simply false. Long ago, the Legal Realists exploded the myth of formalistic value-neutral judging.[23] Having the judicial confirmation process recognize the demise of formalism won't change a thing in how judges behave on the bench.

The argument for considering ideology in judicial selection is simple: people should care about the decisions of the Supreme Court and other federal courts; they affect millions of people's lives in subtle but profound ways. The ideological composition of the court will determine those decisions, and the appropriate place for majoritarian influences in the judicial process is at the selection stage.

CONCLUSION

I bring some personal experience to this topic. Twice during the Clinton years, I was under serious consideration for a federal judgeship. Once, the press reported that I was on a list of three names being considered to fill two vacancies on the federal bench.[24] The other two individuals were picked. Another time, I received a call from the White House Counsel's office that I was being considered for the Ninth Circuit.

In each instance, I was told that I was not selected because the Republican-controlled Senate would find me too liberal and not confirm me. In the latter instance, I was informed that my opposition to Proposition 209, which eliminated affirmative action in California, would likely prevent Republicans from confirming me.

I confess to being disappointed, but not at all surprised; I knew from the outset that ideology always has been a key part of the confirmation process. But now I feel outrage when I hear Republicans say that it is wrong for a Democratic-controlled Senate to look at ideology, when that is exactly what Republicans did for the last six years of the Clinton presidency. . . .

Ultimately, disputes over confirmations are battles over the proper content of the law. This is as it should be, and attention should not be diverted by claims that it is improper to consider a nominee's ideological orientation. Of course, ideology should and must be considered in the judicial selection process.

NOTES

1. Laurence Tribe, *God Save This Honorable Court* 87, 90–91 (1985).
2. Grover Rees, *Questions for Supreme Court Nominees at Confirmation Hearings: Excluding the Constitution*, 17 Ga. L. Rev. 913, 944 (1983).
3. *See also* Jeffrey K. Tulis, *Constitutional Abdication: The Senate, The President, and Appointments to the Supreme Court*, 47 Case W. Res. 1331 (Summer 1997).
4. Rees, *supra* note 2.

5. See Gail Fruchtman, *et al., Questions and Answers*, 84 Law Libr. J. 627, 637 (Summer, 1992); "Background Paper," in *Twentieth Century Fund, Judicial Roulette: Report of the Task Force on Judicial Selection* 77 (1988).
6. *Id.* at 77. See also Bob Woodward & Scott Armstrong, *The Brethren* 56–57 (1979).
7. *See id.* at 74–75.
8. *See* Robert Bork, *The Tempting of America: The Political Seduction of the Law* (1990) 95–100.
9. *See* Robert Bork, *Neutral Principles and Some First Amendment Problems*, 47 Ind. L.J. 1 (1971).
10. *See further* Mark Gitenstein, *Matters of Principle: An Insider's Account of America's Rejection of Robert Bork's Nomination to the Supreme Court* (1992).
11. 121 S.Ct. 545 (2000).
12. It is ironic that those opposed to the use of ideology in the judicial nomination process rarely comment on the fact that *state* judges are elected in almost all the states of the union.
13. This is not so ridiculous a proposition. Justice Hugo Black was a member of the KKK. *See* Gerald T. Dunne, *Hugo Black and the Judicial Revolution* 71–75 (1977).
14. *See, e.g., United States v. Lopez*, 514 U.S. 549 (1995); *United States v. Morrison*, 529 U.S. 598 (2000); *University of Alabama v. Garrett*, 531 U.S. 356 (2001).
15. *See, e.g., Alexander v. Sandoval*, 532 U.S. 275 (2001) (5–4 decision finding no private cause of action under Title VI of 1964 Civil Rights Act against recipients of federal funds for practices that have discriminatory impact in violation of regulations promulgated under that provision); *Circuit City v. Adams*, 532 U.S. 105 (2001) (5–4 decision that Federal Arbitration Act requires arbitration of state law employment discrimination claims); *Buckhannon Board v. West Virginia Department of Health and Human Services*, 532 U.S. 598 (2001) (5–4 decision holding that to be "prevailing party" under attorney fees statute, it is insufficient that plaintiff is catalyst for legislative action).
16. Alexander Bickel, *The Least Dangerous Branch* 16 (1962).
17. This is a difficult proposition to swallow. If judicial decisions could be made so algorithmically, there would be little reason to have a court, let alone any nomination and confirmation process, to begin with! The decision could be made merely according to a set of written equations, or even by a computer. Moreover, if a judge's own values did not affect his or her decisions, there would be no reason for judges to recuse themselves from cases giving rise to conflicts of interest.
18. Stephen Carter, *The Confirmation Mess*, 101 Harv. L. Rev. 1185, 1198 (1988).
19. U.S. Const. art. III § 1 ("The Judges, both of the supreme and inferior Courts, shall hold their Offices during good Behaviour, and shall, at stated Times, receive for their Services, a Compensation, which shall not be diminished during their Continuance in Office").
20. This is a very old principle. Lord Edward Coke, for instance, one of the most important figures in English legal history, wrote, "Honorable and reverend judges and justices, that do or shall sit in high tribunals and courts or

seats of justice . . . fear not to do right to all, and to deliver your opinions justly according to the laws; for feare is nothing but a betraying of the suc-cors that reason should afford. And if you shall sincerely execute justice, be assured . . . that though thereby you may offend a great many favourites, yet you shall have the favourable kindnesse of the Almighty. . . ." Quoted in Catherine Drinker Bowen, The *Lion and The Throne: The Life of Edward Coke* 523 (Atlantic Monthly 1957) (1956). King James I fired Coke as Chief Justice of King's Bench because of Coke's rulings in cases like Dr. Bonham's Case, 8 Co. Rep 113b, 77 Eng. Rep 646 (K.B. 1610), which famously declared that the Court had the power to strike down laws which violated the com-mon law. See Bowen at 314–317, 384–388.

21. Tulis, *supra* note 3 at 1350.
22. *Id.* at 1336; Woodward & Armstrong, *supra* note 14 at 15–16.
23. "Legal realism" refers to a school of thought which sees law as developing not by the discovery of internally operating logical or natural laws, but according to political pressures, experiences, and experiments which result in social structures designed to perpetuate (or to alter) existing sociological or class lines. *See* Karl N. Llewellyn, *A Realistic Jurisprudence—The Next Step,* 30 Harv. L. Rev. 431 (1930). *See further* N.E.H. Hull, *Reconstructing The Origins of Realistic Jurisprudence: A Prequel to The Llewellyn-Pound Exchange over Legal Realism,* 1989 Duke L.J. 1302.
24. Henry Weinstein, "Boxer Recommends L.A. Jurist to Be Nominated for Federal Judgeship," *Los Angeles Times,* Jan. 28, 1995 at B1.

Internet Resources
Visit our Web site at www.mhhe.com/diclerico10 for links and resources relating to Courts.

c h a p t e r 1 4

Civil Liberties

Free Speech

*F*reedom of speech is one of the most important freedoms accorded citizens of the United States. Nowhere is that freedom more highly prized than in its universities, whose central mission—the generation and transmission of knowledge—is predicated upon the free expression of ideas. Thus, it should occasion no surprise that considerable debate erupts on campuses from time to time over the extent to which universities are fostering an environment conducive to free expression.

The most recent debate on this question centers around the matter of student fees— a practice whereby the university imposes mandatory fees on students for the purpose of supporting various student organizations and activities on campus. More specifically, five students at the University of Wisconsin took strong exception to the fact that their student fees were going to support certain campus organizations whose views and purposes they did not share. Indeed, they were so offended by it that they decided to challenge this practice in court.

The first selection consists of portions of an amicus curiae *brief submitted to the U.S. Supreme Court by the American Council on Education on behalf of the University of Wisconsin. It insists that universities have a responsibility to create an environment that fosters a free marketplace of ideas. One of the ways to do so is to support with student fees a host of different campus organizations. Such support, in the view of the American Council on Education, in no way diminishes the free speech of students paying those fees.*

The second selection also contains portions of an amicus curiae *brief submitted to the U.S. Supreme Court—this one by the Pacific Legal Foundation on behalf of the five students. It argues that by requiring students to support, through their fees, organizations with which they disagree, the University of Wisconsin is in fact abridging their right to freedom of speech.*

Mandatory Student Fees Do Not Abridge Freedom of Speech
American Council on Education

I. A UNIVERSITY'S USE OF COMPULSORY FEES TO CREATE A STUDENT ACTIVITY FUND SHOULD BE ANALYZED AS THE CREATION OF A FORUM, RATHER THAN AS COMPELLED SPEECH AND ASSOCIATION

A. A University, as a Marketplace of Ideas, Has a Compelling Interest in Promoting the Presence of a Diversity of Viewpoints

"It is the business of a university to provide that atmosphere which is most conducive to speculation, experiment and creation."[1] A university can provide this atmosphere only by offering an environment in which a rich diversity of ideas, values, and perspectives is championed and challenged. In this sense, "[t]he college classroom with its surrounding environs is peculiarly the 'marketplace of ideas.'"[2]

This marketplace trains future citizens and leaders by providing "wide exposure to that robust exchange of ideas which discovers truth 'out of a multitude of tongues.'"[3] If a university is to provide such training, some members of the academic community will inevitably encounter speech that they find unfamiliar, even abhorrent. Furthermore, learning to tolerate and respond to such speech is an important part of the educational process. "To endure the speech of false ideas or offensive content and then to counter it is part of learning how to live in a pluralistic society, a society which insists upon open discourse towards the end of a tolerant citizenry."[4]

The marketplace extends beyond the classroom to extracurricular activities, which are "a critical aspect of campus life."[5] Education involves more than tests, textbooks, lectures, and libraries. Fundamentally, it is about the development of character.[6] Consequently, education does not end at the classroom door, but permeates campus and university life. As this Court recognizes, a "great deal of learning occurs informally."[7] Indeed, since the nineteenth century,

From the *amicus curiae* brief filed by the American Council on Education in support of the University of Wisconsin in the U.S. Supreme Court case of *Board of Regents, University of Wisconsin v. Scott Southworth* (1999), 5–21.

extracurricular activities have played an increasingly significant role in advancing the core mission of universities:

> Over time . . . extracurricular programs have come to be seen not merely as use-ful services but as an integral part of the educational process itself. Educators point to the dangers of a college that stresses only learning and cognitive skills while ignoring opportunities for students to engage in cooperative activities in which each relies on the efforts of others and is relied upon by others in return. . . . More and more, [extracurricular activities] are regarded not only as a source of enjoyment but as ideal experiences for learning to cooperate and take responsibility for the welfare of one's peers.
> . . . The contemporary college or university does not concentrate only on formal education; it assumes the larger responsibility of promoting human development in all its forms.[8]

. . . In sum, colleges and universities hold a unique position in our society and pursue a correspondingly unique mission. Their business is to provide "that atmosphere which is most conducive to speculation, experiment and creation."[9] This mission can be achieved only by fostering a marketplace of ideas on cam-pus and by ensuring that the resultant diversity of thoughts and perspectives informs the full range of experiences—from course selections to lecture series to student organizations. If a university is barred from this essential business, it cannot prepare its students "to live in a pluralistic society, a society which insists upon open discourse towards the end of a tolerant citizenry."[10]

B. Consistent with the First Amendment, a University Can Use Mandatory Fees to Fund a Neutral Forum That Helps Support a Diverse Variety of Organizations

. . . [T]he University of Wisconsin (and many other colleges and universities) pay fees not to particular groups but to the student government, which then uses the money to fund a wide array of organizations in a viewpoint-neutral manner.[11] "The speech of the offending groups can hardly be attributed to the student government, which funds groups of radically different views."[12] . . .

The University of Wisconsin simply requires its students to support a neutral forum, just as if it "built a large auditorium and held it open for everyone."[13] The fact that this case concerns a fund, rather than a physical space like an auditorium or an amphitheater, does not mean that forum analysis does not apply. . . .

Application of these principles makes clear that a critical difference exists between (a) supporting a forum and (b) supporting the speakers that ultimately use that forum. Thus, in *Widmar v. Vincent*,[14] this Court rejected a university's argument that if it were to allow religious groups to use its buildings it would create an impression that it endorsed religion in violation of the Establishment Clause: "[B]y creating a forum the University does not thereby endorse or pro-mote any of the particular ideas aired there."[15] A student compelled to pay a restoration fee for a university amphitheater can hardly complain that her First Amendment rights are violated because she disagrees with some of the speakers who appear there. She has no greater constitutional cause to complain of a content-neutral student activity fund because she disagrees with some of the organizations it ultimately supports.

If a forum supports organizations in a truly neutral fashion, as is stipulated here, . . . and thereby funds groups that take radically differing positions on the same issues, it cannot be said to endorse or promote any particular group or any specific position.[16] . . .

II. EVEN IF A UNIVERSITY'S USE OF MANDATORY FEES TO FUND STUDENT GOVERNMENT AND ORGANIZATIONS IS ANALYZED UNDER ABOOD-KELLER AS COMPELLED SPEECH AND ASSOCIATION, RATHER THAN AS THE CREATION OF A NEUTRAL FORUM, SUCH A USE OF FEES DOES NOT VIOLATE THE FIRST AMENDMENT

A. The Challenged Use of Mandatory Fees Is Germane to a University's Broad Educational Mission, Including Its Interests in Promoting Diverse Expression and in Providing a Marketplace of Ideas

Abood and *Keller* involve contexts very different from colleges and universities. *Keller* holds that compulsory state bar dues cannot be used to finance ideological activities unrelated to the purposes of the compelled association—regulation of the legal profession and improvement of legal services. Similarly, *Abood* holds that a union may not use a dissenting individual's dues to fund ideological activities not germane to collective bargaining. The purposes of the State Bar in *Keller*, to supervise attorney conduct, and of the union shop in *Abood*, to negotiate contracts, are relatively narrow and definable. The educational mission of a university is substantially broader.[17] ("The goals of the university are much broader than the goals of a labor union or a state bar, and they are inextricably connected with the underlying policies of the First Amendment."[18])

It is the business of a university to create a marketplace of ideas, exposing its students to a broad range of viewpoints on many issues, including the political and the ideological. This happens in classrooms—in courses in history, literature, political science, sociology, philosophy, and many other disciplines. It happens in auditoriums—when guest lecturers speak on ethics, contemporary problems, civil rights, and the like. And it happens in extracurricular activities—in connection with student government, student newspapers, and student organizations identical to those at issue here. Neither state bars nor unions—nor perhaps any institutions other than American colleges and universities—have this broad mission and mandate.

As a result, numerous courts recognize that a university's mission unquestionably reaches the funding of student organizations. Thus, the Second Circuit holds that a university may allocate student activity fees to a group with whose speech some students disagree.[19] *Carroll* recognizes three distinct university interests served by the compulsory fee: "the promotion of extracurricular life, the transmission of skills and civic duty, and the stimulation of energetic campus debate."[20] . . .

B. Courts Should Afford Universities Wide Latitude to Determine Whether the Use of Student Fees Is Germane to Their Educational Mission

Amici respectfully submit that the court below failed to give proper deference to the University of Wisconsin's decision that the use of mandatory fees advances its educational mission. Universities have interests in academic freedom that are a special concern of the First Amendment. This freedom is lost if courts do not afford universities discretion to define the contours of their educational mission and to determine the most effective means of achieving it. Judicial intervention in academic decision making affects not only the academic freedom of the university, but it results as well in a loss of the freedom of the students, faculty, and other members of the academic community, all of whom participate in and help to create the marketplace of ideas.

For these reasons, this Court has recognized that government intervention in the intellectual life of a university is to be avoided.[21] Universities are "characterized by the spirit of free inquiry," and academic freedom gives the university the ability "to determine for itself on academic grounds who may teach, what may be taught, how it shall be taught, and who may be admitted to study."[22] . . .

In this case, the University of Wisconsin—a campus with a rich history of the "robust exchange of ideas"[23]—made a judgment that funding a forum that supports a wide variety of student groups, including some engaged in political and ideological activities, plays an important role in its educational mission. This decision deserves respect, "breathing room," and some significant measure of deference. . . .

III. FORCING THE UNIVERSITY TO DISTINGUISH BETWEEN "EDUCATIONAL" ORGANIZATIONS AND "POLITICAL" OR "IDEOLOGICAL" ORGANIZATIONS RISKS VIOLATING STUDENTS' FIRST AMENDMENT RIGHTS

The court below effectively requires universities to distinguish political from non-political, and ideological from non-ideological organizations, and then to grant or withhold funding based upon these distinctions. Such distinctions may be constitutionally workable in the context of the activities of a union or a state bar, where the government has a narrower interest and where that interest does not include exposure to a diverse marketplace of ideas. Such distinctions emphatically do not work in the context of a university, however, where the government has a broad interest, and where that interest includes exposure to various political and ideological perspectives. Further, in the context of a university campus activities, such distinctions not only fail to work, but they actually create significant constitutional mischief.

Consider a student debate club that sponsors a public forum on presidential impeachment; or a student economic society that hosts a series of speakers on tax reform; or a student group that distributes leaflets asserting that a university discriminates because it hires too few minority professors; or a film society that sponsors a film concerning the events at Tiananmen Square; or an environmental organization that presents a series of lectures on the impact of logging; or a literary studies club that funds a panel discussion of alternative theories of literary criticism, including Marxist, feminist, deconstructionist, and Freudian approaches. At some point it simply becomes impossible to separate the ideological and political from the educational and informative.[24]

Furthermore, a university that attempts to make such distinctions, and then to make funding decisions based upon them, may run afoul of First Amendment prohibitions against content- and viewpoint-based discrimination. In other words, forcing universities to draw these lines does not avoid constitutional difficulties; it compounds them. The University of Wisconsin uses the mandatory activity fee to create a public forum that distributes fees on a content-neutral basis. . . . By supporting groups without regard to the content or viewpoint of their speech, the forum detaches funding decisions from endorsement or condemnation of the political or ideological positions of the different organizations. In contrast, the holding of the *Southworth I* court, which would require the University to refuse funding for groups that are too ideological or political, violates the rule against content and viewpoint discrimination in a public forum. . . .

Faced with a project that calls upon them to do the impossible, with the knowledge that in the effort they might also do the unconstitutional, many universities will respond by funding no student organizations at all or only those that seem to pose no risk whatsoever.[25] As the dissenting judges in *Southworth II* cautioned, such a requirement may "spell the end, as a practical matter, to the long tradition of student-managed activities on these campuses."[26] As funding fails, and as organizations disband, some voices—including, in all likelihood, the most provocative and stimulating, if also the least popular voices—will no longer be heard at our universities. The marketplace of ideas on our campuses will suffer immeasurably.

NOTES

1. *Sweezy v. New Hampshire,* 354 U.S. 234, 263 (1957) (Frankfurter, J., concurring).
2. *Healy v. James,* 408 U.S. 169, 180 (1972) (quoting *Keyishian v. Board of Regents of Univ. of N.Y.,* 385 U.S. 589, 603 (1967)).
3. *Keyishian,* 385 U.S. at 603 (quoting *United States v. Associated Press,* 52 F. Supp. 362, 372 (D.N.Y., 1943)).
4. *Lee v. Weisman,* 505 U.S. 577, 590 (1992).
5. *Widmar v. Vincent,* 454 U.S. 263, 279 n. 2 (1981) (Stevens, J., concurring).
6. See Higher Education Amendments of 1998, Pub. L. No. 105-244, §863, 112 Stat. 1581, 1826 (Congress recognizes that "the development of virtue

and moral character, those habits of mind, heart, and spirit that help young people to know, desire, and do what is right, has historically been a primary mission of colleges and universities. . . .").

7. *Regents of the Univ. of Cal. v. Bakke*, 438 U.S. 265, 313 n. 48 (1978) (opinion of Powell, J.) (quoting William J. Bowen, "Admissions and the Relevance of Race," *Princeton Alumni Weekly* 7, 9 (Sept. 26, 1977)).

8. Derek C. Bok, *Higher Learning* 51–52 (1986). . . .

9. *Sweezy*, 354 U.S. at 263 (Frankfurter, J., concurring).

10. *Lee*, 505 U.S. at 590.

11. The only exception to this procedure may be Wisconsin PIRG, for which funding is authorized by direct student referendum. This brief does not address the separate and different issue raised by this direct funding, although the "germaneness" analysis discussed below would apply to this funding as well.

12. *Southworth II*, 157 F. 3d at 1125.

13. Id. at 1129 (Wood, J., dissenting).

14. 454 U.S. 263 (1981).

15. See also Carolyn Wiggin, Note, *A Funny Thing Happens When You Pay for a Forum: Mandatory Student Fees to Support Political Speech at Public Universities*, 103 Yale L.J. 2009, 2017 (1994) ("[T]he lack of content-based standards . . . enables the system to support a legitimate campus forum, and this in turn creates a distance between those who fund the forum and any particular view expressed within it, thus avoiding unconstitutional forced speech").

16. See Robert M. O'Neil, "Student Fees and Student Rights: Evolving Constitutional Principles," 15 J.C. & U.L. 569, 574 (1999). . . .

17. See *Rounds*, 166 F. 3d at 1039.

18. See also William Walsh, Comment, *Smith v. Regents of the University of California: The Marketplace Is Closed*, 21 J.C. & U.L. 405, 423 (1994) ("[T]he organizations' purposes in *Keller* and *Abood* were much narrower than the university's purpose. It is much easier to see something as 'political or ideological,' and therefore ineligible for funding, because it is unrelated to collective bargaining than it is to distinguish the same from an 'educational mission'").

19. *See Carroll v. Blinken*, 957 F. 2d 991, 992 (2d Cir. 1992).

20. Id. at 1001. . . .

21. See, e.g., *Sweezy*, 354 U.S. at 262 (Frankfurter, J. concurring).

22. Id. at 262–63.

23. *Keyishian*, 385 U.S. at 603.

24. See Smith, 844 P. 2d at 524–25 (Arabian, J., dissenting).

25. An "opt-out refund" procedure might address certain constitutional concerns, see O'Neil, supra, 575, 578, and use of such a procedure certainly should not be foreclosed by this Court. For the reasons set forth in this brief, however, such a procedure should not be required to save the constitutionality of mandatory fees.

26. 157 F. 3d at 1127 (Wood, J., dissenting).

Mandatory Student Fees Violate Students' Right to Free Speech
Pacific Legal Foundation

THE UNIVERSITY HAS NO CONSTITUTIONAL JUSTIFICATION TO COMPEL PAYMENT OF FEES TO PROMOTE STUDENT EXPRESSIVE ACTIVITIES

A. The University Has No Compelling Interest in Coercing Students to Subsidize Voluntary Organizations' Political and Ideological Activities

While a university may well have a compelling interest in *exposing* students to various conflicting viewpoints, it does not have a compelling interest in coercing *support* for those viewpoints.

> [T]he freedom to keep silent as well as to speak is grounded in something broader than a national fear of the state. It is equally the product of our view of personhood, which encompasses what the Supreme Court later referred to as "freedom of thought," "freedom of mind" and a "sphere of intellect and spirit." Were there no state at all, or were it inalterably benign, our conception of what it means to be human would still lead us to respect the individual autonomy of intellect and will enshrined in the First Amendment.[1]

By coercing support for political groups, the university sends a troubling message to students: If students want to advance a political position for which they cannot find support, the government will give them money to propagate their unpopular views. This is an illegitimate lesson for a public university to teach its students. The defendants in *Abood* and *Keller* understood that mandating support for an organization smothers, rather than stokes, contrary speech.*[2] Moreover, the university, let alone the political groups themselves, does not create a free marketplace or forum for the expression of ideas. Rather it requires students to be the financial sponsors of someone else's speech. Indeed, the notion that a free marketplace of ideas can be created and encouraged by involuntary contributions is an oxymoron. The strength of an idea (i.e., its acceptance in the marketplace) is

From the *amicus curiae* brief filed by the Pacific Legal Foundation in support of the plaintiff, Scott Southworth, in the U.S. Supreme Court case of *Board of Regents, University of Wisconsin v. Scott Southworth* (1999), 24–27.

*Two previous cases in which the Supreme Court ruled that non-union teachers and members of a bar association did not have to support the political activities of their groups—*Editors.*

best measured by how many people will volunteer to spread the idea or to help finance its propagation.

The university's position also implies that the First Amendment has only limited application within the confines of a public university campus. As the court below noted,

> far from *serving* the school's interest in education, forcing objecting students to fund objectionable organizations undermines that interest. In some courses students are likely taught the values of individualism and dissent. Yet despite the objecting students' dissent they must fund organizations promoting opposing views or they don't graduate.[3]

If the university really wants students to learn practical civics lessons, it should encourage politically active groups to learn the art of fund-raising. In real political campaigns, opponents of the message do not give money to the cause.

B. A State University May Permit Voluntary Funding of Student Groups as a Less Intrusive Method of Promoting Such Groups on Campus

Universities are free to adopt any system of funding student activities that avoids constitutional defects. The best system, however, is the "positive check-off" voluntary system. Such a check-off could be designed in a number of ways. For example, it could list each recognized student group eligible for funding and permit students to choose which particular groups they wish to subsidize. Alternatively, it could simply provide a single box which, if checked, would mean that the student assents to funding all eligible student groups. By requiring students to designate affirmatively that they wish to fund particular groups, either individually or as a whole, the university advances several compelling goals. First, it requires thought on the part of the student, rather than mindless contributions to groups the student may not even be able to identify. Second, it encourages student groups to organize and articulate their messages clearly so as to attract as much financial support as possible.[4] Third, and most importantly, it sends a strong message to the entire student body that the university respects the constitutional rights of *all* students and has taken the strongest measures possible to protect those rights.[5]

Supporters of compelled funding have derided such a method, complaining that

> funding will soon devolve into a political *popularity* contest. Thus, in a setting where provocative ideas should receive the most support and encouragement, precisely the opposite will occur; student groups will be subject to an ideological referendum, and the most marginal groups will receive the least financial assistance. This is truly Orwellian.[6]

Justice Arabian's reasoning is backwards. What is Orwellian is a situation in which marginal groups are presented to the community as having support where there is none and presented as mainstream rather than extreme. Giving these ideas the cover of legitimacy and acceptability because of coerced subsidization from students who oppose the message perpetrates a great disservice. Students who wish to attract adherents to unconventional ideas must do so by convincing others of the soundness of their theories. Giving these unconventional thinkers the unwilling financial support of their dissenters grants them the means to speak more loudly than their actual support would permit.

CONCLUSION

The students in *West Virginia State Board of Education v. Barnette,* by being forced to salute the flag, were more than exposed to patriotism; they were forced to support it with a raised hand. Like them, the students at UW–Madison were not simply exposed to divergent views, they were forced to reach into their pockets to finance their opponents' views. Ideas that could not win adherence through persuasion and reason were thus kept alive by the state by imposing fees on those who do not support the idea in question. The First Amendment was designed to prevent just such an exercise of state power.

Attempts by the government, whether through a public agency, a legislature, or a court, to force individuals to financially support political and ideological activities with which they disagree have been rejected from the time of Thomas Jefferson to the present. This Court has on numerous occasions protected the rights of teachers, attorneys, and nonunion agency shop fee payers to refrain from supporting speech which they oppose. Students are entitled to no less protection.

NOTES

1. *Carroll v. Blinken,* 957 F. 2d 991, 996 (2d Cir.) cert. denied, 506 U.S. 906 (1992).
2. *Abood v. Detroit Board of Education* 431 U.S. 209 (1977) and *Keller v. State Bar of California* 496 U.S. 1 (1990).
3. *Southworth v. Grebe* 151 F. 3d 728 (1998).
4. The groups benefit in another way: if they suffer a funding shortfall when their opponents are no longer forced to subsidize their activities, the groups will likely turn to their own members to make up the difference. A person who pays a membership fee to belong to one of these groups will have a more personal stake in the group's successful attainment of its objectives. Bevilacqua, *Public Universities, Mandatory Student Activity Fees, and the First Amendment,* 24 J.L. & Educ. 1, 29–30 (1995).
5. La Fetra, "Recent Developments in Mandatory Student Fee Cases," 10 J.L. & Pol. 579, 612–13 (1994).
6. *Smith v. Regents of the University of California,* 4 Cal. 4th 843, 881 (1993) (Arabian, J., dissenting).

Civil Liberties and Terrorism

*D*emocracies confronting major threats to their national security are frequently compelled to go beyond the powers they exercise under normal circumstances. The great challenge, of course, comes in attempting to strike a balance between according the government the necessary freedom of action to meet such threats, while at the same time protecting citizens against the arbitrary exercise of such power.

For the United States, terrorism constitutes the most recent threat to its national security. While this threat predates what has come to be known as 9/11, the destruction of the twin towers of the World Trade Center in New York City nevertheless represented the most devastating act of terrorism directed against us, and served as a catalyst for government action, including passage of the Patriot Act in 2001. Not surprisingly, the sweeping powers granted to the government under this legislation have generated both vigorous critics and ardent defenders.

In the first selection Walter Brasch argues that the Patriot Act is an ill-considered piece of legislation, passed in haste after Congress was stampeded into action by the Bush White House. Moreover, despite the government's repeated protestations to the contrary, he insists that the legislation now on the books allows the government to have access to our possessions and to make use of surveillance, search, and detention procedures— all without anything approaching adequate safeguards for individuals, be they American citizens or legal immigrants.

Robert Bork is no less insistent that the Patriot Act, along with other steps taken by the government, falls well within the bounds of prudent and reasonable actions to combat what he calls a "war like no other we have faced." Indeed, he even argues that in some instances the restrictions do not go far enough. As for the critics, whose rhetoric he claims borders on the hysterical at times, Bork says their complaints variously reflect an inadequate understanding of the law and a failure to grasp what can practically be done by way of protecting individual civil liberties.

230

America's Unpatriotic Acts
Walter M. Brasch

Following 9/11, the nation first went into panic and then revenge. President George W. Bush told Attorney General John Ashcroft, "Make sure this can't happen again."[1] At the top of the Department's Web site is the statement, "The Department of Justice's first priority is to prevent future terrorist attacks."[2]

Congress and the American public gave the government wide latitude to seek out and destroy those responsible. The nation had been attacked; Americans were rightfully frightened. The people believed they may have had to temporarily yield some of their own civil liberties to gain their permanent security. Although understandable in the horror of the events of 9/11, the willing sacrifice of civil liberties would probably have shocked and saddened the nation's founders who wrote our keystone documents under terrors we can't imagine.

Within a week of 9/11, John Ashcroft and his assistants drafted in secret under a cloak of "national security" the Anti-Terrorism Act of 2001.[3] It would soon be renamed the Uniting and Strengthening America by Providing Appropriate Tools Required to Intercept and Obstruct Terrorism Act, better known by the clever acronym, USA PATRIOT Act.[4] The base of the USA PATRIOT Act is three separate acts—the Foreign Intelligence Surveillance Act of 1978 (FISA),[5] passed during the Cold War at a time when there had been increased worldwide terrorism, especially in the Middle East; the Antiterrorism and Effective Death Penalty Act, passed in 1996; and a massive . . . bill that same year that did not meet Congressional approval. . . .

In *Losing America* (2004), Sen. Robert C. Byrd (D-W.Va.), first elected to the Senate in 1958, and one of those who had voted for the PATRIOT Act, boldly declared the PATRIOT Act is "a case in the perils of speed, herd instinct and lack of vigilance when it comes to legislating in the face of crisis." The Congress, wrote Byrd, "basically got stampeded by Attorney General John Aschcroft[,] and the values of freedom, justice and equality received a trampling in the headlong rush."[6]

The House of Representatives passed the bill, 357–66; the Senate passed it 98–1. To critics who would later oppose many of the provisions of the PATRIOT Act, the Department of Justice righteously pointed to the overwhelming vote by Congress to justify the Act—it never referred to the arm-twisting done by

From Walter M. Brasch, America's Unpatriotic Acts (New York: Peter Lang, 2005), chap. 2. Reprinted with permission.

the Bush administration, the deferential attitudes of Congress to presidential authority following 9/11, and the procedures that led to passage of the Act.

Sen. Orrin Hatch (R-Utah), one of the bill's strongest advocates, claimed it passed "because the American people and extraordinary circumstances demanded it."[7]

President Bush enthusiastically signed the bill on October 26, 2001, commenting that his administration took "an essential step in defeating terrorism, while protecting the constitutional rights of all Americans. . . . [It] upholds and respects the civil liberties guaranteed by our Constitution."[8]

. . . The only senator to vote against the bill was Russell Feingold. The nation must "be sure we are not rewarding these terrorists and weakening ourselves by giving up the cherished freedoms that they seek to destroy," Feingold said the day of the vote, emphasizing, "We must redouble our vigilance to ensure our security and to prevent further acts of terror. But we must also redouble our vigilance to preserve our values and the basic rights that make us who we are."[9] Almost every one of the cautions and problems Feingold pointed out in his 5,200-word speech in the Senate were prophetic.

The federal government claims parts of the PATRIOT Act have been successful in giving federal law enforcement the tools it needs to bring about arrests of several persons loyal to al-Qaeda or other terrorists who were in "sleeper cells" in Buffalo, Detroit, Portland, and Seattle. . . .

The conviction of three persons in the Detroit "sleeper cell" was the first major conviction of terrorism following 9/11, and was widely flaunted by John Ashcroft and the Bush administration for almost three years as a major success of the PATRIOT Act. However, by direction of U.S. District Judge Gerald E. Rosen, the Department of Justice initiated a vigorous nine-month posttrial investigation of prosecutorial misconduct, as well as an intense investigation of the original evidence, much of it withheld by the Department of Justice. In September 2004, the Department of Justice asked for a dismissal of all charges of terrorism against two of the four who were convicted; a third was convicted only of document fraud; a fourth had been acquitted. In dismissing the charges, Judge Rosen said the federal prosecutors not only acted outside the limits of the Constitution, but "simply ignored or avoided any evidence or information which contradicted or undermined" their opinion that the four Moroccans were guilty of plotting acts of terrorism. The judge praised the work of the new prosecutors who conducted the investigation.[10] . . .

The PATRIOT Act gave legal authority for the FBI and CIA to share information and evidence (sections 201, 901). Implicit in the intent was that the FBI and CIA, by maintaining their own territorial imperatives, may not have been as efficient in monitoring terrorism as they should have been. Innumerable members of the Bush administration and federal law enforcement agencies have argued that the "wall" between the FBI and CIA, initiated during the 1970s to restrain significant civil liberties violations that arose from domestic spying during the Vietnam era, also allowed significant lapses of intelligence and law enforcement. They argue that the PATRIOT Act has torn down this wall.

In testimony before the National Commission on Terrorist Attacks Upon the United States, John Ashcroft claimed that the "single greatest structural cause for the September 11th problem was the wall that segregated or separated criminal investigators and intelligence agents."[11] . . .

Kate Martin, executive director of the Center for National Security Studies, points out:

> This "wall" metaphor is inaccurate and the existence of legal barriers to sharing information is highly exaggerated. Such talk is used to obscure bureaucratic failures of coordination and communication between the FBI and CIA, as well as inside each agency. . . .
>
> Indeed, to protect civil liberties and guard against the creation of a Gestapo-like agency, the CIA's original charter, the 1947 National Security Act, prohibited the agency from exercising any "police, subpoena, law-enforcement powers, or internal security functions." . . . But this early attempt to prevent the CIA from spying on Americans was not enforced through any law or oversight mechanism, and in fact the intelligence agencies did engage in widespread political spying. . . .
>
> The reforms undertaken since the 1970s to prevent such abuses have been misunderstood as creating a so-called "wall" between law enforcement and intelligence.[12]

The legal mechanisms for coordination between agencies were in place prior to 9/11. The Foreign Intelligence Surveillance Act of 1978 . . . allowed intelligence investigators to "conduct electronic surveillance in the United States against foreign targets under a more lenient standard than is required in ordinary criminal cases, but only if the 'primary purpose' of the surveillance were foreign intelligence rather than criminal prosecution."[13] . . .

The PATRIOT Act also expanded the government's surveillance powers to permit almost unrestricted information-gathering while reducing the oversight function of the courts, but did nothing to break down the non-existent "wall." Under FISA, the government could conduct covert surveillance of individuals but only after seeking an order from a secret court created by the federal government. The court consists of eleven federal district court judges from throughout the country, appointed by the chief justice of the United States, and who serve in addition to their other duties.[14] The court meets at least twice a month behind locked doors on the top floor of the Department of Justice building. If that court denies a request for surveillance, the government may appeal to the three-member Court of Review, its members appointed by the Chief Justice of the United States. However, that appeals court had only one case; the lower court between its creation in 1978 and mid-2004, granted all but one of the government's more than fifteen thousand requests. The court essentially had become a puppet of the executive branch since FISA court judges, under both the original law and its subsequent broadening by the PATRIOT Act, are required to grant FBI surveillance requests if the FBI claims its actions are in accordance with the law. In state actions, individuals have the right to ask local and state courts to quash subpoenas for records. If denied, they may appeal to state supreme courts. No such protection exists under FISA. Individuals and businesses may not be represented in that secret court. The only appeal allowed is one initiated by the government, and all parties are bound by a federal gag order prohibiting any disclosure of such an order even being issued. There is no recourse. . . .

The USA PATRIOT Act reduces judicial oversight of telephone and Internet surveillance. Under the PATRIOT Act, federal law enforcement agencies aren't required to determine if a suspect uses or is likely to use a phone before planting a "bug." Under Sections 214 and 216, the federal government is also authorized to sweep the records of Internet Service Providers (ISPs) and network administrators in both private and public sectors, and may monitor and intercept e-mail and cell phone usage without first being required either to have a court order or to report such activities to judicial oversight. The federal government only has to believe that the information is "relevant," and does not need to show there is a "probable cause," as required under the Fourth Amendment. More important, the federal government can receive such warrants without the courts being allowed to determine if the allegations are truthful. Because the United States is essentially a "wired nation," with almost as many families having access to computers as they do to televisions, the problem of databases and possible privacy intrusions becomes even more severe. America Online (AOL), for instance, has a database of over ninety-two million names, with several identifying characteristics per name, all accessible under the PATRIOT Act.

Subsequent modifications to the Act now allow the government to obtain blanket warrants without identifying who is being monitored or which phones or computers are the target. The Department of Justice says the Act only allows the devices to "reveal the electronic addresses of the users of these media; they do not give law enforcement agents access to the contents of communications that are transmitted over them."[15] However, by knowing each page a person accesses by computer, even if for reasons of curiosity, a person's rights of privacy are violated. Even if a person chooses to purchase an item online, such as a box of dog treats, an electronic address of a specific page will reveal that information. . . .

The PATRIOT Act lowers the standard of proof for a warrant from "probable cause" to the nebulous "reasonable cause," significantly reducing the standard of what is required to obtain a search warrant (Section 218). Senior officials of the Department of Justice had claimed the PATRIOT Act doesn't violate the constitutional guarantees that law enforcement will detain and arrest individuals only for "probable cause." More than a year after the PATRIOT Act had become law, LaRae Quy, FBI spokesperson in San Francisco, said, "We still have to show probable cause for any actions we take. It's not just an agent descending and saying, 'Hey, I want to go in and see what this person is doing.'"[16] Within a month, Mark Corallo of the Department of Justice told the media that not only must there be a "probable cause that the person you are seeking the information for is a terrorist or a foreign spy,"[17] but that law enforcement officials had "to convince a judge that the person for whom you're seeking a warrant is a spy or a member of a terrorist organization."[18]

They were wrong. According to Jameel Jaffer, staff attorney with the American Civil Liberties Union (ACLU):

> [T]he FBI can obtain records . . . merely by specifying to a court that the records are 'sought for' an ongoing investigation. . . . That standard . . . is much lower than the standard required by the Fourth Amendment, which ordinarily prohibits the government from conducting intrusive searches unless it has probable cause to believe that the target of the investigation is engaged in criminal activity.[19]

Before the House Judiciary Committee, John Ashcroft finally admitted that the standard under the PATRIOT Act was "lower than probable cause," and that federal officials could go after citizens who were neither spies nor members of terrorist organizations.[20]

The PATRIOT Act, extending FISA, also allows secret searches to seize an individual's property without notifying that person even after the seizure (Section 806); and "sneak-and-peek" searches (Section 213) without notifying the citizen, to allow a search of the premises while the subjects are away, not just for investigation of potential terrorism cases but also for "any criminal investigation." For almost the entire history of the United States, a legal principle, based upon the Fourth Amendment, demanded that law enforcement, with a few exceptions, "knock and announce" their presence to execute a warrant. Part of that reason is to allow citizens to notify their attorneys, point out irregularities in the warrants (such as a wrong address), or to oversee that the limits of the warrant are not exceeded.

In May 2004, the FBI, with a court warrant obtained through regular procedures, searched the home and office of Brandon Mayfield, a family and immigration lawyer from Oregon. The government seized innumerable "tangible items," including "Spanish documents," which proved to be homework by one of his children. The FBI placed Mayfield into prison as a "material witness," which could have resulted in an indefinite detention with no charges ever being filed, monitored his every move, and announced with "nearly 100 percent certainty" that he was involved in a terrorist attack in Madrid two months earlier that killed almost two hundred and injured about two thousand. The court order was issued on the basis of an FBI claim that a partial fingerprint found on a package of detonator caps was Mayfield's. The Spanish authorities, who provided the fingerprint to the FBI by fax, weren't so sure. Subsequent analysis revealed the Spanish authorities were correct—the fingerprint was that of an Algerian national.

After two weeks in prison, Mayfield, a Muslim and former Army officer, was released. The FBI, which acknowledged it did a sloppy job of processing the print and investigating the case, publicly apologized; John Ashcroft called it "an unfortunate incident." The announced search of Mayfield's home may have been the second search. Steven T. Wax, a federal public defender, and one of Mayfield's attorneys, believes the FBI may have conducted an even more secret search under authority of the PATRIOT Act. The Department of Justice, claiming national security concerns, refused to acknowledge the previous search.

"We need to be safe and secure in our homes, not just from the bad guys but from the government as well," Mayfield told the Portland City Club following his release.[21] A subsequent investigation initiated by the Department of Justice's inspector general, following a complaint by Mayfield, revealed that the FBI may have improperly used the PATRIOT Act to search Mayfield's home without his knowledge.[22] . . .

"In addition to ignoring fundamental Fourth Amendment privacy rights, [the Patriot Act] also greases the slippery slope that was clearly anticipated, but specifically addressed and avoided by the drafters of our Constitution in the threefold separation-of-powers system of government they crafted so magnificently," says Bob Barr, a former CIA intelligence official, U.S. attorney, and conservative congressman who had been a vigorous opponent of the Clinton administration.[23] Barr has repeatedly stated that innumerable provisions of the USA PATRIOT Act "undercut basic conceptions of due process and privacy [and] their effectiveness is questionable."

The PATRIOT Act further gives the government the authority to indefinitely imprison legal immigrants and noncitizens without showing any court probable cause that they are terrorists or suspected of aiding others who are terrorists, and doesn't give the accused the right to challenge the government's assertions (Section 412); and expands the definition of terrorism to allow labeling dissenters as terrorists (Sections 411 and 802).

The PATRIOT Act also grants the FBI almost unlimited and unchecked access to "any tangible things (including books, records, papers, documents, and other items)" from individuals or companies without requiring them to show even minimal evidence of a crime, and places a "chilling effect" upon free speech (Section 215). The Act's sweeping provisions apply not only to homes, businesses, and newsrooms, but also to synagogues, churches, mosques, and other places of religious worship. Under provisions of the PATRIOT Act, the federal government can require libraries to divulge who uses public computers or what books they check out, video stores to reveal what tapes and DVDs customers bought or rented, even grocery and drug stores to disclose what paperbacks or magazines shoppers bought. Before the House Judiciary Committee, John Ashcroft even acknowledged that the federal government could obtain an individual's medical and educational records, and possibly DNA information as well, all without needing a court's determination there was "probable cause" for such a search.[24] . . .

At first, only a few opposed the USA PATRIOT Act. For the same reason Congress passed the bill, the public, politicians, local and state officials, and the media were afraid that by speaking against the Act, or the administration, they would be perceived as being not only unpatriotic but treasonous in the newly declared war on terrorism. It was certainly an impression the Bush administration pushed. Within months, however, some of the public began speaking out. And as the excesses of the PATRIOT Act became known, others began to question its effectiveness in the post-9/11 era.

"Our legislators get carried away sometimes, and go to extremes," said Al Fratzke, a resident of Sun City West, Arizona, and a prisoner of war during World War II; the PATRIOT Act is an extreme reaction to 9/11, he said.[25] Dr. Harry Kraus, Queens College professor emeritus of history, said the PATRIOT Act "is an invasion of our civil rights, our constitutional rights."[26] Former CBS News anchor Walter Cronkite, interviewed by CNN's Larry King, called the USA PATRIOT Act "disastrously severe."[27]

Rep. Don Young (R-Alaska), who had voted for the PATRIOT Act, agrees. Young, in his sixteenth term in the House and that body's ninth ranking member, told a news conference that not only was the Act "not really thought out," but that he was "very concerned that, in our desire for security and our enthusiasm for pursuing supposedly [sic] terrorists, that sometimes we might be on the verge of giving up the freedoms which we are trying to protect."[28]

Before a cheering audience of more than three thousand people in Washington, D.C., slightly more than two years after passage of the PATRIOT Act, former Vice President Al Gore ripped the Bush administration's failure to defend civil liberties:

> I want to challenge the Bush Administration's implicit assumption that we have to give up many of our traditional freedoms in order to be safe from terrorists. Because it is simply not true.
>
> In fact, in my opinion, it makes no more sense to launch an assault on our civil liberties as the best way to get at terrorists than it did to launch an invasion of Iraq as the best way to get at Osama Bin Laden. In both cases, the administration has attacked the wrong target.
>
> In both cases they have recklessly put our country in grave and unnecessary danger, while avoiding and neglecting obvious and much more important challenges that would actually help to protect the country.
>
> In both cases, the administration has fostered false impressions and misled the nation with superficial, emotional and manipulative presentations that are not worthy of American Democracy.
>
> In both cases they have exploited public fears for partisan political gain and postured themselves as bold defenders of our country while actually weakening not strengthening America.[29]

It was a speech that should have been given more than a year earlier, but would now serve as a focal point for opposition to the Bush administration policies.

NOTES

1. Quoted in "After: How America Confronted the September 12 Era," by Steven Brill, *Newsweek*, March 10, 2003; p. 66.
2. See: http://www.lifeandliberty.gov. If we believe the department's official statement, we can only conclude that secondary, less important, responsibilities include investigation and prosecution for racketeering, public corruption, mail fraud, discrimination, and antitrust violations. Further, Justice's mission statement appears to mute the primary function of the Department of Homeland Security.
3. *The 9/11 Commission Report: Final Report of the National Commission on Terrorist Attacks Upon the United States*, p. 328.
4. The Act is identified as P.L. 107-056, 115 STAT. 272. [http://frwebgate.access.gpo.gov/cgibin/getdoc.cgi?dbname=107_cong_public_laws&docid=f:publ056.107.pdf.][http://www.eff.org/Privacy/Surveillance/Terrorism/20011025_hr3162_usa_patriot_bill.html][http://www.wpic.org/privacy/terrorism/hr3162.htm]

5. 50 U.S.C. § 1801

6. Robert C. Byrd, *Losing America: Confronting a Reckless and Arrogant Presidency.*

7. Orrin Hatch, *Confessions of a Citizen Senator* (2002), p. 95.

8. "President Signs Anti-Terrorism Bill," White House news release/transcript; October 26, 2001.[http://www.whitehouse.gov/news/releases/2001/10/200110265.html]. The transcript is also available through the Government Printing Office. [http://frwebgate.access.gpo.gov/cgibin/getdoc.cgi?dbname=2001_presidential_documents&docid=pd29oc01_txt-26]

9. "Statement of U.S. Senator Russ Feingold," U.S. Senate; October 25, 2001. [http://feingold.senate.gov/~feingold/speeches/01/10/102501at.html]. Also available: "Why I Opposed the Anti-Terrorism Bill," by Senator Russ Feingold, *Counterpunch;* October 26, 2001. [http://www.counterpunch.org/feingold1.html]

10. See: "Report Scolds Terrorism Prosecutors; U.S. to Drop Convictions Against Trio in Detroit," by Dan Eggen, *Washington Post;* September 2, 2004; p. A3; "Justice Dept. Seeks End to Its Detroit Terror Case," by Danny Hakim, *New York Times;* September 2, 2004; p. A14; "Experts: Terrorism Trial Full of Errors," by David Ashenfelter, *Detroit Free Press;* September 2, 2004; p. B1; and "Judge Reverses Convictions in Detroit Terrorism Case," by Danny Hakim, *New York Times;* September 3, 2004; p. A12.

11. Quoted in "Mr. Ashcroft's Smear," editorial, *Washington Post;* April 20, 2004; p. A18. Also see: "Statement of Robert S. Mueller II, director, FBI, before the National Commission on Terrorist Attacks Upon the United States; April 14, 2004.
[http://www.fbi.gov/congress/congress04/mueller041404.htm].

12. "Domestic Intelligence and Civil Liberties," by Kate Martin, *SAIS Review,* Winter–Spring 2004, pp. 8–9.

13. "The Truth About the 'Wall'," by Jamie S. Gorelick, *Washington Post;* April 18, 2004; p. B7.

14. The PATRIOT Act increased the number of judges from seven to eleven.

15. "Ten Myths About the USA PATRIOT Act," by Mary Beth Buchanan, U.S. attorney, Western District of Pennsylvania, May 2003, p. 7.

16. Quoted in "Arcada: The Defiant Town Ordinance Penalizes Officials Who Cooperate With PATRIOT Act, But Law May Not Stand Up in Court," by Kevin Fagan, *San Francisco Chronicle;* April 13, 2003; p. 1.

17. Quoted in "Official Counters PATRIOT Act Critics," by Diana Graettinger, *Bangor* (Maine) *Daily News;* April 4, 2003; p. 1.

18. Quoted in "Libraries Post PATRIOT Act Warnings: Santa Cruz Branches Tell Patrons That FBI May Spy on Them," by Bob Egelko and Maria Alicia Gaura, *San Francisco Chronicle;* March 10, 2003; p. 1.

19. "Seeking Truth From Justice," *op. cit.,* pp. 3–4.

20. Testimony of John Ashcroft before the House Judiciary Committee; June 5, 2003. [http://www.house.gov/judiciary/fulltrans060503.htm].

21. Quoted in "Mayfield Recalls 'Dark Nights' as FBI Witness," by Noelle Crombie, *The Oregonian;* June 26, 2004; p. C1. Also see: "Madrid Case Leads

to Lawyer in Oregon," by Noelle Crombie and Mark Larabee, *The Oregonian;* May 7, 2004; p. A1; "Oregon Attorney Arrested Over Possible Tie to Spain Bombings," by Richard B. Schmitt, *Los Angeles Times;* May 7, 2004; p. A1; "American Held in Madrid Bombings," by Susan Schmidt, *Washington Post;* May 7, 2004; p. A1; "Brandon Mayfield's Family Waits for Answers," by Rukmini Callimachi, Associated Press; May 16, 2004; "FBI Exonerates Ore. Attorney," by Thomas Alex Tizon and Richard B. Schmitt, *Los Angeles Times;* May 25, 2004; p. A20; "A Fuzzy Fingerprint Leaves a Lasting Mark," by Thomas Alex Tizon, *Los Angeles Times;* May 29, 2004; p. Al; "Sloppy FBI Investigation Merits More than an Apology," editorial, *News & Record* (Greenville, S.C.); May 31, 2004; p. A10; and "Sensing the Eyes of Big Brother, and Pushing Back," by Timothy Egan, *New York Times;* August 8, 2004; p. A20.

22. "Report to Congress on Implementation of Section 1001 of the USA PATRIOT Act," U.S. Department of Justice, Office of the Inspector General; September 13, 2004.

23. Bob Barr, testimony before the U.S. Senate Committee on the Judiciary, "America after 9/11: Freedom Preserved or Freedom Lost?"; November 18, 2003.
    [http://judiciary.senate.gov/print_testimony.cfm?id=998& wit_id=2874].

24. Oversight Hearing, House of Representatives Committee on the Judiciary, June 5, 2003. [http://www.house.gov/judiciary/fultrans060503.htm]

25. Quoted in "Several in Sun Cities Say PATRIOT Act Goes Too Far," by Erin Reep, Arizona *Daily News-Sun;* July 26, 2003; part II, pp. A1, A5. [Part I, "PATRIOT Act: Scholars Warn of Loss of Liberties," ran on July 25, 2003; pp. A1 and A5.]

26. *Ibid.*

27. CNN transcript 091000CN.V22

28. Quoted in "Alaska Passes Anti-Patriot Resolution," ABC-TV News; May 23, 2003. [http://abcnews.go.com/sections/us/DailyNews/Alaska_patriot 030523.html].

29. "Freedom and Security," *op. cit.*

Liberty and Terrorism
Robert H. Bork

When a nation faces deadly attacks on its citizens at home and abroad, it is only reasonable to expect that its leaders will take appropriate measures to increase security. And, since security inevitably means restrictions, it is likewise only reasonable to expect a public debate over the question of how much individual liberty should be sacrificed for how much individual and national safety.

That, however, is not the way our national debate has shaped up. From the public outcry over the Bush administration's measures to combat terrorism, one might suppose that America is well on the way to becoming a police state. A full-page newspaper ad by the American Civil Liberties Union (ACLU), for instance, informs us that the Patriot Act, the administration's major security initiative, goes "far beyond fighting terrorism" and has "allowed government agents to violate our civil liberties—tapping deep into the private lives of innocent Americans." According to Laura W. Murphy, director of the ACLU's Washington office, Attorney General John Ashcroft has "clearly abused his power," "systematically erod[ing] free-speech rights, privacy rights, and due-process rights." . . .

The charge that our civil liberties are being systematically dismantled must be taken seriously. America has, in the past, overreacted to perceived security threats; the Palmer raids after World War I and the internment of Japanese-Americans during World War II are the most notorious examples. Are we once again jeopardizing the liberties of all Americans while also inflicting particular harm on Muslims in our midst?

Civil libertarians insist that we are. They condemn the indignities of security checks at airports, the tracking of Muslim visitors to the U.S., detentions of suspects for indefinite periods without access to the courts, and, when criminal charges are brought, the government's attempt to limit the accused's access to important evidence. Still worse in their view is the administration's evident intention of using military tribunals to try suspected terrorists. Finally, and most frightening of all to critics, the government has proposed the Terrorism Information Awareness (TIA) program—initially and even more ominously known as the Total Information Awareness program—which would employy

Mr. Bork is a senior fellow at the Hudson Institute. From "Civil Liberties after 9/11" by Robert H. Bork. Reprinted from COMMENTARY, July/August 2003, by permission; all rights reserved.

computers to gather and assess vast amounts of data relating to the transactions of, among others, unknowing American citizens.

There is no denying the rhetorical force of these accusations, or the success with which they have been used by the Left as a rallying cry against President Bush. What is less clear is their validity, not just on their own terms but in relation to the radically altered domestic security situation we have faced since the attacks of 9/11. There may be a case to be made concerning the measures we have taken so far; but it is not the one presented by the critics.

SECURITY AND ETHNIC PROFILING

According to Ibrahim Hooper, a spokesman for the Council on American-Islamic Relations, American Muslims have already lost many of their civil rights. "All Muslims are now suspects," Hooper has protested bitterly. The most salient outward sign of this is said to be the ethnic profiling that now occurs routinely in this country, particularly at airports but elsewhere as well—a form of discrimination widely considered to be self-evidently evil.

For most of us, airport security checks are the only first-hand experience we have with counter-measures to terrorism, and their intrusiveness and often seeming pointlessness have, not surprisingly, led many people to question such measures in general. But minor vexations are not the same as an assault on fundamental liberties. As for ethnic profiling, that is another matter, and a serious one. It is serious, however, not because it is rampant but because it does not exist.

That profiling is wicked *per se* is an idea that seems to have originated in connection with police work, when black civil-rights spokesmen began to allege that officers were relying on race as the sole criterion for suspecting someone of criminal activity. Profiling, in other words, equaled racism by definition. Yet, as Heather Mac Donald has demonstrated in *Are Cops Racist?*, the idea rests on a false assumption—namely, that crime rates are constant across every racial and ethnic component of our society. Thus, if blacks, who make up 11 percent of the population, are subject to 20 percent of all police stops on a particular highway, racial bias must be at fault.

But the truth is that (to stick to this particular example) blacks do speed more than whites, a fact that in itself justifies a heightened awareness of skin color as one of several criteria in police work. Of course, there is no excuse for blatant racism; but, as Mac Donald meticulously documents in case after case around the country, there is by and large no evidence that police have relied excessively on ethnic or racial profiling in conducting their normal investigations.

The stigma attached to profiling where it hardly exists has perversely carried over to an area where it should exist but does not: the war against terrorism. This war, let us remember, pre-dates 9/11. According to Mac Donald, when a commission on aviation security headed by then-Vice President Al Gore was considering a system that would take into account a passenger's national *origin and ethnicity*—by far the best predictors of terrorism—both the Arab lobby and civil libertarians exploded in indignation. The commission duly capitulated—which is why the final Computer-Assisted Passenger Prescreening System (CAPPS) specified that such criteria as national origin, religion, ethnicity, and even gender were not to be taken into consideration.

This emasculated system did manage, even so, to pinpoint two of the September 11 terrorists on the day of their gruesome flight, but prevented any action beyond searching their luggage. As Mac Donald points out, had the system been allowed to utilize all relevant criteria, followed up by personal searches, the massacres might well have been averted.

Ironically, it is the very randomness of the new security checks that has generated so much skepticism about their efficacy. Old ladies, children, Catholic priests—all have been subject to searches of San Quentin-like thoroughness despite being beyond rational suspicion. According to the authorities, this randomness is itself a virtue, preventing would-be terrorists from easily predicting who or what will draw attention. But it is far more probable that frisking unlikely persons has nothing to do with security and everything to do with political correctness. Frightening as the prospect of terrorism may be, it pales, in the minds of many officials, in comparison with the prospect of being charged with racism.

REGISTRATION, TRACKING, AND DETENTION OF VISITORS

Ethnic profiling, it is charged, is also responsible for the unjustified harassment and occasional detention of Arab and Muslim visitors to the United States. This is said to be an egregious violation not only of the rights of such persons but of America's traditional hospitality toward foreign visitors.

An irony here is that the procedures being deplored are hardly new, although they are being imposed with greater rigor. The current system has its roots in the 1950s in the first of a series of statutes ordering the Immigration and Naturalization Service (INS) to require aliens from countries listed as state sponsors of terrorism, as well as from countries with a history of breeding terrorists, to register and be fingerprinted, to state where they will be while in the U.S., and to notify the INS when they change address or leave the country.

Historically, however, the INS has been absurdly lax about fulfilling its mandate. When a visitor with illegal status—someone, for example, thought to have overstayed a student visa or committed a crime—is apprehended, the usual practice of immigration judges has been to release him upon the posting of a bond, unless he is designated a "person of interest." . . .

The procedures are now being adhered to more strictly, and this is what has given rise to accusations of ethnic or religious profiling. But such charges are as beside the point as in the case of domestic police work, if not more so. There is indeed a correlation between detention and ethnicity or religion, but that is because most of the countries identified as state sponsors or breeders of terrorism are, in fact, populated by Muslims and Arabs. . . .

DISCOVERY, DETENTION, AND PROSECUTION OF SUSPECTED TERRORISTS

According to civil libertarians, the constitutional safeguards that normally protect individuals suspected of criminal activity have been destroyed in the case of persons suspected of links with terrorism. This accusation reflects an ignorance both of the Constitution and of long-established limits on the criminal-justice system.

Prior to 1978, and dating back at least to World War II, attorneys general of the United States routinely authorized warrantless FBI surveillance, wire taps, and break-ins for national-security purposes. Such actions were taken pursuant to authority delegated by the President as commander-in-chief of the armed forces and as the officer principally responsible for the conduct of foreign affairs. The practice was justified because obtaining a warrant in each disparate case resulted in inconsistent standards and also posed unacceptable risks. (In one notorious instance, a judge had read aloud in his courtroom from highly classified material submitted to him by the government; even under more conscientious judges, clerks, secretaries, and others were becoming privy to secret materials.)

Attorneys general were never entirely comfortable with these warrantless searches, whose legality had never been confirmed by the Supreme Court. The solution in 1978 was the enactment of the Foreign Intelligence Surveillance Act (FISA). Henceforth, sitting district court judges would conduct secret hearings to approve or disapprove government applications for surveillance.

A further complication arose in the 1980s, however, when, by consensus of the Department of Justice and the FISA court, it was decided that the act authorized the gathering of foreign intelligence only for its own sake ("primary purpose"), and not for the possible criminal prosecution of any foreign agent. The effect was to erect a "wall" between the gathering of intelligence and the enforcement of criminal laws. But last year, the Foreign Intelligence Surveillance Court of Review held that the act did not, in fact, preclude or limit the government's use of that information in such prosecutions. In the opinion of the court, arresting and prosecuting terrorist agents or spies might well be the best way to inhibit their activities, as the threat of prosecution might persuade an agent to cooperate with the government, or enable the government to "turn" him.

When the wall came down, Justice Department prosecutors were able to learn what FBI intelligence officials already knew. This contributed to the arrest of Sami al-Arian, a professor at the University of South Florida, on charges that he raised funds for Palestinian Islamic Jihad and its suicide bombers. Once the evidence could be put at the disposition of prosecutors, al-Arian's longstanding claim that he was being persecuted by the authorities as an innocent victim of anti-Muslim prejudice was shattered.

TREATMENT OF CAPTURED TERRORISTS

According to critics, by depriving certain captured individuals of access to lawyers, and by holding them without filing charges, the government is violating the Geneva Convention's protections of lawful combatants or prisoners of war. This is nonsense.

Four criteria must be met to qualify a person as a lawful combatant. He must be under the command of a person responsible for his subordinates; wear a fixed distinctive emblem recognizable at a distance; carry arms openly; and conduct operations in accordance with the laws and customs of war. The men the United States has captured and detained so far do not meet these criteria.

The government's policy is as follows: if a captured unlawful enemy combatant is believed to have further information about terrorism, he can be held without access to legal counsel and without charges being filed. Once the government is satisfied that it has all the relevant information it can obtain, the captive can be held until the end of hostilities, or be released, or be brought up on charges before a criminal court.

The government chose one of these options when it charged John Lindh, an American citizen who fought with the Taliban in Afghanistan, . . . with crimes. Lindh entered into a plea agreement under which he was sentenced to twenty years in prison. . . .

In a somewhat separate category from Lindh, . . . charged with actual crimes, are the cases of two American citizens who have been detained rather than brought to trial because the government believes they possess undivulged valuable information. Yaser Esam Hamdi remains confined to the Norfolk Naval Brig, and José Padilla is confined at the Consolidated Naval Brig in Charleston. Neither man has yet been charged.

Hamdi filed a petition for habeas corpus challenging the legality of his detention. Although he was captured in Afghanistan, where he was carrying an AK-47 during a time of active military hostilities, and although he was classified by the executive branch as an unlawful enemy combatant, Hamdi claimed the full protections of the Constitution as an American citizen. He argued that his detention without charge and without access to a judicial tribunal or the right to counsel was in violation of the Fifth and Fourteenth Amendments.

The Court of Appeals for the Fourth Circuit held otherwise. Although the detention of U.S. citizens is subject to judicial review, that review must be "deferential." The Constitution explicitly confers war powers on the political branches; in going to war in Afghanistan, the President had relied both on those powers and on Congress's authorization of "all necessary and appropriate force" against nations, organizations, or persons he determined to be involved in terrorist attacks. Hamdi, the court said, was indeed an enemy combatant subject to detention. It elaborated its rationale:

The detention of enemy combatants serves at least two vital purposes. First, detention prevents enemy combatants from rejoining the enemy and continuing to fight against America and its allies. . . . In this respect, "captivity is neither a punishment nor an act of vengeance," but rather "a simple war measure."

Second, detention in lieu of prosecution may relieve the burden on military commanders of litigating the circumstances of a capture halfway around the globe. . . . As the Supreme Court has recognized [in *Johnson* v. *Eisentrager* (1950)], "it would be difficult to devise more effective fettering of a field commander than to allow the very enemies he is ordered to reduce to submission to call him to account in his own civil courts and divert his efforts and attention from the military offensive abroad to the legal defense at home."

Hamdi's petition was denied, as was his right of access to an attorney or to seeing government documents.*

Padilla was arrested upon his arrival at Chicago's O'Hare airport from Pakistan. The government indicted him, claiming he planned acts of terrorism, including the explosion of a radioactive "dirty bomb." When, like Hamdi, he petitioned for habeas corpus, the court held similarly that "the President is authorized under the Constitution and by law to direct the military to detain enemy combatants." Nevertheless, and over the government's objection, the court said it would allow Padilla the assistance of counsel to litigate the facts surrounding his capture and detention. (The government is now appealing this.) At the same time, the court disallowed the presence of counsel at Padilla's interrogations, and averred that the government need only show "some evidence" to prevail.**

Anthony Lewis went ballistic. It is, he wrote, a "fundamental truth" that an individual cannot get justice against the state without the effective help of a lawyer, and this truth was "being challenged in a way that I did not believe was possible in our country." But Lewis was completely wrong. Despite his attempt to conflate the two categories, detention is not punishment; its purpose, rather, is to prevent members of enemy forces from causing harm while hostilities are in progress. Nor is Padilla the subject of a criminal proceeding; criminal law rules do not apply when detention of an enemy is ordered by the President under his war powers. Hundreds of thousands of *lawful* prisoners of war have been held by the United States without the right to a lawyer, and unlawful enemy combatants are entitled to even fewer rights.

This makes perfect sense. A judicial system with rights of due process is crucial to a free society, but it is not designed for the protection of enemies engaged in armed conflict against us. Nor can we divert resources from the conduct of a war to the trial of every POW or unlawful combatant who wants to litigate. Besides, giving someone like Padilla a lawyer would frustrate the

---

*In *Hamdi v. Rumsfeld* (2004), the U.S. Supreme Court ruled that prisoners held at Guantanamo Bay, Cuba must have a "meaningful opportunity" to present a factual argument against detention before a "neutral" military tribunal—*Editors.*

**The U.S. Supreme Court remanded the Padilla case back to the lower court in 2004. It will be reviewed again by the Supreme Court in 2006—*Editors.*

very purpose of his detention, and place American lives in danger. A lawyer's duty, acting within the bounds of ethical behavior, is to create delay and confusion, keeping alive his client's hopes of going free. Armed with such hopes, Padilla would be all the less likely to divulge what he knew, and plans for future terrorist attacks might thereby go undetected.

It might be argued that Padilla is not like other unlawful enemy combatants because he is a U.S. citizen taken on American soil. But the Supreme Court disposed of that distinction as long ago as 1942 in *Ex parte Quirin*. In that case, German would-be saboteurs had entered the U.S. illegally with the intention of attacking war industries and facilities. Upon capture, they sought habeas corpus, claiming a right to trial before a regular court rather than a military tribunal. In denying the petition, the Court deemed it irrelevant that one of the captives claimed U.S. citizenship and was on U.S. soil when apprehended.

This is where there is a role for military tribunals, an institution that has played an important and honorable part in American jurisprudence throughout our history. In *Quirin*, the Court made clear that such tribunals rightly enjoy a separate constitutional track from grand juries and trial by jury. . . .

Consistent with this understanding, military tribunals have been used by several Presidents in time of war. In the Revolutionary War, before there even was a Constitution, George Washington employed them freely. So did Abraham Lincoln in the Civil War, and Franklin D. Roosevelt in World War II. . . .

In any event, the image of military tribunals as drumhead courts manned by stony-faced officers ready to convict regardless of the evidence is a fantasy. In reality, military courts may achieve just and equitable results *more* frequently than the run of civilian juries. Military judges tend to be *more scrupulous* in weighing evidence, in resisting emotional appeals, and in respecting the plain import of the laws. There are no Lance Itos or Johnny Cochrans in military trials. If, as the war against the terrorists drags on, we are forced to have recourse to military tribunals, there may well be clear gains for both justice and security. . . .

But the critics show every sign of being implacable, and in any case the cost of staying with the civil route is likely to be higher. In a district court a defense attorney will almost inevitably demand access to classified information; continued disclosure of such information in court would inform not only Muslim terrorists but all the world's intelligence services of the information we have and our methods of gathering it. If compromising national security is one alternative that may be forced on government by the demand for access to classified material, the other is to drop charges. Neither alternative is acceptable.

THE TERRORIST INFORMATION AWARENESS PROGRAM

Among Menaces to American liberty, this has been widely held to be the most sinister of all. Here is William Safire:

Every purchase you make with a credit card, every magazine subscription you buy and medical prescription you fill, every Web site you visit and e-mail you send or receive, every academic grade you receive, every bank deposit you make, every trip you book and every event you attend—all these transactions and communications will go into what the Defense Department describes as "a virtual, centralized grand database."

To this computerized dossier on your private life from commercial sources, add every piece of information that government has about you—passport application, driver's license and bridge toll records, judicial and divorce records, complaints from nosy neighbors to the F.B.I., your lifetime paper trail plus the latest hidden camera surveillance—and you have the supersnoop's dream.

What is the reality? The Terrorist Information Awareness program (TIA) is still only in a developmental stage; we do not know whether it can even be made to work. If it can, it might turn out to be one of the most valuable weapons in America's war with terrorists.

In brief, the program would seek to identify patterns of conduct that indicate terrorist activity. This entails separating small sets of transactions from a vast universe of similar transactions. Since terrorists use the same avenues of communication, commerce, and transportation that everybody else uses, the objective is to build a prototype of an intelligence system whose purpose would be to find terrorists' signals in a "sea of noise." Taking advantage of the integrative power of computer technology, the system would allow the government to develop hypotheses about possible terrorist activity, basing itself entirely on data that are *already legally available.*

But we may never find out whether the program's objective can be achieved, since TIA has been effectively gutted in advance. Impressed, no doubt, by the ideological breadth of the opposition to TIA, Congress was led to adopt a vague prohibition, sponsored by Democratic Senator Ron Wyden, draining TIA of much of its value. The amendment specifies that the program's technology may be used for military operations outside the U.S. and for "lawful foreign intelligence activities conducted wholly against non-United States persons." By inference, TIA may therefore *not* be used to gather information about U.S. citizens or resident aliens—despite the clear fact that significant number of persons in these categories have ties to terrorist groups.

Writing in *National Journal,* Stuart Taylor, Jr., has offered a hypothetical instance of how the Wyden amendment can cripple intelligence gathering. Suppose the government learns that elements of a deadly gas have been smuggled into the U.S. on flights from Germany by unidentified al-Qaeda operatives during a particular time frame. A TIA-based query of foreign databases might generate a list of possible terrorists. The Wyden amendment, however, would prohibit a search for the names of any who might be Americans, and might even put beyond reach any mixed databases that happened to include Americans. It would similarly bar looking in U.S. databases for passengers on the relevant flights whose names are also on government databases of known or suspected terrorists. Likewise out-of-bounds would be queries directed at legally accessible *commercial* databases—asking, for example, about purchases of canisters suitable for the deployment of the deadly gas. . . .

WHAT REMAINS TO BE DONE

The fact that opponents of the Bush administration's efforts to protect American security have resorted to often shameless misrepresentation and outright scare-mongering does not mean those efforts are invulnerable to criticism. They are indeed vulnerable—for not going far enough.

In addition to the lack of properly targeted security procedures at airports, and the failure to resist the gutting of TIA, a truly gaping deficiency in our arrangements is the openness of our northern and southern borders to illegal entrants. In the south, reportedly, as many as 1,000 illegal aliens *a day* enter through Arizona's Organ Pipe National Monument park, where they have become so brazen that they have cleared their own private roads. In the north, there are plenty of easily accessible and unmanned entry points from Canada. So far, Washington has not adequately responded to calls for more park-ranger staffing and military assistance, let alone addressed the lamentable condition of our immigration procedures in general.

There is, in short, plenty of work to go around. The war we are in, like no other we have ever faced, may last for decades rather than years. The enemy blends into our population and those of other nations around the world, attacks without warning, and consists of men who are quite willing to die in order to kill us and destroy our civilization. Never before has it been possible to imagine one suicidal individual, inspired by the promise of paradise and armed with a nuclear device, able to murder tens or even hundreds of thousands of Americans in a single attack. Those facts justify what the administration has already done, and urgently require more. . . .

Criminal Rights

Courts have a special role to play in our society. Unlike the two political branches of our government—Congress and the Executive—which are most sensitive to majority public opinion, courts must protect and defend minorities. Indeed, courts most often are called upon to ensure that the government acts in a fair and reasonable manner and to make certain that individual rights are protected.

Courts have a particularly important role to play in the protection of criminal rights, for in this area they must see that no injustice is done to the person accused of a crime. In the last thirty years, the U.S. Supreme Court has taken great care in enforcing the constitutional rights of persons accused of a crime. These include such protections as the right to remain silent and the right to counsel. Some of these criminal procedural safeguards have evoked considerable controversy among law-enforcement officials, political leaders, commentators, and the general public. Typically, critics of the criminal justice system point to its failures—failures that either put criminals back on the streets or penalize innocent and unsuspecting people.

The two articles that follow examine the role of the courts in the criminal justice system. In the first article, journalist Bernard Gavzer reports on the views of New York State judge Harold Rothwax, an outspoken critic of today's criminal justice system and author of Guilty: The Collapse of Criminal Justice. According to Judge Rothwax, the criminal justice system, with all its procedural guarantees, is tilted too much in favor of criminal suspects, so much so that he believes "We're in the fight of our lives" to preserve a law-abiding society.

In the second article John Kilwein, a professor of political science at West Virginia University, challenges the views of Judge Rothwax. While conceding that crime continues to be a major problem in the United States, Professor Kilwein argues that it would be unwise to adopt Judge Rothwax's "reforms" of the criminal justice system. Kilwein contends that the real issue in the criminal justice system is whether all citizens are fully protected from the possible abuses and excesses of law-enforcement officials. The many procedural guarantees of the Constitution and the courts, he argues, are merely the means to assure a "fair fight" between a criminal defendant and a criminal justice system that is stacked heavily in favor of the government. Without these guarantees, he contends, there exists the very real possibility that innocent persons might be accused, tried, convicted, and punished without adequate protection of the law.

"We're in the Fight of Our Lives"
Bernard Gavzer

At 2 A.M. on November 20, 1990, Leonardo Turriago was pulled over for speeding by two state troopers. They asked if they could look into his van, and Turriago said they could. Inside, the troopers saw a trunk and asked Turriago about it. He sprang open its lock, then ran away. Opening the trunk, the troopers found the body of a man shot five times.

Turriago was quickly caught. In his apartment, police found 11 pounds of cocaine and guns. The suspect told them where to look for the murder weapon, and it was recovered. Turriago was convicted of second-degree murder and sentenced to 45 years to life.

The defense appealed, saying the troopers had no right to search the van. On June 6, 1996, Turriago's conviction was overturned. A New York appellate court ruled that the police search was not justified and had been coerced.

"Criminal justice in America is in a state of collapse," says Judge Harold J. Rothwax, who has spent 25 years presiding over criminal cases in New York City. "We have formalism and technicalities but little common sense. It's about time America wakes up to the fact that we're in the fight of our lives."

Rothwax believes cases such as Turriago's illustrate that the procedural dotting of every "i" and crossing of every "t" has become more important than the crime's substance. "The bottom line is that criminals are going free," he says. "There is no respect for the truth, and without truth, there can be no justice."

While the search for truth should be the guiding principle of our courts, instead, the judge says, "our system is a carefully crafted maze, constructed of elaborate and impenetrable barriers to the truth." . . .

Practices we have taken for granted—such as the *Miranda* warning, the right to counsel, even unanimous jury verdicts—need to be reconsidered, says the judge. "You know," Rothwax confides, "more than 80 percent of the people who appear before me are probably guilty of some crime."

Rothwax insists there is a fundamental difference between the investigative and the trial stages of a case. The investigative stage is marked by the notion of probable guilt, he asserts, not the presumption of innocence. "Until a defendant goes on trial, he is probably guilty," the judge says, noting that by the time a person reaches trial he has been deemed "probably guilty" several times. "When a person is arrested, indicted by a grand jury, held in detention or

Bernard Gavzer is a contributing editor for *Parade* magazine. From Bernard Gavzer, "We're in the Fight of Our Lives," *Parade*, July 28, 1996, pp. 4–6. Reprinted with permission from *Parade*.

released on bail, it is all based on probable guilt." Rothwax adds, "Once *on trial,* he is presumed innocent." . . .

The positions the judge has staked out in what he regards as his crusade to bring sense to the criminal justice system have shocked those who long associated him with strong liberal causes. A lifelong Democrat, Rothwax was a senior defense trial attorney for the Legal Aid Society in New York and a stalwart of the New York Civil Liberties Union early in his career.

"I represented Lenny Bruce and Abbie Hoffman, the Black Panthers and the Vietnam war protesters," he says, "I am today as much a civil libertarian as ever. But that does not mean I must close my eyes to the devastation that has occurred in criminal justice. We have the crime, but where is the justice? It is all tilted in favor of the criminal, and it is time to bring this into balance."

The interests of the victim weigh solidly in Rothwax's courtroom in the Criminal Court Building in Manhattan. However, he is troubled by some decisions of the U.S. Supreme Court, saying: "Its rulings over the last 35 years have made the criminal justice system incomprehensible and unworkable."

Although neither the Supreme Court nor the Courts of Appeals decide the guilt or innocence of a defendant, they do make rulings on the constitutionality of acts by the police and lower courts and thus have a significant impact on our justice system. Key practices of our current system—which have come about as a result of Supreme Court rulings in recent decades—need to be changed, Rothwax believes. Among them are:

The Miranda Warning. In New York, Alfio Ferro was arrested in 1975 in connection with a fur robbery that turned into a murder. In the lockup, a detective— without saying a word—dropped some of the stolen furs in front of Ferro's cell. Ferro then made incriminating statements that led to his conviction for second-degree murder.

In 1984, an appellate court overturned the conviction, saying that the detective's action amounted to interrogation and violated Ferro's *Miranda* rights. The *Miranda* warning requires that the suspect be told he has a right to remain silent, that any statement he makes might be used against him and that he has the right to have a lawyer present.

"*Miranda* came about because of abuses such as prolonged custodial interrogation, beatings and starving in order to get a confession," says Rothwax. "I think those abuses have been largely dealt with. Now the police officer is put in the position of telling a suspect in a murder or rape, 'Look, you don't have to tell us anything, and that may be the best thing for you.' And it produces a situation in which a proper confession is thrown out because of the way in which it was read or that it wasn't read at the right time."

Rothwax believes *Miranda* can be replaced by the recording of an arrest and interrogation through videotapes, tape recorders and other technology. This would probably show whether a confession or statement was coerced.

The Exclusionary Rule. [In the winter of 1996] Federal Judge Harold Baer Jr. refused to admit as evidence 80 pounds of cocaine and heroin obtained in the arrest of a drug courier in the Washington Heights neighborhood of New York

City. The evidence was excluded because, said Baer, the police had violated the Fourth Amendment protection against unreasonable search and seizure when they searched the car in which the drugs were found.

The police said their search was proper in view of the fact that they saw men hastily loading bags into an out-of-state car in a high drug area in the middle of the night, and the men ran away when the police approached. Judge Baer, however, said just because the men ran off was no reason to suspect them of a crime. In Washington Heights, the judge said, it was not unusual for even innocent people to flee, because police there were regarded as "corrupt, violent and abusive."

Under a growing chorus of criticism, Judge Baer first reversed himself and then asked that the case be assigned to another judge. It was. Rothwax says this is the sort of muddled episode which arises from the exclusionary rule, producing "truth and justice denied on a technicality."

"The Supreme Court has consistently ruled that evidence seized in violation of the Fourth Amendment *should* be excluded from a criminal trial. But if you read the Fourth Amendment, nowhere does it say that *illegally* obtained evidence *must* be excluded," says Rothwax. "In my view, when you exclude or suppress evidence, you suppress the truth."

Judge Rothwax has a remedy: "Make the exclusionary rule *discretionary* instead of mandatory. If it was at the discretion of the judge, there could be a test of reasonableness. A judge could consider factors such as whether a police officer acted with objective reasonableness and subjective good faith. As it is now, the exclusionary rule is irrational, arbitrary and lacks proportion. No wonder that in 90 percent of exclusionary cases, the police don't know what the law is."

The Right to Counsel.   In 1982, Kenneth West of New York, an alleged drug dealer, was suspected of being involved in killing a man who had taken his parking place. His lawyer, at a police lineup, told the police not to question West in his absence. Nothing came of the case for three years. Then police arrested a former cohort of West who said West had been one of the shooters. The informer secretly taped West talking about the killing. West was convicted, but in 1993 the New York Court of Appeals reversed the conviction, saying the secret taping amounted to questioning him without the presence of counsel.

The right to counsel is provided by the Sixth Amendment. "It is essential there be a right to counsel," Judge Rothwax says. "But the amendment doesn't say it has to be during police questioning and investigation. As a result of technicalities over this issue of counsel, I have seen murderers go free. Make it clear that the right to a lawyer shouldn't be a factor in the *investigative* stage but only in pre-trial and trial stages."

Instructions to the Jury.   After closing arguments in the O. J. Simpson murder trial, Judge Ito took great care in telling jurors that Simpson's failure to take the stand in his own defense should in no way be taken to mean anything negative or to draw any other adverse conclusion.

This instruction to the jury occurs in all cases in which the defense asks for it, because of a Supreme Court ruling in 1981 that said not to do so amounted to a violation of the Fifth Amendment. [The Fifth Amendment states that no person shall be forced to testify against himself.] "The Fifth Amendment does not say that one might not draw reasonable inferences from the silence of a defendant," Judge Rothwax says. "I think we must find a way to return to the standard that existed before, that the judge could tell the jury that the failure to explain could amount to an inability to explain."

The judge would like to see other changes made to the jury system. Among them:

1. *Unanimous jury verdicts should no longer be required.* Why? Rothwax cites a murder case he presided over. "It was an overwhelming case of clear guilt. Yet there was a hung jury. One juror was convinced the defendant was not guilty. How did she know? Well, as she explained it, 'Someone that good-looking could not commit such a crime.' We had to retry the case, and the man was quickly found guilty."

   By allowing verdicts to be decided by a vote of 11–1 or 10–2, Rothwax says, there could be a reduced risk that a single juror could cause a retrial or force a compromise in the face of overwhelming evidence of guilt.

2. *Peremptory challenges to prospective jurors should be strictly limited or abolished.* Peremptory challenges allow lawyers to knock someone off the jury without giving any reason. "As we saw in the Simpson case," Rothwax says, "it makes it possible to stack a jury so that the most educated juror is excused, and you end up with a jury that can be manipulated to accept innuendo as evidence."

Judge Rothwax regards the entire conduct of the Simpson trial as an unspeakable insult to the American people, one that left them "feeling wounded and deeply distrustful of the system." He adds: "There was an opportunity to show a vast audience the potential vitality of justice at work. Instead we are assaulted by an obscene circus. We saw proof that the American courtroom is dangerously out of order." . . .

To sit with Rothwax in court, as this writer did, is to get a sense of his urgency for reform. In three hours, there was a procession of men and women charged with felonies from murder to drug dealing. Rothwax was all business, and he was tough with everyone. After 47 cases had been considered and dealt with, the judge turned to me and asked, with irony, about the defendants we had seen: "Did you notice the huge display of remorse?" There hadn't been any. "That's why" he said, "we are in the fight of our lives."

Just Make It a Fair Fight
John C. Kilwein

Crime is a significant problem in this country. In 2000, 15,517 Americans became victims of homicide.[1] Property loss and medical expenses related to crime approach $20 billion per year. Responding to these and other troubling statistics, Congress has "federalized" dozens of crimes that were formerly only state offenses, and state legislatures have passed mandatory-minimum sentence laws that require convicted criminals to spend more time in prison. The U.S. Bureau of Justice Statistics reports that as a result of these changes the number of people incarcerated in federal and state prisons more than quadrupled, increasing from 319,600 in 1980 to 1,406,031 in 2001. In addition, Congress has made it much more difficult for prisoners to use the federal courts, the Constitution, and writ of *habeas corpus* to appeal their convictions. All of this is evidence of a concerted national effort, some might argue excessive effort, to deal with the crime problem.

But efforts such as these are not enough for New York Judge Harold Rothwax. He wants to shock us into taking action in the criminal courts, and in so doing he uses arguments that are based on fear.[2] Judge Rothwax warns Americans, as they read their Sunday papers, of the ominous threats of such dark predators as Leonardo Turriago, who cart murder victims around in the trunks of their automobiles, and who walk the streets thanks to legal "technicalities." But as Judge Rothwax spins his frightening yarn, he fails to tell the reader that the crime rate is actually dropping, in spite of the alleged flaws of the criminal justice system. Violent crime, for example, dropped 10 percent in 2000–2001. Why the paradox?: A *reduction* in crime, while Judge Rothwax thinks we are in "the fight of our lives!"

Judge Rothwax offers us a new system of criminal justice that assumes that all police officers and prosecutors do their jobs in a fair and objective manner, free of any systematic bias against groups or individuals in society. The Rothwax system assumes that prosecutors will base their prosecutorial decisions strictly on legal grounds, ignoring other factors such as political gain or racial animus. Judge Rothwax believes that as a society we have largely solved the problem of police brutality; that American law enforcement officials no longer use uncomfortable detention, physical violence, or psychological coercion to secure convictions. The Rothwax system assumes that criminal defendants in

John C. Kilwein is a professor of political science at West Virginia University. He wrote this article especially for *Points of View* in 1997 and revised it in 2000 and again in 2003.

the United States have more legal representation than they deserve, and that the system would benefit from reducing the formal rules that lawyers bring to the pre-trial process. Unfortunately, the real world of American criminal justice is far more complex than the "good vs. evil" morality play suggested by Judge Rothwax.

THE GOVERNMENT VS. THE CRIMINAL DEFENDANT: A FAIR FIGHT?

The legal system in the United States is based on the belief that the best way for a court to discover the truth in a legal dispute is to allow the parties to battle it out in the courtroom before a jury or judge. The judge acts as an independent and objective arbiter or referee who makes sure that the disputants battle fairly by following the rules of law. The disputants are responsible for developing the case they will bring into the courtroom, and they understandably have a strong incentive to seek out any evidence or witnesses that might assist them. The disputants also have the right to challenge the veracity of their opponents' presentations. The confrontation in court between these two competing sides, each presenting a very different version of a contested dispute, will, in theory, maximize the likelihood that the truth will come out.[3] Of course, the difficult job for the judge or the jury is sifting through the two accounts to arrive at a sense of what actually took place and what justice should be.

When applied to disputes involving a crime, the disputants in the adversarial system are the defendant, or the person charged with committing the crime, and the state. The state, rather than the victim, is the litigant in criminal cases because, by definition, crimes not only harm victims, they also harm and threaten society as a whole. In a criminal case, therefore, the battle to be played out in the courtroom is between a person charged with a crime and a prosecutor who represents the interests of society—a battle that strains the notion of a fair fight. The government clearly has a lot more advantages than the criminal defendant. The extent of this mismatch is underscored by the fact that prosecutors have available to them the machinery of government, including the vast investigative powers of law enforcement, whereas defendants must do it on their own.

The American justice system takes into account this disparity, however, by providing the defendant with certain procedural rights and advantages that are intended to equalize the courtroom battle in criminal cases. This system assumes that when a powerful litigant, the state, faces a weaker litigant, the defendant, there is a high probability of a wrongful conviction of an innocent person unless the state follows procedures designed to make it a fair fight. And in our criminal legal tradition, there is no greater miscarriage of justice than sending innocent individuals to prison or to their death. Modern-day criminal procedure protections seek to prevent such an outcome.

Among the equalizers built into the American legal system are the presumption of innocence, the beyond-a-reasonable-doubt standard of proof; the prohibitions against unreasonable search and seizure, forced self-incrimination, excessive bail, excessive fines, double jeopardy, and cruel and unusual punishment; and the right to counsel, to a trial by jury, to a public and speedy trial, to speak at trial, to confront and cross-examine hostile witnesses, to present favorable witnesses, and to access the writ of *habeas corpus*. Some of these "equalizers" have been incorporated into our system as part of formal documents, or constitutions, that act as the blueprints for our American governments, while others were added as our criminal justice system evolved and became part of our legal tradition.

For Judge Rothwax the balance between the state and the criminally accused is fundamentally flawed. Criminal defendants are not the "weak sisters" in a criminal trial; the state is. For Judge Rothwax, a "liberal" judiciary led by the U.S. Supreme Court has conspired to create new and extreme rights for the defendant. These extravagant rights, moreover, make it extremely difficult for the prosecutor and the police to do their jobs. Seemingly guilty defendants are released from custody because their defense lawyers exploited some constitutional technicality. The murder trial of O. J. Simpson is given as a case in point. Overworked, underpaid, and inept prosecutors fumbled before a group of highly paid "dream team" defense lawyers, who exploited every procedural technicality to achieve a verdict of innocence.

Judge Rothwax offers up an alternative system of criminal justice that tips the balance in the courtroom battle toward the side of the prosecution by limiting a defendant's right to counsel, altering the presumption of innocence, increasing the power of police to search for proof of criminality and to interrogate defendants, allowing more evidence favoring the prosecution's case to be admitted in court, and altering the nature of jury deliberations in criminal trials. In short, the Rothwax system makes it easier for the prosecution to prove to a jury that a criminal defendant is guilty as charged and deserving of punishment.

THE "SUSPECT RIGHTS" OF SUSPECTS

The Presumption of Innocence

Our legal system recognizes that a criminal dispute is more serious than a civil dispute. In criminal law, society has the capacity to publicly punish the convicted criminal, using several forms of punishment. First, the defendant faces the shame and consequences associated with being declared a convicted criminal, including the loss of certain freedoms and rights, as for example, access to a variety of licenses or the freedom to perform certain jobs. Second, criminal conviction can bring with it the possibility of substantial monetary fines, often in the thousands of dollars. Third, criminal conviction can result in a complete loss of freedom through incarceration, with all the unintended consequences of life behind bars, a violent world often filled with physical assault, rape, and other indignities. Finally, in thirty-eight states and at the federal level, defendants charged with capital crimes face the ultimate punishment of being put to death by the state.

Given the seriousness of being charged with a crime, the American legal system confers on the defendant an important protection: the presumption of innocence. The primary purpose of this rule is to prevent a wrongful conviction that sends an innocent person to prison or to death. There is a simple, yet profound logic behind this rule. When a criminal victimizes an individual, society intervenes to find, try, and punish the criminal. The harm suffered by the victim can never be undone, but some solace comes from the fact that the state takes a direct interest in resolving the criminal dispute. On the other hand, when the state wrongfully punishes an innocent defendant, the victimization is absolute. There is no solace available to the innocent person since the perpetrator is the state. This perspective gives rise to the old saw that it is better to let ten guilty persons go free, than to send one innocent individual to prison or death. For Judge Rothwax, however, that old saw is apparently a bit rusty and should be replaced by a new motto: The criminal justice system almost never convicts the wrong person; and those guilty individuals who are set free are threatening us all.

Judge Rothwax makes a distinction between the investigative (pre-trial) and trial stages of the criminal process. Rothwax argues that, during the investigative stage, defendants are assumed to be guilty by the police and the prosecutor or they would not have been arrested and indicted in the first place. He concludes that when defendants appear before his bench, they are probably guilty of the charges or their cases would never have reached his court. In short, Judge Rothwax gives the state the benefit of the doubt that it only prosecutes clearly guilty people. This perspective is troubling because it ignores the basic idea behind adversarial justice: Legal conflicts are not pre-judged but decided through the courtroom battle.

While it is true that the great majority of police officers and prosecutors are honest people who play by the rules and who have no desire to harm innocent people, Rothwax's position ignores a number of very real problems. The most obvious problem of the proposed system is that it fails to take into account that justice officials can and do make mistakes, and the importance of the trial process in detecting these honest errors. Second, Judge Rothwax ignores the fact that a minority of justice officials, however small, are lazy, dishonest, corrupt, racist, or some combination of these. Examples of these troubling behaviors abound in our criminal justice system. In 2003, the Republican governor of Illinois, George Ryan, took the unprecedented action of commuting the death sentences of all men and women on death row, 167 prisoners, to life imprisonment. Governor Ryan based his decision on his research into the machinery of Illinois' capital justice system, which left him with serious questions about its inherent fairness.[4] Ryan cited misconduct by prosecutors and police officers as factors that can lead to unjust capital sentences. A year earlier in Los Angeles, police officers admitted to systematically committing crimes to convict innocent individuals.[5] The Los Angeles District Attorney's Office took the unprecedented action of seeking the reversal of forty felony convictions, because it had clear evidence that those convictions were based on the false testimony of the errant officers.

In 1997, an internal U.S. Department of Justice investigation revealed that agents of the highly respected F.B.I. crime laboratory altered evidence and skewed testimony to assist prosecutors.[6] In Texas and West Virginia false testimony given by an incompetent and dishonest medical examiner sent at least six innocent men to prison.[7] To avoid the embarrassment and political fallout of being unable to convict the perpetrators of an arson fire with multiple deaths in New York[8] and the killing of a police officer in Houston,[9] prosecutors in both cities tenaciously pursued capital murder charges against apparently innocent individuals, while ignoring or concealing exculpatory evidence in the prosecution's possession. And evidence that some police officers and prosecutors target young black and Hispanic men for questionable arrest and prosecution comes to light with alarming clarity, as in the case of Carlton Brown.[10]

The case of Carlton Brown is particularly enlightening. Mr. Brown, who is black, is paralyzed from the chest down following injuries he sustained while under arrest in New York City's 63rd Precinct. Charged with driving with a suspended license, Mr. Brown contended that the arresting officers, after becoming irritated with his demands for information on his arrest, smashed his head, while he was handcuffed, into a bulletproof, double-plate glass window and severely injured his spine. The two police officers involved with his arrest countered that Mr. Brown had hurt himself falling down in the police station. The police officers were charged, tried before a judge, and acquitted. In a subsequent civil proceeding, however, the city of New York agreed to pay Mr. Brown $4.5 million in civil damages, a record-setting pre-trial settlement. Needless to say, such a settlement calls into question Judge Rothwax's confidence in the criminal justice system's ability to function in an unbiased manner. Our system of justice assumes that people, including law enforcement officials, are not angels[11] or saints; nor are they infallible; and it builds in protections, like the presumption of innocence, accordingly. The Rothwax system depends on an angelic conversion among these officials, an unlikely occurrence now or ever.

Miranda, the Right to Remain Silent and the Right to Counsel

Judge Rothwax reserves some of his harshest criticism for the U.S. Supreme Court's 1966 decision in *Miranda v. Arizona*.[12] In that decision the Court ruled that a confession made by Ernest Miranda, who was charged with kidnapping and raping an eighteen-year-old woman, was unconstitutionally obtained by police interrogators.[13] Extending its ruling beyond the immediate circumstances of the arrest and interrogation of Miranda, the Court required that henceforth all police officers and prosecutors must inform defendants of their rights to remain silent and to have counsel.[14] Commenting on state law enforcement officials, the Court observed,

> The use of physical brutality and violence is not, unfortunately, relegated to the past or to any part of the country. Only recently in Kings County [Brooklyn Borough], New York, the police brutally beat, kicked and placed lighted cigarette butts on the back of a potential witness under interrogation for the purpose of securing a statement incriminating a third party.[15]

The Court added that, although not using physical violence, other police inter-rogators use psychological abuse and lies to trick defendants into confessing to crimes.

Seen as an indictment against all police officers and prosecutors, the decision in *Miranda* was, and, as highlighted by Judge Rothwax, still is very unpopular within the law enforcement community.[16] This is unfortunate because, as Chief Justice Warren argued in the opinion, the *Miranda* requirements do not prevent good law enforcement officers from doing their job. Indeed, as pointed out by Warren, agents of the F.B.I. had already been using the warnings and were still able to investigate and assist in the conviction of federal defendants. What the warnings were designed to do was prevent an innocent defendant from confess-ing in order to bring an end to an abusive interrogation. The fact of the matter is that police officers who do not abuse defendants have nothing to fear from the *Miranda* requirements.

The *Miranda* decision also sought to make effective two important equaliz-ers in the Bill of Rights: the prohibition against self-incrimination and the right to counsel. The right against self-incrimination, or the right to remain silent, is based on an old common law principle that the state cannot force defendants to testify against themselves. Rather, the state makes the charges and must prove its case. Although the right to counsel came later in the Anglo-American legal tradition, it is based on the belief that it is unreasonable to expect ordinary persons to understand the legal implications of statements they might make or actions they might take in the pre-trial stage, actions that might again lead to their wrongful conviction. The *Miranda* requirement was based on the reason-able assumption that illiterate or uninformed defendants probably are not aware of these protections and therefore the state has a responsibility to inform them.

Judge Rothwax argues against this necessity, contending that, because defense attorneys step in and convince their clients to do otherwise, *Miranda* prevents the police from securing confessions from cooperative defendants. Apparently Judge Rothwax is opposed to the general principle of informed consent; that is, that defendants should know what they are doing before they say anything or confess. Judge Rothwax also seems to believe that the abuse of defendants while in police custody, cited by Chief Justice Warren in *Miranda*, is no longer a problem. Unfortunately, evidence suggests that, in his zeal to get tougher on crime and criminals, Judge Rothwax is ignoring the fact that abuses continue in the interrogation stage of the pre-trial process. An example from Rothwax's own hometown underscores this conclusion.[17] Police officers in New York's 24th Precinct arrested a seventeen-year-old white male for a mis-demeanor. He refused to confess. The defendant was held in a jail cell for two nights. At one point, he was placed in a van and chained in the sweltering heat. At another point a police officer waved his gun in front of the defendant and threatened to "shoot his dick off." One wonders if the cameras in the precinct, called for by Judge Rothwax to protect against such abuse, would have cap-tured this particular "Kodak moment"! The evidence suggests that this incident is not a random occurrence, in New York or nationally. Amnesty International has cited ninety cases of police brutality allegedly perpetrated by officers of the New York Police Department alone. Similar charges by other watchdog groups have been leveled at other departments around the country.[18]

Sometimes law enforcement officers use less violent forms of coercion in the interrogation room. For example, in 1999, F.B.I. agents lied to Wen Ho Lee, a Department of Energy employee suspected of spying for China, by informing him that he had failed a lie detector test, when, in fact, he had registered a score indicating he was telling the truth.[19] Building on this lie, the agents then told Mr. Lee that if he did not provide them with a confession, he would likely die in the electric chair.

For most first-time defendants the pre-trial process can be a very frightening experience. Defendants, innocent or guilty, who cannot post bail are held in jail until their trial. The pace of some criminal justice systems can be glacial, taking up to two years for a case to make it to trial. This delay, moreover, can be used to entice or coerce a defendant into making a confession, even a false one. For example, a prosecutor can offer defendants awaiting trial a plea bargain that gives them credit for time served while awaiting trial in exchange for a guilty plea. Given this offer, an innocent defendant might make a false confession, assuming that the conviction is a small price to pay for immediate release from prison.[20] The deal may be especially appealing if the defendant considers that a guilty verdict by jury at trial could yield an even stiffer sentence. Interrogations are also daunting for a defendant unfamiliar with the law. And although the great majority of questionings are conducted by professional officers observing all relevant constitutional requirements, the fact remains that police officers have substantially more experience in the process than do defendants, thereby increasing the probability that defendants will unwittingly damage their own case. In these and every other pre-trial situation, defendants would be at a severe disadvantage without legal representation.

In the end, the Rothwax system would punish the ignorant, the weak, and the poor. Wealthy or more highly educated defendants, who have a basic understanding of the legal system, are more likely to know they have the right to remain silent and to make informed choices about its use. Likewise, sophisticated defendants who are not intimidated by pre-trial detention and rough treatment are also more likely to refuse to assist the police in developing the state's case against them. Moreover, defendants with long-standing criminal records are also likely to be especially cognizant of their right to remain silent. In addition, multiple offenders who have experienced the daily violence of the corrections system are probably less likely to be frightened into confessing as the result of a difficult interrogation.

The most troubling aspect of Rothwax's system, however, from the point of view of equal justice for all, is that it rewards wealthier criminal defendants. Individuals who can afford to hire a lawyer and post bail are able to avoid the various forms of pre-trial pressure since they can await trial in the comfort of their own homes; and, with the advice of counsel, they are more likely to remain silent, thereby putting the government to its full task of convicting them without their assistance. It is quite possible, therefore, that the system proposed by Judge Rothwax will have the unintended consequence of convicting more innocent, first-time criminal defendants, while releasing those defendants with experience and/or money. These potential biases do not seem to concern Judge Rothwax. Like some American generals in Vietnam, Judge Rothwax seems to be singularly concerned only with body counts: So what if these new convictions are gained at the expense of fairness? They're convictions; and that's what counts! A justice system that operates in this manner has abandoned any pretense of being blind to a defendant's wealth or social status. It is a justice system more likely to convict an innocent defendant whose real crime is that he or she lives in the South Bronx rather than on Long Island.

The Exclusionary Rule

The exclusionary rule is an American invention, created by the U.S. Supreme Court in 1914.[21] It was designed to resolve the question of what should be done when a police officer or prosecutor violates the constitutional protections of defendants who have been the targets of illegal searches or interrogations. By making this ruling, the Supreme Court, using a classic American "free-market" approach, has ruled that such evidence is tainted and must therefore be excluded from trial. The exclusionary rule, the Court has argued, removes any incentive for law enforcement officials to engage in unconstitutional and illegal activities, since ill-gotten gains cannot be used in court.

Since the Bill of Rights makes no mention of this rule in the Fourth Amendment's prohibition against unreasonable searches and seizures, Judge Rothwax contends that the rule is an illegitimate hindrance to the criminal justice system's operation. He argues that excluded evidence prevents the court from getting the total truth surrounding a case. To accept this logic, however, one must, again, accept, as Rothwax clearly does, that in the rule's absence, police officers or prosecutors are unlikely to violate the Fourth or Fifth Amendments in their search for evidence or confessions. Given the examples of illegal police conduct cited, it is difficult to share Justice Rothwax's views of the motives and actions of the police.

Judge Rothwax is also upset because the exclusionary rule has, in his view, been used by judges in an overly technical and picky manner, with good cases being thrown out because investigating officers forgot to "dot the i's and cross the t's." He blames the "liberal" U.S. Supreme Court for decisions that favor criminal defendants. The Supreme Court of 2003, however, is, in fact, a very conservative one, particularly in its decisions dealing with the rights of criminal defendants. Since the mid-1970s, the U.S. Supreme Court has consistently shifted the constitutional advantage in criminal matters away from criminal defendants toward the police and prosecution. Specifically, in terms of the exclusionary rule, the Court has ruled in ways that enable prosecutors to use more questionable evidence and confessions against criminal defendants. Two examples highlight this shift. In *U.S. v. Havens,*[22] the Court allowed illegally obtained evidence to be used in trial to discredit testimony during cross-examination. And in *Nix v. Williams,*[23] the Court ruled that tainted evidence can be used against the defendant if the trial court judge concludes that evidence would inevitably have been discovered. Still, this very pro-police U.S. Supreme Court drew the line by refusing to overturn Miranda when given the opportunity in *Dickerson v. U.S.*[24]

Peremptory Challenges and Unanimous Jury Verdicts

Judge Rothwax's remaining indictments of the present criminal justice system deal with criminal juries. Responding to the controversy surrounding the O. J. Simpson murder trial, he criticizes the defense team's use of peremptory challenges to eliminate prospective jurors.[25] He argues that the Simpson defense team used such challenges to seat a jury that could easily be fooled by courtroom pyrotechnics. Whether this is true or not is a matter of conjecture, but it should be noted that Judge Rothwax ignores the fact that the prosecution had the same opportunity to affect the makeup of the jury. In reality, peremptory challenges help both sides in the courtroom battle, and thus we can assume that their removal would potentially hurt both sides as well. In 1997, for example, a videotape surfaced that was used as a training device for assistant prosecutors in Philadelphia.[26] The tape shows a senior prosecutor counseling his trainees to exclude black citizens from serving on criminal juries because they are distrustful of the police and therefore less likely to convict. The tape tells the trainees they should especially avoid placing young black women on their juries, because they are very bad for the prosecution's case. Although this episode remains to be investigated, and the attorney featured in the video vehemently denies having done anything illegal or morally wrong, the advice presented on this tape would appear to violate a Supreme Court ruling prohibiting race from being used as a factor in selecting jurors. More fundamentally, this example calls into question Judge Rothwax's contention that the justice system has solved the problem of systemic racism.

Judge Rothwax also opposes the requirement that a criminal jury reach a verdict of guilt unanimously, suggesting instead that we should allow a jury to convict a defendant with a substantial majority, such as a vote of 11–1 or 10–2. In fact, the practice of jury unanimity[27] is merely a legal custom and not an explicit constitutional right, and the U.S. Supreme Court has established that, if states choose, they can allow juries to reach their decision with a clear, non-unanimous verdict.[28] Given the Supreme Court's view on this issue, Judge Rothwax's gripe, then, is with the legal system of the state of New York, which apparently has decided to continue the practice of jury unanimity, and not with the rulings of the so-called "liberal" U.S. Supreme Court in Washington.

WE FACE THE CHOICE OF OUR LIVES

The late Senator Sam Ervin once said, "In a free society you have to take some risks. If you lock everybody up, or even if you lock up everybody you think might commit a crime, you'll be pretty safe, but you won't be free."[29] To this one might add, "And you might end up getting locked up yourself!"

This country was shaped in part by a healthy concern for the potential abuses of governments. The U.S. Bill of Rights and the civil liberty protections of the state constitutions were created to ensure certain fundamental protections for all citizens. These guarantees were designed to withstand the shifting winds created by agitated majorities. Judge Rothwax is not the first American, nor will he likely be the last, to tell his fellow citizens that we live in a particularly dangerous time and that to survive we must forgo the "luxury" of our civil liberties.

Judge Rothwax is wrong. The guarantees created by James Madison and the Constitution are not luxuries. Rather, they make up a very battered constitutional firewall that barely protects us from the police state that he, cynical politicians, and a very conservative U.S. Supreme Court seem to be inching toward. These civil liberties are not excessive; if anything, they provide too little protection for the realities of daily life in an increasingly urban, multicultural society facing the twenty-first century.

Of course, many Americans share Judge Rothwax's concern over criminal predators like Leonardo Turriago who prey on their fellow citizens. These violent criminals should be punished severely. But the same level of concern ought to be expressed in regard to how today's criminal justice system treats black, Hispanic, American Indian, poor, and uneducated Americans. Americans ought to be concerned about the rights of innocent, hardworking Americans who are harassed, injured, maimed, or killed every day by abusive police officers for being in the "wrong" neighborhood or driving too "nice" a car. Judge Rothwax's system will not win the war against the Leonardo Turriagos of the world; it will likely create more Carlton Browns.

NOTES

1. Federal Bureau of Investigation, *Uniform Crime Report*, 2000.
2. Bernard Gavzer, "We're in the Fight of Our Lives." *Parade* (July 28, 1996): 4–6.
3. In other countries, such as most of the nations of continental Europe, an inquisitorial system of justice is used. In this system, it is the judge who determines the direction of the trial by calling witnesses, examining evidence and drawing final conclusions of fact. When compared to an adversarial justice system, inquisitorial disputants and, more importantly, their lawyers play a much less active role in affecting the composition of the case. Instead of a courtroom battle, the inquisitorial trial might be likened to a trip to the principal's office to determine who did what to whom and what should be done about it.
4. Jodi Wilgoren, "Citing Issue of Fairness, Gov. Clears out Death Row in Ill." *The New York Times* (January 12, 2003).
5. James Sterngold, "Los Angeles Police's Report Cites Vast Command Lapses." *The New York Times* (March 2, 2000): A14.
6. David Johnston, "Report Criticizes Scientific Testing at FBI Crime Lab." *The New York Times* (April 16, 1997): A1.

7. Mark S. Warnick, "A Matter of Conviction." *Pittsburgh Post-Gazette* (September 24, 1995): A1.

8. Bob Herbert, "Brooklyn's Obsessive Pursuit." *The New York Times* (August 21, 1994): E15.

9. "Mexican Once Nearly Executed Wins Freedom in Texas." *The New York Times* (April 17, 1997): A8.

10. Bob Herbert, "Savagery Beyond Sense." *The New York Times* (October 18, 1996): A12.

11. James Madison, the leading figure in the development of the U.S. Constitution and Bill of Rights, commented on the need for checks on human behavior associated with the affairs of the state in *Federalist* No. 51: "If men were angels, no government would be necessary. If angels were to govern men, neither external nor internal controls on government would be necessary."

12. 384 U.S. 436.

13. Both sides conceded that, during the interrogation, the police did not use any force, threats, or promises of leniency if Miranda would confess. Both sides also conceded that at no point did the police inform Miranda that he had a constitutional right to refuse to talk to the police and that he could have counsel if he so desired.

14. Thus yielding the famous *Miranda* warnings:
    - You have the right to remain silent.
    - Anything you say can and will be used against you in a court of law.
    - You have a right to a lawyer.
    - If you can't afford a lawyer one will be provided to you.
    - If you say at any point that you do not want to talk to the police the interrogation must cease.

15. 384 U.S. 446.

16. It is worth noting that critics of the Miranda decision often ignore the fact that Ernesto Miranda did not go unpunished as a result of the Court's action. Instead, he was prosecuted by the State of Arizona in a second trial, without the use of his confession, and was convicted and sentenced to prison.

17. *Economist* (July 13, 1996): 29.

18. Ibid.

19. David Ignatius, "Tricks, Lies and Criminal Confessions." *The Washington Post National Weekly Edition* (January 24, 2000): 26.

20. It is important to note that only about 10 percent of criminal cases are resolved through the formal trial process. Most criminal convictions in this country are the result of plea bargaining between the defendant and the prosecutor.

21. *Weeks v. U.S.,* 232 U.S. 383 (1914).

22. 446 U.S. 620 (1980).

23. 467 U.S. 431 (1984).

24. 530 U.S. 428 (2000).

25. When a jury is used as the fact finder in a criminal case, the defense and prosecution have a significant role in determining who will sit on the jury.

In the jury selection process both sides can challenge a prospective juror in two ways. A challenge for cause is used when an attorney can show the court that there are tangible characteristics of the prospective jurors that make them biased and warrant their removal from consideration; lawyers have an unlimited ability to challenge for cause. A peremptory challenge allows a lawyer to remove a potential juror without giving a reason; each lawyer in a case gets a limited number of these. But peremptory challenges are not as peremptory as their name implies. The Supreme Court has ruled that lawyers cannot use them to systematically exclude all blacks or women from consideration for jury service.

26. Michael Janofsky, "Under Siege, Philadelphia's Criminal Justice System Suffers Another Blow." *The New York Times* (April 10, 1997): A9.
27. Jury unanimity is another balancer. It is based on the notion that the prosecutor should be required to present a case that convinces all jurors that the defendant is guilty beyond a reasonable doubt.
28. *Johnson v. Louisiana,* 406 U.S. 356 (1972), and *Apodaco v. Oregon,* 406 U.S. 404 (1972).
29. Quoted in Richard Harris, *Justice.* New York: Avon, 1969, p. 162.

Internet Resources

Visit our Web site at www.mhhe.com/diclerico10 for links and resources relating to Civil Liberties.

chapter 15

Civil Rights

Affirmative Action

For at least four decades, the federal government and many state governments have pursued a policy of "affirmative action," which requires government agencies and many public and private groups to take positive steps to guarantee nondiscrimination and a fair share of jobs, contracts, and college admissions for racial minorities and women. The underlying assumption of these requirements has been that because racial minorities, particularly African-Americans, have been historically discriminated against, special efforts must be made to correct past discriminatory policies and practices and to assure greater opportunities in the future.

In recent years, affirmative action has become a hot-button issue, often generating heated debate between proponents and opponents. The debate revolves around these fundamental questions: Should minorities and women, because of past discrimination, be given special consideration in employment, admission to colleges and universities, government contracts, and the like; or should race and gender be ignored, even if the result leads to a lack of diversity and opportunity in many fields?

To balance the competing interests in affirmative action and discrimination cases, the Supreme Court has set forth certain principles in judging the legitimacy of actions designed to guarantee equal opportunity. These include requirements that affirmative action programs serve a "compelling state interest" and be "narrowly tailored" to accomplish their goal.

In 2003, the Court sought to apply these principles in two cases in the state of Michigan. In the first case, Gratz v. Bollinger, *the court reviewed the affirmative action process with regard to undergraduate admissions at the University of Michigan. The court ruled that the admissions process did not meet the requirements of compelling interest or narrowly tailored remedy, thus invalidating affirmative action measures taken by the school in undergraduate admissions. However, in the second case,* Grutter v. Bollinger, *involving an affirmative action program in the law school admission process, the Court did accept the school's underlying rationale of accomplishing "diversity" as a legitimate state interest. Hence, in the latter case, the affirmative action program was upheld.*

The two selections below are from the Grutter *case, in which affirmative action in law school admission was at issue. The first selection, taken from the majority opinion, is written by Associate Justice Sandra Day O'Connor, one of the more senior members of the court and a supporter of affirmative action. The second selection is a dissenting opinion written by Associate Justice Clarence Thomas, one of the newest members of the court and its only African-American.*

Although the outcome of the law school case clearly points in the direction of court acceptance of narrowly tailored affirmative action programs, the narrowness of the court majority (a five to four decision) points out how vulnerable the policy of affirmative action might be at a time when future appointments to the Supreme Court are on the horizon.

Law School Admissions: The Case for Affirmative Action
Sandra Day O'Connor

This case requires us to decide whether the use of race as a factor in student admissions by the University of Michigan Law School is unlawful. . . .

Before this Court, as they have throughout this litigation, respondents assert only one justification for their use of race in the admissions process: obtaining "the educational benefits that flow from a diverse student body." . . . In other words, the Law School asks us to recognize, in the context of higher education, a compelling state interest in student body diversity. . . .

The Law School's educational judgment that such diversity is essential to its educational mission is one to which we defer. The Law School's assessment that diversity will, in fact, yield educational benefits is substantiated by respondents and their *amici*. Our scrutiny of the interest asserted by the Law School is no less strict for taking into account complex educational judgments in an area that lies primarily within the expertise of the university. Our holding today is in keeping with our tradition of giving a degree of deference to a university's academic decisions, within constitutionally prescribed limits. . . .

We have long recognized that, given the important purpose of public education and the expansive freedoms of speech and thought associated with the university environment, universities occupy a special niche in our constitutional tradition. . . . In announcing the principle of student body diversity as a compelling state interest, Justice Powell invoked our cases recognizing a constitutional dimension, grounded in the First Amendment, of educational autonomy: "The freedom of a university to make its own judgments as to education includes the selection of its student body." *Bakke*, 438 U.S. at 312. From this premise, Justice Powell reasoned that by claiming "the right to select those students who will contribute the most to the 'robust exchange of ideas,'" a university "seek[s] to achieve a goal that is of paramount importance in the fulfillment of its mission." Our conclusion that the Law School has a compelling interest in a diverse student body is informed by our view that attaining a diverse student body is at the heart of the Law School's proper institutional mission, and that "good faith" on the part of a university is "presumed" absent "a showing to the contrary." 438 U.S., at 318–319.

Sandra Day O'Connor was associate justice of the Supreme Court. Excerpted from the majority opinion in *Grutter v. Bollinger* 539 U.S. 306 (2003). Some notes and references have been deleted to maintain continuity in the text—*Editors*.

As part of its goal of "assembling a class that is both exceptionally academically qualified and broadly diverse," the Law School seeks to "enroll a 'critical mass' of minority students." . . . The Law School's interest is not simply "to assure within its student body some specified percentage of a particular group merely because of its race or ethnic origin." *Bakke,* 438 U.S., at 307 (opinion of Powell, J.). That would amount to outright racial balancing, which is patently unconstitutional. . . . Rather, the Law School's concept of critical mass is defined by reference to the educational benefits that diversity is designed to produce.

These benefits are substantial. As the District Court emphasized, the Law School's admissions policy promotes "cross-racial understanding," helps to break down racial stereotypes, and "enables [students] to better understand persons of different races." . . . These benefits are "important and laudable," because "classroom discussion is livelier, more spirited, and simply more enlightening and interesting" when the students have "the greatest possible variety of backgrounds." . . .

The Law School's claim of a compelling interest is further bolstered by its *amici,* who point to the educational benefits that flow from student body diversity. In addition to the expert studies and reports entered into evidence at trial, numerous studies show that student body diversity promotes learning outcomes, and "better prepares students for an increasingly diverse workforce and society, and better prepares them as professionals." Brief for American Educational Research Association et al. as *Amici Curiae* 3. . . .

These benefits are not theoretical but real, as major American businesses have made clear that the skills needed in today's increasingly global marketplace can only be developed through exposure to widely diverse people, cultures, ideas, and viewpoints. Brief for 3M et al. as *Amici Curiae* 5; Brief for General Motors Corp. as *Amicus Curiae* 3–4. What is more, high-ranking retired officers and civilian leaders of the United States military assert that, "[b]ased on [their] decades of experience," a "highly qualified, racially diverse officer corps . . . is essential to the military's ability to fulfill its principle mission to provide national security." Brief for Julius W. Becton, Jr. et al. as *Amici Curiae* 27. . . .

We have repeatedly acknowledged the overriding importance of preparing students for work and citizenship, describing education as pivotal to "sustaining our political and cultural heritage" with a fundamental role in maintaining the fabric of society. *Plyler v. Doe,* 457 U.S. 202, 221 (1982). This Court has long recognized that "education . . . is the very foundation of good citizenship." *Brown v. Board of Education,* 347 U.S. 483, 493 (1954). For this reason, the diffusion of knowledge and opportunity through public institutions of higher education must be accessible to all individuals regardless of race or ethnicity. The United States, as *amicus curiae,* affirms that "[e]nsuring that public institutions are open and available to all segments of American society, including people of all races and ethnicities, represents a paramount government objective." Brief for United States as *Amicus Curiae* 13. And, "[n]owhere is the importance of such openness more acute than in the context of higher education." *Ibid.* Effective participation by members of all racial and ethnic groups in the civic life of our Nation is essential if the dream of one Nation, indivisible, is to be realized.

Moreover, universities, and in particular, law schools, represent the training ground for a large number of our Nation's leaders. . . . Individuals with law degrees occupy roughly half the state governorships, more than half the seats in the United States Senate, and more than a third of the seats in the United States House of Representatives. . . . The pattern is even more striking when it comes to highly selective law schools. A handful of these schools accounts for 25 of the 100 United States Senators, 74 United States Courts of Appeals judges, and nearly 200 of the more than 600 United States District Court judges.

In order to cultivate a set of leaders with legitimacy in the eyes of the citizenry, it is necessary that the path to leadership be visibly open to talented and qualified individuals of every race and ethnicity. All members of our heterogeneous society must have confidence in the openness and integrity of the educational institutions that provide this training. As we have recognized, law schools "cannot be effective in isolation from the individuals and institutions with which the law interacts." . . . Access to legal education (and thus the legal profession) must be inclusive of talented and qualified individuals of every race and ethnicity, so that all members of our heterogeneous society may participate in the educational institutions that provide the training and education necessary to succeed in America.

The Law School does not premise its need for critical mass on "any belief that minority students always (or even consistently) express some characteristic minority viewpoint on any issue." . . . To the contrary, diminishing the force of such stereotypes is both a crucial part of the Law School's mission, and one that it cannot accomplish with only token numbers of minority students. Just as growing up in a particular region or having particular professional experiences is likely to affect an individual's views, so too is one's own, unique experience of being a racial minority in a society, like our own, in which race unfortunately still matters. The Law School has determined, based on its experience and expertise, that a "critical mass" of underrepresented minorities is necessary to further its compelling interest in securing the educational benefits of a diverse student body. . . .

We find that the Law School's admissions program bears the hallmarks of a narrowly tailored plan. As Justice Powell made clear in *Bakke*, truly individualized consideration demands that race be used in a flexible, nonmechanical way. It follows from this mandate that universities cannot establish quotas for members of certain racial groups or put members of those groups on separate admissions tracks. . . . Nor can universities insulate applicants who belong to certain racial or ethnic groups from the competition for admission. *Ibid.* Universities can, however, consider race or ethnicity more flexibly as a "plus" factor in the context of individualized consideration of each and every applicant. . . .

We are satisfied that the Law School's admissions program, like the Harvard plan described by Justice Powell, does not operate as a quota. Properly understood, a "quota" is a program in which a certain fixed number or proportion of opportunities are "reserved exclusively for certain minority groups." . . . Quotas "'impose a fixed number or percentage which must be attained, or which cannot be exceeded,'" . . . and "insulate the individual from comparison with all other candidates for the available seats." *Bakke, supra,* at 317 (opinion of

Powell, J.). In contrast, "a permissible goal . . . require[s] only a good-faith effort . . . to come within a range demarcated by the goal itself," *Sheet Metal Workers v. EEOC, supra,* at 495, and permits consideration of race as a "plus" factor in any given case while still ensuring that each candidate "compete[s] with all other qualified applicants," . . .

That a race-conscious admissions program does not operate as a quota does not, by itself, satisfy the requirement of individualized consideration. When using race as a "plus" factor in university admissions, a university's admissions program must remain flexible enough to ensure that each applicant is evaluated as an individual and not in a way that makes an applicant's race or ethnicity the defining feature of his or her application. The importance of this individualized consideration in the context of a race-conscious admissions program is paramount. See *Bakke supra,* at 318, n. 52 (opinion of Powell, J). . . .

Here, the Law School engages in a highly individualized, holistic review of each applicant's file, giving serious consideration to all the ways an applicant might contribute to a diverse educational environment. The Law School affords this individualized consideration to applicants of all races. There is no policy, either *de jure* or *de facto,* of automatic acceptance or rejection based on any single "soft" variable. . . . [T]he Law School awards no mechanical, predetermined diversity "bonuses" based on race or ethnicity. . . . Like the Harvard plan, the Law School's admissions policy "is flexible enough to consider all pertinent elements of diversity in light of the particular qualifications of each applicant, and to place them on the same footing for consideration, although not necessarily according them the same weight," *Bakke, supra,* at 317 (opinion of Powell, J.).

We also find that, like the Harvard plan Justice Powell referenced in *Bakke,* the Law School's race-conscious admissions program adequately ensures that all factors that may contribute to student body diversity are meaningfully considered alongside race in admissions decisions. With respect to the use of race itself, all underrepresented minority students admitted by the Law School have been deemed qualified. By virtue of our Nation's struggle with racial inequality, such students are both likely to have experiences of particular importance to the Law School's mission, and less likely to be admitted in meaningful numbers on criteria that ignore those experiences. . . .

The Law School does not, however, limit in any way the broad range of qualities and experiences that may be considered valuable contributions to student body diversity. To the contrary, the 1992 policy makes clear "[t]here are many possible bases for diversity admission," and provides examples of admittees who have lived or traveled widely abroad, are fluent in several languages, have overcome personal adversity and family hardship, have exceptional records of extensive community service, and have had successful careers in other fields. . . . The Law School seriously considers each "applicant's promise of making a notable contribution to the class by way of a particular strength, attainment, or characteristic—e.g., an unusual intellectual achievement, employment experience, nonacademic performance, or personal background," . . . All applicants have the opportunity to highlight their own potential diversity contributions through the submission of a personal statement, letters of recommendation, and an essay describing the ways in which the applicant will contribute to the life and diversity of the Law School.

What is more, the Law School actually gives substantial weight to diversity factors besides race. The Law School frequently accepts nonminority applicants with grades and test scores lower than underrepresented minority applicants (and other nonminority applicants) who are rejected. . . . This shows that the Law School seriously weighs many other diversity factors besides race that can make a real and dispositive difference for nonminority applicants as well. By this flexible approach, the Law School sufficiently takes into account, in practice as well as in theory, a wide variety of characteristics besides race and ethnicity that contribute to a diverse student body . . . .

We are mindful . . ., that "[a] core purpose of the Fourteenth Amendment was to do away with all governmentally imposed discrimination based on race," *Palmore v. Sidoti*, 466 U.S. 429, 432 (1984). Accordingly, race-conscious admissions policies must be limited in time. This requirement reflects that racial classifications, however compelling their goals, are potentially so dangerous that they may be employed no more broadly than the interest demands. Enshrining a permanent justification for racial preferences would offend this fundamental equal protection principle. We see no reason to exempt race-conscious admissions programs from the requirement that all governmental use of race must have a logical end point. The Law School, too, concedes that all "race-conscious programs must have reasonable durational limits." . . .

In the context of higher education, the durational requirement can be met by sunset provisions in race-conscious admissions policies and periodic reviews to determine whether racial preferences are still necessary to achieve student body diversity. Universities in California, Florida, and Washington State, where racial preferences in admissions are prohibited by state law, are currently engaged in experimenting with a wide variety of alternative approaches. Universities in other States can and should draw on the most promising aspects of these race-neutral alternatives as they develop. . . .

The requirement that all race-conscious admissions programs have a termination point "assure[s] all citizen that the deviation from the norm of equal treatment of all racial and ethnic groups is a temporary matter, a measure taken in the service of the goal of equality itself." *Richmond v. J.A. Croson Co.*, 488 U.S., at 510 (plurality opinion). . . .

We take the Law School at its word that it would "like nothing better than to find a race-neutral admissions formula" and will terminate its race-conscious admissions program as soon as practicable. See Brief for Respondents Bollinger et al. 34; *Bakke, supra*, at 317–318 (opinion of Powell, J.) (presuming good faith of university officials in the absence of a showing to the contrary). It has been 25 years since Justice Powell first approved the use of race to further an interest in student body diversity in the context of public higher education. Since that time, the number of minority applicants with high grades and test scores has indeed increased. . . . We expect that 25 years from now, the use of racial preferences will no longer be necessary to further the interest approved today.

Law School Admissions: The Case Against Affirmative Action
Clarence Thomas

Frederick Douglass, speaking to a group of abolitionists almost 140 years ago, delivered a message lost on today's majority:

"[I]n regard to the colored people, there is always more that is benevolent, I perceive, than just, manifested towards us. What I ask for the negro is not benevolence, not pity, not sympathy, but simply *justice*. The American people have always been anxious to know what they shall do with us. . . . I have had but one answer from the beginning. Do nothing with us! Your doing with us has already played the mischief with us. Do nothing with us! If the apples will not remain on the tree of their own strength, if they are worm-eaten at the core, if they are early ripe and disposed to fall, let them fall! . . . . And if the negro cannot stand on his own legs, let him fall also. All I ask is, give him a chance to stand on his own legs! Let him alone! . . . [Y]our interference is doing him positive injury." . . .

Like Douglass, I believe blacks can achieve in every avenue of American life without the meddling of university administrators. Because I wish to see all students succeed whatever their color, I share, in some respect, the sympathies of those who sponsor the type of discrimination advanced by the University of Michigan Law School (Law School). The Constitution does not, however, tolerate institutional devotion to the status quo in admissions policies when such devotion ripens into racial discrimination. . . .

* * *

The Constitution abhors classifications based on race, not only because those classifications can harm favored races or are based on illegitimate motives, but also because every time the government places citizens on racial registers and makes race relevant to the provision of burdens or benefits, it demeans us all. . . .

. . . I believe what lies beneath the Court's decision today are the benighted notions that one can tell when racial discrimination benefits (rather than hurts) minority groups, . . . and that racial discrimination is necessary to remedy general societal ills. This Court's precedents supposedly settled both issues, but clearly the majority still cannot commit to the principle that racial classifications

Clarence Thomas is associate justice of the U.S. Supreme Court. Excerpted from a dissenting opinion in *Grutter v. Bollinger* 539 U.S. 306 (2003). Some notes and references have been deleted to maintain continuity in the text—*Editors.*

are *per se* harmful and that almost no amount of benefit in the eye of the beholder can justify such classifications.

. . . I must contest the notion that the Law School's discrimination benefits those admitted as a result of it. The Court spends considerable time discussing the impressive display of *amicus* support for the Law School in this case from all corners of society. But nowhere in any of the filings in this Court is any evidence that the purported "beneficiaries" of this racial discrimination prove themselves by performing at (or even near) the same level as those students who receive no preferences. . . .

The silence in this case is deafening to those of us who view higher education's purpose as imparting knowledge and skills to students, rather than a communal, rubber-stamp, credentialing process. The Law School is not looking for those students who, despite a lower LSAT score or undergraduate grade point average, will succeed in the study of law. The Law School seeks only a facade—it is sufficient that the class looks right, even if it does not perform right.

The Law School tantalizes unprepared students with the promise of a University of Michigan degree and all of the opportunities that it offers. These overmatched students take the bait, only to find that they cannot succeed in the caldron of competition. And this mismatch crisis is not restricted to elite institutions . . . Indeed, to cover the tracks of the aestheticists, this cruel farce of racial discrimination must continue—in selection for the Michigan Law Review, . . . and in hiring at law firms and for judicial clerkships—until the "beneficiaries" are no longer tolerated. While these students may graduate with law degrees, there is no evidence that they have received a qualitatively better legal education (or become better lawyers) than if they had gone to a less "elite" law school for which they were better prepared. And the aestheticists will never address the real problems facing "underrepresented minorities," instead continuing their social experiments on other people's children.

Beyond the harm the Law School's racial discrimination visits upon its test subjects, no social science has disproved the notion that this discrimination "engender[s] attitudes of superiority or, alternatively, provoke[s] resentment among those who believe that they have been wronged by the government's use of race." *Adarand*, 515 U.S., at 241 (Thomas, J., concurring in part and concurring in judgment). "These programs stamp minorities with a badge of inferiority and may cause them to develop dependencies or to adopt an attitude that they are 'entitled' to preferences." *Ibid.*

It is uncontested that each year, the Law School admits a handful of blacks who would be admitted in the absence of racial discrimination. . . . Who can differentiate between those who belong and those who do not? The majority of blacks are admitted to the Law School because of discrimination, and because of this policy all are tarred as undeserving. This problem of stigma does not depend on determinacy as to whether those stigmatized are actually the "beneficiaries" of racial discrimination. When blacks take positions in the highest places of government, industry, or academia, it is an open question today whether their skin color played a part in their advancement. The question itself is the stigma—because either racial discrimination did play a role, in which case the person may be deemed "otherwise unqualified," or it did not, in which case asking the question itself unfairly marks those blacks who would succeed without discrimination. Is this what the Court means by "visibly open"?

Finally, the Court's disturbing reference to the importance of the country's law schools as training grounds meant to cultivate "a set of leaders with legitimacy in the eyes of the citizenry" through the use of racial discrimination deserves discussion. As noted earlier, the Court has soundly rejected the remedying of societal discrimination as a justification for governmental use of race. . . . For those who believe that every racial disproportionality in our society is caused by some kind of racial discrimination, there can be no distinction between remedying societal discrimination and erasing racial disproportionalities in the country's leadership caste. And if the lack of proportional racial representation among our leaders is not caused by societal discrimination, then "fixing" it is even less of a pressing public necessity.

The Court's civics lesson presents yet another example of judicial selection of a theory of political representation based on skin color—an endeavor I have previously rejected. . . . The majority appears to believe that broader utopian goals justify the Law School's use of race, but "[t]he Equal Protection Clause commands the elimination of racial barriers, not their creation in order to satisfy our theory as to how society ought to be organized." *DeFunis,* 416 U.S., at 342 (Douglas, J., dissenting). . . .

The Court also holds that racial discrimination in admissions should be given another 25 years before it is deemed no longer narrowly tailored to the Law School's fabricated compelling state interest. While I agree that in 25 years the practices of the Law School will be illegal, they are, for the reasons I have given, illegal now. The majority does not and cannot rest its time limitation on any evidence that the gap in credentials between black and white students is shrinking or will be gone in that timeframe. In recent years there has been virtually no change, for example, in the proportion of law school applicants with LSAT scores of 165 and higher who are black. In 1993 blacks constituted 1.1% of law school applicants in that score range, though they represented 11.1% of all applicants. Law School Admission Council, National Statistical Report (1994) (hereinafter LSAC Statistical Report). In 2000 the comparable numbers were 1.0% and 11.3%. LSAC Statistical Report (2001). No one can seriously contend, and the Court does not, that the racial gap in academic credentials will disappear in 25 years. Nor is the Court's holding that racial discrimination will be unconstitutional in 25 years made contingent on the gap closing in that time.

Indeed, the very existence of racial discrimination of the type practiced by the Law School may impede the narrowing of the LSAT testing gap. An applicant's LSAT score can improve dramatically with preparation, but such preparation is a cost, and there must be sufficient benefits attached to an improved score to justify additional study. Whites scoring between 163 and 167 on the LSAT are routinely rejected by the Law School, and thus whites aspiring to admission at the Law School have every incentive to improve their score to levels above that range. . . . [I]n 2000, 209 out of 422 white applicants were rejected in this scoring range). Blacks, on the other hand, are nearly guaranteed admission if they score above 155 . . . (63 out of 77 black applicants are accepted with LSAT scores above 155). As admission prospects approach certainty, there is no incentive for the black applicant to continue to prepare for the LSAT once he is reasonably assured of achieving the requisite score. It is far from certain that the LSAT test-taker's behavior is responsive to the Law School's admissions policies. Nevertheless, the possibility remains that this racial discrimination will help fulfill the bigot's prophecy about black underperformance—just as it confirms the conspiracy theorist's belief that "institutional racism" is at fault for every racial disparity in our society.

I therefore can understand the imposition of a 25-year time limit only as a holding that the deference the Court pays to the Law School's educational judgments and refusal to change its admissions policies will itself expire. At that point these policies will clearly have failed to "'eliminat[e] the [perceived] need for any racial or ethnic'" discrimination because the academic credentials gap will still be there. . . .

* * *

For the immediate future, however, the majority has placed its imprimatur on a practice that can only weaken the principle of equality embodied in the Declaration of Independence and the Equal Protection Clause. "Our Constitution is color-blind, and neither knows nor tolerates classes among citizens." *Plessy v. Ferguson*, 163 U.S. 537,559 (1896) (Harlan, J., dissenting). It has been nearly 140 years since Frederick Douglass asked the intellectual ancestors of the Law School to "[d]o nothing with us!" and the Nation adopted the Fourteenth Amendment. Now we must wait another 25 years to see this principle of equality vindicated. I therefore respectfully dissent from the remainder of the Court's opinion and the judgment.

Gender Equity

The modern era in civil rights has been unprecedented in the advancement of rights for minorities and women: elimination of racial segregation; removal of racial, gender, and disability discrimination in employment, school admissions, and other areas; and the extension of the vote to millions of Americans. Yet, in the face of much progress, there are areas in civil rights policy where opinion is strongly divided. One such area is gender equity in sports.

In 1972, Congress passed the Education Act Amendment. Title IX of this act prohibits discrimination against women on college campuses in housing, financial assistance, faculty and staff hiring and pay,and most contentious of all, athletics. It is the latter area—gender equity in sports—that is the subject of the two essays in this section.

The main issue in regard to Title IX is the requirement that women be given athletic opportunities in proportion to their numbers at particular colleges and universities. Thus, if a college campus is 50 percent male, 50 percent female, then according to current interpretations of Title IX, the male–female ratio in sponsored sports must also be 50–50. This proportionality requirement has led some schools to eliminate athletic opportunities for men, as in the case of men's wrestling, to make room for more women.

The regulations regarding implementation of Title IX were changed in 2005 to permit colleges and universities to determine, via the Internet, student "interest" in sports as a means of meeting the proportionality requirement. However, some in college sports, including the NCAA, have interpreted this action as reducing the impact of Title IX. Regardless of the outcome of this new controversy, the fundamental issue remains: Is Title IX a fair way to proceed in achieving equality in sports?

In the essays that follow, the authors discuss the merits of eliminating or changing Title IX rules. The first author, John Irving, a prominent writer and a part-time wrestling coach, while conceding the value of Title IX, argues that it is simply unfair in application. According to Irving, men's teams should not have to suffer in order to meet a proportionality test that is, at best, unreasonable. The second author, law professor Joanna Grossman, disagrees, insisting that not only has Title IX permitted women to make unprecedented gains in sports—gains that they would likely not have obtained without it—but also that the current array of critics of Title IX are setting up a smoke screen to hide the real problem in providing equity for both men and women in sports—the favored position of college football.

Wrestling with Title IX
John Irving

Title IX, the federal law that prohibits sex discrimination in educational programs receiving federal assistance, may be in for an overhaul. This week
[January 27, 2003] a committee appointed by the Bush administration will hold
its final meetings before submitting its recommendations for changing the law
to Secretary of Education Rod Paige. Since Title IX was enacted in 1972, it has
been the subject of debate—much of it misguided—about its application to college athletics. At issue now is how to alter the law—or not—so that, as Secretary
Paige has put it, we can find ways of "expanding opportunities to ensure fairness for all college athletes."

I hope the commission will realize that what's wrong with Title IX isn't
Title IX. What's wrong is that, in practice, there are two Title IX's. The first Title
IX was the one passed by Congress in 1972 to put an end to sex discrimination
in schools—good for the original Title IX! The second Title IX, the one currently
enforced, is the product of a policy interpretation in 1979 by the Department
of Education's Office for Civil Rights (but never debated or approved by
Congress)—and which is functioning as a gender quota law.

In its prohibition against sex discrimination, the 1972 law expressly states
as "exceptions" any "preferential or disparate treatment because of imbalance
in participation" or any "statistical evidence of imbalance." In English, this
means that Congress recognized that the intent of Title IX was not to establish
gender quotas or require preferential treatment as reparation for past discrimination. Smart thinking—after all, the legislation was intended to prohibit discrimination against either sex.

But what happened in 1979—and in subsequent re-evaluations of the law—
has invited discrimination against male athletes. The 1979 interpretation required
colleges to meet at least one of the following three criteria that the number of athletes from each sex be roughly equivalent to the number of students enrolled; that
colleges demonstrate a commitment to adding women's sports; and that they
prove that the athletic interests of female students are effectively accommodated.
The problems lie in complying with the first criterion. In order to achieve gender
proportionality, men's collegiate sports are being undermined and eliminated.
This was never the intention of Title IX.

John Irving is a novelist and former wrestler. "Wrestling with Title IX," by John Irving from
The New York Times, January 28, 2003. Reprinted with author's permission.

The proportionality rule stipulates that the ratio of male to female athletes be proportionate to the ratio of male to female students at a particular college. On average, females make up about 56 percent of college enrollment, males 44 percent; for most colleges to be in compliance with proportionality, more than half the athletes on team rosters must be women. Can you imagine this rule being applied to all educational programs—classes in science, engineering, accounting, medicine or law? What about dance, drama or music—not to mention women's studies?

In 1996, the Department of Education further bolstered the proportionality zealots by requiring colleges to count every name on a team's roster—scholarship and nonscholarship athletes, starters and nonstarters. It is this ruling that has prompted a lawsuit by the National Wrestling Coaches Association, the Committee to Save Bucknell Wrestling, the Marquette Wrestling Club, the Yale Wrestling Association, and the National Coalition for Athletics Equity, all of whom argue that the 1996 rules exceed the Department of Education's statutory authority "by effectively mandating the very discrimination that Title IX prohibits."

Why are wrestlers so upset about this? The number of collegiate wrestling programs lost to Title IX compliance is staggering; this is especially alarming because, since 1993, wrestling has been a rapidly growing sport at the high-school level. Data compiled by Gary Abbott, director of special projects at USA Wrestling, indicates that in 2001, there were 244,984 athletes wrestling in high school; only 5,966 got to wrestle in the National Collegiate Athletic Association. Not to put too fine a point on it: there is only one N.C.A.A. spot for every 41 high-school wrestlers. The numbers have been going downhill for a while. In 1982, there were 363 N.C.A.A. wrestling teams with 7,914 wrestlers competing; in 2001, there were only 229 teams with fewer than 6,000 wrestlers. Yet, in that same period, the number of N.C.A.A. institutions has increased from 787 to 1,049. No wonder wrestlers are unhappy.

As for the virtual elimination of walk-ons (nonscholarship athletes) in many men's sports, and the unrealistic capping of male team rosters—again, to make the number of male athletes proportional to the number of females—the problem is that athletic programs are going to absurd lengths to fill the unfilled rosters for women's teams. But women, statistically, aren't interested in participating in intercollegiate athletics to the degree that men are. J. Robinson, wrestling coach at the University of Minnesota, cites intramural sports, which are wholly interest driven, as an example. In a column about Title IX published in the Chronicle of Higher Education, Robinson wrote that "men outnumber women 3-1 or 4-1 on the intramural field."

Don't we need to know the exact numbers for how many women are interested in playing college sports now? But the Women's Sports Foundation, an advocacy group that favors maintaining proportionality, opposes conducting surveys of incoming students—that is, expressly to gauge interest in athletics. These surveys, they say, would force "female athletes to prove their interest in sports in order to obtain the right to participate and be treated fairly." But men would fill out the same surveys.

One suggestion that the presidential commission is considering is counting the available spots on teams, rather than the actual participants. The Women's Sports Foundation rejects this idea, arguing that it counts "ghost female participants." However, the foundation has no objection to counting interest that isn't there.

In fact, those women's groups opposed to tampering with either the 1979 interpretation or the 1996 ruling, which endorses the proportionality arm of Title IX, often argue that there are three ways (at least on paper) for an institution to comply with Title IX—not just proportionality. But only proportionality can be measured concretely. A 1996 clarification letter from the Department of Education refers to the proportionality test as a "safe harbor"—meaning that this simple-to-apply numerical formula can assure an athletic director and a university president that their institution is in compliance and not subject to legal action. In other words, proportionality is not only wrong—it's lazy.

Some women's advocates argue that it is not proportionality that forces athletic directors to cut men's teams; they blame the budget excesses of Division I football and men's basketball. But there are countless examples where money was not the issue in the case of the sport that was dropped. Marquette University had a wrestling team that was completely financed by alumni and supporters; yet the sport was dropped in 2001, to comply with gender equity. (Marquette has no football team.)

Boston College dropped three sports that had only part-time coaches and offered no scholarships; these sports could easily have been sponsored by fundraising. Keep in mind, too, that the majority of male college teams dropped in the 1990s were from Division II and Division III programs, which don't have big-time football or men's basketball.

Furthermore, many Division I football and basketball programs earn millions of dollars a year, enough to support all the other sports programs—men's and women's. Moreover, most schools with high-profile football programs are schools where women's teams have thrived. (Witness the Big 10, the S.E.C., the Big 12 and other Division I athletic conferences, which have produced both winning football teams as well as great women's teams in other sports.)

While eliminating men's sports like wrestling, where the interest in participation is increasing, athletic programs go begging to find women athletes to fill the vacancies on an ever-expanding number of women's teams.

One of the most ludicrous examples of this was the attempt by Arizona State University in Tempe—a cactus-studded campus in the middle of the Sonoran Desert—to add a competitive women's rowing team. There's not a lot of water in Arizona. But the school asked the city to create a body of water (by flooding a dry gulch) on which the team could practice. Because of a lack of funds, the school had to drop the plan. This is probably just as well; taxpayer dollars would have financed scholarships either to rowers from out of state or to teach Arizona women (most of whom have never held an oar) how to row. But Arizona State is to be commended. It not only worked to meet the numerical demands of proportionality, it tried to adhere to the original spirit of Title IX by adding opportunities for women, not by cutting opportunities for men.

To apply the rule of proportionality to men's and women's collegiate athletics amounts to a feminist form of sex discrimination. And I won't be dismissed by that other argument I've heard (ad nauseam) from those women's advocates unwilling to let proportionality go—namely, that to oppose proportionality, or even the crudest enforcement of Title IX to eliminate men's sports programs, is tantamount to being antifeminist and hostile to women in sports. Don't try to lay that on me.

I *am* a women's advocate. I have long been active in the pro-choice movement; my principal political commitment is my longstanding and continuing role as an abortion-rights advocate. But I'm also an advocate of fairness. What is unfair is not Title IX—it is Title IX's enforcement of proportionality, which discriminates against men.

In 1992, Brian Picklo, a walk-on, asked the Michigan State Wrestling coach, Tom Minkel, if he could try out for the team. Picklo had wrestled for only two years in high school and never qualified for state tournaments. Minkel thought Picklo's chances of wrestling in the Big 10 were "slim to none." But Picklo became a two-time Division I All-American, and he won the Big 10 title at 190 pounds. In most wrestling programs across the country today, Brian Picklo wouldn't be allowed to be a walk-on.

Title IX, the original legislation, was conceived as a fairness-for-all law; it has been reinvented as a tool to treat men unfairly. Advocates of proportionality claim that universities that are not "proportional" are breaking the law, but they're not breaking the original law.

The Women's Sports Foundation has accused the presidential commission of politicizing Title IX. But Title IX was politicized by the Department of Education in 1979 and 1996—during Democratic administrations. Is it only now political because a Republican administration is taking a closer look at the way Title IX is applied? (I make this criticism, by the way, as a Democrat. I'd have a hard time being an abortion rights advocate in the Bush administration, wouldn't I?)

Based on 2001 membership data—raw data from the National Federation of State High Schools, and from the N.C.A.A.—for every single N.C.A.A. sports opportunity for a woman, there are 17 high school athletes available to fill the spot; for a man, there are 18. Isn't that equal enough? In fact, women have more opportunity to compete in college than men do. Yet the attitude represented by the Women's Sports Foundation, and other women's groups, is that women are far from achieving gender equity; by their continuing endorsement of proportionality in collegiate athletics, these women's advocates are being purely vindictive.

Years ago, I was playing in a Little League baseball game when an umpire made what I thought was a memorable mistake. Later, in another game, he made it again. I realized it was no mistake at all—he meant to say it. Instead of hollering "Play ball!" at the start of the game, this umpire shouted "Play fair!"

Keep Title IX; eliminate proportionality. Play fair.

Preserve, Not Reverse, Equity for Women in College Athletics
Joanna Grossman

The year 2003 marked the thirtieth anniversary of the passage of Title IX of the Education Amendments of 1972. . . . Title IX is a federal statute banning sex discrimination in educational programs receiving federal financial assistance. . . .

Title IX has been used to challenge gender inequity in a variety of contexts: sexual harassment; pregnancy; school admissions, testing, and scholarships; and, most controversially, school athletics. It is the statute's impact on collegiate athletics that has garnered it its highest praise, as well as its harshest criticism.

Critics have called for amendments of Title IX and its regulations that would make its demand for gender equity—particularly in the realm of college athletics—less strict. Among those critics is the Bush Administration, whose lackluster defense of the statute in a recent lawsuit reveals its utter lack of commitment to gender equity in athletics. (On this issue, the President is perhaps continuing the legacy of his father—who made headlines as vice-president for suggesting in a 1981 speech that Title IX had simply gone too far in the field of athletics.)

The Administration and other critics of Title IX, however, are wrong, and should be opposed. Title IX has turned out to be one of the most important pieces of protection for women against sex discrimination—and in particular, a crucial way to ensure women's equality in college athletics. Rather than going too far, it has held an important line—a line that should not now be moved backwards.

THE HISTORY OF TITLE IX AND ITS REGULATIONS RELEVANT TO COLLEGE ATHLETICS

In 1975, it was made clear that Title IX applied to athletics, as well as to other aspects of education—and the controversy that has plagued this application of the statute began.

That year, the Department of Health, Education, and Welfare (the predecessor to today's Department of Education) issued regulations to implement Title IX. The regulations required institutions to provide "equal athletic opportunity for members of both sexes."

Joanna Grossman is associate professor of law at Hofstra University. From Joanna Grossman, "On the Thirtieth Anniversary of Title IX, We Need to Preserve, Not Reverse, Its Guarantee of Equity for Women in College Athletics." This column originally appeared on www.FindLaw.com on June 18, 2002, pp. 1–6.

This general standard was supplemented by ten factors to be considered in determining whether equal opportunity was in fact being provided. The first of these factors—and the one most frequently at issue in litigation—asks "whether the selection of sports and levels of competition effectively accommodate the interests and abilities of both sexes."

In a 1979 Policy Interpretation, HEW broke down this factor further, into a three-prong test. Under that test, an institution can show effective accommodation by proving one of three things: First, it can show that it provides athletic opportunities to men and women substantially proportionate to their overall enrollment. Second, it can show that it is engaged in a continuing practice of program expansion with respect to the underrepresented sex (almost always women). Third, it can show that it has fully and effectively accommodated the interests and abilities of the members of the underrepresented sex.

In 1995, the Department of Education sent a "clarification" of the Policy Interpretation to thousands of interested parties. The clarification explained, among other things, that although proportionality alone can provide a "safe harbor" for institutions able to demonstrate it, they are also free to comply with the other prongs of the test instead.

The new clarification also said that institutions were authorized, though not required to eliminate teams, or cap team size, as a way of achieving gender proportionality. (For example, eliminating the men's lacrosse team could be a way to address the fact that there was no women's lacrosse team.)

Finally, the clarification said that participation opportunities should be measured based on actual athletes rather than "slots"—a healthy dose of realism that meant schools had to focus on women athletes, not theoretical possibilities that there could be women athletes.

TITLE IX'S IMPACT ON WOMEN'S SPORTS: OVERWHELMINGLY POSITIVE

There has been a dramatic increase in athletic participation of girls and women since Title IX was enacted. Every available statistic bears this out.

For instance, participation by high school girls in varsity sports has risen from one in twenty-seven to one in two-and-a-half. Meanwhile, participation by college female athletes has risen from under 30,000 to more than 150,000. Interestingly, during the same thirty years, participation by male athletes, at both the high school and college levels, has risen as well, though not nearly as dramatically.

While cause and effect are hard to pinpoint, Title IX litigation and administrative enforcement have clearly been important to these developments. However, there are still important areas of inequity.

For instance, an estimated 80 percent of high schools and colleges run athletic programs that do not comply with Title IX. And, of course, men's athletic programs continue to receive much more money for athletic scholarships, recruiting, coaching, and general operations than women's athletic programs do. In addition, female coaches get paid a fraction of what male coaches earn, and only two percent of the head coaching jobs for men's teams. . . .

MORE THAN PROPORTIONALITY ALONE: OTHER WAYS TO SATISFY TITLE IX

In the popular media, the three-prong test of the Title IX regulations has been reduced to a single idea—a requirement of proportionality. The media also suggests that the only way schools achieve proportionality is by cutting men's "minor" sports—like wrestling, swimming, and gymnastics—in order to bring the overall opportunities for men down to the level of women's.

As noted above, the "clarification" does allow men's programs to be cut in order to achieve equality. But in fact, the reality is quite different—as the fact that male athletes have prospered, rather than being harmed, over the last thirty years can attest.

As the clarification also notes, proportionality is only one way to comply with Title IX. Schools can also comply by showing a good-faith effort to expand opportunities for women. Alternatively, they can show that women's interests and abilities are fully accommodated, even though that means they have significantly fewer actual roster spots or teams. More than two-thirds of the schools involved in Title IX cases before the Department of Education during a recent five-year period chose to comply with one of these alternative prongs, rather than by instituting gender proportionality.

Moreover, for schools who do try to achieve proportionality, only some of them accomplish it by cutting men's teams or capping team size. Two-thirds of colleges and universities have not cut any men's teams at all in their efforts to achieve gender equity. (And many schools have cut both women's and men's teams in certain sports, like gymnastics, wrestling, and field hockey, and replaced them with more popular sports like soccer and track.)

But where schools have cut men's teams purportedly to comply with Title IX, those decisions have often been the target of litigation. Male athletes on teams that have been cut have alleged reverse discrimination, claiming that the decision to eliminate their particular team was made solely on the basis of sex.

However, every case bringing a reverse discrimination claim has ultimately been unsuccessful. As the relevant courts have often noted, when a school reallocates resources to remedy past inequity against women, it does not commit a new act of reverse discrimination. Thus, the school does not violate either Title IX or the Equal Protection Clause.

After all, if the remedy for discrimination were called "reverse discrimination" and forbidden, Title IX would be effectively unenforceable. If cutting men's teams were not sometimes an option, then it would be impossible for schools to cure past discrimination without dramatically expanding their budget for athletics, an option not available to most schools.

This conclusion may sound harsh, but consider the situation. A school has a men's lacrosse team and a men's hockey team, and no women's teams in either sport. It can't afford new teams, so it cuts men's lacrosse and creates women's hockey. Although the male lacrosse players will be understandably aggrieved (and so will would-be women's lacrosse players, who never had and never will have a team), the outcome is more fair than the status quo—and that is because of Title IX.

THE CURRENT ASSAULT ON TITLE IX, AND THE ADMINISTRATION'S FAILURE TO DEFEND IT

In February 2002, the National Wrestling Coaches' Association filed a lawsuit against the Department of Education. The Association alleges that the interpretation of Title IX embodied in the Policy Guidance and its subsequent clarification—and still currently in use—is unlawful.

More specifically, the Association argues that this interpretation of the statute authorizes intentional discrimination against male athletes. (Thus, the Association is making the same "reverse discrimination" argument that has failed every time it has been raised before.) Based on this argument, the Association is seeking an order declaring that the Policy Interpretation—and the three-part test it propounded—is invalid and unenforceable.

The Bush Administration had the opportunity in this lawsuit to mount a strong defense of Title IX and its regulations regarding athletics. The argument could have been based on law—consider the many suits dismissing similar "reverse discrimination" claims—not just on policy preferences. Yet instead, the Administration filed a motion to dismiss that cited only narrow technical defects in the lawsuit as a basis for throwing it out of court.

The government's brief is carefully worded to avoid any defense of Title IX on the merits. In fact, the implicit message is to the contrary—that the plaintiffs are wrong only in their choice of defendant (they have sued the government, not the schools), rather than on the merits.

That this Administration will not fight to protect Title IX is clear. So those who support the statute—and more generally, who support equality in women's high school and college athletics—will have to fight for it instead, and fight against the Administration if necessary.

THE RHETORICAL BATTLE OVER TITLE IX

Title IX's critics have tried to score rhetorical points by convincing the public, first, that Title IX's insistence on gender equity is misplaced. They make several arguments, but none are convincing.

First, they claim that women are naturally less interested in sports than men. But in fact, the evidence shows that women's interest in sport is not innately fixed, but dynamic and affected by tangible factors such as playing opportunities and available resources—as well as intangible factors like public opinion and culture.

Watching senior women soccer stars triumph, for example, can motivate a freshman high school girl to follow up on her athletic ambitions. If all the seniors had been cheerleaders and homecoming queens, she might have sacrificed the same ambitions to the ever-present urge to fit in. Are women "naturally" less interested in sports, or "socially" less interested? If the phenomenon is social, it can change.

And it has. Consider the eight-fold rise in female athletic participation at the high school level and the five-fold increase at the college level over the last 30 years—the lifetime of Title IX. It is pretty good—indeed, overwhelming— evidence that opportunities create athletes as much as biology does.

Second, critics often claim that greedy female athletes are responsible for the downfall of men's minor sports. (In our previous scenario, for instance, the men's lacrosse team has been sacrificed so the women's hockey team could be created.)

This argument, too, is unfair and inaccurate. It is unfair for the equality reason given above; women's hockey and lacrosse players should not both have to suffer so men's lacrosse players can prosper. It is inaccurate because of, in a word, football.

The greed and excess, both in terms of participation opportunities and resource allocation, endemic to men's collegiate football programs is by far the greatest reason that other men's sports get the sack. Football, with its unnecessarily large number of players and scholarships (an average of 94 per NCAA Division I team, compared with only 53 per NFL team), eats up the lion's share of athletic resources, which adversely impacts both men's minor sports and women's sports.

And when football is the culprit, there is no equality justification for the loss. The men's lacrosse team loses out simply because the brawnier sport wins out. A man who loses his lacrosse team due to emphasis on football should be upset about the gender-policing of his institution, which prefers more "masculine" sports. In contrast, a man who loses his lacrosse team due to Title IX can at least see that it was unfair that women never had such a team in the first place. But schools themselves feed these misperceptions, often expressly citing Title IX as the reason for cutting a particular men's team.

The reason men's teams must sometimes be cut is because for decades they have received more resources than they should have. Men had almost unlimited opportunities to participate in sports *because* women were denied them, and this denial freed up money the men's teams could use. This artificially inflated allocation of resources—due in large part to stereotypes about women and their lack of interest and ability in sports—does not create an entitlement to have such resources continue.

Ideally, men and women should both have a team in every sport and if the behemoth of football did not consume such huge resources, that might be possible. But if a new women's team must be created at the expense of an old male team, that is only fair. Women are not saying that years of men-only sports should be compensated with the same number of years of women-only sports. Rather, they are only asking for equality today.

Passage of the Nineteenth Amendment (granting women the right to vote) diluted the male vote by half, but nonetheless did not constitute an act of "reverse discrimination." Neither does a reallocation of resources for collegiate sports away from the sex that has historically had plentiful opportunities, and toward the sex that has had few.

Abortion

*P*robably *no domestic issue has polarized the nation more during the last thirty years than abortion. It has proved to be a hotly contested subject in state and national elections and has been the occasion for repeated mass demonstrations in our nation's capital. That abortion has aroused such strong feelings is not surprising, for some see the right to privacy at stake even as others insist that the real issue is the taking of human life.*

In the first selection, Susan Estrich and Kathleen Sullivan argue that, if the decision on abortion is taken out of the hands of the mother, then she will necessarily be forced to surrender autonomy over both her body and family decisions. Government intrusion into these spheres would constitute an intolerable infringement on the fundamental right to privacy—a view shared by the Supreme Court when it upheld a woman's right to an abortion in Roe v. Wade *(1973).*

In the second essay, James Bopp and Richard Coleson contend that the Roe v. Wade *decision was a glaring example of judicial power gone wild, with the justices manufacturing a right to privacy in the Constitution where it was nowhere to be found. In doing so, the Court not only violated its own stated criteria for determining what qualifies as a fundamental right, but also arrogated to itself a power which the people alone may exercise. Bopp and Coleson further argue that the right to abortion should be rejected on moral as well as legal grounds, and they also challenge pro-choice claims that the outlawing of abortions would have harmful social consequences for women.*

Abortion Politics
The Case for the Right to Privacy
Susan R. Estrich and Kathleen M. Sullivan

I. THE EXISTENCE OF A LIBERTY INTEREST

A. Reproductive Choice Is Essential to a Woman's Control of Her Destiny and Family Life

Notwithstanding the abortion controversy, the Supreme Court has long acknowledged an unenumerated right to privacy as a species of "liberty" that the due process clauses protect.[1] The principle is as ancient as *Meyer v. Nebraska*[2] and *Pierce v. Society of Sisters*,[3] which protected parents' freedom to educate their children free of the state's controlling hand. In its modern elaboration, this right continues to protect child rearing and family life from the overly intrusive reach of government.[4] The modern privacy cases have also plainly established that decisions whether to bear children are no less fundamental than decisions about how to raise them. The Court has consistently held since *Griswold v. Connecticut*[5] that the Constitution accords special protection to "matters so fundamentally affecting a person as the decision whether to bear or beget a child," and has therefore strictly scrutinized laws restricting contraception.[6] Roe held that these principles extend no less to abortion than to contraception.

The privacy cases rest, as Justice Stevens recognized in *Thornburgh*, centrally on "'the moral fact that a person belongs to himself [or herself] and not others nor to society as a whole.'"[7] Extending this principle to the abortion decision follows from the fact that "[f]ew decisions are . . . more basic to individual dignity and autonomy" or more appropriate to the "private sphere of individual liberty" than the uniquely personal, intimate, and self-defining decision whether or not to continue a pregnancy.[8]

In two senses, abortion restrictions keep a woman from "belonging to herself." First and most obviously, they deprive her of bodily self-possession. As Chief Justice Rehnquist observed in another context, pregnancy entails "profound

Susan R. Estrich is Robert Kingsley Professor of Law at the University of Southern California, and Kathleen M. Sullivan is Richard E. Lang Professor of Law and Dean of Stanford University Law School. This selection is from Susan R. Estrich and Kathleen M. Sullivan, "Abortion Politics: Writing for an Audience of One," *University of Pennsylvania Law Review*, 138:125–32, pp. 150–55 (1989). Copyright © 1989 by the University of Pennsylvania. Reprinted by permission. Notes have been renumbered to correspond with edited text.

physical, emotional, and psychological consequences."[9] To name a few, pregnancy increases a woman's uterine size 500–1,000 times, her pulse rate by 10 to 15 beats a minute, and her body weight by 25 pounds or more.[10] Even the healthiest pregnancy can entail nausea, vomiting, more frequent urination, fatigue, back pain, labored breathing, or water retention.[11] There are also numerous medical risks involved in carrying pregnancy to term: of every 10 women who experience pregnancy and childbirth, 6 need treatment for some medical complication, and 3 need treatment for major complications.[12] In addition, labor and delivery impose extraordinary physical demands, whether over the 6-to-12 hour or longer course of vaginal delivery, or during the highly invasive surgery involved in a cesarean section, which accounts for one out of four deliveries.[13]

By compelling pregnancy to term and delivery even where they are unwanted, abortion restrictions thus exert far more profound intrusions into bodily integrity than the stomach-pumping the Court invalidated in *Rochin v. California*,[14] or the surgical removal of a bullet from a shoulder that the Court invalidated in *Winston v. Lee*.[15] "The integrity of an individual's person is a cherished value of our society"[16] because it is so essential to identity: as former Solicitor General Charles Fried, who argued for the United States in *Webster*, recognized in another context: "[to say] that my body can be used is [to say] that I can be used."[17]

These points would be too obvious to require restatement if the state attempted to compel abortions rather than to restrict them. Indeed, in colloquy with Justice O'Connor during the *Webster* oral argument, former Solicitor General Fried conceded that in such a case, liberty principles, although unenumerated, would compel the strictest view. To be sure, as Mr. Fried suggested, restrictive abortion laws do not literally involve "laying hands on a woman."[18] But this distinction should make no difference: the state would plainly infringe its citizens' bodily integrity whether its agents inflicted knife wounds or its laws forbade surgery or restricted blood transfusions in cases of private knifings.[19]

Apart from this impact on bodily integrity, abortion restrictions infringe a woman's autonomy in a second sense as well; they invade the autonomy in family affairs that the Supreme Court has long deemed central to the right of privacy. Liberty requires independence in making the most important decisions in life.[20] "The decision whether or not to beget or bear a child" lies at "the very heart of this cluster of constitutionally protected choices,"[21] because few decisions can more importantly alter the course of one's life than the decision to bring a child into the world. Bearing a child dramatically affects "'what a person is, what [s]he wants, the determination of [her] life plan, of [her] concept of the good'" and every other aspect of the "'self-determination . . . [that] give[s] substance to the concept of liberty.'"[22] Becoming a parent dramatically alters a woman's educational prospects,[23] employment opportunities,[24] and sense of self.[25] In light of these elemental facts, it is no surprise that the freedom to choose one's own family formation is "deeply rooted in this Nation's history and tradition."[26]

Today, virtually no one disputes that these principles require heightened scrutiny of laws restricting access to contraception.[27] But critics of *Roe* sometimes argue that abortion is "different in kind from the decision not to conceive in the first place."[28] Justice White, for example, has asserted that, while the liberty interest is fundamental in the contraception context,[29] that interest falls to minimal after conception.[30]

Such a distinction cannot stand, however, because no bright line can be drawn between contraception and abortion in light of modern scientific and medical advances. Contraception and abortion are points on a continuum. Even "conception" itself is a complex process of which fertilization is simply the first stage. According to contemporary medical authorities, conception begins not with fertilization, but rather six to seven days later when the fertilized egg becomes implanted in the uterine wall, itself a complex process.[31] Many medically accepted contraceptives operate after fertilization. For example, both oral contraceptives and the intra-uterine device (IUD) not only prevent fertilization but in some instances prevent implantation.[32] Moreover, the most significant new developments in contraceptive technology, such as RU486, act by foiling implantation.[33] All such contraceptives blur the line between contraception and abortion.

In the absence of a bright physiological line, there can be no bright constitutional line between the moments before and after conception. A woman's fundamental liberty does not simply evaporate when sperm meets ovum. Indeed, as Justice Stevens has recognized, "if one decision is more 'fundamental' to the individual's freedom than the other, surely it is the postconception decision that is the more serious."[34] Saying this much does not deny that profound evolutionary changes occur between fertilization and birth. Clearly, there is some difference between "the freshly fertilized egg and . . . the 9-month-gestated . . . fetus on the eve of birth."[35] But as *Roe v. Wade* fully recognized, such differences go at most to the weight of the state's justification for interfering with a pregnancy; they do not extinguish the underlying fundamental liberty.

Thus *Roe* is not a mere "thread" that the Court could pull without "unravel[ing]" the now elaborately woven "fabric" of the privacy decisions.[36] Rather, *Roe* is integral to the principle that childbearing decisions come to "th[e] Court with a momentum for respect that is lacking when appeal is made to liberties which derive merely from shifting economic arrangements.[37] The decision to become a mother is too fundamental to be equated with the decision to buy a car, choose optometry over ophthalmology, take early retirement, or any other merely economic decision that the government may regulate by showing only a minimally rational basis.

B. Keeping Reproductive Choice in Private Hands Is Essential to a Free Society

Even if there were any disagreement about the degree of bodily or decisional autonomy that is essential to personhood, there is a separate, alternative rationale for the privacy cases: keeping the state out of the business of reproductive decision making. Regimentation of reproduction is a hallmark of the totalitarian state, from Plato's Republic to Hitler's Germany, from Huxley's *Brave New World to Atwood's A Handmaid's Tale.* Whether the state compels reproduction or prevents it, "totalitarian limitation of family size . . . is at complete variance with our constitutional concepts."[38] The state's monopoly of force cautions against any official reproductive orthodoxy.

For these reasons, the Supreme Court has long recognized that the privacy right protects not only the individual but also our society. As early as *Meyer*[39] and *Pierce,*[40] the Court acknowledged that "[t]he fundamental theory of liberty" on which a free society rests "excludes any general power of the State to standardize" its citizens.[41] As Justice Powell likewise recognized for the Moore plurality, "a free society" is one that avoids the homogenization of family life.[42]

The right of privacy, like freedoms of speech and religion, protects conscience and spirit from the encroachment of overbearing government. "Struggles to coerce uniformity of sentiment," Justice Jackson recognized in *West Virginia State Board of Education v. Barnett,*[43] are the inevitably futile province of "our totalitarian enemies."[44] Preserving a private sphere for childbearing and childbearing decisions not only liberates the individual; it desirably constrains the state.[45]

Those who would relegate all control over abortion to the state legislatures ignore these fundamental, systematic values. It is a red herring to focus on the question of judicial versus legislative control of reproductive decisions, as so many of *Roe's* critics do. The real distinction is that between private and public control of the decision: the private control that the courts protect through *Griswold* and *Roe,* and the public control that the popular branches could well usurp in a world without those decisions.

Precisely because of the importance of a private sphere for family, spirit, and conscience, the framers never intended to commit all moral disagreements to the political arena. Quite the contrary:

> The very purpose of a Bill of Rights was to withdraw certain subjects from the vicissitudes of political controversy, to place them beyond the reach of majorities and officials and to establish them as legal principles to be applied by the courts. One's right to life, liberty, and property, to free speech, a free press, freedom of worship and assembly, and other fundamental rights may not be submitted to vote; they depend on the outcome of no elections.[46]

Such "withdrawal" of fundamental liberties from the political arena is basic to constitutional democracy as opposed to rank majoritarianism, and nowhere is such "withdrawal" more important than in controversies where moral convictions and passions run deepest. The inclusion of the free exercise clause attests to this point.[47]

The framers also never intended that toleration on matters of family, conscience, and spirit would vary from state to state. The value of the states and localities as "laborator[ies for] . . . social and economic experiments"[48] has never extended to "'experiments at the expense of the dignity and personality of the individual.'"[49] Rather as Madison once warned, "'it is proper to take alarm at the first experiment on our liberties. We hold this prudent jealousy to be the first duty of citizens, and one of [the] noblest characteristics of the late Revolution.'"[50]

Roe v. Wade thus properly withdrew the abortion decision, like other decisions on matters of conscience, "from the vicissitudes of political controversy." It did not withdraw that decision from the vicissitudes of moral argument or social suasion by persuasive rather than coercive means.[51] In withdrawing the abortion decision from the hot lights of politics, Roe protected not only persons but the processes of constitutional democracy. . . .

II. THE POLITICAL PROCESS: NOT TO BE TRUSTED

On October 13, 1989, the *New York Times* declared that the tide had turned in the political process on abortion.[52] The Florida legislature, in special session, rejected a series of proposals to restrict abortion, and Congress voted to expand abortion funding for poor women to cases of rape and incest. And most stunningly of all, the Attorney General of Illinois on November 2, 1989, settled a pending challenge to Illinois' abortion clinic regulation rather than risk winning his case in the United States Supreme Court. These events have triggered the assessment that the post-*Webster* pro-choice mobilization has succeeded. Which raises the question: why not leave these matters to the political process?

The short answer, of course, is that we don't leave freedom of speech or religion or association to the political process, even on good days when the polls suggest they might stand a chance, at least in some states. The very essence of a fundamental right is that it "depend[s] on the outcome of no elections."[53]

The long answer is, as always, that fundamental liberties are not occasions for the experimentation that federalism invites. The right to abortion should not depend on where you live and how much money you have for travel.[54] And, regardless of our recent, at long-last successes, the reality remains that the political process is to be trusted the least where, as here, it imposes burdens unequally.

The direct impact of abortion restrictions falls exclusively on a class of people that consists entirely of women. Only women get pregnant. Only women have abortions. Only women will endure unwanted pregnancies and adverse health consequences if states restrict abortions. Only women will suffer dangerous, illegal abortions where legal ones are unavailable. And only women will bear children if they cannot obtain abortions.[55] Yet every restrictive abortion law has been passed by a legislature in which men constitute a numerical majority. And every restrictive abortion law, by definition, contains an unwritten clause exempting all men from its strictures.

As Justice Jackson wrote, legislators threaten liberty when they pass laws that exempt themselves or people like them: "The framers of the Constitution knew, and we should not forget today, that there is no more effective practical guaranty against arbitrary and unreasonable government than to require that the principles of law which officials would impose upon a minority must be imposed generally."[56] The Supreme Court has long interpreted the equal protection clause to require even-handedness in legislation, lest the powerful few too casually trade away for others key liberties that they are careful to reserve for themselves.

For example, in striking down a law permitting castration of recidivist chicken thieves but sparing white collar embezzlers the knife, the Court implied that, put to an all-or-nothing choice, legislators would rather sterilize no one than jeopardize a politically potent class.[57] In the words of Justice Jackson: "There are limits to the extent to which a legislatively represented majority may conduct biological experiments at the expense of the dignity and personality and natural powers of a minority—even those who are guilty of what the majority defines as crimes."[58]

At least there should be. Relying on state legislatures, as Chief Justice Rehnquist would, to protect women against "abortion regulation reminiscent of the dark ages,"[59] ignores the fact that the overwhelming majority of "those who serve in such bodies"[60] are biologically exempt from the penalties they are imposing.

The danger is greater still when the subject is abortion. The lessons of history are disquieting. Abortion restrictions, like the most classic restrictions on women seeking to participate in the worlds of work and ideas, have historically rested on archaic stereotypes portraying women as persons whose "paramount destiny and mission . . . [is] to fulfill the noble and benign office of wife and mother."[61] Legislation prohibiting abortion, largely a product of the years between 1860 and 1880, reflected *precisely* the same ideas about women's natural and proper roles as other legislation from the same period, long since discredited, that prohibited women from serving on juries or participating in the professions, including the practice of law.[62] And modern studies have found that support for laws banning abortion continues to be an outgrowth of the same stereotypical notions that women's only appropriate roles are those of mother and housewife. In many cases, abortion laws are a direct reaction to the increasing number of women who work outside of the home.[63] Those involved in anti-abortion activities tend to echo the well-known views of Justice Bradley in *Bradwell*:

> Men and women, as a result of . . . intrinsic differences, have different roles to play. Men are best suited to the public world of work, whereas women are best suited to rearing children, managing homes, and loving and caring for husbands. . . . Mothering, in their view, is itself a full-time job, and any woman who cannot commit herself fully to mothering should eschew it entirely.[64]

But the lessons of history are not limited to the powers of enduring stereotypes. History also makes clear that a world without *Roe* will not be a world without abortion but a world in which abortion is accessible according to one's constitutional case. While affluent women will travel to jurisdictions where safe and legal abortions are available, paying whatever is necessary, restrictive abortion laws and with them, the life-threatening prospect of back-alley abortion, will disproportionately descend upon "those without . . . adequate resources" to avoid them.[65] Those for whom the burdens of an unwanted pregnancy may be the most crushing—the young, the poor, women whose color already renders them victims of discrimination—will be the ones least able to secure a safe abortion.

In the years before *Roe*, "[p]oor and minority women were virtually pre-cluded from obtaining safe, legal procedures, the overwhelming majority of which were obtained by white women in the private hospital services on psy-chiatric indications."[66] Women without access to safe and legal abortions often had dangerous and illegal ones. According to one study, mishandled criminal abortions were the leading cause of maternal deaths in the 1960s,[67] and mortal-ity rates for African-American women were as much as nine times the rate for white women.[68] To trust the political process to protect these women is to ignore the lessons of history and the realities of power and powerlessness in America today.

In the face of such lessons, those who would have us put our faith in the political process might first want to look a little more closely at the victories which are said to support such a choice. The Florida legislature's rejection of proposed abortion restrictions came days *after* the state's highest court held that the State Constitution protects the right to choose abortion, rendering the entire session, by the press's verdict before it began, symbolic at best. The session was still a triumph, but hardly one in which the courts were beside the point. And while extending funding to cases of rape and incest would have been a step forward, the narrowness of the victory and the veto of the resulting legislation should give pause, at least.[69]

We believe that energizing and mobilizing pro-choice voters, and women in particular, is vitally important on its own terms. We hope, frankly, that with apportionment approaching in 2000, that mobilization will affect issues well beyond abortion. We hope more women will find themselves running for office and winning. We hope pro-choice voters and the legislators they elect will attack a range of issues of particular importance to women, including the atten-tion that children receive after they are born.

But we have no illusions. We will lose some along the way. Young and poor and minority women will pay most dearly when we do. That's the way it is in politics. That's why politics should not dictate constitutional rights. . . .

NOTES

1. The right of privacy is only one among many instances in which the Court has recognized rights that are not expressly named in the Constitution's text. To name just a few other examples, the Court has recognized unenu-merated rights to freedom of association, see *National Association for the Advancement of Colored People v. Alabama*, 357 U.S. 449, 466 (1958); to equal protection under the Fifth Amendment due process clause, see *Bolling v. Sharpe*, 347 U.S. 497, 500 (1954); to travel between the states, see *Shapiro v. Thompson*, 394 U.S. 618, 638 (1966); to vote, see *Harper v. Virginia Bd. of Elections*, 383 U.S. 663, 665–66 (1966); *Reynolds v. Sims*, 377 U.S. 533, 554 (1964); and to attend criminal trials, see *Richmond Newspapers Inc. v. Virginia*, 448 U.S. 555, 579–80 (1980).
2. 262 U.S. 390 (1923).

3. 268 U.S. 510 (1925).
4. See, e.g., *Moore v. City of East Cleveland*, 431 U.S. 494, 503–06 (1977) (plurality opinion) (noting a constitutional right to live with one's grandchildren); *Loving v. Virginia*, 388 U.S. 1, 12 (1967) (affirming a right to interracial marriage).
5. 381 U.S. 479 (1965).
6. *Eisenstadt v. Baird*, 405 U.S. 438, 453 (1972).
7. *Thornburgh v. American College of Obstetricians & Gynecologists*, 476 U.S. 747, 777 n.5 (1985) (Stevens, J., concurring) (quoting former Solicitor General Fried, "Correspondence," 6 *Phil. & Pub. Aff.* 288–89 (1977)).
8. *Thornburgh*, 476 U.S. at 772.
9. *Michael M. v. Sonoma County Superior Court*, 480 U.S. 464, 471 (1981).
10. See J. Pritchard, P. McDonald & N. Gant, *Williams Obstetrics*, 181–210, 260–63 (17th ed. 1985) [hereinafter *Williams Obstetrics*].
11. See *Id.*
12. See R. Gold, A. Kenney & S. Singh, *Blessed Events and the Bottom Line: Financing Maternity Care in the United States*, 10 (1987).
13. See D. Danforth, M. Hughey & A. Wagner, The *Complete Guide to Pregnancy*, 228–31 (1983); S. Romney, M. J. Gray, A. B. Little, J. Merrill, E. J. Quilligan & R. Stander, *Gynecology and Obstetrics: The Health Care of Women*, 626–37 (2d ed. 1981).
14. 342 U.S. 165 (1952).
15. 470 U.S. 753 (1985).
16. *Id.* at 760.
17. C. Fried, *Right and Wrong*, 121 n.* (1978).
18. "Transcript of Oral Argument in Abortion Case," *N.Y. Times*, Apr. 27, 1989, at B12, col. 5.
19. Likewise, a state would surely infringe reproductive freedom by compelling abortions even if it became technologically possible to do so without "laying hands on a woman."
20. See *Whalen v. Roe*, 429 U.S. 589, 599–600 (1977).
21. *Carey v. Population Serv. Int'l*, 431 U.S. 678, 685 (1977).
22. *Thornburgh v. American College of Obstetricians & Gynecologists*, 476 U.S. 747, 777 n.5 (1985) (Stevens, J., concurring) (quoting C. Fried, *Right and Wrong*, 146–47 (1978)).
23. Teenage mothers have high dropout rates: 8 out of 10 who become mothers at age 17 or younger do not finish high school. See Fielding, *Adolescent Pregnancy Revisited*, 299 Mass. Dep't Pub. Health, 893, 894 (1978).
24. Control over the rate of childbirth is a key factor in explaining recent gains in women's wages relative to men's. See Fuchs, "Women's Quest for Economic Equality," 3 *J. Econ. Persp.* 25, 33–37 (1989).
25. This fact is evident even if the biological mother does not raise her child. Relinquishing a child for adoption may alleviate material hardship, but it is psychologically traumatic. See Winkler & VanKeppel, *Relinquishing Mothers in Adoption: Their Long-Term Adjustment, Monograph* No. 3, Institute of Family Studies (1984).

26. *Moore v. City of East Cleveland,* 431 U.S. 494, 503 (1977) (plurality opinion).
27. The United States has conceded before the Supreme Court that the *Griswold* line of cases was correctly decided. See *Brief for the United States as Amicus Curiae Supporting Appellants,* 11–13; *Webster v. Reproductive Health Serv.,* 1109 S.Ct. 3040 (1989) (No. 88-605); "Transcript of Oral Argument in Abortion Case," *N.Y. Times,* Apr. 27, 1989, at B13, col. 1 (Argument of former Solicitor General Fried on behalf of the United States).
28. *Thornburgh,* 476 U.S. at 792 n.2 (White, J., dissenting).
29. See *Eisenstadt v. Baird,* 405 U.S. 438, 463–64 (1972) (White, J., concurring in result); *Griswold v. Connecticut,* 381 U.S. 479, 502–03 (1965) (White, J., concurring in judgment).
30. See *Thornburgh,* 476 U.S. at 792 n.2 (White, J., dissenting) (arguing that the fetus's presence after conception changes not merely the state justification but "the characterization of the liberty interest itself").
31. See *Williams Obstetrics,* supra note 10, at 88–91; Milby, "The New Biology and the Question of Personhood: Implications for Abortion," *9 Am. J.L. & Med.* 31, 39–41 (1983). Indeed, the American College of Obstetricians & Gynecologists, the preeminent authority on such matters, has adopted the following official definition of conception: conception consists of "the implantation of the blastocyst [fertilized ovum]" in the uterus, and thus is "not synonymous with fertilization." *Obstetric-Gynecologic Terminology* 229, 327 (E. Hughes ed. 1972). Such a definition is not surprising in view of the fact that less than half of fertilized ova ever successfully become implanted. See "Post-Coital Contraception," 1 *The Lancet* 855, 856 (1983).
32. See R. Hatcher, E. Guest, F. Stewart, G. Stewart, J. Trussell, S. Bowen & W. Gates, *Contraceptive Technology,* 252–53, 377 (14th rev. ed. 1988) [hereinafter *Contraceptive Technology*]; *United States Department of Health and Human Services, IUDs: Guidelines for Informed Decision-Making and Use* (1987).
33. See *Contraceptive Technology,* supra note 32, at 378; Nieman, Choate, Chrousas, Healy, Morin, Renquist, Merriam, Spitz, Bardin, Balieu & Loriaux, "The Progesterone Antagonist RU486: A Potential New Contraceptive Agent," 316 *N. Eng. J. Med.* 187 (1987). RU486 is approved for use in France but not in the United States.
34. *Thornburgh,* 476 U.S. at 776 (Stevens, J., concurring).
35. *Id.* at 779.
36. "Transcript of Oral Argument in Abortion Case," *N.Y. Times,* April 27, 1989, at B12, col. 5 (former Solicitor General Fried, arguing on behalf of the United States). Counsel for Appellees gave the following complete reply: "It has always been my personal experience that when I pull a thread, my sleeve falls off." *Id.* at B13, col. 1 (argument of Mr. Susman).
37. *Thornburgh,* 476 U.S. at 775 (Stevens, J., concurring) (citing *Griswold v. Connecticut,* 381 U.S. 479, 502–03 (1965) (White, J., dissenting)).
38. *Griswold,* 381 U.S. at 497 (Goldberg, J., concurring).
39. *Meyer v. Nebraska,* 262 U.S. 390 (1923).
40. *Pierce v. Society of Sisters,* 268 U.S. 510 (1925).
41. *Id.* at 535.

42. See *Moore v. City of East Cleveland*, 431 U.S. 494, 503 n.11 (1977) (quoting from a discussion of *Griswold* in Pollak, "Thomas I. Emerson, Lawyer and Scholar: *Ipse Custodiet Custodes*," 84 Yale L.J. 638, 653 (1975)).
43. 319 U.S. 624 (1943).
44. *Id.* at 640–41.
45. See generally Rubenfeld, "The Right of Privacy," 102 *Harv. L. Rev.* 737, 804–07 (1989) (arguing that the constitutional right of privacy protects individuals from being turned into instrumentalities of the regimenting state, or being forced into a state-chosen identity).
46. *Barnette*, 319 U.S. at 638.
47. Justice Douglas wrote:

> The Fathers of the Constitution were not unaware of the varied and extreme views of religious sects, of the violence of disagreement among them, and of the lack of any one religious creed on which all men would agree. They fashioned a charter of government which envisaged the widest possible toleration of conflicting views.

   United States v. Ballard, 322 U.S. 78, 87 (1944). See also *Webster*, 109 S. Ct. at 3085 & n.16 (Stevens, J., concurring in part and dissenting in part) (noting that "the intensely divisive character of much of the national debate over the abortion issue reflects the deeply held religious convictions of many participants in the debate").
48. *New State Ice Co. v. Liebmann*, 285 U.S. 262, 311 (1932) (Brandeis, J., dissenting).
49. *Poe v. Ullman*, 367 U.S. 497, 555 (1961) (Harlan, J., dissenting) (quoting *Skinner v. Oklahoma*, 316 U.S. 535, 546 (1942) (Jackson, J., concurring)).
50. *Everson v. Board of Educ.*, 330 U.S. 1, 65 (1947) (Appendix, Rutledge, J., dissenting) (quoting Madison, *Memorial and Remonstrance Against Religious Assessments*).
51. Nor, of course, did it bar political efforts to reduce the abortion rate through noncoercive means, such as funding sex education and contraception, or providing economic security to indigent mothers.
52. See Apple, "An Altered Political Climate Suddenly Surrounds Abortion," *N.Y. Times*, Oct. 13, 1989, at A1, col. 4; see also Berke, "The Abortion-Rights Movement Has Its Day," *N.Y. Times*, Oct. 15, 1989, § 4 at 1, col. 1.
53. *West Virginia Bd. of Educ. v. Barnette*, 319 U.S. 624, 638 (1943).
54. Even if only 10 or 11 states were to preclude abortion within their borders, many women would be held hostage there by the combination of geography, poverty, and youth. This situation would be no more tolerable than the enforcement of racial segregation in a "mere" ten or eleven states in the 1950s.
55. See *Michael M. v. Sonoma County Superior Court*, 450 U.S. 464, 473 (1981) ("[V]irtually all of the significant harmful and inescapably identifiable consequences of teenage pregnancy fall on the young female").
56. *Railway Express Agency v. New York*, 336 U.S. 106, 112 (1949) (Jackson, J., concurring).
57. See *Skinner v. Oklahoma*, 316 U.S. 535 (1942). Cf. Epstein, "The Supreme Court, 1987 Term: Foreword: Unconstitutional Conditions, State Power,

and the Limits of Consent," 102 *Harv. L. Rev.* 4 (1988) (arguing that enforcement of unconstitutional conditions doctrine similarly functions to put legislatures to an all-or-nothing choice).

58. *Skinner,* 316 U.S. at 546 (Jackson, J., concurring).
59. *Webster,* 109 S. Ct. at 3045.
60. *Id.*
61. *Bradwell v. Illinois,* 83 U.S. (16 Wall.) 130, 142 (1873) (Bradley, J., concurring).
62. See J. Mohr, *Abortion in America: The Origins and Evolution of National Policy. 1800–1900,* at 168–72 (1978). To many of the doctors who were largely responsible for abortion restrictions, "the chief purpose of women was to produce children; anything that interfered with that purpose, or allowed women to 'indulge' themselves in less important activities, threatened . . . the future of society itself." Id. at 169. The view of one such 19th-century doctor drew the parallel even more explicitly: he complained that "the tendency to force women into men's places" was creating the insidious new idea that a woman's "ministrations . . . as a mother should be abandoned for the sterner rights of voting and law making." Id. at 105; see also L. Gordon, *Woman's Body, Woman's Right: A Social History of Birth Control in America* (1976) (chronicling the social and political history of reproductive rights in the United States).
63. See generally K. Luker, *Abortion and the Politics of Motherhood,* 192–215 (1984) (describing how the abortion debate, among women, represents a "war" between the feminist vision of women in society and the homemaker's world view); Luker, "Abortion and the Meaning of Life," in *Abortion: Understanding Differences* 25, 31–33 (S. Callahan & D. Callahan eds. 1984) (concluding that "[b]ecause many prolife people see sex as literally sacred, *and because, for women, procreative sex is a fundamental part of their "career* . . . abortion is, from their [the prolife] point of view, to turn the world upside down").
64. Luker, *supra* note 63, at 31. It is, of course, precisely such stereotypes, as they are reflected in legislation, which have over and over again been the focus of this Court's modern equal protection cases. See, e.g., *Califano v. Goldfarb,* 430 U.S. 199, 206–07 (1977) ("Gender-based differentiation . . . is forbidden by the Constitution, at least when supported by no more substantial justification than 'archaic and overbroad' generalizations."); *Weinberger v. Wiesenfeld,* 420 U.S. 636, 645 (1975) ("Gender-based generalizations" that men are more likely than women to support their families "cannot suffice to justify the denigration of the effects of women who do work. . . ."); *Stanton v. Stanton,* 421 U.S. 7, 14 (1975) ("A child, male or female, is still a child. No longer is the female destined solely for the home and the rearing of the family, and only the male for the marketplace and the world of ideas."); *Frontiero v. Richardson,* 441 U.S. 677, 684 (1973) ("[O]ur Nation has had a long and unfortunate history of sex discrimination . . . which in practical effect put women, not on a pedestal, but in a cage.").
65. *Griswold v. Connecticut,* 318 U.S. 479, 503 (1965) (White, J., concurring).
66. *Polgar & Fried,* "The Bad Old Days: Clandestine Abortions Among the Poor in New York City Before Liberalization of the Abortion Law," 8 *Fam. Plan.*

Persp. 125 (1976); see also Gold, "Therapeutic Abortions in New York: A 20-Year Review," 55 Am J. Pub. Health 964, 66 (1965) (noting that the ratio of legal hospital abortions per live birth was 5 times more for white women than for women of color, and 26 times more for white women than for Puerto Rican women in New York City from 1951–62); Pilpel, "The Abortion Crisis," in *The Case for Legalized Abortion Now* 97, 101 (Guttmacher ed. 1967) (noting that 93% of in-hospital abortions in New York State were performed on white women who were able to afford private rooms).

67. See Niswander, "Medical Abortion Practice in the United States," in *Abortion and the Law,* 37, 37 (D. Smith ed. 1967).

68. See Gold, *supra* note 66, at 964–65.

69. Requiring prompt reporting of cases of rape and incest to criminal authorities, measured in terms of days if not hours, as the White House has suggested, is to ignore study after study that has found precisely such cases among the least often reported to the police. Yet late reporting, which should be encouraged, becomes grounds to deny funding, and excludes altogether those who fear, often with reasons, to report at all. The pain and suffering of brutal victimization and of an unwanted pregnancy are in no way affected by the speed of the initial criminal report. A small victory, indeed.

President Bush vetoed the legislation on October 21, 1989. The House vote to override was 231–191, short of the necessary two-thirds majority. See 135 *Cong. Rec.* H7482-95 (daily ed. Oct. 25, 1989).

Abortion on Demand Has No Constitutional or Moral Justification
James Bopp Jr. and Richard E. Coleson

I. THE ABSENCE OF A CONSTITUTIONAL RIGHT TO ABORTION

Abortion is not mentioned in the United States Constitution. Yet, in *Roe v. Wade*,[1] the United States Supreme Court held that there is a constitutional right to abortion.

How could the Court justify such a decision? Actually, it never did. The Court simply *asserted* that the "right of privacy . . . is broad enough to encompass a woman's decision whether or not to terminate her pregnancy."[2] Leading constitutional scholars were outraged at the Court's action in *Roe* and vigorously argued that the Court had no constitutional power to create new constitutional rights in this fashion.[3] And, of course, many people were incensed that a whole class of innocent human beings—those awaiting birth—was stripped of all rights, including the right to life itself.

Why does it matter whether abortion is found in the Constitution? Why shouldn't the United States Supreme Court be free to create new constitutional rights whenever it chooses? The answers lie in the carefully designed structure of our democracy, whose blueprints were drawn over two centuries ago by the framers of the Constitution and ratified by the People. This design is explained below as the foundation for rejecting abortion on demand on a constitutional basis.

But what of abortion on demand as a legislative issue? Even if there is no constitutional right to abortion, how much should state legislatures restrict abortion? The answer lies in the states' compelling interest in protecting innocent human life, born or preborn. This interest is given scant attention by abortion rights advocates. Rather, they envision an extreme abortion-on-demand regime; but their societal vision is overwhelmingly rejected by public opinion. As shown below, the states constitutionally may and morally should limit abortion on demand.

James Bopp Jr. is an attorney in the law firm of Bopp, Coleson, & Bostrom, Terre Haute, Indiana, and general counsel to the National Right to Life Committee, Inc. Richard E. Coleson is an associate with Bopp, Coleson, & Bostrom and general counsel, Indiana Citizens for Life, Inc. This article was written especially for *Points of View* in 1992.

A. The People Have Created a Constitutional Democracy with Certain Matters Reserved to Democratic Control and Other Matters Constitutionally Protected

The United States Constitution begins with the words "We the People of the United States . . . do ordain and establish this Constitution for the United States of America."[4] Thus, our Republic is founded on the cornerstone of democratic self-governance—all authority to govern is granted by the People.[5] The only legitimate form of government is that authorized by the People; the only rightful authority is that which the People have granted to the institutions of government.[6]

The People have chosen to authorize a regime governed by the rule of law, rather than rule by persons.[7] The supreme law of the land is the Constitution,[8] the charter by which the People conferred authority to govern and created the governing institutions. Thus, the only legitimate form and authority for governance are found in the Constitution.

The constitutional grant of governing authority was not a general grant but one carefully measured, balanced, and limited. Three fundamental principles underlie the Constitution: (1) the People have removed certain matters from simple majority rule by making them constitutional rights but have retained other matters to be democratically controlled through their elected representatives[9], (2) the People have distributed governmental powers among three branches of government, with each limited to its own sphere of power[10]; and (3) the People have established a federal system in which the power to regulate certain matters is granted to the national government and all remaining power is retained by the states or by the People themselves.[11]

Because these fundamental principles were violated by the Supreme Court in *Roe v. Wade*,[12] leading constitutional scholars condemned the decision. Law professors and dissenting Supreme Court Justices declared that the Court had seized power not granted to it in the Constitution, because (1) it had created new constitutional rights, which power only the People have,[13] (2) it had acted as a legislature rather than as a court,[14] and (3) it had trespassed into an area governed by the states for over two centuries.[15] The scholarly rejection of *Roe v. Wade* continues to the present.[16]

Although the Court's power grab in *Roe* was a seizure less obvious to the public than tanks in the street, it has nevertheless been rightly characterized as a "limited *coup d'état*."[17] The Court seized from the People a matter they had left to their own democratic governance by declaring a constitutional right to abortion without establishing any connection between the Constitution and a right to abortion. Richard Epstein attacked the Court's *Roe* decision thus, "*Roe* . . . is symptomatic of the analytical poverty possible in constitutional litigation."[18] He concluded: "[W]e must criticize both Mr. Justice Blackmun in *Roe v. Wade*. . . and the entire method of constitutional interpretation that allows the Supreme Court . . . both to 'define' and to 'balance' interests on the major social and political issues of our time."[19]

B. To Determine Which Matters Are Constitutionally Removed from Democratic Control, the Supreme Court Has Developed Tests to Determine Fundamental Rights

The Court did not violate the Constitution in *Roe* simply because there is no *express* mention of abortion in the Constitution. There are matters which the Constitution does not *expressly* mention which the Supreme Court has legitimately found to be within some express constitutional protection. But where the Court employs such constitutional analysis, it must clearly demonstrate that the newly recognized constitutional right properly falls within the scope of an express right. This requires a careful examination and explanation of what the People intended when they ratified the particular constitutional provision in question. It was the Roe Court's failure to provide this logical connection between the Constitution and a claimed right to abortion which elicited scholarly outrage.

Under the Supreme Court's own tests, the Court had to find that the claimed right to abortion was a "fundamental" right in order to extend constitutional protection to it under the Fourteenth Amendment, the constitutional provision in which the Court claimed to have found a right to abortion.[20] The Fourteenth Amendment guarantees that no "State [shall] deprive any person of life, liberty, or property, without due process of law."[21] While the provision on its face seems to guarantee only proper legal proceedings before a state may impose capital punishment, imprisonment, or a fine, the Court has assumed the authority to examine activities asserted as constitutional rights to determine whether—in the Court's opinion—they fall within the concept of "liberty."[22] The notion that the Court may create new constitutional rights at will by reading them into the "liberty" clause of the Fourteenth Amendment could readily lead to a rejection of the foundational constitutional premise of the rule of law, not of persons. If a handful of Justices can place whatever matters they wish under the umbrella of the Constitution—totally bypassing the People and their elected representatives—then these Justices have constituted themselves as Platonic guardians,[23] thereby rejecting the rule of law for the rule of persons. What would prevent a majority of the Supreme Court from declaring that there is a constitutional right to practice, e.g., infanticide or polygamy (matters which the states have historically governed)?

This danger has caused many scholars to reject the sort of analysis which allows five Justices (a majority of the Court) to read new constitutional rights into the "liberty" clause.[24] It led the Court in earlier years to forcefully repudiate the sort of analysis the Court used in *Roe v. Wade.*[25] This danger has caused the current Court to establish more rigorous tests for what constitutes a constitutional right to prevent the Supreme Court from "roaming at large in the constitutional field."[26] These tests had been established at the time of *Roe,* but were ignored in that case.[27]

The Court has developed two tests for determining whether a new constitutional right should be recognized. The first test asks whether an asserted fundamental right is "implicit in the concept of ordered liberty."[28] The second test—a historical test—is whether the right asserted as "fundamental" is "so rooted in the traditions and conscience of our people as to be ranked as fundamental."[29] The historical test is the one now primarily relied upon by the Court.

C. Applying the Proper Test for Determining Constitutional Rights Reveals That Abortion Is Not a Constitutional Right

In *Roe*, the Court should have determined whether or not there is a constitutional right to abortion by asking whether it has historically been treated as "implicit in the concept of ordered liberty" in this nation or whether it has been "deeply rooted [as a right] in this Nation's history and tradition."

The *Roe* opinion itself recounted how abortion had been regulated by the states by statutory law for over a century and before that it had been regulated by the judge-made common law inherited from England.[30] In fact, the period from 1860 to 1880—the Fourteenth Amendment was ratified in 1868[31]—saw "the most important burst of anti-abortion legislation in the nation's history."[32] Therefore, the framers of the Fourteenth Amendment and the People who ratified it clearly did not intend for the Amendment to protect the right to abortion, which was considered a crime at the time.

Now Chief Justice Rehnquist stated well the case against *Roe's* right to abortion in his 1973 dissent to that decision:

> To reach its result, the Court necessarily has had to find within the scope of the Fourteenth Amendment a right that was apparently completely unknown to the drafters of the Amendment. As early as 1821, the first state law dealing directly with abortion was enacted by the Connecticut Legislature. By the time of the adoption of the Fourteenth Amendment in 1868, there were at least 36 laws enacted by state or territorial legislatures limiting abortion. While many states have amended or updated their laws, 21 of the laws on the books in 1968 remain in effect today. Indeed, the Texas statute struck down today was, as the majority notes, first enacted in 1857 and has remained substantially unchanged to the present time.
>
> There apparently was no question concerning the validity of this provision or of any of the other state statutes when the Fourteenth Amendment was adopted. The only conclusion possible from this history is that the drafters did not intend to have the Fourteenth Amendment withdraw from the states the power to legislate with respect to this matter.[33]

Thus, applying the Court's own tests, it is clear that there is no constitutional right to abortion. As a result, the Supreme Court has simply arbitrarily declared one by saying that the right of privacy—previously found by the Court in the "liberty" clause—"is broad enough to encompass a woman's decision whether or not to terminate her pregnancy."[34] In so doing, the Court brushed aside the restraints placed on it by the Constitution, seized power from the People, and placed within the protections of the Constitution an abortion right that does not properly belong there.

One thing is clear from this nation's abortion debate: abortion advocates do not trust the People to decide how abortion should be regulated.[35] However, in rejecting the voice of the People, abortion partisans also reject the very foundation of our democratic Republic and seek to install an oligarchy—with the Court governing the nation—a system of government rejected by our Constitution.

II. THE INTEREST IN PROTECTING INNOCENT HUMAN LIFE

Abortion rights advocates generally ignore one key fact about abortion: abortion requires the willful taking of innocent human life. Abortion involves not merely the issue of what a woman may do with her body. Rather, abortion also involves the question of what may the woman do with the body of another, the unborn child.

A. The People Have an Interest in Protecting Preborn Human Life

The fact that human life begins at conception was well-known at the time the Fourteenth Amendment was ratified in 1868. In fact it was precisely during the time when this Amendment was adopted that the medical profession was carrying the news of the discovery of cell biology and its implications into the legislatures of the states and territories. Prior to that time, science had followed the view of Aristotle that the unborn child became a human being (i.e., received a human soul) at some point after conception (40 days for males and 80–90 days for females).[36] This flawed scientific view became the basis for the "quickening" (greater legal protection was provided to the unborn from abortion after the mother felt movement in the womb than before) distinction in the common law received from England, which imposed lesser penalties for abortions performed prior to "quickening." With the scientific discovery of cell biology, however, the legislatures acted promptly to alter abortion laws to reflect the newly established scientific fact that individual human life begins at conception.

Victor Rosenblum summarized the history well:

> Only in the second quarter of the nineteenth century did biological research advance to the extent of understanding the actual mechanism of human reproduction and of what truly comprised the onset of gestational development. The nineteenth century saw a gradual but profoundly influential revolution in the scientific understanding of the beginning of individual mammalian life. Although sperm had been discovered in 1677, the mammalian egg was not identified until 1827. The cell was first recognized as the structural unit of organisms in 1839, and the egg and sperm were recognized as cells in the next two decades. These developments were brought to the attention of the American state legislatures and public by those professionals most familiar with their unfolding import—physicians. It was the new research findings which persuaded doctors that the old "quickening" distinction embodied in the common and some statutory law was unscientific and indefensible.[37]

About 1857, the American Medical Association led the "physicians' crusade," a successful campaign to push the legal protection provided for the unborn by abortion laws from quickening to conception.[38]

What science discovered over a century before *Roe v. Wade* was true in 1973 (when *Roe* was decided) and still holds true today. For example, a recent textbook on human embryology declared:

> It is the penetration of the ovum by a spermatozoon and the resultant mingling of the nuclear material each brings to the union that constitutes the culmination of the process of *fertilization* and *marks the initiation of the life of a new individual.*[39]

However, abortion rights advocates attempt to obscure the scientific evidence that individual human life begins at conception by the claiming that conception is a "complex" process and by confusing contraception with abortion.[40]

The complexity of the process of conception does not change the fact that it marks the certain beginning of individual human life.[41] Moreover, the complex process of conception occurs in a very brief time at the beginning of pregnancy.[42]

Furthermore, the fact that some so-called "contraceptives" actually act after conception and would be more correctly termed "abortifacients" (substances or devices causing abortion, i.e., acting to abort a pregnancy already begun at conception) does nothing to blur the line at which individual human life begins. It only indicates that some so-called "contraceptives" have been mislabelled.[43] Such mislabelling misleads women, who have a right to know whether they are receiving a contraceptive or are having an abortion.

The "spin"[44] which abortion advocates place on the redefinition of "contraception" is deceptive in two respects. First, there is a clear distinction between devices and substances which act before conception and those which act after conception. This was admitted by Planned Parenthood itself (before it became involved in advocating, referring for, and performing abortions) in a 1963 pamphlet entitled *Plan Your Children*: "An abortion kills the life of a baby after it has begun. . . . Birth control merely postpones the beginning of life."[45]

Second, even if there were no "bright physiological line . . . between the moments before and after conception"[46] this does not mean there can be no constitutional line.[47] At *some point* early in pregnancy, scientific truth compels the conclusion that individual human life has begun. If the indistinction is the real problem, then abortion advocates should be joining prolife supporters in protecting unborn life from a time when there is certitude.[48] However, abortion partisans are not really interested in protecting unborn human life from the time when it may be certain that it exists. They are seeking to justify absolute, on-demand abortion throughout pregnancy.

B. Abortion Rights Advocates Envision an Abortion-on-Demand Regime Unsupported by the People

Abortion rights proponents often argue that our democratic Republic must sanction abortion on demand lest women resort to dangerous "back-alley" abortions. The claims of abortion advocates that thousands of women died each year when abortion was illegal are groundless fabrications created for polemical purposes.[49] In reality, the Surgeon General of the United States has estimated that only a handful of deaths occurred each year in the United States due to illegal abortions.[50] Even since *Roe,* there are still maternal deaths from legal abortions.[51] As tragic as the death of any person is, it must be acknowledged that women who obtain illegal abortions do so by choice and most women will choose to abide by the law. In contrast, preborn human beings are destroyed—without having a choice—at the rate of about 1.5 million per year in the United States alone.[52]

Abortion supporters also resort to the practice of personally attacking prolifers and making false charges about them.[53] A founding member of what is now called the National Abortion Rights Action League (NARAL) chronicles how prolifers were purposely portrayed as Catholics whenever possible, in an attempt to appeal to latent (and sometimes overt) anti-Catholic sentiment in certain communities.[54] It is also routinely claimed that opposition to abortion is really an attempt to "keep women in their place"[55]—to subjugate them—as if requiring fathers to support their children subjugates them. And prolifers are depicted as forcing what are merely their religious views upon society,[56] despite the fact that the United States Supreme Court has held that opposition to abortion "is as much a reflection of 'traditionalist' values towards abortion, as it is an embodiment of the views of any particular religion."[57] Those attempting so to "poison the well," by attacking prolife supporters with untruthful allegations, ignore the fact that polls consistently show that abortion opinion is rather evenly divided in our country within all major demographic groups. For example, women are roughly equally divided on the subject, as are whites, non-whites, Republicans and Democrats.[58] Abortion advocates also ignore the fact that most prolifers simply are opposed to the taking of what they consider (and science demonstrates) to be innocent human life.

Of even greater risk than the risk to a few women who might choose to obtain illegal abortions is the effect of abortion on demand—for any or no reason—on society. Abortion cheapens the value of human life, promotes the idea that it is permissible to solve one's problems at the expense of another, even to the taking of the other's life, legitimizes violence (which abortion is against the unborn) as an appropriate solution for problems, and exposes a whole class of human beings (those preborn) to discrimination on the basis of their age or place of residence (or sometimes their race, gender, or disability).

The regime which abortion-on-demand advocates envision for our society is a radical one. Their ideal society is one where abortions may be obtained for any reason, including simply because the child is the wrong sex; where a husband need not be given any consideration in (or even notice of) an abortion decision involving a child which he fathered; where fathers are shut out even when the child to be aborted might be the only one a man could ever have; where parents could remain ignorant of their daughter's abortion, even when she is persuaded to abort by counselors at an abortion mill whose practitioners care only about financial gain, practice their trade dangerously, and never bother to follow up with their patients; where abortion may be used as a means of birth control; where abortionists do not offer neutral, scientific information about fetal development (and about resources for choosing alternatives to abortion) to women considering abortion; where women are not given adequate time to consider whether they really want an abortion; where abortion is available right up to the time of birth; and where our taxes are used to pay for abortion on demand.[59]

The American People reject such a regime. In fact, polls show that an overwhelming majority would ban well over 90 percent of all abortions that are performed.[60] For example a Boston Globe national poll . . . revealed that:

> Most Americans would ban the vast majority of abortions performed in this country. . . .
>
> While 78 percent of the nation would keep abortion legal in limited circumstances, according to the poll, those circumstances account for a tiny percentage of the reasons cited by women having abortions.
>
> When pregnancy results from rape or incest, when the mother's physical health is endangered and when there is likely to be a genetic deformity in the fetus, those queried strongly approve of legal abortion.
>
> But when pregnancy poses financial or emotional strain, or when the woman is alone or a teen-ager—the reasons given by most women seeking abortions—an overwhelming majority of Americans believes abortion should be illegal, the poll shows.[61]

Yet *Family Planning Perspectives*, a publication of the Alan Guttmacher Institute, which is a research arm of the Planned Parenthood Federation, reveals that these are precisely the reasons why over 90 percent of abortions are performed.[62]

Thus, it is little wonder that the Supreme Court's effort to settle the abortion question with its decision in *Roe v. Wade* has utterly failed. That there is not an even greater groundswell of public opposition to abortion must be attributed to the fact that many Americans are not aware that *Roe* requires virtual abortion on demand for the full nine months of pregnancy.[63] Many people still believe that abortion is only available in the earliest weeks of pregnancy and that abortions are usually obtained for grave reasons, such as rape and incest, which abortion rights advocates always talk about in abortion debates. Of course, such "hard" cases make up only a tiny fraction of all abortions, and many state abortion laws, even before *Roe*, allowed abortions for such grave reasons. It is clear, therefore, that the People reject the radical abortion-on-demand regime promoted by abortion rights advocates.

III. CONCLUSION: STATES CONSTITUTIONALLY MAY AND MORALLY SHOULD LIMIT ABORTION ON DEMAND

One of the principles underlying our liberal democratic Republic is that we as a People choose to give the maximum freedom possible to members of our society. John Stuart Mill's essay *On Liberty*,[64] a ubiquitous source on the subject, is often cited for the principle that people ought to be granted maximum liberty—almost to the degree of license. Yet, Mill himself set limits on liberty relevant to the

abortion debate. Mill wrote his essay *On Liberty* to assert "one very simple principle," namely, "[t]hat the only purpose for which power can be rightfully exercised
over any member of a civilized community, against his will, is to prevent harm to
others."[65] Thus, under Mill's principles, abortion should go unrestricted only if it
does no harm to another. But that, of course, is precisely the core of the abortion
debate. If a fetus is not really an individual human being until he or she is born,
then the moral issue is reduced to what duty is owed to potential life (which is still
a significant moral issue). If however, a fetus is an individual human being from
the moment of conception (or at least some time shortly thereafter), then the
unborn are entitled to legal protection. Ironically, the United States Supreme Court
neglected this key determination—when human life begins—in its *Roe* decision.[66]

Science, of course, has provided the answer to us for well over a hundred
years. Indeed, modern science and technological advances have impressed
upon us more fully the humanity and individuality of each unborn person. As
Dr. Liley has said:

> Another fallacy that modern obstetrics discards is the idea that the pregnant
> woman can be treated as a patient alone. No problem in fetal health or disease
> can any longer be considered in isolation. At the very least two people are
> involved, the mother and her child.[67]

In fact, since *Roe,* the technology for improving fetal therapy is advancing exponentially.[68] In sum, modern science has shown us that:

> The fetus as patient is becoming more of a reality each year. New medical ther-
> apies and surgical technology increasingly offer parents a new choice when a
> fetus has a particular disorder. Recently, the only choices were abortion, early
> delivery, vaginal versus a cesarean delivery, or no intervention. We are now
> able to offer medical and/or surgical intervention as a viable alternative to a
> number of infants. With advancing technologies, it is clearly evident that many
> new and exciting therapies lie just ahead for the fetus.[69]

Because all civilized moral codes limit the liberty of individuals where the
exercise of liberty would result in the taking of innocent human life, arguments
that abortion is necessary to prevent the subjugation of women must also be
rejected.[70] It cannot logically be considered the subjugation of anyone to prevent
him or her from taking innocent human life; otherwise, society could not prevent infanticide, homicide, or involuntary euthanasia. No civilized society could
exist if the unjustified killing of one citizen by another could not be prosecuted.

Nor do abortion restrictions deny women equality by denying them the
same freedom which men have. Men do not have the right to kill their children,
nor may they force women to do so. Thus, abortion rights advocates are really
arguing for a right that men don't have, and, indeed, no one should have—
the right to take innocent human life.

Society has recognized that in some situations men and women should be
treated differently, because they are biologically different and are, therefore, not
similarly situated for constitutional purposes. For example, the Supreme Court
decided in 1981 that a statute that permitted only men to be drafted was not

unconstitutional because "[m]en and women . . . are simply not similarly situated for purposes of a draft or registration for a draft."[71] The same principle, however, made constitutional a Navy policy which allowed women a longer period of time for promotion prior to mandatory discharge than was allowed for men.[72] The Supreme Court in this case found that "the different treatment of men and women naval officers . . . reflects, not archaic and overbroad generalizations, but, instead, the demonstrable fact that male and female line officers . . . are not similarly situated."[73] Because men and women are not similarly situated—by the dictates of nature rather than by society or the law—with respect to pregnancy, it is neither a denial of equality to women nor the subjugation of women to provide legal protection for unborn human beings.[74]

It is essential to a civilized society to limit liberties where reasonably necessary to protect others. Thus, government has required involuntary vaccination to prevent a plague from decimating the community,[75] military conscription to prevent annihilation of the populace by enemies,[76] and the imposition of child support—for 18 years—upon fathers unwilling to support their children.[77] These and other limits on freedom are not the subjugation of citizens, but are the essence of life in a community.

In sum, the states constitutionally may and morally should limit abortion on demand.

NOTES

1. 410 U.S. 113 (1973).
2. *Id.* at 153.
3. See *infra*, notes 13–19 and accompanying text.
4. U.S. Const., preamble.
5. In the landmark case of *Marbury v. Madison*, 1 Cranch 137, 176 (1803), the United States Supreme Court explained, "That the people have an original right to establish, for their future government, such principles, as, in their own opinion, shall most conduce to their own happiness is the basis on which the whole American fabric has been erected. See also The Declaration of Independence, para. 2 (U.S. 1776); *The Federalist*, No. 49 (J. Madison).
6. *Marbury*, 1 Cranch at 176 ("The original and supreme will [of the People] organizes the government, and assigns to different departments their respective powers. It may either stop here, or establish certain limits not to be transcended by those departments. The government of the United States is of the latter description.").
7. See, e.g., id. at 163 ("The government of the United States has been emphatically termed a government of laws, and not of men."); *Akron v. Akron Center for Reproductive Health*, 462 U.S. 416, 419–20 (1983) (We are a "society governed by the rule of law.").
8. *Marbury*, 1 Cranch at 177 ("Certainly all those who have framed written constitutions contemplate them as forming the fundamental and paramount law of the nation. . . ."); *id.* at 179 ("[T]he constitution of the United

States confirms and strengthens the principle, supposed to be essential to all written constitutions, that a law repugnant to the constitution is void; and that courts, as well as other departments, are bound by that instrument.").

9. The Constitution enumerates certain rights; the creation of additional constitutionally protected rights is through amending the Constitution, which depends upon establishing public support for such a right by a supermajority of the People acting through their elected representatives. U.S. Const., art. V. Cf. Bork, "Neutral Principles and Some First Amendment Problems," 47 *Ind. L. J.* 1, 3 (1971).

10. U.S. Const., art. I, § 1, art. II, § 1, art. III, § 1.

11. U.S. Const., amend. IX ("The enumeration in the Constitution, of certain rights, shall not be construed to deny or disparage others retained by the people."), amend. X ("The powers not delegated to the United States by the Constitution, nor prohibited by it to the States, are reserved to the States respectively, or to the people.").

12. 410 U.S. 113.

13. Ely, "The Wages of Crying Wolf: A Comment on *Roe v. Wade,*" 82 Yale L.J. 920, 947 (1973) (*Roe* was "a very bad decision. Not because it [would] perceptibly weaken the Court . . . and not because it conflict[ed] with [his] idea of progress. . . . It [was] bad because it [was] bad constitutional law, or rather because it [was] not constitutional law and [gave] almost no sense of an obligation to try to be.") (emphasis in the original). *Doe v. Bolton,* 410 U.S. 179, 222 (1973) (White, J., dissenting in this companion case to *Roe*) (The Court's action is "an exercise of raw judicial power. . . . This issue, for the most part, should be left with the people and to the political processes the people have devised to govern their affairs.").

14. The *Michigan Law Review,* in an edition devoted to abortion jurisprudence, contained two passages which summarize the scholarly critiques well. In the first, Richard Morgan wrote:

> Rarely does the Supreme Court invite critical outrage as it did in *Roe* by offering so little explanation for a decision that requires so much. The stark inadequacy of the Court's attempt to justify its conclusions . . . suggests to some scholars that the Court, finding no justification at all in the Constitution, unabashedly usurped the legislative function.

Morgan, "*Roe v. Wade* and the Lesson of the Pre-*Roe* Case Law," 77 *Mich. L. Rev.* 1724, 1724 (1979). The editors of the journal concluded from their survey of the literature on *Roe,* "[T]he consensus among legal academics seems to be that, whatever one thinks of the holding, the opinion is unsatisfying." "Editor's Preface," 77 *Mich. L. Rev.* (no number) (1979).

15. *Roe,* 400 U.S. at 174–77 (Rehnquist, J., dissenting).

16. See, e.g., Wardle, "'Time Enough': *Webster v. Reproductive Health Services* and the Prudent Pace of Justice," 41 *Fla. L. Rev.* 881, 927–49 (1989); Bopp & Coleson, "The Right to Abortion: Anomalous, Absolute, and Ripe for Reversal," 3 *B.Y.U. J. Pub. L.* 181, 185–92 (1989) (cataloging critiques of *Roe* in yet another critique of *Roe*).

17. Bork, *supra* note 9, at 6.
18. Epstein, "Substantive Due Process by Any Other Name: The Abortion Cases," 1973 *Sup*. Ct. Rv. 159, 184.
19. *Id*. at 185.
20. The Court acknowledged this duty in Roe itself, but failed to apply the usual tests for determining what rights are rightfully deemed "fundamental." *Roe*, 410 U.S. at 152.
21. U.S. Const., amend. XIV, § 1, cl. 3.
22. *Roe v. Wade*, 410 U.S. 113, revived this sort of "substantive due process" analysis in recent years.
23. The Greek philosopher Plato advocated rule by a class of philosopher-guardians as the ideal form of government. A. Bloom, *The Republic of Plato*, 376c, lines 4–5, 412b–427d (1968).
24. See, e.g., Ely, *supra* note 13; Bork, *supra* note 9.
25. In repudiating an earlier line of "substantive due process" (i.e., finding new rights in the "liberty" clause of the Fourteenth Amendment) cases symbolized by *Lochner v. New York*, 198 U.S. 45 (1905), the Supreme Court declared that the doctrine "that due process authorizes courts to hold laws unconstitutional when they believe the legislature has acted unwisely, has been discarded." *Ferguson v. Skrupa*, 372 U.S. 726, 730 (1963). The Court concluded in *Ferguson*, "We have returned to the original constitutional proposition that courts do not substitute their social and economic beliefs for the judgment of legislative bodies, who are elected to pass laws." *Id*.
26. *Griswold v. Connecticut*, 381 U.S. 479, 502 (1965) (Harlan, J., concurring.)
27. Cf. *Duncan v. Louisiana*, 391 U.S. 145, 149–50 n.14 (1968), with *Roe v. Wade*, 410 U.S. at 152, and *Moore v. City of East Cleveland*, 431 U.S. 494, 503–04 n.12 (1977). See also Ely, *supra* note 13, at 931 n.79 (The *Palko* test was of "questionable contemporary vitality" when *Roe* was decided).
28. *Roe*, 410 U.S. at 152 (quoting *Palko v. Connecticut*, 302 U.S. 319, 325 (1937)) (quotation marks omitted).
29. *Palko*, 302 U.S., at 325 (quoting *Snyder v. Massachusetts*, 291 U.S. 97, 105 (1934)) (quotation marks omitted).
30. *Roe*, 410 U.S. at 139.
31. *Black's Law Dictionary*, 1500 (5th ed. 1979).
32. J. Mohr, *Abortion in America: The Origins and Evolution of National Policy 1800–1900*, 200 (1978). These laws were clearly aimed at protecting preborn human beings and not just maternal health, *id*. at 35–36, so that medical improvements bringing more maternal safety to abortions do not undercut the foundations of these laws, as *Roe* alleged. *Roe*, 410 U.S. at 151–52.
33. *Roe*, 410 U.S. at 174–77 (Rehnquist, J., dissenting) (citations and quotation marks omitted).
34. *Id*. at 153.
35. Cf. Estrich & Sullivan, "Abortion Politics: Writing for an Audience of One," 138 *U. Pa. L. Rev*. 119, 150–55 (1989), with *Webster v. Reproductive Health Services*, 109 S. Ct. 3040, 3058 (1989) (plurality opinion). In *Webster*, the plurality opinion declared:

> The goal of constitutional adjudication is to hold true the balance between that which the Constitution puts beyond the reach of the democratic process and that which it does not. We think we have done that today. The dissent's suggestion that legislative bodies, in a Nation where more than half of our population is women, will treat our decision today as an invitation to enact abortion regulation reminiscent of the dark ages not only misreads our views but does scant justice to those who serve in such bodies and the people who elect them.

    Id. (citation omitted).

36. *Roe,* 410 U.S. at 133 n.22.
37. *The Human Life Bill: Hearings on S. 158 Before the Subcomm. on Separation of Powers of the Senate Comm. on the Judiciary,* 97th Cong., 1st Sess. 474 (statement of Victor Rosenblum). See also Dellapenna, "The History of Abortion: Technology, Morality, and Law," 40 *U. Pitt. L. Rev.* 359, 402–04 (1979).
38. J. Mohr, *supra* note 32, at 147–70. This 19th-century legislation was designed to protect the unborn as stated explicitly by 11 state court decisions interpreting these statutes and implicitly by 9 others. Gorby, "The 'Right' to an Abortion, the Scope of Fourteenth Amendment 'Personhood,' and the Supreme Court's Birth Requirement," 1979 S. *Ill, U.L.J.* 1, 16–17. Twenty-six of the 36 states had laws against abortion as early as 1865, the end of the Civil War, as did six of the ten territories. Dellapenna, *supra* note 37, at 429.
39. B. Patten, *Human Embryology,* 43 (3rd ed. 1969) (emphasis added). See also L. Arey, *Developmental Anatomy,* 55 (7th ed. 1974); W. Hamilton & H. Mossman, *Human Embryology,* 1, 14 (4th ed. 1972); K. Moore, *The Developing Human: Clinically Oriented Embryology,* 1, 12, 24 (2nd ed. 1977); *Human Reproduction, Conception and Contraception,* 461 (Hafez ed., 2nd ed. 1980); J. Greenhill & E. Friedman, *Biological Principles and Modern Practice of Obstetrics,* 17, 23 (1974); D. Reid, K. Ryan & K. Benirschke, *Principles and Management of Human Reproduction,* 176 (1972).
40. See, e.g., Estrich & Sullivan, *supra* note 35, at 128–29. While a complete discussion of cell biology, genetics and fetology is beyond the scope of this brief writing, the standard reference works cited by Estrich & Sullivan verify the fact that individual human life begins at conception.
41. *Supra,* note 39.
42. *Id.*
43. By its etymology (*contra + conception,* i.e., against conception) and traditional and common usage, the term *"contraception"* properly refers to "[t]he prevention of conception or impregnation," Dorland's *Illustrated Medical Dictionary,* 339 (24th ed. 1965), or a "deliberate prevention of conception or impregnation," *Webster's Ninth New Collegiate Dictionary,* 284 (1985).
44. Estrich & Sullivan, *supra* note 35, at 1.
45. Planned Parenthood International, *Plan Your Children* (1963).
46. Estrich & Sullivan, *supra* note 35, at 129.
47. At oral arguments in *Webster v. Reproductive Health Services,* 109 S. Ct. 3040 (1989), Justice Antonin Scalia could see a distinction between contraception and abortion, remarking, "I don't see why a court that can draw that line

[between the first, second, and third trimesters of pregnancy] cannot separate abortion from birth control quite readily."

48. For example, the West German Constitutional Court in 1975 set aside a federal abortion statute which was too permissive, for it "did not sufficiently protect unborn life." M. Glendon, *Abortion and Divorce in Western Law*, 33 (1987). The West German court began with the presumption that "at least after the fourteenth day, developing human life is at stake." *Id.* at 34.

49. B. Nathanson, *Aborting America*, 193 (1979). Nathanson, a former abortionist and early, organizing member of the National Association for the Repeal of Abortion Laws (NARAL, now known as the National Abortion Rights Action League), says:

> In N.A.R.A.L. . . . . it was always "5,000 to 10,000 deaths a year [from illegal abortion]." I confess that I knew the figures were totally false. . . . In 1967, with moderate A.L.I.-type laws in three states, the federal government listed only 160 deaths from illegal abortion. In the last year before the [*Roe*] era began, 1972, the total was only 39 deaths. Christopher Tietze estimated 1,000 maternal deaths as the outside possibility in an average year before legalization; the actual total was probably closer to 500.

Id. at 193. Nathanson adds that even this limited "carnage" argument must now be dismissed "because technology has eliminated it." *Id.* at 194 (referring to the fact that even abortions made illegal by more restrictive abortion laws will generally be performed with modern techniques providing greater safety, and antibiotics now resolve most complications).

50. U.S. Dept. of Health and Human Services, *Centers for Disease Control Abortion Surveillance*, 61 (annual summary 1978, issued Nov. 1980) (finding that there were 39 maternal deaths due to illegal abortion in 1972, the last year before *Roe*).

51. Deaths from legally induced abortions were as follows: 1972 = 24, 1973 = 26, 1974 = 26, 1975 = 31, 1976 = 11, 1977 = 17, 1978 = 11. *Id.* During the same period, deaths from illegal abortions continued as follows: 1972 = 39, 1973 = 19, 1974 = 6, 1975 = 4, 1976 = 2, 1977 = 4, 1978 = 7. *Id.*

52. See, e.g., Henshaw, Forrest & Van Vort, "Abortion Services in the United States, 1984 and 1985," 19 *Fam. Plan. Persps.* 64, table 1 (1987) (at the rate of roughly 1.5 million abortions per year for the 18 years from 1973 to 1990, there have been about 27 million abortions in the U.S.A.).

53. Estrich & Sullivan, *supra* note 35, at 152–54.

54. B. Nathanson, *The Abortion Papers: Inside the Abortion Mentality*, 177–209 (1983).

55. Estrich & Sullivan, *supra* note 35, at 152–54.

56. See, e.g., *id.* at 153 n.132.

57. *Harris v. McRae*, 448 U.S. 297, 319 (1980).

58. See generally R. Adamek, *Abortion and Public Opinion in the United States* (1989).

59. These are some of the radical positions urged by abortion rights partisans in cases such as *Roe v. Wade*, 410 U.S. 113, *Planned Parenthood of Central Missouri v. Danforth*, 428 U.S. 52 (1976), and *Thornburgh v. American College of Obstetricians and Gynecologists*, 476 U.S. 747 (1986).

60. "Most in US favor ban on majority of abortions, poll finds," *Boston Globe,* March 31, 1989, at 1, col. 2–4.

61. *Id.*

62. Torres & Forrest, "Why Do Women Have Abortions?" 20 *Fam. Plan. Persps.,* 169 (1988). Table 1 of this article reveals the following reasons and percentages of women giving their most important reason for choosing abortion: 16% said they were concerned about how having a baby would change their life; 21% said they couldn't afford a baby now; 12% said they had problems with a relationship and wanted to avoid single parenthood; 21% said they were unready for responsibility; 1% said they didn't want others to know they had sex or were pregnant; 11% said they were not mature enough or were too young to have a child; 8% said they had all the children they wanted or had all grown-up children; 1% said their husband wanted them to have an abortion; 3% said the fetus had possible health problems; 3% said they had a health problem; less than .5% said their parents wanted them to have an abortion; 1% said they were a victim of rape or incest; and 3% gave another, unspecified reason. (Figures total more than 100% due to rounding off of numbers.) It is significant to note, also, that 39% of all abortions are repeat abortions. Henshaw, "Characteristics of U.S. Women Having Abortions, 1982–1983," 19 *Fam. Plan. Persps.* 1, 6 (1987).

63. *Roe* held that a state may prohibit abortion after fetal viability, but that it may not do so where the mother's "life or health" would be at risk. 410 U.S. at 165. In the companion case to *Roe, Doe v. Bolton,* the Supreme Court construed "health" in an extremely broad fashion to include "all factors—physical, emotional, psychological, familial, and the woman's age—relevant to the well-being of the patient." 410 U.S. 179, 195 (1973). The breadth of these factors makes a "health" reason for an abortion extremely easy to establish, so that we have virtual abortion on demand for all nine months of pregnancy in America. Moreover, there are physicians who declare that if a woman simply seeks an abortion she *ipso facto* has a "health" reason and the abortion may be performed. *McRae v. Califano,* No. 76-C-1804 (E.D.N.Y. Transcript, August 3, 1977, pp. 99–101) (Testimony of Dr. Jane Hodgson) (Dr. Hodgson testified that she felt that there was a medical indication to abort a pregnancy if it "is not wanted by the patient.").

64. J. Mill, *On Liberty* (Atlantic Monthly Press edition 1921).

65. *Id.* at 13. It should be noted that Mill's contention that society should never use its power to protect the individual from the actions of himself or herself is hotly disputed. See, e.g., J. Stephen, *Liberty, Equality, Fraternity* (R. White ed. 1967) (the 1873 classic response to Mill); P. Devlin, *The Enforcement of Morals* (1974).

66. *Roe,* 410 U.S. at 159 ("We need not resolve the difficult question of when life begins.").

67. H. Liley, *Modern Motherhood* 207 (1969).

68. "Technology for Improving Fetal Therapy Advancing Exponentially," *Ob. Gyn. News,* Aug. 1–14, 1987, at 31.

69. P. Williams, "Medical and Surgical Treatment for the Unborn Child," in *Human Life and Health Care Ethics,* 77 (J. Bopp ed. 1985).

70. Estrich & Sullivan, *supra* note 35, at 152–54. In legal terms, this argument is an equal protection one. See *id.* at 124 n.10. However, equal protection of the laws is only constitutionally guaranteed to those who are equally situated, and the Supreme Court has held that treating pregnancy differently from other matters does not constitute gender-based discrimination. *Geduldig v. Aiello*, 417 U.S. 484, 496–97 n.20 (1974). For a further discussion of this point, see Bopp, "Will There Be a Constitutional Right to Abortion After the Reconsideration of *Roe v. Wade?*" 15 *J. Contemp. L.* 131, 136–41 (1989). See also Smolin, "Why Abortion Rights Are Not Justified by Reference to Gender Equality: A Response to Professor Tribe," 23 *John Marshall L. Rev.* 621 (1990).
71. *Rostker v. Goldberg*, 453 U.S. 57 (1981).
72. *Schlesinger v. Ballard*, 419 U.S. 498 (1975).
73. *Id.* at 508.
74. Bopp, "Is Equal Protection a Shelter for the Right to Abortion?" in *Abortion, Medicine and the Law* (4th ed. 1991).
75. *Jacobson v. Massachusetts*, 197 U.S. 11 (1905).
76. *The Selective Service Draft Law Cases*, 245 U.S. 366 (1918).
77. See, e.g., *Sistare v. Sistare*, 218 U.S. 1 (1910). All states have recognized this obligation by passage of the Uniform Reciprocal Enforcement of Support Act. See Fox, "The Uniform Reciprocal Enforcement of Support Act," 12 *Fam. L.Q.* 113, 113–14 (1978).

 /diclerico10

Internet Resources

Visit our Web site at www.mhhe.com/diclerico10 for links and resources relating to Civil Rights.